Singapore

"All you've got to do is decide to go
and the hardest part is over.

So go!"

TONY WHEELER, COFOUNDER – LONELY PLANET

Ria de Jong

Contents

Dragon statue at Haw Par Villa p130
Chinese-mythology theme park

COVID-19

We have re-checked every business in this book before publication to ensure that it is still open after the COVID-19 outbreak. However, the economic and social impacts of COVID-19 will continue to be felt long after the outbreak has been contained, and many businesses, services and events referenced in this guide may experience ongoing restrictions. Some businesses may be temporarily closed, have changed their opening hours and services, or require bookings; some unfortunately could have closed permanently. We suggest you check with venues before visiting for the latest information.

Building facade in Little India p83
Colourful sights and delicious food

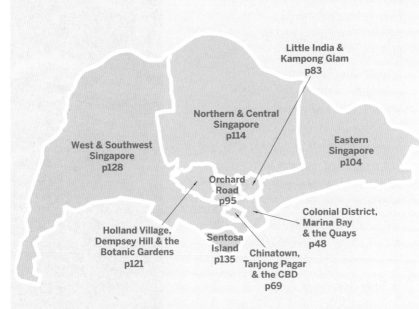

Little India &
Kampong Glam
p83

Northern & Central
Singapore
p114

West & Southwest
Singapore
p128

Eastern
Singapore
p104

Orchard
Road
p95

Colonial District,
Marina Bay
& the Quays
p48

Holland Village,
Dempsey Hill & the
Botanic Gardens
p121

Sentosa
Island
p135

Chinatown,
Tanjong Pagar
& the CBD
p69

Right: Buddha
Tooth Relic
Temple (p72)

WELCOME TO
Singapore

Small enough to feel intimate yet big enough to retain a degree of mystery, Singapore is a place I love discovering again and again. The city sometimes feels like it's travelling at a breakneck speed into tomorrow with its futuristic architecture, high-speed efficiency and shiny image, but you only need to take a small step off the main drag to get a dose of its rich history and culture. Then there's the food: nothing stills my beating heart quite like perfectly grilled satay and an ice-cold Tiger Beer.

By Ria de Jong, Writer
🐦 @ria_in_transit 📷 @ria_in_transit
For more about our writers, see p224

Singapore's Top Experiences

1 THE ISLAND OF FEASTING

Singapore takes food very seriously. From cheap hawker fare to Michelin-starred fine dining, food-enamoured Singaporeans queue for it, Instagram the hell out of it and passionately debate whether it's 'die, die, must try' – Singlish slang for 'to die for'. A food odyssey awaits.

Above: Newton Food Centre (p98)

PREMSHREE PILLAI/FLICKR CREATIVE COMMONS BY-NC-ND 2.0 ©

Odette

With three shiny Michelin stars, chef Julien Royer knows how to deliver an out-of-body gastronomic experience. From the muted pink interiors, floating aerial installation, glass-enclosed kitchen, perfect French-inspired menu and immaculate service – it's five (well, three) stars all the way. p61

Right: Pigeon Fabien Deneour

RUSLAN KALNITSKY/SHUTTERSTOCK ©

TANG YAN SONG/SHUTTERSTOCK ©

Newton Food Centre

Rachel Chu got her first taste of Singaporean hawker fare here in the 2018 blockbuster *Crazy Rich Asians*, and it's the perfect spot to begin your Singapore food journey. Check the local favourites board at the entrance, bags a table and order up a storm. p98

Hong Kong Soya Sauce Chicken Rice & Noodle

The world's first hawker to be awarded a Michelin star, humble Hawker Chan is now part of a shiny, fast growing franchise. However, things haven't changed much at the original location in Chinatown Complex, bar the snazzy new sign, and the tender soy sauce chicken is definitely worth the wait. p73

PLAN YOUR TRIP

2 KNOCK-OUT VISTAS

With it's abundance of modern, shiny skyscrapers and iconic landmark buildings (think the gravity-defying floating ship silhouette of Marina Bay Sands), it's no surprise that as night falls and the city lights twinkle punters clamour for the best viewing seats in town – preferably perched with a cold drink in hand.

CÉ LA VI Skybar

Views from Marina Bay Sands' cantilevered rooftop are breathtaking, on a clear day you can spot Malaysia inland and Indonesia out to sea. It's worth arriving early to nab a piece of prime viewing real estate in the Sky Lounge, from here the city vista will smack you in the face plus you can peer across the world-famous infinity pool. p64

Below: The view from CÉ LA VI

Smoke and Mirrors

Atop the imposing National Gallery Singapore, this swanky bar offers a spectacular view framed by towering skyscrapers, over the Padang and onwards to Marina Bay Sands. Bonus that the bartenders take their tipples seriously – expect your drink to be same level knockout as the view. p63

Above left: Smoke and Mirrors

ION Sky

If you need to clear your head during a heady day of Orchard Road retail therapy, use your shopping receipts (you'll need to have spent S$20 at ION Orchard that day) to book yourself a ride up to the clouds. The view from the 56th level is a sight to behold, and just worth the palava of getting a ticket. p97

Top right: View from ION Sky

3 HISTORICAL HAUNTS

History buffs will feverishly devour Singapore's highly acclaimed and impeccably executed world-class museums. Dive in and discover priceless regional treasures, learn about the melting pot of cultures which call this island home and of course how it all came to be.

National Museum of Singapore

There's nothing stuffy about Singapore's National Museum, here staid exhibits have made way for cutting-edge multimedia galleries that take visitors on a vivid journey through Singapore's action-packed history. p54

Below: National Museum of Singapore

RIA DE JONG/LONELY PLANET ©

Chinatown Heritage Centre

Garner a snapshot of the harsh, and often dangerous, reality of the Chinese immigrants who gave this neighbourhood its name. p71

Above: Chinatown Heritage Centre

Battlebox

Hidden under Fort Canning Hill's lush foliage, this mazelike 26-room underground WWII bunker is where some of Singapore's most historic moments unfolded. p57

Right: Battlebox

4 GREAT GREENWAYS

CHONNIKARNKAMSING/SHUTTERSTOCK ©

Above: MacRitchie Reservoir (p118)

Singapore's 'City in a Garden' masterplan has seen a network of parks, gardens and nature reserves connecting and greening this once concrete-heavy metropolis. Lace up your walking shoes, pack plenty of water, douse yourself in mosquito repellent and set off to discover the island's swathes of wilderness.

MacRitchie Reservoir

A hike through this patch of dense rainforest, which teams with a mind-blowing array of flora and fauna (do not to feed the monkeys), is elevated to new heights with the sweeping views from the 25m-high Treetop Walk. p118

Southern Ridges

Take in jungle and city vistas as you meander on forest-canopy walkways, over the sculptural Henderson Waves bridge and through manicured gardens on this 10km walking trail connecting Kent Ridge Park to Mt Faber and the Labrador Nature Reserve. p134

Sungei Buloh Wetlands Reserve

If you're hoping to spot some wildlife in the wilderness, a trip to this wetland reserve should be top of your list. In amongst the mangroves, mudflats, ponds and forest, you'll easily spot migratory birds, mudskippers, monitor lizards and possibly an estuarine crocodile. p131

5 ARCHITECTURAL MARVELS

A meander through the Colonial District will have you admiring several imposing historical treasures but a quick glance across Marina Bay and you'll be awed by futuristic, out-of-this-world designs. Neighbourhood districts are dotted with ornate temples, terraced shophouses and the somewhat visually soothing uniformly designed public housing estates (HBDs).

Peranakan Terrace Houses

You'll spot decorated shophouses in many of the city's heritage areas, but none are as photogenic as the beauties you'll find lining Koon Seng Road. p107

Top left: Shophouses on Koon Seng Rd

Moshe Safdie's Masterpieces

Celebrated Israeli-Canadian Moshe Safdie designed the iconic ship-shaped Marina Bay Sands. His glass-domed Jewel is bliss for design-lovers. p55

Above left: Jewel at Changi (p113)

Gardens by the Bay

Singapore's S$1 billion 'super park' is home to over one million plants, all accompanied by such contemporary architecture that it feels like a sci-fi garden of the future. p53

Above: Gardens by the Bay

6 SEASIDE BREEZES

With a sweatbox-esque climate nearly all year round, Singaporeans love nothing more than heading to the country's many coastal parks, beaches and off-shore islands for a breath of cool sea breeze. It's not just lazing under palms trees, unless of course you want to, as there're plenty of beachside haunts for adrenaline junkies, history buffs and foodies which will add some thrill to your chill.

Above: Coastal boardwalk on Pulau Ubin; Top: Cycling in East Coast Park

East Coast Park

Perfect for cycling, ocean frolicking and beachside picnics, this 15km stretch of seafront parkland is the perfect spot to relax by doing as little or as much as you like. The East Coast Lagoon Food Village is famous for its seafood and satay hawker fare, best enjoyed with the sand still between your toes. p108

Sentosa Island

Sentosa is Singapore's carefully planned, all-ages playground – a world-class sprawl of theme parks, luxe resorts and a subterranean casino. There's something for everyone, from marine life at SEA Aquarium to blockbuster rides and a historic British fort. Palm-fringed beach bars seemingly beg you to stop in for a sundowner. p135

Pulau Ubin

Singapore's rustic island getaway offers a glimpse of the *kampong* (village) life that was a big part of Singapore as recently as the 1960s. Hop aboard a chugging bumboat (motorised sampan) from Changi, and explore old-growth mangrove swamps, cycle past tin-roof shacks, ramshackle shrines and lazing monitor lizards before ending the day with a simple seafood meal by the sea. p142

What's New

Singapore has its eyes firmly on the future. Moving past the COVID-19 pandemic, the island city-state continues to adapt and morph at a blistering pace, evident not just in the number of ongoing government infrastructure projects but the opening of luxury hotels, dining establishments, bars and leisure facilities. Onwards and upwards.

Singapore Botanic Gardens Gallop Extension

Adding 8 hectares to the already impressive 74-hectare pocket of botanical lushness (p123), the Gallop Extension includes a nature-inspired playground and two conserved black and white bungalows which house the Botanical Art Gallery and Forest Discovery Centre @ OCBC Arboretum.

Sembawang Hot Spring Park

Converted from a single tap in the ground (BYO bucket) to a cascading footbath pool, complete with side seating. As Singapore's only public hot spring, it's the perfect place to revive tired tootsies...and boil eggs!

Rail Corridor

Not for the faint-hearted, the 24km Green Corridor trail spans the island from top to bottom, following the disused Singapore–Malaysia rail route. Major upgrading works are now completed and visitors can access the entire length of this urban oasis.

Changi Chapel & Museum

Recently revamped, this tranquil chapel and museum (p106) eloquently tell the sombre stories of prisoners interned in Changi Prison camp during the Japanese occupation. A perfect setting for remembrance and reflection.

LOCAL KNOWLEDGE

WHAT'S HAPPENING IN SINGAPORE

Ria de Jong, Lonely Planet Writer

Singapore's population more than doubled from 2.4 million in 1980 to a smidge under 5.7 million in 2020, an increase driven in no small part by waves of foreign workers. Indeed, non-Singaporeans now constitute almost half of the nation's headcount. According to the ruling People's Action Party (PAP), large-scale immigration has been essential to the country's economic growth. For a growing number of Singaporeans, however, it's seen as the cause of numerous woes, from overcrowded transport to rising living costs. There is also a sentiment that 'foreign talent' are taking jobs away from locals, a common social media theme, which has lead to the government gradually tightening the flow of foreign workers. During the global Covid-19 pandemic the cramped living conditions of migrant labourers housed in boarding dormitories came under global scrutiny. The virus spread rapidly through the dormitories resulting in their occupants being separated from the community. Many workers returned to their home countries, causing a labour shortage on the island.

Supertree Observatory

Get a bird's-eye perspective of the spectacular Gardens by the Bay (p53) from the newly opened rooftop deck, perched 50m atop the tallest sci-fi Supertree.

Changi Jurassic Mile

Take a walk amongst life-sized dinosaurs on the Changi Airport connector, which joins Changi Airport to East Coast Park. The towering beasts are accompanied by handy information panels and safari-themed music.

HydroDash

Singapore's first floating aqua park is located in the calm waters off Sentosa's Palawan Beach. Get ready for a full body workout as you slide, bounce, leap and of course, get soaking wet.

Jurong Lake Gardens

Singapore's new national gardens in the heartlands sprawls over 90 hectares and compromises a number of gardens. Highlights include the tranquil Chinese Garden and the nature inspired Forest Ramble playgarden.

National Orchid Garden

Immerse yourself in the National Orchid Garden's (p123) newest attraction, the Tropical Montane Orchidetum. Follow windy paths through a 'secret ravine' and be awed by over 1000 species of orchids and hybrids in an ethereal cooled glasshouse.

Changi Experience Studio

Located in futuristic Jewel (p113) at Changi, this fun, interactive virtual experience allows guests to step behind the scenes and discover everything there is to know about the world's most highly awarded airport.

FAST FACTS

Drinks trend Craft cocktails

Number of wild otter families 10

Offshore islands 64

Population 5.69 million

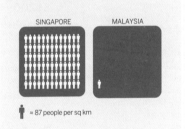

SINGAPORE   MALAYSIA

≈ 87 people per sq km

Dempsey Hill

This former British Army barracks has recently upped its game on the food front with several highly anticipated restaurant openings joining an already packed stable of feted dining establishments, including Peranakan Michelin-starred Candlenut.

Need to Know

For more information, see Survival Guide (p181)

Currency
Singapore dollar (S$)

Languages
English (primary), Mandarin, Bahasa Malaysia, Tamil

Visas
Generally issued 90-day entry on arrival. Citizens of India, Myanmar and certain other countries must obtain a visa before arriving.

Money
ATMs and moneychangers are widely available. Credit cards are accepted in most shops and restaurants.

Mobile Phones
You can buy a tourist SIM card for around S$15 from post offices, convenience stores and telco stores – by law you must show your passport. Local carriers include:

M1 (www.m1.com.sg)

SingTel (www.singtel.com)

StarHub (www.starhub.com)

Time
Singapore Time (GMT/UTC plus eight hours)

Tourist Information
Singapore Visitors Centre @ Orchard (Map 216; ☑1800 736 2000; www.yoursingapore.com; 216 Orchard Rd; ⊙8.30am-9.30pm; ☎; Ⓜ Somerset) Knowledgeable staff to help you organise tours, buy tickets and book hotels.

Daily Costs

Budget: Less than S$200
➡ Dorm bed: S$20–45

➡ Meals at hawker centres and food courts: around S$6

➡ One-hour foot reflexology at People's Park Complex: S$25

➡ Ticket to a major museum: S$6–20

Midrange: S$200–400
➡ Double room in midrange hotel: S$150–300

➡ Singapore Ducktour: S$37

➡ Two-course dinner with wine: S$80

➡ Cocktail at a decent bar: S$18–25

Top End: More than S$400
➡ Four- or five-star double room: S$300–700

➡ Food Playground cooking course: S$119

➡ Dégustation in top restaurant: S$250 or more

➡ Theatre ticket: S$150

Advance Planning

Two months before Book big-ticket events such as the Formula One race. Reserve a table at a hot top-end restaurant.

One month before Book a bed if you're planning to stay in a dorm over the weekend.

One week before Look for last-minute deals on Singapore accommodation and check for any events or festivals. Book a posh hotel brunch or high tea.

Websites

Lonely Planet (www.lonely planet.com/singapore) Destination information, hotel reviews, traveller forum and more.

Your Singapore (www.your singapore.com) Official tourism board website.

Honeycombers (www.thehoney combers.com) A good online guide to Singapore, covering events, eating, drinking and shopping.

City Nomads (www.citynomads. com) A handy website with reviews and event listings.

Sistic (www.sistic.com.sg) One-stop shop for tickets to concerts and shows in Singapore; useful events calendar, too.

WHEN TO GO

Singapore is tropical and humid year-round. School holidays fall in June and July, the hottest (and haziest) time.

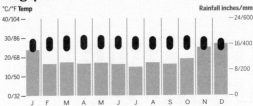

Singapore

Arriving in Singapore

Changi Airport MRT trains run into town from the airport from 5.30am to 11.18pm; public buses run from 6am to midnight. Both the train and bus trips cost from S$1.69. The airport shuttle bus (adult/child S$9/6) runs 24 hours a day. A taxi into the city will cost anywhere from S$20 to S$40, and up to 50% more between midnight and 6am, plus airport surcharges. A four-seater limousine taxi is S$55, plus a S$15 surcharge per additional stop.

HarbourFront Ferry Terminal MRT trains into town cost from S$1.40. A taxi will cost from S$8 to S$13, plus any surcharges.

Woodlands Train Checkpoint Taxis into town cost from S$22 to S$25, plus any surcharges.

For more on **arrival** see 182

HOW LONG TO STAY FOR?

Singapore is stopover central for long-haul flights and most people stay a day or two. That may be enough to scratch the surface, but if you want to get beyond mall-trawling Orchard Rd, spend at least four days here: you'll get to see the top sights, eat at some of the best hawker places, be surprised by the nature reserves and have time to properly explore Singapore's booming cafe and bar scenes.

Sleeping

Staying in Singapore is expensive. Budget travellers can stay in hostel rooms for S$25 a night. Newer midrange hotels are lifting the game with better facilities and good, regular online deals. Luxury digs are expensive but plentiful and among the world's best, with options from colonial and romantic to architecturally cutting-edge.

Lonely Planet (lonelyplanet.com /singapore/hotels) Hotel reviews on Lonely Planet's website.

LateRooms (www.laterooms. com) Great deals on rooms; book now then pay when you stay.

StayinSingapore (www.stayin singapore.com) Hotel-booking website dedicated to Singapore, managed by the Singapore Hotel Association.

For more on **sleeping** see p153

Getting Around

Singapore is the easiest city in Asia to get around. Maps on the walls in MRT stations show the surrounding area – great for figuring out which exit to use. Get the credit-card-sized electronic EZ-Link card to use on MRT trains and local buses. Just tap on and off at the sensors. You can buy one, and top up your card's credit, at all MRT stations. The smartphone app gothere. sg will guide you from your location to your destination via different public transport options; and offers an approximate taxi fare guide.

Bus Go everywhere the trains do and more. Great for views. Runs from 6am till midnight, plus some later night buses from the city.

MRT The local subway – the most convenient way to get around between 5.30am and midnight.

Taxis These are fairly cheap if you're used to Sydney or London prices, though there are hefty surcharges during peak hours and from midnight to 6am. Flag one on the street or at a taxi stand. Good luck getting one on rainy days.

For more on **getting around** see p183

First Time Singapore

For more information, see Survival Guide (p181)

Checklist

➡ Ensure your passport is valid for at least six months past your arrival date

➡ Check airline baggage restrictions

➡ Organise travel insurance

➡ Inform your credit-/debit-card company of your travels

➡ Book your accommodation and any big-ticket events or restaurants

➡ Check that you'll be able to use your mobile (cell) phone

What to Pack

➡ Hat, sunglasses and sunscreen – and an umbrella

➡ Mosquito repellent, especially if planning to explore nature reserves

➡ Electrical adaptor

➡ A smart outfit and a decent pair of shoes for higher-end restaurants and bars

➡ Swimwear

➡ A photocopy of your passport photo page, stored separately from your passport

Top Tips for Your Trip

➡ Buy an EZ-Link card, an electronic travel card accepted on MRT trains, local buses and the Sentosa Express monorail, and by most taxis. Options include one-, two- or three-day 'Singapore Tourist Pass' cards, which offer unlimited travel on buses and trains.

➡ Combination tickets for some sights (eg Singapore Zoo and Night Safari) can save you money.

➡ Leave rigorous outdoor activities for early morning or late afternoon to avoid the sweltering midday heat.

➡ Party early: there's no shortage of bars offering good-value happy-hour deals, mostly between 5pm and 8pm or 9pm.

➡ Carry a packet of tissues: you won't find serviettes (napkins) at hawker centres, so you'll need these to 'chope' (save) your seat before lining up for food.

What to Wear

Singapore is hot and humid so pack clothes that are light and comfortable. Shorts, T-shirts and flip-flops are acceptable almost everywhere, though higher-end restaurants and bars call for more stylish attire; consider bringing at least one evening dress or long-sleeved shirt and trousers, and dress shoes. You'll need a pair of trainers or hiking boots if tackling the nature reserves, and it's always a good idea to carry a small, portable umbrella for those sudden tropical downpours, especially during the monsoon season (November to January).

Be Forewarned

Singapore is one of the world's safest and easiest travel destinations, but be aware of the following:

Drugs Penalties for the illegal import or export of drugs are severe and include the death penalty.

Mosquitoes Outbreaks of mosquito-borne illnesses, such as dengue fever, do occur, especially during the wet season, and there have also been a number of zika cases confimed in Singapore: wear mosquito repellent, especially if visiting nature reserves.

Public Transport Eating and drinking is prohibited on public transport.

Money

ATMs and moneychangers are widely available. Credit cards are accepted in most shops and restaurants.

For more information, see p188.

Taxes & Refunds

Singapore applies a 7% GST to goods and services. Most prices in shops and food outlets will have GST already included – the symbol ++ shows GST and service charge (10%) is not included in the displayed price and will be added to the final bill. This is common in hotels, restaurants and luxury spas.

For more information, see p42.

Merlion statue (p59)

BATTEREK MEDIA/SHUTTERSTOCK © SCULPTOR: SCULPTOR: LIM NANG SENG

Tipping

Tipping is generally not customary in Singapore. It's prohibited at Changi Airport.

Hotels Unnecessary at budget places. At higher-end establishments, consider tipping porters S$2 to S$5 for luggage help and housekeeping S$2 for room cleaning.

Restaurants Many add a 10% service charge, in which case tipping is discouraged. A small tip is still appreciated when a staff member has gone out of their way. Don't tip at hawker centres and food courts.

Taxis Not expected, although it's courteous to round up or tell the driver to keep the change.

Etiquette

Loss of Face Singaporeans are sensitive to retaining face in all aspects of their lives. Being confrontational or angry with a local makes them lose face and you look rude.

Uncles & Aunties It is common to address middle-aged and elderly people as 'Uncle' or 'Auntie' as a sign of respect, even if they are not related or known to you.

Chopsticks Do not stick chopsticks upright in a bowl of rice. It is reminiscent of funeral rites and considered bad luck.

Hands Use your right hand to greet, wave, eat or interact with someone of Malay, Indonesian or Indian descent as the left hand is associated with restroom use.

Head & Feet The head is considered sacred by many so avoid touching someone else's. In contrast, the feet are considered dirty and directly pointing them at someone may cause offence.

Language

Singapore has no less than four official languages: English, Bahasa Malaysia, Mandarin and Tamil. English is the first language of instruction in the majority of schools and English speakers will generally find it very easy to communicate with locals. Exceptions to the rule include some older Singaporeans and some newer arrivals, especially people from mainland China.

For more information on Singlish, see p179.

Perfect Days

Day One

Colonial District, Marina Bay & the Quays (p48)

 Start your Singapore fling with a local breakfast of *kaya* (coconut jam) toast, runny eggs and strong *kopi* (coffee) at **Ya Kun Kaya Toast** before taking a riverside stroll at the **Quays** for a jaw-dropping panorama of brazen skyscrapers and refined colonial buildings. Dive into the brilliant **Asian Civilisations Museum** or keep walking to the **National Museum of Singapore**, the **Peranakan Museum** or the new **National Gallery Singapore**.

 Lunch Peranakan at National Kitchen by Violet Oon (p60).

Chinatown, Tanjong Pagar & the CBD (p69)

While the area feels touristy, the **Sri Mariamman Temple**, **Buddha Tooth Relic Temple** and **Thian Hock Keng Temple** offer genuine glimpses into everyday neighbourhood life. Head up **Pinnacle@ Duxton** for a bird's-eye view of the city skyline and beyond, or de-stress with super-cheap reflexology at **People's Park Complex**. Either way, follow up with a pre-dinner tipple on **Amoy St**, **Club St** or **Ann Siang Rd**.

Dinner Knockout Asian fusion at Ding Dong (p76).

Northern & Central Singapore (p114)

Early dinner done, catch a taxi to the fantastic **Night Safari**, where you have a date with a cast of majestic and curious creatures. Ride the quiet tram through the park and hop off for atmospheric walks past tigers, leopards and swooping bats.

Day Two

Little India & Kampong Glam (p83)

 Little India will erase every preconceived notion of Singapore as a sterile, OCD metropolis. Weathered tailors stitch and sew by the side of the road, and the air is thick with cumin and Bollywood soundtracks. Take in the colours and chanting of **Sri Veeramakaliamman Temple** and buy a sari at **Tekka Centre**. Learn more about the area's fascinating backstory at the **Indian Heritage Centre**.

 Lunch Choose-your-own-spice-level adventure at Lagnaa Barefoot Dining (p89).

Orchard Road (p95)

Escape the afternoon heat in the air-conditioned comfort of the malls on **Orchard Rd**. This is one of the world's most famous shopping meccas. Hunt down rare Singaporean prints and books at **Antiques of the Orient** and cognoscenti threads at **Robinsons the Heeren** and **In Good Company**. Shopped out, it's time for a refreshing cocktail at rooftop **Bar Canary** or beers on heritage beauty **Emerald Hill Rd**.

Dinner Breezy, bayside hawker grub at Satay by the Bay (p60).

Colonial District, Marina Bay & the Quays (p48)

If you're dining at Satay by the Bay, you're already at **Gardens by the Bay**. Give yourself plenty of time to explore Singapore's incredible new botanic gardens, including the Flower Dome and Cloud Forest conservatories. The gardens' Supertrees are especially spectacular during the nightly light show (7.45pm and 8.45pm).

Javanese art at the Asian Civilisations Museum (p50)

ION Orchard Mall (p101) on Orchard Road

Day Three

Northern & Central Singapore (p114)

 Wake up early to join the orang-utans for **Jungle Breakfast with Wildlife** at the world-class **Singapore Zoo**. There's lots of ground to cover so jump on the guided tram to get the lay of the land. Note feeding times as the animals are more active then and you have the opportunity to get up-close and personal.

 Lunch Pick from one of the on-site eateries at the Singapore Zoo (p116).

Sentosa Island (p135)

After all that wildlife, it's time for some pure, unadulterated fun on Singapore's pleasure island, **Sentosa**. Tackle rides from heart-racing and sedate at movie theme park **Universal Studios**; eye-up creatures great and small at the spectacular **SEA Aquarium**; or book an indoor sky-dive at **iFly**.

Dinner Authentic Greek on the marina at Mykonos on the Bay (p138).

Sentosa Island (p135)

Slow down the pace with even-ing drinks on a palm-fringed Sentosa beach. Options include family-friendly **Coastes** or the more secluded **Tanjong Beach Club**. If you're travel-ling with kids, consider catching the popular **Wings of Time** show, a multimillion-dollar sound, light and laser extravaganza.

Day Four

Islands & Day Trips (p141)

 For a taste of 1950s Singapore, head to Changi to catch a bumboat across to **Pulau Ubin**. Rent a bicycle and cycle the island's peaceful, jungle-fringed roads, passing tin-shacked houses and quirky shrines, and walk along a mangrove board-walk. There's even a mountain-bike park with trails for varying skill levels.

Lunch Pick a seafood restaurant around **Pulau Ubin pier**.

Eastern Singapore (p104)

Once you've finished exploring sleepy Pulau Ubin, catch a bumboat back to Singapore. If it's not too late, pay a visit to the moving **Changi Museum & Chapel**, which recounts the suffering and resilience of those who endured Singapore's Japanese occupation. If it is too late, wan-der the shops at **Changi Village**, stopping for a beer at **Little Island Brewing Co**.

Dinner Delectable white-pepper and chilli crab in red-light Geylang at No Signboard Seafood (p109).

Colonial District, Marina Bay & the Quays (p48)

 Come evening, swap tranquil nostalgia for neon-lit excess in **Geylang**, a red-light district juxtaposed with temples, mosques and some of the best food in Singapore. Head back into town and end the night at trendy rooftop bar **Smoke and Mirrors**, atop the **National Gallery Singapore**, where you can enjoy commanding views of the Marina Bay Sands spectacular nightly light-and-laser show.

Month By Month

January

**The year kicks off with
extreme Hindu devotion
and indie music.**

☆ St Jerome's
Laneway Festival

A popular one-day
music festival (http://
singapore.lanewayfestival.
com) serving up top-tier
indie acts from across the
world at Gardens by the
Bay. Acts span rock, folk
and electronica.

February

**Chinese New Year is a big
deal in Singapore. The
occasion is celebrated
with a two-day holiday and
loud, intense, colourful
festivity.**

Chinese New Year

Dragon dances, parades and
wishes of '*gong xi fa cai*'
('I hope that you gain lots
of money') mark the start
of the Chinese New Year
(February 2022; January
2023). Chinatown lights up,
especially Eu Tong Sen St
and New Bridge Rd, and the
'River Hongbao' (www.river
hongbao.sg) at Marina Bay
features market and food
stalls, shows and fireworks.

Thaipusam

Hindus head from Sri
Srinivasa Perumal Temple
on Serangoon Rd to Sri
Thendayuthapani Temple
on Tank Rd carrying *ka-
vadis* (heavy metal frames
decorated with peacock
feathers, fruit and flowers)
during this dramatic festival (www.thaipusam.sg).

Chingay

Held over two nights dur-
ing the first weekend of
Chinese New Year, Chingay
(www.chingay.org.sg) de-
livers Singapore's biggest
street parade. It's a flam-
boyant multicultural affair
featuring lion dancers,
floats and other cultural
performers. Buy tickets in
advance for a seat in the
viewing galleries, or battle
the crowds for a place at
the roadside barriers.

March

**The northeast monsoon
peters out and the
mercury starts rising.**

Singapore
International
Jazz Festival

Held at Marina Bay Sands,
the three-day Sing Jazz
(www.sing-jazz.com)
delivers established and
emerging jazz talent from
around the world. Past
acts have included Jamie
Cullum, India Arie and
Natalie Cole.

April

**Temperatures continue
to rise in April, however,
fairly predictable
afternoon thunderstorms
cool things down.**

🔒 Affordable
Art Fair

A three-day expo (www.
affordableartfair.com/
singapore) with more
than 40 local and inter-
national galleries show-
casing art priced between
S$100 and S$15,000 from
hundreds of artists. Held
at the F1 Pit Building, the
event also takes place in
November.

May

It's the quiet month leading towards the peak of the 'summer' heat and the busy school holidays.

 ### Vesak Day

Buddha's birth, enlightenment and death are celebrated with various events, including the release of caged birds to symbolise the setting free of captive souls. The centres of activity are the Buddha Tooth Relic Temple and Kong Meng San Phor Kark See Monastery.

June

School holidays coupled with blockbuster sales equal big crowds. It's one of the hottest months.

Great Singapore Sale

The Great Singapore Sale (www.greatsingaporesale.com.sg) runs from early June to late July. Retailers around the island cut prices (and wheel out the stuff they couldn't sell earlier in the year). There are bargains to be had if you can stomach the crowds. Go early!

Hari Raya Puasa

Also known as Hari Raya Aidilfitri, this festival celebrates the end of the Ramadan fasting month (dates change annually). Head to Kampong Glam for nightly feasts during Ramadan.

Singapore International Festival of Arts

A world-class offering (http://sifa.sg/sifa) of mostly dance and drama curated by Ong Keng Sen, one of Singapore's most respected theatre practitioners. Runs from late June to early September.

July

The dry months continue, and so do the school holidays.

Singapore Food Festival

A two-week celebration (www.yoursingapore.com) of all things edible and Singaporean. Events taking place across the city include tastings, special dinners and food-themed tours.

August

National Day, Singapore's best-known event, is held every August. Even the unpatriotic love it because it's a public holiday.

Singapore National Day

Held on 9 August, Singapore National Day (www.ndp.org.sg) is a hugely popular spectacle of military parades, civilian processions, air-force fly-bys and fireworks. Tickets are snapped up well in advance, however, you can watch all the aerial acts from Marina Bay Sands.

Hungry Ghost Festival

This festival marks the day when the souls of the dead are released to walk the earth for feasting and entertainment. The Chinese put offerings of food on the street and light fires. Chinese operas and other events are held.

Beerfest Asia

Asia's biggest beer event (www.beerfestasia.com) pours more than 500 types of brews, from both international heavyweights and craft microbreweries. Events include DJs and live music.

Singapore Night Festival

Spectacular light projections, plus interactive installations, performance art, cabaret, comedy and more. The festival (www.nightfest.sg) is held over two weekends.

September

With the Formula One night race the hottest ticket on the annual calendar, it does mean that hotels jack up prices.

Formula One Grand Prix

The Formula One Grand Prix night race (www.singapore-f1-grand-prix.com) screams around Marina Bay. Off-track events include international music acts. Book accommodation months in advance and be prepared to pay through the nose.

Mid-Autumn Festival

Also known as the Lantern Festival, the Mid-Autumn (or Moon Cake) Festival is celebrated with lanterns in Chinatown and locals nibbling on moon cakes. Takes place on the full moon of the eighth lunar month.

Navarathiri

Dedicated to the wives of Siva, Vishnu and Brahma, the Hindu festival of 'Nine

Nights' includes traditional Indian dancing. The Sri Thendayuthapani Temple, Sri Mariamman Temple and Sri Srinivasa Perumal Temple are the main activity hubs.

October

October is an inter-monsoon period. Thunderstorms are frequent but extreme weather is rare.

✨ Deepavali

Rama's victory over the demon king Ravana is celebrated during the 'Festival of Lights'. Little India is ablaze with lights for a month, culminating in a huge street party on the eve of the holiday.

November

As always, Singapore's cultural calendar is packed with religious events.

✨ Thimithi

At this eye-opener of a fire-walking ceremony, Hindu devotees prove their faith by walking across glowing coals at the Sri Mariamman Temple.

December

A sense of festivity (and monsoon rains) permeates the air as the year winds down.

☆ ZoukOut

ZoukOut (www.zoukout. com) is Singapore's biggest outdoor dance party, held over two nights on Siloso Beach, Sentosa. Expect A-list international DJs.

Top: Performer at Chingay (p22)
Bottom: River Hongbao festival, Chinese New Year (p22)

KOBBY DAGAN/SHUTTERSTOCK ©

HUNTERGOL HP/SHUTTERSTOCK ©

With Kids

Singapore is one of the easiest Asian countries in which to travel with children – it's safe and clean, with efficient public transport. Kids are welcome everywhere, and there are facilities and amenities catering to children of all ages. Oh, and don't be surprised if locals fawn over your little ones!

Animal Kingdom

Singapore Zoo, Night Safari, River Safari & Jurong Bird Park

Kids can get up close and personal with orang-utans and cheeky proboscis at Singapore Zoo (p116), watch antelopes trot past at Night Safari (p117), press up against giant manatees at River Safari (p119), or feed Technicolor parrots at Jurong Bird Park (p131). Interactive shows at all venues (except River Safari) crank up the excitement.

Island Thrills

Sentosa Island

Whole days in the sun is what you get at attraction-packed Sentosa (p135). Older kids will get a kick out of the rides at Universal Studios (p137), while young tikes can frolic on the beach or get splash happy at Adventure Cove Waterpark (p140).

Pulau Ubin

This small, relatively flat island is the perfect place to spend a day cycling and exploring. Kids will love the **Sensory Trail** (☑6542 4108; www.nparks.gov.sg) and Chek Jawa Wetlands (p142), both filled with plenty of flora and fauna. Kids bikes are available for hire, as are child seats and helmets.

Kid-Friendly Culture

National Gallery Singapore

Imaginations run wild at the Keppel Centre for Art Education (p52), a wonderful facility dedicated to nurturing children's creativity and curiosity. Kids are encourage to interact with artworks and also create their own masterpieces. Check the website – youth programs are run throughout the year.

Botanic Blockbusters

Gardens by the Bay

As if the space-age bio domes, crazy Supertrees and bird's-eye Skyway weren't enthralling enough, Singapore's jaw-dropping botanical masterpiece (p53) is home to a one-hectare Children's Garden, complete with motion-sensor wet-play zones and giant tree houses.

Rainy-Day Mall Trawls

Orchard Road

Where do you go when it's pouring down with rain? Mall-packed Orchard Rd (p95), of course. You'll find cinemas, Imax screens and, of course, Toys 'R' Us. There's no shortage of quality food courts, cafes and underground walkways to keep you dry.

Ride a Duck

Singapore Duck Tours

The embarrassingly fun Singapore Ducktours (p31) transports visitors on a brightly coloured amphibious former military vehicle. The tour is informative, loud and over the top, especially when the vehicle drives off-road into Marina Bay!

Like a Local

From taking the MRT out into the 'heartlands', to knowing where to go for cheap beer or a bargain foot rub, you don't have to look too hard for an authentic local experience.

Cheap Beer

Coffeeshops

When Singaporeans say 'coffeeshop', they aren't referring to a place for cappuccinos, but rather a food court. Peppered throughout the island are these large collections of food stalls under one roof. Many run late into the night, and some are open 24 hours. While the ambience isn't flashy, you'll get a large bottle of Tiger for S$7, alfresco seating and decent food. Each MRT station has a neighbouring coffeeshop. You won't go wrong if you head to Geylang – there's always somewhere to plonk yourself for a beer, grub and hyperactive street life.

Happy Hour

Travellers bemoan the expensive drinks in Singapore. While it is true that they are, you can still have cheap drinks if you know where and when to go. Most bars offer a happy hour, starting anytime from noon to 9pm. Deals range from 'one-for-one' (two for the price of one) drinks to S$10 cocktails and pints.

Local Obsessions

Foot Reflexology

This Chinese form of relaxation involves lying in a chair and letting the masseur knead and press all the pressure points on your feet. In theory, the different bits of your foot are connected to vital organs, and getting the circulation going is good for you. In reality, it can be bloody painful. Most malls have a foot reflexology place. One Chinatown favourite is People's Park Complex (p82), a mall packed with cheap, no-frills reflexology stalls open late.

Brunch

Given Singapore's work-hard attitude, it's natural that weekend brunch has evolved into such a local passion (not to mention the coolest place to be seen in daylight hours). Any nosh spot worth its hot-spot credentials peddles a dedicated brunch menu – usually a pick of dishes off the standard breakfast and lunch menus. Sessions normally run from 11am to between 3pm and 5pm. The golden rule: if you can't book a table, go early.

The Heartlands

Orchard Rd and the CBD area offer plenty for the tourist, but the city's residential neighbourhoods proffer a stronger dose of local culture. Pick any MRT station to stop at and you'll usually emerge in a local mall. Wander away from the mall and you'll see local life in a big way: wet markets, local coffeeshops, tailors, barbers, Chinese medical halls and the like. Lively neighbourhoods include Tampines, Jurong, Bishan, Toa Payoh and Ang Mo Kio.

Shop 24/7

Bored at 2am? Jump into a taxi and head to the Mustafa Centre (p93) in Little India. This popular complex sells everything. Cameras, diamonds, Bollywood DVDs, underwear, toys, spices, food and more.

Reservoir (p118) – don't miss the 250m-long Treetop Walk.

For Free

It's possible to savour some of Singapore's top offerings, from evocative artefacts to million-dollar light shows, without reaching for your wallet. And then there's always the simple pleasure of hitting the city's diverse neighbourhoods, where daily life is the best show in town.

Museums & Galleries

Baba House

You'll need to book ahead, but the reward for your effort is a free, engrossing tour of one of Singapore's most elegantly restored Peranakan homes (p72). Once the domain of a wealthy Straits Chinese family, its architecture and furnishings offer an intimate glimpse into old Singaporean life.

Gillman Barracks

This rambling art outpost (p130) with 11 commercial galleries is a civilised way to spend a late afternoon, browsing free temporary exhibitions of works produced by some of the world's most coveted creatives. You'll find great nosh here to.

Natural Highs

Exploring Singapore's swath of nature reserves and parks is both free and invigorating. Singapore's Botanic Gardens (p123) is one of the country's greatest attractions and not only is it free, it also hosts free tours and seasonal opera performances. The Southern Ridges (p134) is another winner, with forest canopy strolling, striking architectural features and breathtaking views. If you like monkeys, you'll spot plenty on a wander along the shady forest pathway around MacRitchie

Street Life

Chinatown

Chinatown is a visceral jungle of heady temples, medicinal curiosities, heritage shophouses and still-wriggling market produce. It costs nothing to explore the architecture of places such as the Sri Mariamman Temple (p73) and Buddha Tooth Relic Temple (p72), the gut-rumbling Chinatown Complex market (p75), or the contemporary exhibitions at pocket-sized Utterly Art (p79).

Little India

Singapore's most refreshingly unruly inner neighbourhood offers an intense dose of colours, sounds and scents. Soak up the hypnotic energy of Sri Veeramakaliamman Temple (p85), the fairy-tale architecture of Abdul Gafoor Mosque (p86), and the riotously colourful shops and stalls of Dunlop and Buffalo Sts.

Entertainment

Esplanade – Theatres on the Bay

Singapore's iconic arts centre (p66) has no shortage of free events, from live-music gigs to art exhibitions and film screenings. Don't miss the million-dollar view from the rooftop garden.

Gardens by the Bay

While the domed conservatories and OCBC Skyway come at a cost, the rest of Singapore's showpiece city-centre gardens (p53) are free, from the Heritage Gardens to Marc Quinn's 'floating' sculpture, *Planet*. Topping it off is the twice-nightly Garden Rhapsody sound-and-light show.

Marina Bay Sands

Like Gardens by the Bay, MBS (p55) razzle-dazzles with Spectra, its own twice-nightly, spectacular light, laser and water show choreographed to a stirring score. The best view is from the CBD side of Marina Bay.

Plan Your Trip
Under the Radar Singapore

With a well-worn tourist trail, and often just a few days to complete it in, many visitors only manage to tick off Singapore's must-see highlights. However, if you dare to deviate off the path Singapore is more than happy to divulge many of its best-kept secrets.

Best Under the Radar Attractions

Lian Shan Shuang Lin Monastery
Stunning monastery just 15 minutes from the city centre. (p118)

Lorong Buangkok
The city's last remaining mainland *kampong* (village) in the island's north. (p120)

Gillman Barracks
A former British military camp turned contemporary arts enclave. (p130)

Lee Kong Chian Natural History Museum
A jaw-dropping display of Southeast Asia's biologically diverse ecosystem complete with specimens and high-tech exhibits. (p130)

Singapore City Gallery
Singapore's mind-boggling 50 year transformation conveniently located steps from Chinatown. (p73)

Singapore & Tourism

Singapore hosts a large number of business and leisure travellers, with on average 169,000 on the little red dot at any one time, most staying three to four days. With such a short stay, many may expect Singapore's main sights and tourist areas to be routinely crowded, however thankfully this is not often the case.

The majority of Singapore's attractions are located in different districts resulting in visitors being well distributed across the island. Add to that the city's top-notch transit system which can move crowds around swiftly, efficiently, and most importantly, cooly. Even Singapore's further afield attractions, like the world-famous Singapore Zoo (p116) and Night Safari (p117), are easily accessible via designated tour buses from the CBD and closest MRT station.

The government and tourism board continues to pour money into infrastructure, the MRT system opens new stations year on year, and the rejuvenation and redevelopment of key attractions and precincts. These initiatives benefit the locals and at the same time continue to draw tourists, whether for their first visit or their fifth.

Kranji Farmlands

One thing Singapore does not have a lot of is space, and in recent years it has spent a tonne investing in urban farming. Think vertical, high-tech, artificial intelligence operated indoor farm, which the island hopes will ramp up local food production and ensure the nation's food security.

Interestingly, however, you can still find small pockets of thriving farmers doing it the old-fashioned way in the island's far northwest. Not your typical farmlands, there's not a cow or rolling green hill in sight, but well worth the jaunt for a unique experience.

Bollywood Veggies (p133) grows organic produce, with a side of education, and also dishes up delectable farm-to-table nosh at its onsite bistro. Other area highlights include Hay Dairies Goat Farm (p133) and the slightly more offbeat Jurong Frog Farm (p133), complete with frog meat sampling.

If you've travelled out this far from the CBD it's also worth making a detour to Thow Kwang Pottery Jungle (p132). Here you can fossick through a maze of rooms, each filled to the brim with brightly coloured ceramics, and also check out Singapore's oldest surviving dragon kiln. Although the kiln only gets fired up a few times a year, you can still head inside on a guided tour.

As Kranji is quite a distance from the city, and you'll be making numerous stops, the easiest way to spend a day exploring is by hiring a car and driver. Grab offers a hire service via its app starting from S$60 for one hour and $200 for four hours. Alternatively, you can order taxis as you go but you may experience long waits due to the countryside's remote location.

Jalan Besar

Sandwiched between Little India and Kampong Glam, this micro-burb foodie enclave, its name means 'big or wide road' in Malay, has somehow coasted under most visitors' radars. Chockfull of stunning shophouses, vibrant street art, funky cafes and famous local eats its definitely worth a look-see.

Architecture buffs will fall in love with the repetitive beauty of 18 pre-war shophouses (p88) along Petain Road. There is so much to take in, from the vibrant Peranakan tiles, nature-inspired pillar bas-reliefs and hyper-ornate window decorations. Keep your eyes peeled for the numerous other design gems throughout this area, as well as a continuing evolving street art scene.

Many of the area's newer inhabitants have paid homage to their predecessors, including one of Singapore's most lauded coffee spots and roastery. Chye Seng Huat Hardware (p88), yep you guessed it, has taken over an art deco former hardware shop to serves up hip third-wave coffee offerings from and all the paraphernalia to brew your own at home.

A few steps away, Druggists (p88) shares a building with the Singapore Chinese Druggists Association, but you'll only find beer, and a few other drinks, here. That said, the 23 taps pour an interesting selection of rotating craft brews – well worth wetting your whistle with.

Unmissable local foodie haunts include steamy bowls of fragrant laksa at Sungei Road Laksa (p89), try to avoid the lunchtime rush, the glorious mess that is a meal at Beach Road Scissor Cut Curry Rice (p88), and finally little parcels of dim sum happiness at **Swee Choon Tim Sum** (☑6225 7788; www.sweechoon.com; 183-193 Jln Besar; dishes S$1.40-9; ◷11am-2.30pm & 6pm-6am Mon, Wed-Sat, 10am-3pm & 6pm-6am Sun; Ⓜ Jalan Besar, Rochor). Swee Choon Tim Sum roars into the wee hours of the morning so make a beeline for it if you're in need of a late-night feast.

Guided Tours & River Cruises

Although Singapore is one of the world's easiest cities for self-navigation, guided tours can open up the city and its history in unexpected ways. Tours and cruises span everything from fun, family-friendly overviews to specialised themed adventures.

Bumboat on the Singapore River

Neighbourhood Tours

Original Singapore Walks

These popular **tours** (☑ 6325 1631; www.singaporewalks.com; adult S$32-60, child 7-12yr S$15-30; ⊙ 9am-6pm Mon-Fri) deliver irreverent, knowledgable on-foot excursions through various districts and war-related sites, lasting from 2½ to three hours. Most tours do not require a booking; simply check the website for meeting times and places.

Chinatown Trishaw Night Tour

This **Chinatown tour** (☑ in the US 1-702-648-5873; www.viator.com; adult/child under 13yr S$88/66) includes dinner, a traditional Chinese medicine hall visit, a trishaw ride through the night market and a bumboat river cruise. Hotel pick-ups and drop-offs are provided.

Trishaw Uncle

An old-fashioned **trishaw ride** (Map p210; ☑ 6337 7111; www.trishawuncle.com.sg; Albert Mall Trishaw Park, Queen St; 30min tour adult/child from S$39/29, 45min tour S$49/39; ⓜ Bugis) through Bugis and Little India, with the 45-minute tour also taking in the Singapore River. The trishaw terminal is on Queen St, between the Fu Lu Shou Complex and Albert Centre Market and Food Centre.

Hop-On, Hop-Off Tours

City Sightseeing

This double-decker, open-top **tourist bus** (www.singapore7.com; adult/child S$43/33) runs several routes, passing major tourist areas such as Orchard Rd, the Botanic Gardens, Little India, Kampong Glam, Boat and Clarke Quays, Marina Bay Sands and Chinatown. Tickets are valid for 24 hours, allowing you to hop on and off as many times as you like.

SIA Hop-On

Singapore Airlines' **tourist bus** (Map p202, G3; ☑ 6338 6877; www.siahopon.com; Suntec Hub, Suntec Mall; 24hr ticket Singapore Airlines passengers adult/child S$19.50/14.50, nonpassengers S$39/29) traverses the main tourist arteries every 15 to 60 minutes daily, over four different lines. Trips start from Suntec Hub, with the first bus departing at 8.30am and the last bus departing at 6pm, terminating back at Suntec Hub at 7.10pm. Buy tickets from the driver; see the website for route details.

River Tours

Singapore Ducktours

Jump into a remodelled WWII amphibious Vietnamese war craft for a surprisingly informative and engaging one-hour **tour** (Map p202, G3; ☑6338 6877; www.ducktours. com.sg; 01-330 Suntec City, 3 Temasek Blvd; adult/child under 13yr S$37/27; ☺9am-6.30pm; ⓂEsplanade) that traverses land and water. The route focuses on Marina Bay and the Colonial District. The ticket kiosk and departure point is in Tower 5 of Suntec City, directly facing the Nicoll Hwy.

Singapore River Cruise

The 40-minute bumboat **cruises** (Map p202, C4; ☑6336 6111; www.rivercruise.com. sg; bumboat river cruise adult/child S$25/15; ⓂClarke Quay) that ply the stretch between the Quays and Marina Bay depart from several places along the Singapore River. The running commentary is a little cringe-inducing, but the trip itself is relaxing, with spectacular views of the skyline and Marina Bay.

Themed Tours

Betel Box: The Real Singapore Tours

These **insider tours** (Map p214, D3; ☑6247 7340; www.betelboxtours.com; 200 Joo Chiat Rd, tours S$50-80; ⓂPaya Lebar) include culture and heritage walks, city kick scootering and food odysseys through historic Joo Chiat (Katong), Kampong Glam and Chinatown, and a Friday night tour through red-light Geylang.

Explore at your own pace with our neighbourhood walks and Local Life features.
➡ Colonial District, Marina Bay & the Quays (p58)
➡ Chinatown (p74)
➡ Local Life: Tiong Bahru (p78)
➡ Little India (p86)
➡ Local Life: Jalan Besar (p88)

Jane's SG Tours

Specialising in **tours** (www.janestours. com; group tours S$30-80) of colonial black-and-white private homes across the island, Jane offers rare insights you may not usually be afforded as a tourist. Her other tours, covering architecture, history, religions, botany and culture are also popular – it's best to book a month in advance.

East West Planners

Exploring the city's iconic dishes and where best to eat them, these bespoke, top-end **tours** (Map p202, E1; ☑9674 5861; www.eastwestplanners.com; 03-03 Tan Chong Tower, 15 Queen St; ☺8.30am-5.30pm Mon-Fri; ⓂBras Basah, Bencoolen) are aimed at the more affluent visitor – prices and itineraries are available on request.

Walking Tours

Bukit Brown Tour

Take a **walking tour** (www.facebook.com/ groups/bukitbrown) through one of Singapore's most historic, wild and beautiful cemeteries, currently under threat from development.

Charlotte Chu Tours

See how locals live, work, eat and play on these **tours** (☑8101 1003; charlottechutours@ gmail.com; 3hr tour S$240) of lesser-known aspects of Singapore's history, heritage and culture.

VICHY DEAL/SHUTTERSTOCK ©

Maxwell Food Centre (p77)

Dining Out

Singaporeans are obsessed with makan *(food), from talking incessantly about their last meal, to feverishly photographing, critiquing and posting about it online. It's hardly surprising – food is one of Singapore's greatest drawcards, the nation's melting pot of cultures creating one of the world's most diverse, drool-inducing culinary landscapes.*

Hawker Centres, Kopitiams & Food Courts

Singapore's celebrated hawker centres, *kopitiams* and food courts serve up knockout street food at wallet-friendly prices.

Hawker centres are usually standalone, open-air (or at least open-sided) structures with a raucous vibe and rows of stalls peddling any number of different local cuisines.

Often found in air-conditioned shopping malls, food courts are basically air-conditioned hawker centres with marginally higher prices, while coffeeshops, also called

kopitiams (*tiam* is Hokkien for 'shop'), are open shopfront cafes, usually with a handful of stalls and roaming 'aunties' or 'uncles' taking drinks orders.

Hawker Centre Etiquette

➡ Bag a seat first, especially if it's busy. Sit a member of your group at a table, or 'chope' (save) your seat by laying a packet of tissues there. Don't worry if there are no completely free tables; it's normal to share with strangers.

➡ If there's a table number, note it as the stall owner uses it as a reference for food delivery.

➡ If the stall has a 'self service' sign, you'll have to carry the food to the table yourself. Otherwise, the vendor brings your order to you.

➡ Ignore wandering touts who try to sit you down and plonk menus in front of you.

➡ It's customary to return your tray once finished, although there are a few roaming cleaners who'll take your empty dishes.

Beyond Hawker

Singapore's restaurant scene is booming. From celebrated local chefs' restaurants, such as Violet Oon's National Kitchen by Violet Oon (p60) and Janice Wong's 2am Dessert Bar (p124), the city has an ever-expanding legion of top-notch, celebrity-chef nosheries. Iggy's (p99) remains one of Asia's most coveted destination restaurants, with French chef Julien Royer's new offering Odette (p61) providing lofty competition.

Most exciting is Singapore's new breed of lively eateries, which, alongside trailblazers such as Kilo (p91), deliver sharp, produce-driven menus in an altogether more relaxed setting. Among the best are Australian grill Burnt Ends (p76) and Japanese *izakaya* **Neon Pigeon** (Map p206; ☑6222 3623; www.neonpigeonsg.com; 1A Keong Saik Rd; small dishes S$9-25, large dishes S$16-48; ☺6pm-midnight Mon-Sat; ☎; Ⓜ Outram Park, Chinatown), two of a string of newcomers that have transformed Chinatown and Keong Saik into dining 'it' spots.

Singapore Specialities

CHINESE

Cantonese is the best known of the regional Chinese cuisines, with typical dishes including *xiao long bao* (dumplings filled with a piping hot soup) and dim sum – also known as yum cha – snack-type dishes usually eaten at lunchtime or as a Sunday brunch in large, noisy restaurants. Practically Singapore's national dish, Hainanese chicken rice is a soulful mix of steamed fowl and rice cooked in chicken stock, and served with a clear soup, slices of cucumber and ginger, chilli and soy dips.

Many of Singapore's Chinese are Hokkien, infamously coarse-tongued folk whose hearty noodle dishes include *char kway teow* (stir-fried noodles with cockles, Chinese sausage and dark sauces), *bak chor mee* (noodles with pork, meat balls and fried scallops) and *hokkien mee* (yel-

PLAN YOUR TRIP DINING OUT

NEED TO KNOW

Price Range

Most restaurant prices will have 17% added to them at the end: a 10% service charge plus 7% for GST, indicated by ++ on menus. The following price ranges represent the cost of a single dish or a main course, including service charge and GST.

$ less than S$10

$$ S$10–S$30

$$$ more than S$30

Opening Hours

➡ Hawker centres, food courts, coffee-shops: 7am to 10pm, sometimes 24hrs

➡ Midrange restaurants: 11am to 11pm

➡ Top-end restaurants: noon to 2.30pm and 6pm to 11pm

Reservations

➡ Book a table for expensive and 'hot' restaurants.

➡ Make bookings for midrange restaurants for Friday to Sunday nights.

Tipping

Tipping is unnecessary in Singapore, as most restaurants impose a 10% service charge – and nobody ever tips in hawker centres. That said, many do leave a discretionary tip for superlative service at higher-end restaurants.

low Hokkien noodles with prawn, served either fried or in a rich prawn-based stock).

Seafood is a speciality of Teochew cuisine, with fish *maw* (a fish's swim bladder) cropping up alarmingly often. The classic Teochew comfort food is rice porridge, served with fish, pork or frog (the last is a Geylang favourite).

INDIAN

Spicy, South Indian food dominates Singapore, with a typical dish being thali, often a large mound of rice served with various vegetable curries, *rasam* (hot, sour soup) and a dessert. Local Chinese love Indian *roti prata* – a flat bread cooked with oil on a hotplate and served with a curry sauce. Try a *roti telur* (*prata* cooked with an egg) or a *roti tissue* (ultra-thin *prata* cooked with margarine and sugar and served in a cone shape).

Other South Indian vegetarian dishes include *masala dosa,* a thin pancake rolled around spiced vegetables. Its carnivorous, halal (Muslim) equivalent is *murtabak,* paper-thin dough filled with egg and minced mutton.

MALAY & INDONESIAN

The cuisines of Malaysia and Indonesia are similar, with staples including satay – grilled kebabs of chicken, mutton or beef dipped in a spicy peanut sauce. Both *ayam goreng* (fried chicken) and *rendang* are popular, as are *nasi goreng* (fried rice) and *nasi lemak* (coconut rice served with anchovies, peanuts and a curry dish). The Sumatran style of Indonesian food bends much more towards curries and chillies. *Nasi padang,* from the Minangkabau region of West Sumatra, consists of a wide variety of spicy curries and other smaller dishes served with rice. Simply pick and choose what you want and it's dolloped on a plate.

PERANAKAN

Peranakan food is a unique fusion of Chinese ingredients and Malay sauces and spices. It's commonly flavoured with shallots, chillies, *belacan* (Malay fermented prawn paste), peanuts, preserved soybeans and galangal (a ginger-like root). Thick coconut milk is used to create the sauce that flavours the prime ingredients. Typical dishes include *otak-otak* (a paste-like combo of fish, coconut milk, chilli, galangal and herbs, wrapped and grilled in a banana leaf) and *ayam buah keluak* (chicken stewed with dark, earthy nuts imported from Indonesia to produce a rich sauce). Equally scrumptious is the distinctive Peranakan laksa (noodles in a savoury coconut-milk gravy with fried tofu and bean sprouts).

VEGETARIAN & VEGAN

Little India teems with vegetarian food, and most food courts and hawker centres offer at least some vegetarian options.

Be aware that interpretations of 'vegetarian' food can vary. 'Vegetable soup' can contain both chicken and prawn. Be highly specific when ordering food – don't just say 'vegetarian', but stress that you eat 'no meat, no seafood'.

Vegans may find life a little more difficult, though, since the consumption of dairy and other animal by-products is relatively limited, usually all you have to do is ensure there are no eggs.

Cooking Courses

A highly recommended cooking school exploring Singapore's classic dishes is Food Playground (p81). Courses usually run for three hours and can be tailored for budding cooks with dietary restrictions.

Top Guides and Blogs

Start with KF Seetoh's superb *Makansutra,* the bible of hawker centre food, then visit www.sg.dining.asiatatler.com for high-end restaurant news and reviews. Also check out the following respected food blogs:

www.ieatishootipost.sg On-the-ball foodie Leslie Tay reviews mainly hawker food around the island.

www.sethlui.com Seth scours the island for the best fare. Whichever neighbourhood you're visiting, he's been there and written about it.

www.misstamchiak.com Blogging about the Singapore food scene for over 10 years, Miss Tam Chiak loves to share her foodie adventures.

Eating by Neighbourhood

Colonial District, Marina Bay & the Quays (p60) Covers all bases, from celebrity fine-diners to food courts and tucked-away foodie gems.

Chinatown, Tanjong Pagar & the CBD (p73) Old-school hawker centres and trendy eateries.

Little India & Kampong Glam (p87) Cheap, authentic Indian in Little India; old-school Malay and trendy global eats in Kampong Glam.

Orchard Road (p97) Superlative food courts, trendy brunch cafes and high-end destination restaurants.

Eastern Singapore (p109) Home to local food hubs Joo Chiat (Katong) and Geylang.

Holland Village, Dempsey Hill & the Botanic Gardens (p124) Chic bistros and leafy garden restaurants.

Northern & Central Singapore (p119) Local dining experiences, from chilli crab at a HDB (public housing) complex to a gourmet market.

Sentosa Island (p138) Everything from fine-dining hideaways to fish and chips on the beach.

Pulau Ubin (p143) A few simple restaurants in the main street.

Southern Islands (p144) There are no restaurants on the islands so you will need to bring your own food.

West & Southwest Singapore (p132) Lush settings and top-notch Thai and Peranakan.

Lonely Planet's Top Choices

Odette (p61) Expertly crafted French creations in a perfectly pastel dining room.

Burnt Ends (p76) Meat grilled to perfection in cool Keong Saik.

National Kitchen by Violet Oon (p60) Peranakan cuisine in the stunning National Gallery Singapore.

Gluttons Bay (p60) Lip-smacking hawker fare and a festive vibe on Marina Bay.

Best by Budget

$

Gluttons Bay (p60) Hawker classics in an easy-to-navigate setting on Marina Bay.

A Noodle Story (p73) Ramen with a Singaporean twist in Chinatown.

Gandhi Restaurant (p87) Quick, authentic Indian in Little India.

$$

National Kitchen by Violet Oon (p60) Celebrating Singapore's finest flavours at the National Gallery Singapore.

Coconut Club (p75) Crispy *nasi lemak* on Ann Siang Rd.

Lian He Ben Ji Claypot Rice Pots of freshly cooked gooey goodness in Chinatown Complex (p77).

$$$

Kilo (p91) Flavourful fusion fare and a dinner-club vibe in Lavender.

Odette (p61) Modern French cuisine in pretty pastel surrounds in the National Gallery Singapore.

Iggy's (p99) Orchard Rd's most desirable culinary address.

Momma Kong's (p76) Delicious crab from a family of chilli-crab geeks in Chinatown.

Best by Cuisine

Chinese & Peranakan

Paradise Dynasty (p98) Superlative dumplings and hand-pulled noodles.

Song Fa Bak Kut Teh (p60) Steamy pork-rib soul soup.

National Kitchen by Violet Oon (p60) Much-loved Peranakan favourites in a sublime setting.

Indian

Lagnaa Barefoot Dining (p90) Flexible spice levels in Little India.

Gandhi Restaurant (p87) Flavour-packed thali, *dosa* and *uttapam* bites.

StraitsKitchen (p99) A high-end regional buffet off Orchard Rd.

Malay & Indonesian

Tambuah Mas (p98) Made-from-scratch Indonesian on Orchard Rd.

Zam Zam (p90) Old-school *murtabak* in the shadow of Sultan Mosque.

Coconut Club (p75) Upscale *nasi lemak* on Ann Siang Hill.

International & Fusion

Kilo (p91) Strictly seasonal Italian-Japanese and a killer upstairs lounge.

Cicheti (p90) Contemporary Italian dishes made with hand-picked market produce.

Smokey's BBQ (p110) Authentic, American-style barbecue in laid-back Joo Chiat (Katong).

Best for Romance

Jaan (p62) Cutting-edge French high above the Colonial District.

Halia (p126) Ginger-spiked menu in a tropical garden wonderland.

2am Dessert Bar (p124) Show-stopping desserts paired with wine and cocktails.

Best Hawker Centres & Food Courts

Maxwell Food Centre (p77) Chinatown's most tourist-friendly hawker centre.

Chinatown Complex (p77) The hardcore hawker experience.

Takashimaya Food Village (p98) A fabulous basement food hall on Orchard Rd.

Best for Crab

Momma Kong's (p76) Good deals, huge buns and Singapore's freshest Sri Lankan crabs.

No Signboard Seafood (p109) Superlative white-pepper crab in red-light Geylang.

Mellben Seafood (p120) Modern hawker-style set-up serving delicious crab.

Best for Brunch

PS Cafe (p76) Airy colonial setting with top-notch breakfast delights.

Wild Honey (p99) Filling all-day breakfasts from around the world on Orchard Rd.

Common Man Coffee Roasters (p61) Near Robertson Quay, it's known island over for scrumptious breakfasts and addictive coffee.

Best for Old-School Singapore

Red Star (p75) Retro yum cha on the edge of Chinatown.

Colbar (p132) Hainanese-style Western classics in a former officers' mess in western Singapore.

Samy's Curry Restaurant (p125) Aromatic curries served canteen-style in leafy Dempsey Hill.

ZDL/SHUTTERSTOCK ©

Drinking alfresco

Bar Open

From speakeasy cocktail bars to boutique beer stalls to artisan coffee roasters, Singapore is discovering the finer points of drinking. The clubbing scene is no less competent, with newcomers including a futuristic club in the clouds, a basement hot spot fit for the streets of Tokyo, and a techno refuge in Boat Quay.

Cocktail Bars & Lounges

Forget the sling. From the sesame-infused complexity of the 'gomashio' at Operation Dagger (p77), to the nature infused 'antz' at Native (p82), Singapore's new breed of cocktail bars are shaking and stirring bold and thrilling libations. Locavore tendencies shine through in the likes of Jekyll & Hyde's (p80) Mr Bean (vodka, Lao Ban bean curd and *kaya*), while the meticulous dating of drinks at speakeasy 28 HongKong Sreet (p63) is testament to a deepening reverence for the history and craft of cocktail making.

Pubs & Microbreweries

Singapore's beer scene is coming of age, with more bars, cafes and restaurants jumping on the craft-brew bandwagon. Even Chinatown Complex is in on the act, home to Singapore's first hawker-centre craft-beer stalls, the Good Beer Company (p80) and Smith Street Taps (p80). In stock is Singapore's own award-winning Jungle Beer (www.junglebeer.com), kick-started by four college friends determined to make beer with flavours that reflect local geography. It's not the only microbrewery in town either, with brewery-bar hybrids Alchemist Beer Lab (p64), Level 33 (p64) and Little Island Brewing Co. (p112) keeping things nuanced and local.

Cafes and Coffee Roasters

While old-school *kopitiams* (coffeeshops) have been serving *kopi* (coffee) for generations, Singapore's speciality coffee scene is a more recent phenomenon. Inspired by Australia's artisanal coffee culture, contemporary cafes such as Ronin (p64), Atlas Coffeehouse (p126) and Maison Ikkoku (p92) are brewing ethically sourced seasonal beans, using either espresso machines or 'third wave' brewing techniques such as Japanese siphons and AeroPress. Also on the increase are cafes sourcing and roasting their own beans, the best of which include Chye Seng Huat Hardware (p88) and Nylon Coffee Roasters (p77).

Clubbing

Zouk (p65) remains the city's best-known club, and its annual **ZoukOut** (www.zoukout.com), a massive dance party held each December, attracts 40,000 revellers and A-list DJs. Dance clubs proliferate around the Quays area, among them Attica (p65) and hidden, techno-pumping Headquarters by the Council (p65). Beyond this, check out **Super 0** (www.super0.sg), which runs top-notch pop-up dance parties, usually towards the end of the year. For updated listings, hit www.timeoutsingapore.com/clubs or www.e-clubbing.com.

Deals & Discounts

Singapore is an expensive city to drink in; a fact not helped by a 25% alcohol tax hike in 2014. A beer at most city bars will set you back between S$10 and S$18, with cocktails commonly ringing in between S$20 and S$30.

That said, many bars offer decent happy-hour deals, typically stretching from around 5pm to 8pm, sometimes starting earlier and finishing later. Most deals offer two drinks for the price of one or cheaper 'house pours'. On Wednesday, 'ladies' night' promotions offer cheaper (sometimes free) drinks to women.

Of course, those who don't mind plastic tables and fluorescent lights can always

NEED TO KNOW

Prices
Regular bars add 17% to your bill: 10% for service charge, 7% for GST. You'll see this indicated by '++' on drink lists.

Opening Hours
Bars 3pm to 1am or 3am
Cafes 10am to 7pm
Clubs 10pm to 3am or 5am

Entry Fees
Unless you know someone at the door or a member, at the hottest clubs you'll have to queue up. You can avoid the cover charge for some bars and clubs if you go early.

hang out with the locals at hawker centres and coffeeshops, swilling S$7 bottles of Tiger Beer.

Drinking & Nightlife by Neighbourhood

Colonial District, Marina Bay & the Quays (p63) Skyscraper bars and clubs, colonial legends, and party-people bars, pubs and clubs at the Quays.

Chinatown, Tanjong Pagar & the CBD (p77) Hip cafes, slinky cocktail lounges, hawker beer stalls, Neil St gay bars, and after-work-drinks hub Club St.

Little India & Kampong Glam (p91) Raffish pubs, artisan coffee and hidden cocktail dens.

Orchard Road (p99) Mall-bound tea purveyors and cafes, hotel bars and a bar-lined heritage street.

Eastern Singapore (p112) Local beer and cider hang-outs and relaxed beach-side bars.

Holland Village, Dempsey Hill & the Botanic Gardens (p126) Cafe-bistro hybrids in Dempsey Hill and raucous expat bars in Holland Village.

Northern & Central Singapore (p120) Old-school coffeeshops and a secret garden oasis.

Sentosa Island (p139) Beach bars with palms, sand and the odd pool.

West & Southwest Singapore (p132) Languid, old-school drinking in a veteran military mess.

Lonely Planet's Top Choices

Smoke and Mirrors (p63) Cocktails with a view to knock your socks off.

Operation Dagger (p77) Spectacular cocktails in bustling Club St and Ann Siang Hill.

28 HongKong Street (p63) Chronological cocktails in an unmarked lounge off Boat Quay.

Chye Seng Huat Hardware (p88) Hardware store turned coffee roaster in hip Jalan Besar.

Atlas (p92) A 1920s cocktail lounge with a 12m-high gin wall in Bugis.

Best Cocktails

Tippling Club (p77) Boundary-pushing libations from the bar that raised the bar.

28 HongKong Street (p63) Passionate mixologists turning grog into greatness.

Native (p82) Surprising ingredients and clever twists in trendy Amoy St.

Ah Sam Cold Drink Stall (p64) Sneaky cocktail den above Boat Quay.

Manhattan (p99) Long-forgotten cocktails are given a new lease on life in this Orchard Rd heavyweight.

Best Clubs

Zouk (p65) A multivenue classic smack in the centre of Circular Quay.

Headquarters by the Council (p65) Thumping techno and house beats in this Boat Quay shophouse.

Cherry (p101) Step back to the 1980s in this Orchard Rd basement dance club.

Best for Views

Smoke and Mirrors (p63) Point-blank views of the Marina Bay skyline.

1-Altitude (p64) The world's tallest alfresco bar, in the heart of the CBD.

CÉ LA VI SkyBar (p64) A seamless city and island panorama from Marina Bay Sands' cantilevered rooftop.

Lantern (p64) Stylish rooftop sipping with million-dollar views of Marina Bay.

Best for Beers

Level 33 (p64) Slurp made-on-site beers 33 floors above the city.

Good Beer Company (p80) A rotating cast of craft suds in a Chinatown hawker centre.

Druggists (p88) Twenty-three taps pouring craft brews in trendy Jalan Besar.

Little Island Brewing Co. (p112) Local microbrews in laid-back Changi village.

Alchemist Beer Lab (p64) Eight gleaming beer towers pouring infusion-flavoured liquid gold.

Best for Coffee

Chye Seng Huat Hardware (p88) Superlative espresso, filter coffee, on-site roasting and classes.

Nylon Coffee Roasters (p77) A small, mighty espresso bar and roaster in up-and-coming Everton Park.

Ronin (p64) Serving strong brews behind large, dark doors near Boat Quay.

Atlas Coffeehouse (p126) Industrial-styled cafe serving top-notch coffee moments from Botanic Gardens MRT.

Coffee Break (p79) Singapore *kopi* meets hipster flavours in this Amoy St hawker stall.

Best for Lingering

Tanjong Beach Club (p139) Sand, palms and a lap pool at Sentosa's more tranquil end.

Middle Rock (p120) A secluded tropical oasis in the middle of Bishan Park.

Coastal Settlement (p112) A lush, green hideaway cafe-bar-restaurant in sleepy, verdant Changi.

Best Heritage Settings

Raffles Hotel (p64) Sip a sling (if only for the novelty value) where Somerset Maugham once slumbered.

Post Bar (p65) It's worth getting dressed up for drinks in this colonial dame.

Colbar (p132) Knock back beers at a nostalgic colonial officers' mess.

Black Swan (p80) Swill martinis in a deco-licious CBD bar-cum-lounge.

Best Wine Bar

Wine Connection (p65) Diverse and interesting wines at affordable prices at Robertson Quay.

Entertainment & Activities

You're never short of a hot night out in Singapore. There's live music, theatre and adrenalin-pumping activities year-round, while at certain times of the year the Little Red Dot explodes into a flurry of car racing, cultural festivals and hot-ticket music events.

Theatre

Esplanade – Theatres on the Bay (p66) is one of the brightest spots in Singapore's vibrant theatre and dance scene. Visiting Broadway musicals take to the stage at Marina Bay Sands (p55), and local theatre groups such as Wild Rice (p92) and the Singapore Repertory Theatre (p66) regularly put up local plays as well as the occasional adaptation.

Live Music

Sure, a lot of average cover bands grace hotel bars, but an enthusiastic local music scene also thrives (to a point). Esplanade – Theatres on the Bay hosts regular free performances, and is the home of the **Singapore Symphony Orchestra** (SSO; Map p202; ☑6602 4245; www.sso.org.sg; 01-02 Victoria Concert Hall, 11 Empress Pl; ⊙10am-6pm Mon-Fri; ⓜCity Hall). Festival–themed cafe chain. Singapore also attracts a growing number of international acts, with top-tier talent showcased at both the **Singapore International Jazz Festival** (www.sing-jazz.com; ⊙Mar-Apr) and the indie-music favourite **St Jerome's Laneway Festival** (http://singapore.lanewayfestival.com; ⊙Jan/Feb).

Chinese Opera

Also known by the Malay term *wayang* (performance), Chinese opera includes indoor performances and street opera, the latter usually staged during religious events such as the **Hungry Ghost Festival** (⊙Aug/Sep). Although its popularity has decreased over time, the centuries-old tradition is kept alive by groups such as the Chinese Theatre Circle (p80).

Film

Singaporeans love to watch movies and, at around S$12.50 per ticket, it's great value. Multiplex cinemas abound, with many located in larger malls. Beyond them, the historic Rex Cinemas (p92) runs Bollywood films, while the annual **Singapore International Film Festival** (www.sgiff.com; ⊙Nov) screens independent and art-house films. Singapore's cinemas are notoriously chilly, so remember to wear something warm inside.

Thrills & Spills

The fast-paced **Rugby Sevens** (www.singapore7s.com.sg) tournament usually hits town in April, but was rescheduled in 2021 due to Covid-19; check the website for the latest information. The **Formula One Grand Prix** (www.singapore-f1-grand-prix.com) roars through in September. Hands-on sporting events include December's increasingly popular Singapore Marathon. Around the year, there's no shortage of options for thrill seekers, whether it's indoor skydiving, zip-lining on Sentosa, wakeboarding in East Coast Park, or cycling the rustic island Pulau Ubin.

Spas & Massage

Pampering is big business in Singapore, from hole-in-the-wall reflexology stalls to luxe day spas. Midrange to high-end spas can be found in most malls and five-star hotels, with Spa Esprit (p101) a popular beauty empire. At the other end of the scale, People's Park Complex (p82) has no shortage of places offering very affordable reflexology, shiatsu, and even feet-nibbling fish. Rates vary from around S$25 for a foot massage to over S$200 for a full-day package.

Lonely Planet's Top Choices

Universal Studios (p137) Gold standard rides for the young and young at heart.

Singapore Dance Theatre (p93) Classical and contemporary performances by Singapore's premier dance company.

BluJaz Café (p92) Swinging sax in a bohemian pub.

Comedy Masala (p66) Side-splitting laughs at Tuesday stand-up at Boat Quay.

Pulau Ubin (p142) Time-warped Pulau Ubin is a cycling paradise.

Best for Theatre

Singapore Repertory Theatre (p66) A world-class repertoire that includes seasonal Shakespeare at Fort Canning Park.

Wild Rice (p92) Reinterpreted classics, new works and striking sets.

TheatreWorks (p66) New commissions and international collaborations.

Necessary Stage (p112) Locally flavoured, thought-provoking theatre.

Best for Live Music

BluJaz Café (p92) Consistently good jazz and blues in Kampong Glam.

Crazy Elephant (p66) Rock and blues in party-central Clarke Quay.

Esplanade – Theatres on the Bay (p66) Polished performances from classical to rock.

Best for Film

VivoCity (p133) State-of-the-art audiovisual, Gold Class seating, and both Hollywood and independent flicks.

Screening Room (p80) Cult classics in an intimate suite in Chinatown.

Rex Cinemas (p92) Hip-shaking Bollywood hits on the edge of Little India.

Best for Pampering

Remède Spa (p101) Luxe treatments just off Orchard Rd.

People's Park Complex (p82) Low-cost rubs in atmospheric Chinatown.

Spa Esprit (p101) Oil-based therapies in an Orchard Rd apothecary.

Kenko Wellness Spa (p82) Good spa massages without blowing the budget.

Best for Hikes

Southern Ridges (p134) User-friendly trails with panoramic views.

MacRitchie Reservoir (p118) Monkeys, monitor lizards and a canopy walk.

Bukit Timah Nature Reserve (p118) Walking and biking trails through wild, primary rainforest.

Chestnut Park (p119) Hiking trails running parallel to the mountain-bike trails – over 8km of them.

Best for Kicks

iFly (p140) Freefall 9000ft without the need for a plane.

G-Max Reverse Bungy (p68) Is it a bird or a plane? It's you, hurled into the air at 200km/h.

Universal Studios (p137) Brave the world's tallest duelling roller coasters.

Ultimate Drive (p68) Tear through Singapore in a fast and sexy Italian car.

Best for Cycling

Chestnut Park (p119) Over 8km of biking trails plus two skill parks located in the forest.

East Coast Park (p108) Dedicated bike paths, flat terrain and soothing sea breezes.

Pulau Ubin (p142) A rustic island getaway made for bikes.

NEED TO KNOW

Prices

➡ From S$20 to S$70 for a ticket to a local theatre production.

➡ It's often free to watch home-grown bands at local venues; some places have a small cover charge.

➡ International music acts are expensive.

➡ Big-budget musical tickets cost S$65 to S$200.

➡ Expect to pay through the nose during the Singapore Airshow in February and the Formula One season in September – hotel prices often triple.

➡ Single-day grandstand tickets to the F1 start at S$128, but if you're on a budget, you can get walkabout tickets from S$78.

SAM'S STUDIO/SHUTTERSTOCK ©

Shoppes at Marina Bay Sands (p67)

🛍 Treasure Hunt

While its shopping scene mightn't match the edge of Hong Kong's or Bangkok's, Singapore is no retail slouch. Look beyond the malls and you'll find everything from sharply curated local boutiques to vintage map peddlers and clued-in contemporary galleries.

Malls & Boutiques

Singapore's iconic malls come in all styles and sizes, from shiny, high-tech temples such as ION Orchard Mall (p101) to budget throwbacks such as Far East Plaza (p102). Orchard Rd is Singapore's mall epicentre, with the greatest breadth and depth of stores, from high-street chains to decadent couture. While luxury brands are generally more expensive in Singapore than they are in Hong Kong, the UK or Europe, some stores offer discounts of between 10% and 15% for big spenders, so it's always worth asking.

For an altogether more idiosyncratic experience, hit the city's independent boutiques, which stock anything from lesser-known and emerging fashion labels to inspired design objects and harder-to-find books. You'll find small but thriving scenes in Tiong Bahru and Jalan Besar, as well as on Haji Lane in Kampong Glam.

Electronics

While Singapore is not the cut-price electronics nirvana it used to be, it can offer a few savings for those who do their homework and bargain successfully. Know the price of things before you start shopping around, then browse and compare. Always ask vendors what they can do to sweeten the deal; at the very least, they should be able to throw in a camera case or some memory cards, for example.

Electronics mall Sim Lim Square (p93) is well-known for its range and negotiable prices, though it's also known for taking the

PLAN YOUR TRIP TREASURE HUNT

NEED TO KNOW

Opening Hours

Malls 10am to 10pm

Mustafa Centre 24 hours

Retail stores 11am to 9pm or 10pm

Bargaining & Returns

Prices are usually fixed, except at markets and some tourist shops. If you do haggle, stay good-humoured, not causing everyone to lose face. Singaporean shops don't accept returns. Exchanges are accepted if items have original tags and packaging.

Taxes & Refunds

Departing visitors can get a refund of the 7% GST on their purchases, under the following conditions:

➡ Minimum spend of $100 at one retailer on the same day for no more than three purchases.

➡ You have a copy of the Electronic Tourist Refund Scheme (eTRS) ticket issued by the shop. Alternatively you can use a debit or credit card as a token to track your purchases; no need to pay with the card, it will just keep a tally.

➡ You scan your eTRS ticket or token bank card at the self-help kiosks at the airport or cruise terminal. If inspection of the goods is required as indicated by the eTRS self-help kiosk, you will have to present the goods, with the original receipt and your boarding pass, at the Customs Inspection Counter. Smaller stores may not participate in the GST refund scheme.

uninitiated for a ride, not to mention for occasionally selling 'new' equipment that isn't quite new: a quick internet search will bring up blacklisted businesses.

The best deals are on computers and cameras, with prices often 20% lower than in major stores. During sale periods, it's not unusual to score a computer or camera for around half the recommended retail price.

Arts & Antiques

If you're after art or antiques, it pays to know your original piece from your cheap copy. For Asian antiques, the best places to head to are Chinatown, Dempsey Rd or Tanglin Shopping Centre (p102). Deep-

pocketed collectors of contemporary Asian art should scour gallery hubs Gillman Barracks (p130) and the Old Hill Street Police Station (p59). For more affordable art by local and regional artists, check out Utterly Art (p81) and the **Affordable Art Fair** (☑6220 5682; www.affordableartfair.com/singapore; ☉Apr & Nov), the latter showcasing the work of local creatives such as Billy Ma. For goods with a distinctive Singapore flavour, try treasure-trove, junk cupboard Tong Mern Sern Antiques (p81), jam-packed **Polar Arts of Asia** (Map p216; ☑9835 5955; 02-16 Far East Shopping Centre, 545 Orchard Rd; ☉11am-5.30pm Mon-Fri, till 3.30pm Sat; Ⓜ Orchard) or wonderful Antiques of the Orient (p102).

Crafts & Fabrics

Little India is a good spot to pick up spices, decorative items and saris – you'll find a large choice of saris at Tekka Centre (p87), with finer options at nearby **Nalli** (Map p210; ☑6299 3949; www.nallisingapore.com.sg; 10 Buffalo Rd; ☉10am-9pm; Ⓜ Little India). Kampong Glam is the place to go for Persian rugs. There's no shortage of vendors on Arab St, where you'll also find Sifr Aromatics (p93), a modern take on the area's old-school perfume merchants. For colourful Peranakan garments and traditional batik fabrics, head east to the neighbourhood of Katong.

Shopping by Neighbourhood

Colonial District, Marina Bay & the Quays (p67) Interconnected malls, discount electronics and in-the-know fashion, books and art.

Chinatown, Tanjong Pagar & the CBD (p81) Antiques, food, medicines, local art and a fashion boutique.

Little India & Kampong Glam (p93) Spices, incense and saris in Little India; rugs, perfumes and indie boutiques in Kampong Glam.

Orchard Road (p101) Singapore's mall-lined shopping epicentre.

Eastern Singapore (p113) Traditional wares, from Peranakan clothing, slippers and porcelain to batik and Malaysian and Indonesian food.

Holland Village, Dempsey Hill & the Botanic Gardens (p127) High-end art and antiques in ex-military Dempsey Hill.

West & Southwest Singapore (p133) MRT-connected megamalls at HarbourFront and Jurong East.

Lonely Planet's Top Choices

Orchard Road (p95) You'll find everything on Singapore's world-famous retail strip.

Raffles Hotel Arcade (p67) One-stop souvenir shopping in an iconic locale.

Little India (p93) Five-foot ways redolent of spices and dripping with atmosphere.

Antiques of the Orient (p102) Take home a little slice of Singapore history.

Best Luxury Malls

ION Orchard Mall (p101) High-end labels in Singapore's most striking mall.

Jewel (p113) International and local brands set in a flash architectural setting at Changi Airport.

Shoppes at Marina Bay Sands (p67) Bayside luxury and the world's first floating Louis Vuitton store.

Paragon (p102) Coveted brands and a dedicated children's floor.

Hilton Shopping Gallery (p102) Harder-to-find A-listers in a tranquil setting.

Best Midrange Malls

313@Somerset (p102) High-street staples and an upbeat vibe right above Somerset MRT.

ION Orchard Mall (p101) Everything from H&M to Uniqlo and Zara in the heart of Orchard Rd.

VivoCity (p133) Midrange labels galore at Singapore's biggest mall.

Tanglin Shopping Centre (p102) Cute boutiques bring in the expats and yuppies.

Best Local & Independent Designers

In Good Company (p101) Lauded home-grown fashion label with a geometric modern aesthetic.

Supermama (p94) Stunning, locally designed Singaporean-themed giftware.

Beyond The Vines (p103) Stylish local boutique offering functional and luxurious basics in soothing, pastel hues.

Forum (p102) Cult-status, multi-label threads from street to chic.

i.t (p103) Hip designers in a Hong Kong concept store at Wisma Atria.

Best for Souvenirs

Raffles Hotel Arcade (p67) The Raffles gift shop has everything from vintage poster prints to tea and tomes.

Antiques of the Orient (p102) Beautiful old maps, prints and photos of Singapore and the region.

Rumah Bebe (p113) Peranakan fashion, accessories and craft in Joo Chiat (Katong).

Tea Chapter (p79) Beautiful loose-leaf teas and tea sets in Chinatown.

Best for Arts & Antiques

Tanglin Shopping Centre (p102) Quality Asian antiques and art in an old-school mall.

Chan + Hori Contemporary (p130) Well-respected commercial gallery of mostly contemporary, emerging Singaporean talent.

Utterly Art (p81) Affordable regional art in a tiny Chinatown gallery.

Shang Antique (p126) Evocative temple artefacts and vintage Asian knick-knacks in salubrious Dempsey Hill.

Best for Tech

Sim Lim Square (p93) Six levels of electronics at Singapore's biggest tech mall.

Mustafa Centre (p93) No shortage of electronic gizmos, available 24 hours a day.

Cathay Photo (p68) For all things camera-related.

Best for Design

Supermama (p94) Contemporary designer pieces with a Singaporean theme.

Bynd Artisan (p127) Bespoke stationery and handmade leather journals.

Scene Shang (p94) Asian designs with a contemporary twist from small items to furniture pieces.

Explore Singapore

SINGAPORE'S TOP EXPERIENCES

Buddha Tooth Relic Temple (p72)

Neighbourhoods at a Glance

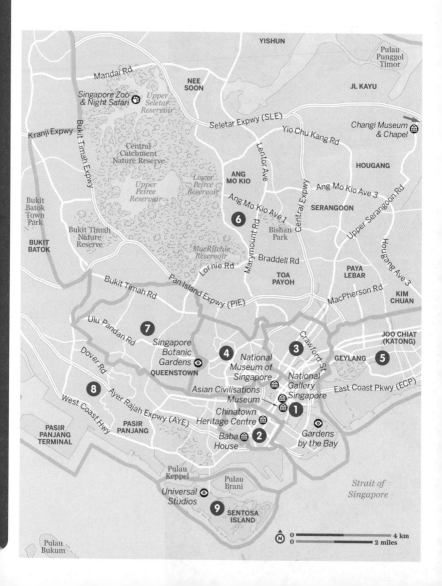

YISHUN

Pulau Punggol Timor

Mandai Rd

NEE SOON

JL KAYU

Singapore Zoo & Night Safari

Upper Seletar Reservoir

Seletar Expwy (SLE)

Yio Chu Kang Rd

Changi Museum & Chapel

Kranji Expwy

HOUGANG

Central Catchment Nature Reserve

Lentor Ave

ANG MO KIO

Ang Mo Kio Ave 3

Bukit Timah Expwy

Lower Peirce Reservoir

Upper Serangoon Rd

Upper Peirce Reservoir

Ang Mo Kio Ave 1

SERANGOON

Bukit Batok Town Park

Marymount Rd

Central Expwy

Bishan Park

6

BUKIT BATOK

Bukit Timah Nature Reserve

Hougang Ave 3

MacRitchie Reservoir

Braddell Rd

PAYA LEBAR

KIM CHUAN

Lornie Rd

TOA PAYOH

Bukit Timah Rd

Pan Island Expwy (PIE)

MacPherson Rd

Ulu Pandan Rd

7

JOO CHIAT (KATONG)

Singapore Botanic Gardens

4

National Museum of Singapore

3

GEYLANG

5

Dover Rd

QUEENSTOWN

Crawford St

National Gallery Singapore

Asian Civilisations Museum

East Coast Pkwy (ECP)

8

Ayer Rajah Expwy (AYE)

Chinatown Heritage Centre

1

West Coast Hwy

PASIR PANJANG

PASIR PANJANG

Baba House

2

Gardens by the Bay

PASIR PANJANG TERMINAL

Pulau Keppel

Pulau Brani

Strait of Singapore

Universal Studios

9

SENTOSA ISLAND

Pulau Bukum

N

0   4 km
0   2 miles

❶ Colonial District, Marina Bay & the Quays p48

The former British administrative enclave is home to a swathe of colonial architecture, museums and the track for the Formula One night race. High rollers try their luck at Marina Bay. Bisecting it all, the Singapore River also connects the three quays – home to restaurants, clubs and bars.

❷ Chinatown, Tanjong Pagar & the CBD p69

While Singapore's Chinatown may be a tamer version of its former self, its temples, heritage centre, and booming restaurant and bar scene make the trip there worthwhile. The CBD is best known for its stunning, ever-evolving skyline: rooftop bars jostle with old-school temples, all set against the financial heart that funds Singapore.

❸ Little India & Kampong Glam p83

Little India is Singapore trapped in its gritty past – it's frenetic, messy and fun. Spice traders spill their wares across its five-foot ways and Indian labourers swarm into the area each weekend. Kampong Glam, the former home of the local sultan, is an eclectic mix of Islamic stores and eateries, hipster bars and boutiques.

❹ Orchard Road p95

If you worship the gods of retail, pay your respects at this seemingly endless row of malls. For a slice of history, take a stroll along Emerald Hill Rd, a heritage strip lined with pretty Peranakan houses.

❺ Eastern Singapore p104

Geylang is an incongruous combo of temples, mosques, brothels and cult-status local eateries. East Coast Park is perfect for cycling and picnics by the beach, while nearby Joo Chiat (Katong) is steeped in Peranakan culture. At the extreme tip of the island, you'll find moving exhibits at Changi Museum & Chapel and bumboats to Pulau Ubin.

❻ Northern & Central Singapore p114

From treetop walks in MacRitchie Reservoir to the hiking and biking trails of Chestnut Park, there's plenty to keep lovers of the outdoors busy. If hiking isn't your thing, seek out grand temples and the Singapore Zoo, Night Safari and the newer River Safari.

❼ Holland Village, Dempsey Hill & the Botanic Gardens p121

Chic, salubrious Holland Village may not be a must for visitors, but its boutiques, cafes and lunching ladies offer a revealing slice of expat life. Even leafier is historic Dempsey Hill, a converted barracks laced with antiques dealers, boutiques, cafes and languid bistros. Upstaging them both is the Botanic Gardens, an invigorating blend of rare orchids, precious rainforest and romantic dining.

❽ West & Southwest Singapore p128

Walk the stunning Southern Ridges, and drop into Gillman Barracks for fabulous free art. Further west are the family-friendly attractions of the Jurong Bird Park and the Science Centre.

❾ Sentosa Island p135

Singapore's good-time island is dedicated to unabashed fun, from ambitious theme parks and a breathtaking aquarium to zip lines and cool beach bars.

NEIGHBOURHOODS AT A GLANCE

Colonial District, Marina Bay & the Quays

Neighbourhood Top Five

❶ Asian Civilisations Museum (p50) Admiring Southeast Asia's finest collection of pan-Asian treasures while discovering the historical connections among the cultures of Asia.

❷ Gardens by the Bay (p53) Leaping into a sci-fi future at Singapore's spectacular botanic garden.

❸ Marina Bay Sands (p55) Pondering Singaporean ambition from the top of one of the world's greatest engineering feats.

❹ National Museum of Singapore (p54) Time travelling through Singapore's history at this engrossing museum.

❺ Peranakan Museum (p55) Exploring the colour-saturated culture of the Peranakans.

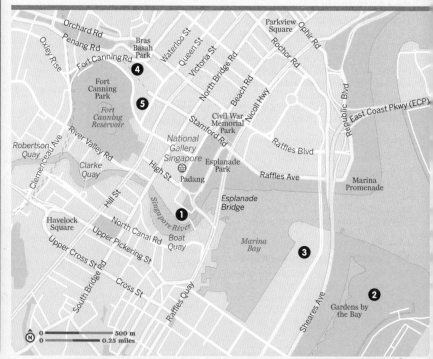

For more detail of this area see Map p202 and p204 ➡

Explore: Colonial District, Marina Bay & the Quays

This is the heart of Singapore: a showcase of grand colonial buildings, modern architectural marvels, superlative museums and parks, and pulsating riverside restaurants, bars and clubs.

The City Hall MRT station bolts the neighbourhood together and is a perfect starting point. Wander northwest along Stamford Rd towards the museums. Head in the opposite direction for booming Marina Bay, home of Marina Bay Sands, Gardens by the Bay and Esplanade – Theatres on the Bay. Around City Hall MRT itself are the iconic edifices of colonialism, among them Raffles Hotel and St Andrew's Cathedral.

Further south are the three riverside quays, best saved for night-time. You'll find a few quality drinking dens among the touristy bars at Boat Quay, no shortage of party people at raucous Clarke Quay, and a more grown-up crowd at Roberston Quay. Rising behind Clarke Quay is idyllic Fort Canning Park.

Local Life

→**Foreign enclaves** Eat, drink and shop Yangon-style at Peninsula Plaza (p67), Singapore's unofficial Little Burma and hub frequented by the city-state's influx of migrant workers.

→**Get moving** Strap on your running shoes and join locals for an early morning walk or jog through Marina Bay. The loop around the bay area is about 3.5km long; you can extend your walk by heading into the Quays.

→**Marina Barrage** The 'green roof' of Marina Barrage (p57) is a popular hang-out for Singaporean families, love-struck couples and kite enthusiasts. The curvaceous strip of lawn offers breathtaking views of the city skyline and the Strait of Singapore. For the full effect, head here just before sunset.

Getting There & Away

→**MRT** The MRT is centred on City Hall, an interchange station that's also connected via underground malls towards the Esplanade, from where you can cut across to Marina Bay. Raffles Place (East–West Line) is the next stop for the Quays. The Bayfront MRT (Downtown Line) serves Marina Bay Sands, Gardens by the Bay and Fort Canning.

→**Bus** The area is well connected by bus. Key stops are outside Raffles Hotel and outside St Andrew's Cathedral along North Bridge Rd. Bus 2 takes you down Victoria and Hill Sts. Buses 51, 61, 63 and 80 go along North Bridge Rd. For Beach Rd, take buses 100, 107 or 961. Along Bras Basah Rd, take buses 14, 16, 77 or 111.

Lonely Planet's Top Tip

Many of Singapore's museums offer free tours, which run on a first-come-first-served basis, and some also sell combined tickets that will save you a few bucks. Most bars in the area have happy-hour specials from 5pm to 8pm or 9pm. During these hours, drinks are either buy-one-get-one-free or heavily discounted. Several bars and clubs run weekly 'Ladies Nights' – usually on Wednesday – where women enjoy free entry and, sometimes, free booze (sorry boys).

⊙ Best Sights

→ National Gallery Singapore (p52)
→ Gardens by the Bay (p53)
→ National Museum of Singapore (p54)
→ Asian Civilisations Museum (p50)

For reviews, see p55.

✕ Best Places to Eat

→ National Kitchen by Violet Oon (p60)
→ Odette (p61)
→ Artichoke (p60)
→ Gluttons Bay (p60)

For reviews, see p60. →

🍷 Best Places to Drink

→ Smoke and Mirrors (p63)
→ Lantern (p64)
→ 28 HongKong St (p63)
→ Ronin (p64)

For reviews, see p63.

TOP EXPERIENCE
EXPLORE THE ASIAN CIVILISATIONS MUSEUM

The remarkable Asian Civilisations Museum houses the region's most comprehensive collection of pan-Asian treasures. Over three levels, its beautifully curated galleries explore Singapore's heritage as a port city and the connections, history, cultures and religions of Southeast Asia, China, the Indian subcontinent and Islamic west Asia. These aspects are then further explored in the context of Asia and the rest of the world.

Tang Shipwreck

Having sunk more than 1000 years ago, the Tang Shipwreck offers an insight into the history of trade throughout Asia in the 9th century. Laden with exquisite objects and over 60,000 Tang dynasty ceramics, its discovery was literally like finding hidden treasure. The mesmerising sea of Changsha bowls buoys a replica wooden plank boat, held together by coconut husk rope. Don't bother trying to see your reflection in the ornate bronze mirrors – their silvery alloy has been blackened from centuries underwater. One was even an antique before setting sail – it's now over 2000 years old!

Trade

As people migrated around the region, so did their ideas, tastes and goods. The collection of porcelain is especially strong, covering the history of the different regions in which it was produced. Don't miss the intense blue-and-white Chinese and Middle Eastern ceramics – a highlight is the elephant-shaped hookah base. It started life as a boring old water pitcher but was transformed with metal and

DON'T MISS

➡ Tang Shipwreck's 1000-year-old booty

➡ Trade Gallery's blue-and-white Chinese and Middle Eastern ceramics

➡ Chinese monochrome ceramics

➡ Imposing terracotta head of Bodhisattva

PRACTICALITIES

➡ Map p202, E6

➡ ☎ 6332 7798

➡ www.acm.org.sg

➡ 1 Empress Pl

➡ adult/child under 6yr S$8/free, 7-9pm Fri half price

➡ ⏰10am-7pm Sat-Thu, to 9pm Fri

➡ Ⓜ Raffles Place

silver to create this stunning object. One for slightly different tastes is the brightly coloured boar's-head tureen and underdish – complete with open nostrils for the steam to escape, it must have made quite the spectacle on its owner's dinner table. It wasn't all about porcelain in the Tang dynasty era, though – the intricate silver tea set was made in China and is one of the few remaining still with its original box.

Ancient Religions

Ancient Indian religions also spread throughout Asia from the 3rd century BCE, specifically Hinduism and Buddhism, and this gallery showcases the changes in religious images that occurred as the new was meshed with the old. Be enthralled by the commanding presence of the terracotta head of a Bodhisattva, whose mane of hair, beard and headdress is incredibly detailed. This gallery is still a work in progress as the museum intends to delve further into the transformations of these religions and others in Asia.

Chinese Ceramics

The Chinese Ceramics collection offers a huge range of baked clay objects, from rudimentary pots to fine porcelain objects, showcasing some of China's most esteemed artistic legacies. Learn the history of the different areas, kilns and techniques, as well as the many uses for these products. The burial and rituals section is particularly interesting – some may even find the crude, miniature figurines for Han tombs slightly disturbing. Don't miss the monochrome ceramics, which lack any decorations or patterns, and are strangely calming – the Xing whitewares are the most beautiful.

EMPRESS PLACE BUILDING

The Asian Civilisations Museum's handsome home is the Empress Place Building. Designed by British architect John Frederick Adolphus McNair and built in 1865 using Indian convict labour, it originally housed the colonial British government offices. Architecture buffs will appreciate its elegant fusion of neo-Palladian classicism and tropical touches like the timber louvered shutters and wide shaded porch. Two new wings were added in 2015; designed by Singaporean architect and design firm Greenhilli, these modern additions to complement and integrate beautifully with the existing buildings.

TOP TIPS

➡The 3rd-level galleries are only accessible from the stairs and the lift at the rear of the building.

➡Mornings are the quietest time to visit to avoid crowds.

➡If you enter via the River Entrance, make sure you exit out the main lobby doors to see the building's impressive facade.

JENNY ZHANG/SHUTTERSTOCK © ARCHITECTS: STUDIOMILOU

TOP EXPERIENCE

GET ARTY AT NATIONAL GALLERY SINGAPORE

Ten years in the making, the S$530 million National Gallery is a befitting home for what is one of the world's most important surveys of colonial and post-colonial Southeast Asian art. Housed in the historic City Hall and Old Supreme Court buildings, its 8000-plus collection of 19th-century and modern Southeast Asian art fills two major gallery spaces.

The Buildings

Unified by a striking aluminum and glass canopy, Singapore's former City Hall and Old Supreme Court buildings are now joined to create the country's largest visual arts venue spanning a whopping 64,000 sq metres. Enter via the St Andrew's Rd door to get a real appreciation of how these colonial giants have been seamlessly connected. Tours are held daily; don't miss the court holding cells, where many of Singapore's accused waited to hear their fates.

Permanent Galleries

Titled 'Siapa Nama Kamu?' (Malay for 'what is your name?'), the DBS Singapore Gallery showcases a comprehensive overview of Singaporean art from the 19th century to today. Be mesmerised by *Portrait of Lee Boon Ngan* before having your mind bent by *Chair,* remade especially for the gallery. The UOB Southeast Asia Gallery examines the art and artistic contexts of the greater Southeast Asian region. Be confronted by Raden Saleh's wall-filling Forest Fire and fright-inducing Wounded Lion.

For the Kids

Young culture vultures shouldn't miss the National Gallery's Keppel Centre for Art Education, which delivers innovative, multisensory art experiences for kids.

DON'T MISS

➡ Raden Saleh's *Forest Fire* and *Wounded Lion*
➡ *Chair,* by Matthew Ngui
➡ View from the 6th floor Padang Deck

PRACTICALITIES

➡ Map p202, E4
➡ www.nationalgallery.sg
➡ St Andrew's Rd
➡ adult/child S$20/15
➡ ⏱10am-7pm Sun-Thu, to 10pm Fri & Sat
➡ 🛜
➡ Ⓜ City Hall

TOP EXPERIENCE
BE AMAZED IN GARDENS BY THE BAY

Welcome to the botanic gardens of the future, a land of space-age bio-domes, high-tech Supertrees and whimsical sculptures. Costing S$1 billion and sprawling across 101 hectares of reclaimed land, Gardens by the Bay is an ambitious masterpiece of urban planning, as thrilling to architecture buffs as it is to nature lovers.

The Conservatories

Housing 217,000 plants from 800 species, the asymmetrical conservatories rise like giant paper nautilus shells beside Marina Bay. The Flower Dome replicates a dry, Mediterranean climate, and is home to sophisticated restaurant Pollen (p63), which sources ingredients from the Gardens. Cloud Forest Dome is a steamy affair, re-creating the tropical montane climate found between 1500m and 3000m. Its centrepiece is a 35m-high mountain with waterfall.

Supertrees & Sculptures

Sci-fi meets botany at the Supertrees, 18 steel-clad concrete structures adorned with 162,900 plants. Actually massive exhausts for the Gardens' bio-mass steam turbines, they generate electricity to cool the conservatories. Walk across the 22m-high OCBC Skyway connecting six Supertrees at Supertree Grove (pictured), where tickets are purchased. Daily at 7.45pm and 8.45pm, the Supertrees become the glowing protagonists of Garden Rhapsody, a light-and-sound show.

The most visually arresting of the Gardens' numerous artworks is Mark Quinn's colossal, *Planet*. Created in 2008 and donated to Gardens by the Bay, the sculpture is a giant seven-month-old infant, fast asleep and seemingly floating above the ground. This illusion is nothing short of brilliant, especially considering the bronze bubba comes in at a hefty 7 tonnes. The work was modelled on Quinn's own son.

DON'T MISS

→ Flower Dome and Cloud Forest Dome
→ Supertree Grove
→ *Planet* sculpture

PRACTICALITIES

→ Map p204, C2
→ ✆ 6420 6848
→ www.gardensbythebay.com.sg
→ 18 Marina Gardens Dr
→ gardens free, conservatories adult/child under 13yr S$28/15, OCBC Skyway adult/child under 13yr S$8/$5
→ ⏲ 5am-2am, conservatories & OCBC Skyway 9am-9pm, last ticket sale 8pm
→ 📶
→ Ⓜ Bayfront

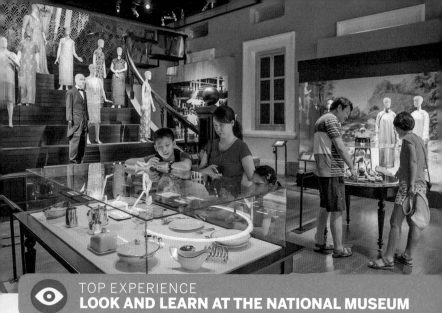

TOP EXPERIENCE
LOOK AND LEARN AT THE NATIONAL MUSEUM

Imaginative, prodigiously stocked and brilliantly designed, the National Museum of Singapore is good enough to warrant two visits. Recently revamped, the space ditches staid exhibits for lively multimedia galleries that bring Singapore's jam-packed biography to vivid life.

Galleries

Spanning six centuries and peppered with historical artefacts and personal accounts, the History Gallery will have you peering into opium dens, confronting harrowing tales of Japanese occupation and even smelling the stench of the old Singapore River! On level two, exhibitions magically re-create snapshots of everyday life in Singapore over the past 100 years – from the buzz and fashion of the colonial era, to stories of resilience and hope from war survivors, and the aspirations and dreams of a child growing up. It's rounded off with the emergence of Singapore as a nation through arts and culture. The final exhibition, Desire and Danger, showcases exquisite 19th-century botanical watercolours commissioned by Singapore's first resident and commandant, William Farquhar. Adding further layers of enlightenment are the museum's top-notch temporary exhibitions, which cover subjects as diverse as post-independence art to the history of Singapore motor racing.

The Building

The superb neoclassical wing, built in 1887 as the Raffles Library and Museum, boasts a breathtaking rotunda, lavished with 50 panels of stained glass. A sleek extension features a Glass Passage, with revealing views of the dome's exterior, as well as its own dramatic, 16m-high Glass Rotunda.

DON'T MISS

➡ History gallery and the Desire and Danger exhibition

➡ Life in Singapore: The Past 100 Years galleries

➡ Temporary exhibitions

➡ Architecture

PRACTICALITIES

➡ Map p202, D2

➡ ☎ 6332 3659

➡ www.national museum.sg

➡ 93 Stamford Rd

➡ adult/child, student & senior S$15/10

➡ ⏲10am-7pm, last admission 6.30pm

➡ P 🛜

➡ Ⓜ Dhoby Ghaut, Bencoolen

SIGHTS

NATIONAL GALLERY SINGAPORE   GALLERY
See p52.

GARDENS BY THE BAY   GARDENS
See p53.

ASIAN CIVILISATIONS MUSEUM   MUSEUM
See p50.

**NATIONAL MUSEUM
OF SINGAPORE**   MUSEUM
See p54.

★MARINA BAY SANDS   CASINO
Map p204 (www.marinabaysands.com; Marina
Bay; ☎; MBayfront) Designed by Israeli-born
architect Moshe Safdie, Marina Bay Sands
is a sprawling hotel, casino, mall, theatre,
exhibition and museum complex. Star of
the show is the Marina Bay Sands hotel
(p157), its three 55-storey towers connected
by a cantilevered SkyPark (p64). Head up
for a drink and stellar views at CÉ LA VI
(p64), before catching a show at the Master-
Card Theatres or doing serious damage to
your credit card at the Shoppes (p67).

★PERANAKAN MUSEUM   MUSEUM
Map p202 (☎6332 7591; www.peranakan
museum.org.sg; 39 Armenian St; adult/child under
7yr S$10/free, 7-9pm Fri half price; ⊙10am-7pm,
to 9pm Fri; MCity Hall, Bras Basah) This is the
best spot to explore the rich heritage of the
Peranakans (Straits Chinese descendants).
Thematic galleries cover various aspects
of Peranakan culture, from the traditional
12-day wedding ceremony to crafts, spirituality and feasting. Look out for intricately
detailed ceremonial costumes and beadwork, beautifully carved wedding beds and
rare dining porcelain. An especially curious
example of Peranakan fusion culture is a
pair of Victorian bell jars in which statues
of Christ and the Madonna are adorned
with Chinese-style flowers and vines. The
museum shop stocks embroidered bags,
Peranakan-style *kebayas* (traditional blouse
dresses) and ceramics, and books spanning
Peranakan history, food and architecture.

RAFFLES HOTEL   NOTABLE BUILDING
Map p202 (☎6337 1886; www.raffleshotel.com; 1
Beach Rd; MCity Hall, Esplanade) Although its
resplendent lobby is only accessible to hotel and restaurant guests, Singapore's most
iconic slumber palace is worth a quick visit
for its magnificent ivory frontage, famous
Sikh doorman and lush, hushed tropical
grounds. The hotel started life in 1887 as
a modest 10-room bungalow fronting the
beach (long gone thanks to land reclamation) and unveiled a new chapter in August
2019, when it reopened after nearly two
years of significant renovations (the cost of
which is a tightly held secret).

Behind the hotel were the Sarkies brothers, immigrants from Armenia and proprie-
tors of two other grand colonial hotels – the
Strand in Yangon (Rangoon) and the Eastern & Oriental in Penang. The hotel's heyday
began in 1899 with the opening of the main
building, the same one that guests stay in today. Before long, 'Raffles' became a byword

MARINA BAY SANDS

Love it or hate it, it's hard not to admire the sheer audacity of Singapore's S$5.7 billion
Marina Bay Sands. Perched on the southern bank of Marina Bay, the sprawling hotel,
casino, theatre, exhibition centre, mall and museum is the work of Israeli-born architect
Moshe Safdie. Star of the show is Marina Bay Sands (p157) hotel, its three 55-storey
towers inspired by propped-up playing cards and connected by a cantilevered, 1.2-
hectare SkyPark.

SkyPark offers one gob-smacking panorama. Its world-famous infinity pool is off-limits
to non-hotel guests, but the Observation Deck (p64) is open to all. The deck is completely
exposed, so use sunscreen and wear a hat, and avoid heading up on wet days.

Marina Bay Sands' attention-seeking tendencies extend to the nightly **Spectra**
(☎6688 8868; Event Plaza, Promenade; ⊙8pm & 9pm Sun-Thu, 8pm, 9pm & 10pm Fri & Sat;
MBayfront) FREE, a 15-minute extravaganza of interweaving lasers, water screens,
fountain jets and video projections set to a pumping soundtrack. While its 'journey as a
multicultural society into the cosmopolitan city theme' is hard to follow, there's no deny-
ing the technical brilliance of the show. Best views are from the city side of Marina Bay.

for oriental luxury ('A legendary symbol for all the fables of the Exotic East', went the publicity blurb) and was featured in novels by Joseph Conrad and Somerset Maugham. The famous Singapore Sling was first concocted here by bartender Ngiam Tong Boon in 1915, and (far less gloriously) a Singaporean tiger, escaped from a travelling circus nearby, was shot beneath the Billiard Room in 1902. A shabby relic by the 1970s, the property dodged the wrecking ball in 1987 with National Monument designation, reopening in 1991 after a S$160-million facelift.

ARTSCIENCE MUSEUM   MUSEUM

Map p204 (☑6688 8826; www.marinabaysands.com/museum; Marina Bay Sands; average prices adult/child under 13yr S$17/12, under 2yr free; ◷10am-7pm, last admission 6pm; Ⓜ Bayfront) Designed by prolific Moshe Safdie and looking like a giant white lotus, the lily pond–framed ArtScience Museum hosts major international travelling exhibitions in fields as varied as art, design, media, science and technology. Expect anything from explorations of deep-sea creatures to retrospectives of world-famous industrial designers.

FORT CANNING PARK   PARK

Map p202 (www.nparks.gov.sg; bounded by Hill St, Canning Rise, Clemenceau Ave & River Valley Rd; Ⓜ Dhoby Ghaut, Clarke Quay, Fort Canning) When Raffles rolled into Singapore, locals steered clear of Fort Canning Hill, then called Bukit Larangan (Forbidden Hill) out of respect for the sacred shrine of Sultan Iskandar Shah, ancient Singapura's last ruler. Today, the hill is better known as Fort Canning Park, a lush retreat from the hot streets below. Take a stroll in the shade of truly enormous trees, amble through the spice garden or ponder Singapore's wartime defeat at the Battlebox museum (p57).

MINT MUSEUM OF TOYS   MUSEUM

Map p202 (☑6339 0660; www.emint.com; 26 Seah St; adult/child S$15/7.50; ◷9.30am-6.30pm, last Sat of month to 9.30pm; Ⓜ City Hall, Esplanade) Nostalgia rules at this slinky ode to playtime, its four skinny floors home to over 50,000 vintage toys. You'll see everything from rare Flash Gordon comics and supersonic toy guns to original Mickey Mouse dolls and oh-so-wrong golliwogs from 1930s Japan. Stock up on whimsical

QUAYS OF THE CITY

The stretch of riverfront that separates the Colonial District from the CBD is known as the Quays. The Singapore River now connects the three quays together. A walk along them offers an eye-opening view of the changes that have impacted Singapore's trade through the years: from the dirt and grit of the once-filthy waterways to the gleaming steel and glass of today's financial district.

Boat Quay (Map p202; Ⓜ Raffles Place, Clarke Quay) Closest to the former harbour, Boat Quay was once Singapore's centre of commerce, and remained an important economic area into the 1960s. By the mid-1980s, many of the shophouses were in ruins as businesses moved elsewhere on the island. Declared a conservation zone by the government, the area became a major entertainment district filled with touristy bars, shops and menu-clutching touts luring the masses into their waterside restaurants. Discerning punters ditch these for the growing number of clued-in cafes and drinking dens dotting the streets behind the main strip.

Clarke Quay (Map p202; www.clarkequay.com.sg; 🕾; Ⓜ Clarke Quay, Fort Canning) Named after Singapore's second colonial governor, this is the busiest and most popular of the quays, its plethora of bars, restaurants and clubs pulling in the pleasure seekers every night. How much time you spend in Clarke Quay really depends upon your personal taste in aesthetics. If pastel hues, Dr Seuss–style design and lad-and-ladette hang-outs are your schtick, you'll be well in your element. Fans of understated cool, however, should steer well clear.

Robertson Quay (Map p202; Ⓜ Clarke Quay, Fort Canning) At the furthest reach of the river, Robertson Quay was once used for the storage of goods. Now some of the old godown (warehouses) have found new purpose as bars and members-only party places. The vibe here is more 'grown up' than Clarke Quay, attracting a 30-plus crowd generally more interested in wining, dining and conversation. A handful of notable riverside hang-outs have also popped up further west of Saiboo St.

toys at the lobby shop or celebrate adulthood with a stiff drink at the adjacent **Mr Punch Rooftop Bar** (Map p202; ☑6339 6266; www.mrpunch.com; ⊘3-11.30pm Mon-Thu, to 2am Fri, 11am-11.30pm Sat, to 6pm Sun; ⓂCity Hall, Esplanade). Enjoy free admission on the last Saturday of the month from 6.30pm till 9.30pm.

NATIONAL LIBRARY
LIBRARY

Map p202 (☑6332 3255; www.nlb.gov.sg; 100 Victoria St; ⊘10am-9pm; Ⓟ⚡; ⓂBugis, Bras Basah) Designed by Malaysian architect and ecologist Ken Yeang, this white, curvaceous brains trust is home to numerous facilities, including a reference library, lending library and drama centre. For visitors, the real draws are the display of beautiful maps of Asia on level 10 (some dating back to the 16th century), and the library's program of free exhibitions. If you have little ones in tow, head to the forest-themed children's library in the basement for some story-time R&R.

MARINA BARRAGE
PARK

Map p204 (☑6514 5959; www.pub.gov.sg/marinabarrage; 8 Marina Gardens Dr; ⊘24hr; ☐400, ⓂBayfront) Singaporean ingenuity in action, Marina Barrage is both a flood-control dam of the Marina Channel and a gorgeous park with commanding skyline views. The on-site Sustainable Singapore Gallery includes fascinating photos and archival footage of the Singapore River before its extreme makeover, as well as a nifty working model of the Marina Barrage itself. The park's lawn is dotted with locals flying their colourful kites.

ST ANDREW'S CATHEDRAL
CHURCH

Map p202 (☑6337 6104; www.cathedral.org.sg; 11 St Andrew's Rd; ⊘9am-5pm; ⓂCity Hall) Funded by Scottish merchants and built by Indian convicts, this wedding cake of a cathedral stands in stark contrast to the glass and steel surrounding it. Completed in 1838 but torn down and rebuilt in its present form in 1862 after lightning damage, it's one of Singapore's finest surviving examples of English Gothic architecture. Interesting details include the tropics-friendly *porte-cochère* (carriage porch) entrance – designed to shelter passengers – and the colourful stained glass adorning the western wall.

8Q SAM
MUSEUM

Map p202 (☑6589 9580; www.singaporeartmuseum.sg; 8 Queen St; adult/student & senior S$6/3, 6-9pm Fri free; ⊘10am-7pm Sat-Thu, to 9pm Fri; ⓂBras Basah, Bencoolen) Named after its address, the younger sibling of the **Singapore Art Museum** (SAM; Map p202; 71 Bras Basah Rd; ⓂBras Basah), is undergoing a significant revamp until 2023. Snoop around four floors of contemporary art, from quirky installations and video art to mixed-media statements.

BATTLEBOX
MUSEUM

Map p202 (☑6338 6133; www.battlebox.com.sg; 2 Cox Tce; adult/child S$18/9; ⊘tours 1.30pm, 2.45pm & 4pm Mon, 9.45am, 11am, 1.30pm, 2.45pm & 4pm Tue-Sun; ⓂDhoby Ghaut) Take a tour through the Battlebox, the former command post of the British during WWII, and get lost in the eerie and deathly quiet 26-room underground complex. War veterans and Britain's Imperial War Museum helped re-create the authentic bunker environs; life-size models re-enact the fateful surrender to the Japanese on 15 February 1942. Japanese Morse codes are still etched on the walls. Enthusiasts can also join the **Of Graves, Guns & Battles tour** (adult/child S$32/15), which includes Fort Canning Hill, every Monday and Thursday at 2pm (except public holidays).

SINGAPORE FLYER
FERRIS WHEEL

Map p204 (☑6333 3311; www.singaporeflyer.com.sg; 30 Raffles Ave; adult/child under 13yr S$33/21; ⊘ticket booth 8am-10pm, wheel 8.30am-10.30pm, last ride 10pm; ⓂPromenade) Las Vegas' High Roller may have since stolen its 'World's Biggest Observation Wheel' title, but Singapore's 165m-tall Ferris wheel continues to serve up a gobsmacking panorama. On a clear day, the 30-minute ride will have you peering out over the Colonial District, CBD and Marina Bay, the high-rise housing sprawl to the east and out to the ship-clogged South China Sea. The wheel's construction is documented in an on-site multimedia display, Journey of Dreams.

SINGAPORE TYLER PRINT INSTITUTE
GALLERY

(STPI; ☑6336 3663; www.stpi.com.sg; 41 Robertson Quay; ⊘10am-7pm Mon-Fri, 9am-6pm Sat, free guided tours 11.30am Tue & Thu, 2pm Sat; ⓂFort Canning) FREE Established by the American master printmaker Kenneth E Tyler, the STPI collaborates with both established and emerging artists to create contemporary, often surprising, art based on printmaking and paper. Both local and

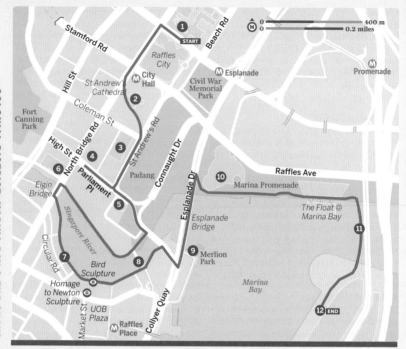

Neighbourhood Walk
Colonial to Cutting Edge

START RAFFLES HOTEL
END MARINA BAY SANDS
LENGTH 4KM; FOUR TO FIVE HOURS

Start at ❶**Raffles Hotel** (p55), taking in the magnificent ivory frontage, colonial arcades and tropical gardens. Head along North Bridge Rd and turn left into elegant ❷**St Andrew's Cathedral** (p57), used as an emergency hospital during WWII. Going south down St Andrew's Rd you'll pass City Hall and the Old Supreme Court, housing the ❸**National Gallery Singapore** (p52). Behind it, along Parliament Pl, is the ❹**New Supreme Court** (p59), a sci-fi statement co-designed by Sir Norman Foster's company Foster + Partners. Return to the St Andrew's Rd corner, and look below where it curves to the left, where the ❺**Victoria Theatre & Concert Hall** (p59) stands, one of Singapore's first Victorian Revivalist buildings. Before it is the original Raffles statue, which once stood at the Padang. Hang a right to walk along the bank of the Singapore River, one of the best spots to take in the CBD's

powerhouse towers. They're significantly taller than the multicoloured ❻**Old Hill St Police Station** (p59) on the corner of Hill St, proclaimed a 'skyscraper' upon completion in 1934. The building houses several high-end art galleries. Cross Elgin Bridge and head down to ❼**Boat Quay** (p56), its riverfront shophouses now home to bars, restaurants and snap-happy tourists. Look out for the area's great sculptures, including Fernando Botero's *Bird* and Salvador Dalí's *Homage to Newton*. Following the river further east you'll pass ❽**Cavenagh Bridge**, constructed in Scotland and reassembled in Singapore in 1869. Soaring beside it is the mighty Fullerton Hotel, Singapore's general post office until 1996. Take a 'wacky' photo with the famous ❾**Merlion statue** (p59), then head north along the Esplanade Bridge towards ❿**Esplanade – Theatres on the Bay** (p66). Continue east along Marina Promenade to the ⓫**Helix Bridge**, where the impressive views of the Singapore skyline are upstaged by those from the Sands SkyPark atop ⓬**Marina Bay Sands** (p55).

international names are showcased in the gallery, while the Saturday guided tour takes place in the printing workshop itself.

MERLION · MONUMENT

Map p202 (1 Fullerton Rd; Ⓜ Raffles Place) Back in the 1980s, someone at the tourism board created a myth about a half fish, half lion, and the gawking tourists helped seal its status as an iconic (nobody said it was pretty) Singapore sight. While visiting this S$165,000 concrete creature isn't in itself worth your time, the Marina Bay views make the trip worthwhile. Don't forget to jump on a boat cruise for a complete circuit of Singapore's changing waterways.

OLD HILL STREET POLICE STATION · GALLERY

Map p202 (formerly MICA Building; 140 Hill St; ◷10am-7pm; Ⓜ Clarke Quay, Fort Canning) **FREE** An architectural pin-up famed for its Technicolor shutters and neo-Renaissance design, the Old Hill Street Police Station houses a string of well-known commercial art galleries representing successful regional artists. These include **Art-2 Gallery** (☑6338 8713; www.art2.com.sg; 01-03 Old Hill Street Police Station; ◷11am-7pm Mon-Fri) and the **Cape of Good Hope** (☑6733 3822; www.capeofgoodhope.com.sg; 01-06 Old Hill St Police Station; ◷11am-7pm Mon-Sat, noon-6pm Sun). Here you'll also find **Redot Fine Art Gallery** (☑6222 1039; www.redotgallery.com; 01-08 Old Hill St Police Station; ◷noon-7pm Tue-Sat), the only gallery in Singapore specialising in Australian Indigenous art.

ARMENIAN CHURCH · CHURCH

Map p202 (www.armeniansinasia.org; 60 Hill St; ◷9am-6pm; Ⓜ City Hall) The Armenians were the first Christian community to build a permanent place of worship in Singapore – this handsome, neoclassical number was designed by eminent colonial architect George Coleman. Consecrated in 1836 and dedicated to St Gregory the Illuminator, the building features a Greek cruciform plan and elegant Roman Doric columns and pilasters. The tower and spire were added in the 1850s.

Pushing up orchids in the graveyard is Agnes Joaquim, discoverer of Singapore's national flower – the Vanda Miss Joaquim orchid.

CRICKET, COURTS & CULTURE: THE PADANG & AROUND

The open field of the **Padang** (Map p202; Ⓜ City Hall, Esplanade) is where eager batsmen play cricket in the tropical heat, cheered on by members of the Singapore Cricket Club in the pavilion. At the opposite end of the field is the Singapore Recreation Club. Cricket is still played on the weekends.

This rather prosaic spot has darker historical significance, as it was here that the invading Japanese herded the European community together before marching them off to Changi Prison. Apart from the reconstructed monstrosity that is the Singapore Recreation Club (it looks like something made from kids' building blocks), the Padang is flanked by a handsome collection of colonial buildings and assorted monuments, all of which can be enjoyed on a leisurely stroll.

At the Padang's southern end is the **Victoria Theatre & Concert Hall** (Map p202; ☑6908 8810; www.vtvch.com; 11 Empress Pl; ◷10am-9pm; Ⓜ Raffles Place). Recently restored, it was once the town hall. Built in 1827, the **Old Parliament House** (The Arts House; Map p202; ☑6332 6900; www.theartshouse.sg; 1 Old Parliament Lane; ◷10am-10pm; Ⓜ City Hall) is Singapore's oldest government building. Originally a private mansion, it became a courthouse, then the Assembly House of the colonial government and, finally, the Parliament House for independent Singapore. It's now an arts centre called Arts House.

Along St Andrew's Rd, the Old Supreme Court (built in 1939) and City Hall (which dates from 1929) have now been morphed into the resplendent National Gallery Singapore (p52). Situated next door is the **New Supreme Court** (Map p202; ☑6336 0644; 1 Supreme Court Lane; Ⓜ City Hall), its disc-shaped crown a new-millennium answer to its older sibling's dome. It was in the City Hall building that Lord Louis Mountbatten announced Japanese surrender in 1945 and Lee Kuan Yew declared Singapore's independence in 1965. Looking on quite reverently is neo-Gothic St Andrew's Cathedral (p57), the last but not least, of the Padang area's colonial beauties.

EATING

The handful of restaurants in the National Gallery Singapore brings some top-notch dining options to the Colonial District, while those who have a thing for celeb restaurants will be in their element in Marina Bay Sands. Head to the Quays for an endless choice of breezy waterfront restaurants and bars.

★GLUTTONS BAY HAWKER $
Map p202 (www.makansutra.com; 01-15 Esplanade Mall, 8 Raffles Ave; dishes from S$4.50; ◎5pm-2am Mon-Thu, to 3am Fri & Sat, 4pm-1am Sun; MEsplanade, City Hall) Selected by the *Makansutra Food Guide,* this row of alfresco hawker stalls is a great place to start your Singapore food odyssey. Get indecisive over classics like oyster omelette, satay, barbecue stingray and carrot cake (opt for the black version).

Its central, bayside location makes it a huge hit, so head in early or late to avoid the frustrating hunt for a table.

SONG FA BAK KUT TEH CHINESE $
Map p202 (☑6533 6128; www.songfa.com.sg; 11 New Bridge Rd; dishes S$3.20-11.50; ◎9am-9.15pm Tue-Sun; MClarke Quay) If you need a hug, this cult-status eatery delivers with its *bak kut teh.* Literally 'meat bone tea', it's a soothing concoction of fleshy pork ribs simmered in a peppery broth of herbs, spices and whole garlic cloves. The ribs are sublimely soft, sweet and melt-in-the-mouth, and staff will happily refill your bowl with broth.

Be in by 11.45am at lunch or before 7pm at dinner or else head to the back of the queue.

SATAY BY THE BAY HAWKER $
Map p204 (☑6538 9956; www.gardensbythebay. com.sg; Gardens by the Bay, 18 Marina Gardens Dr; dishes from S$4; ◎stall hours vary, drinks stall 24hr; MBayfront) Gardens by the Bay's own hawker centre has an enviable location, alongside Marina Bay and far from the roar of city traffic.

Especially evocative at night, it's known for its satay, best devoured under open skies on the spacious wooden deck. As you'd expect, prices are a little higher than at more local hawker centres, with most dishes costing S$8 to S$10.

YET CON CHINESE $
Map p202 (☑6337 6819; 25 Purvis St; chicken rice S$6; ◎11am-9.30pm; MCity Hall, Esplanade) Retro Yet Con has been serving up superlative Hainanese chicken rice since 1940. Don't come expecting designer decor or charming service. Just come for the chicken, which is tender, packed with flavour and served to faithful suits, old-timers and 20-something food nerds by stern-looking aunties. Don't be put off by the crowds either – turnover is usually fast.

RASAPURA MASTERS HAWKER $
Map p204 (☑6688 6888; www.marinabaysands. com; B2-50 Shoppes at Marina Bay Sands, 2 Bayfront Ave; dishes from S$5; ◎24hr, stall hours vary; ☎; MBayfront) If you prefer your hawker grub with a side of air-con, head to this bustling, gleaming food court in the Marina Bay Sands mall's basement. Its stalls cover most bases, from Japanese ramen and Korean kimchi to Hong Kong roast meats and local *bak kut teh* (porkbone tea soup). Tuck in while you watch kids attempt to skate on the rink next door.

Dishes average around S$8 to S$12 – more expensive than local hawker centres but still a bargain in this corner of town.

★NATIONAL KITCHEN BY VIOLET OON PERANAKAN $$
Map p202 (☑9834 9935; www.violetoon.com; 02-01 National Gallery Singapore, 1 St Andrew's Rd; dishes S$15-42; ◎noon-2.30pm & 6-9.30pm, high tea 3-4.30pm; MCity Hall) Chef Violet Oon is a national treasure, much loved for her faithful Peranakan (Chinese-Malay fusion) dishes – so much so that she was chosen to open her latest venture inside Singapore's showcase National Gallery (p52). Feast on made-from-scratch beauties like sweet, spicy *kueh pie ti* (pastry cups stuffed with prawns and yam beans), dry laksa and beef rendang. Bookings two weeks in advance essential.

True to its name, the restaurant also touches on Singapore's other culinary traditions, from Indian and Eurasian to Hainanese. The high tea offers a wonderful sampling of Violet's signature flavours – the perfect afternoon break. There are several other **branches** in town, including one at Clarke Quay (Map p202; ☑9834 9935; 01-18, 3B River Valley Rd; ◎6-10.30pm; MClarke Quay, Fort Canning) – the National Gallery outlet is the best, though.

PURVIS STREET FOOD OUTLETS

Not one to lose out to its neighbour Seah St, Purvis St (MCity Hall, Esplanade) packs it in with a whole heap of restaurants, many of them excellent. Those with deep pockets will want to splash out on Italian at **Garibaldi** (Map p202; 6837 1468; www.garibaldi.com.sg; 01-02, 36 Purvis St; mains S$28-88, set lunch from S$39; noon-2.30pm & 6.30pm-12.30am) or French at **Gunther's** (Map p202; 6338 8955; www.gunthers.com.sg; 01-03, 36 Purvis St; set lunch S$38, mains S$28-125; noon-2.30pm & 6.30-10pm Mon-Fri, 6.30-10pm Sat), while carnivores will love **Salted and Hung** (Map p202; 6358 3130; www.saltedandhung.com.sg; 12 Purvis St; dishes S$12-65, chef's sharing menu S$75, set lunch from S$25; 11.30am-2pm & 5-10pm Mon-Fri, 11.30am-3.30pm & 6-10pm Sat;) for nose-to-tail dining. The chicken rice at old-school, 50-odd-year-old Yet Con (p60) is superb and you can shovel in Thai food at **Jai Thai** (Map p202; 6336 6908; www.jai-thai.com; 27 Purvis St; dishes S$6-14; 11.30am-3pm & 6-9.30pm). The French fare at **Saveur** (Map p202; 6333 3121; www.saveur.sg; 01-04, 5 Purvis St; mains S$15-30, set lunch/dinner S$22.90/29.90; noon-9.30pm) is both tasty and filling, and surprisingly cheap for this area.

ARTICHOKE
MEDITERRANEAN $$

(6336 6949; www.artichoke.com.sg; 161 Middle Rd; dishes S$8-38; 6.30-9.45pm Tue-Fri, 11.30am-2.45pm & 6.30-9.45pm Sat, 11.30am-2.45pm Sun; MBras Basah, Bencoolen) Sequestered in a cosy building behind an old church, cafe-style Artichoke is the stamping ground of street-smart chef Bjorn Shen. His schtick is Middle Eastern cuisine with radical twists, whether it's grilled octopus paired with truffles, chickpea hummus and pickled peppers, chicken skewers served with Lebanese pickles and garlic whip, or house-smoked salmon dip. Sharing plates make it a good spot for foodie friends.

Doors open at 4pm for 'hang time' when super crispy chicken wings are served with finger-licking sauces and well-priced drinks. Artichoke's dinner menu kicks off from 6pm.

SUPER LOCO
CUSTOMS HOUSE
MEXICAN $$

Map p204 (6532 2090; www.super-loco.com/customshouse; 01-04 Customs House, 70 Collyer Quay; mains S$8-23; noon-midnight Mon-Fri, 5pm-midnight Sat; ; MRaffles Place, Downtown) With a perfect harbourside location and fashionable string lights, this Mexican restaurant injects a laid-back vibe into Singapore's super-corporate CBD.

Tacos are the house speciality and the *de cangrejo* with tangy soft-shell crab and pineapple is a winner; wash it down with a margarita (choose from 10 flavours!) while admiring the in-your-face Marina Bay Sands view.

COMMON MAN
COFFEE ROASTERS
CAFE $$

(6836 4695; www.commonmancoffeeroasters.com; 22 Martin Rd; mains S$14-29; 7.30am-6pm; ; MFort Canning) While this airy, industrial-cool cafe roasts and serves top-class coffee, it also serves seriously scrumptious grub.

Produce is super fresh and the combinations simple yet inspired, from all-day brekkie winners like filo-wrapped soft-boiled eggs paired with creamy hummus, feta, olives, cucumber and tomato, to a lunchtime quinoa salad with grilled sweet potato, spinach, mint, coriander, goat cheese and honey-raisin yoghurt.

WAH LOK
CHINESE $$

Map p202 (6311 8188; www.carltonhotel.sg; Level 2, Carlton Hotel, 76 Bras Basah Rd; dim sum S$5.40-12, mains S$22-40; 11.30am-2.30pm & 6.30-10.30pm Mon-Sat, 11am-2.30pm & 6.30-10.30pm Sun; ; MCity Hall, Bras Basah) This plush Cantonese classic serves one of Singapore's best dim sum lunches. There are no trolley-pushing aunties here, just a dedicated yum cha menu and gracious staff ready to take your order (must eats include the *xiao long bao* soup dumplings, and baked barbecued-pork buns).

There are two lunch sittings per day on weekends; best book a week ahead to dine then.

★ODETTE
MODERN FRENCH $$$

Map p202 (6385 0498; www.odetterestaurant.com; 01-04 National Gallery Singapore, 1 St Andrew's Rd; lunch from S$98, dinner from S$228;

⊙noon-1.30pm Tue-Sat, 7-9pm Mon-Sat; 🖋; Ⓜ City Hall) Muscling in on Singapore's saturated fine dining scene, this modern French restaurant had people talking even before the first dish left the kitchen. With former Jaan chef Julien Royer at the helm, menus are guided by the seasons and expertly crafted.

The space is visually stunning, with a soft colour palette and floating aerial installation by local artist Dawn Ng. Book at least a month in advance and have your credit card ready.

⭐**JUMBO SEAFOOD**   CHINESE $$$

Map p202 (📞6532 3435; www.jumboseafood. com.sg; 01-01/02 Riverside Point, 30 Merchant Rd; dishes from S$14, chilli crab per kg around S$78; ⊙noon-2.15pm & 6-11.15pm; Ⓜ Clarke Quay) If you're lusting after chilli crab – and you should be – this is a good place to indulge. The gravy is sweet and nutty, with just the right amount of chilli. Make sure you order some *mantou* (fried buns) to soak up the gravy.

While all of Jumbo's outlets have the dish down to an art, this one has the best riverside location.

One kilo of crab (or 1.5kg if you're especially hungry) should be enough for two. Book ahead if heading in later in the week.

JAAN   FRENCH $$$

Map p202 (📞6837 3322; www.jaan.com.sg; Level 70, Swissôtel The Stamford, 2 Stamford Rd; lunch/dinner set menus from S$88/238; ⊙noon-2.30pm & 7-10.30pm Mon-Sat; 🖋; Ⓜ City Hall, Esplanade) Seventy floors above the city, chic and intimate Jaan is home to British chef Kirk Westaway, sous chef to his predecessor French chef Julien Royer. Since taking the reins, Westaway has dazzled diners with his artisanal cuisine and added a Michelin star to his accolades. Menu changes seasonally, flavours are revelatory and presentation utterly theatrical. Always book ahead, and request a window seat.

THE ART OF HIGH TEA

For a little afternoon delight (with your clothes on), it's hard to beat a session of high tea. Not only is it a civilised antidote to Singapore's high speed and higher temperatures, it's the perfect midafternoon recharge. Although most luxury hotels are in on the act, not all high teas are created equal. Pick the right spots and you practically have yourself a late lunch, your steaming pots of delicate tea (or flutes of Champagne, if you insist) accompanied by a veritable feast of sweet and savoury morsels.

Singapore's best high tea is arguably at plush, waterfront lounge, **Landing Point** (Map p202; 📞6333 8388; www.fullertonbayhotel.com; Fullerton Bay Hotel, 80 Collyer Quay; high tea per adult S$45, with glass of Champagne S$65, per child S$22; ⊙9am-midnight Sun-Thu, to 1am Fri & Sat, high tea 3-5.30pm Mon-Fri, noon-3pm & 3.30-6pm Sat & Sun; 🛜; Ⓜ Raffles Place). Book ahead (one day for weekdays, two weeks for weekends), style up and go with an empty stomach. Blue-ribbon TWGz teas are a fine match for luxe bites, like cucumber sandwiches with *ikura* (roe), melt-in-your-mouth Boston lobster tarts and scandalously rich dark-chocolate tarts. You won't be able to stop at one, which is just as well, as your three-tier stand will be gladly replenished.

The Landing Point's most serious competitor is Ritz-Carlton's **Chihuly Lounge** (Map p204; 📞6434 5288; www.ritzcarlton.com/en/hotels/singapore; Ritz-Carlton Millenia Singapore, 7 Raffles Ave; high tea from S$49; ⊙9am-1am, high tea weekday noon-5pm, weekend 2.30-5pm; 🛜; Ⓜ Promenade), whose eight-course version keeps the preened and the coiffered nibbling on an equally sublime array of bites. Aptly, the light-filled lounge is graced with an original Dale Chihuly glass sculpture. It forms part of the hotel's renowned collection of modern art, valued at around S$5 million and including works from the likes of Andy Warhol, David Hockney and Frank Serra. Teapot empty and belly full, head to the concierge desk for a guide to the masterpieces. Book ahead (two days for weekdays, a week or two for weekends).

KOPI CULTURE

There are few things more Singaporean than kicking back at a *kopitiam* (coffeeshop) with an old-school *kopi* (coffee). Its distinctive taste comes from the way the beans are prepared: roasted with sugar and margarine. The result is a coffee that's dark and strong, with the smooth caramel and butter character of its roasting companions. *Kopi* is either drunk black or mixed with condensed or evaporated milk.

Try this *kopi* primer. Note that these terms can also be applied to *teh* (tea).

Kopi Coffee with condensed milk. No sugar, but the condensed milk makes it sweet.

Kopi-O Black coffee with sugar.

Kopi-O kosong Black coffee without sugar (kosong is Malay for nothing or zero).

Kopi-C Coffee with evaporated milk and sugar (the C is for Carnation, a popular evaporated milk brand).

Kopi-C kosong Coffee with evaporated milk, but no sugar.

Kopi peng Iced coffee with condensed milk.

Kopi gao Literally, 'thick' coffee (think double espresso).

Kopi poh A 'light' coffee.

WAKU GHIN
JAPANESE $$$

Map p204 (📞6688 8507; www.marinabaysands. com/restaurants/celebrity-chefs/waku-ghin; L2-01 Shoppes at Marina Bay Sands, 2 Bayfront Ave, access via lift A or B; dégustation S$450; ⓧ5.30pm & 8pm seatings; Ⓜ Bayfront) The refinement and exquisiteness of the 10-course dégustation menu by acclaimed chef Tetsuya Wakuda is nothing short of breathtaking. Expect to fork out nearly S$1000 for the pleasure of treating a party of two; more if you plan to toast to the occasion with more than tap water. The newly awarded Michelin star has only added to this elusive restaurant's appeal.

POLLEN
EUROPEAN $$$

Map p204 (📞6604 9988; www.pollen.com.sg; Flower Dome, Gardens by the Bay, 18 Marina Gardens Dr; mains S$39-68, 5-course dinner tasting menu S$168; ⓧnoon-2.30pm & 6-9.30pm Wed-Mon, Pollen Terrace cafe 9am-9pm; Ⓜ Bayfront) Inside Gardens by the Bay's Flower Dome (free entry when dining), posh Pollen is the Singapore spin-off of London's lauded Pollen Street Social. Its menus deliver artful, produce-driven European flavours with subtle Asian inflections. The three-course set lunch (S$55) is good value, while the upstairs cafe serves high tea (S$38) from 3pm to 5pm Wednesday to Monday (book two weeks ahead). Pollen runs a frequent courtesy shuttle service between the restaurant and the Gardens' main arrival plaza.

 # DRINKING & NIGHTLIFE

★28 HONGKONG STREET
COCKTAIL BAR

Map p202 (www.28hks.com; 28 Hongkong St; ⓧ5.30pm-1am Mon-Thu, to 3am Fri & Sat; Ⓜ Clarke Quay) Softly lit 28HKS plays hide and seek inside an unmarked 1960s shophouse. Slip inside and into a slinky scene of cosy booths and passionate mixologists turning grog into greatness. Marked with their alcohol strength, cocktails are sublime, among them the refreshing 'planter's punch' with rum, grenadine, citrus and Darjeeling tea. House-barreled classics, hard-to-find beers and lip-smacking grub seal the deal.

★SMOKE AND MIRRORS
BAR

Map p202 (📞9234 8122; www.smokeandmirrors. com.sg; 06-01 National Gallery Singapore, 1 St Andrew's Rd; ⓧ3pm-midnight Mon-Fri, noon-2am Sat & Sun; Ⓜ City Hall) This chic bar offers the best view of Singapore. Perched on the top of the National Gallery, Smoke and Mirrors looks out over the Padang to Marina Bay Sands and is flanked by skyscrapers on either side. Arrive before sunset so you can sit, drink in hand, and watch the city transition from day to night. Book ahead and request front-row seats.

If you can't tear yourself away for dinner, there are some tasty treats on the bar menu; most are surprisingly reasonably priced for the location. Outdoor tables have a minimum spend of S$45 per person and tables change over every two hours.

★ LANTERN   BAR

Map p202 (☎6333 8388; www.fullertonbayhotel. com; Fullerton Bay Hotel, 80 Collyer Quay; ☺8am-1am Sun-Thu, to 2am Fri & Sat; ℳRaffles Place) It may be lacking in height (it's dwarfed by the surrounding CBD buildings) and serve its drinks in plastic glasses (scandalous!), but Lantern remains a magical spot for a sophisticated evening toast. Why? There are the flickering lanterns, the shimmering, glass-sided pool – for Fullerton Bay Hotel (p156) guests only – and the romantic views over Marina Bay.

To avoid disappointment, consider booking a table two to three days ahead, especially on weekends.

CÉ LA VI SKYBAR   BAR

Map p204 (☎6508 2188; www.sg.celavi.com; Level 57, Marina Bay Sands Hotel Tower 3, 10 Bay-front Ave; ☺noon-late; ℳBayfront) Perched on Marina Bay Sands' cantilevered SkyPark, this bar offers a jaw-dropping panorama of the Singapore skyline and beyond. A dress code kicks in from 6pm (no shorts, singlets or flip-flops) and live DJ sets pump from 7pm. Tip: skip the S$30 entry fee to the **Sands SkyPark Observation Deck** (Map p204; ☎6688 8826; adult/child under 13yr S$23/17; ☺9.30am-10pm Mon-Thu, to 11pm Fri-Sun) – come here, order a cocktail and enjoy the same view! Entry is via the lobby of the Marina Bay Sands hotel.

RONIN   CAFE

Map p202 (http://ronin.sg; 17 Hongkong St; ☺8am-6pm Mon-Fri, to 7.30pm Sat & Sun; ℳClarke Quay) Ronin hides its talents behind a dark, tinted-glass door. Walk through and the Brutalist combo of grey concrete, exposed plumbing and low-slung lamps might leave you expecting some tough-talking interrogation. Thankfully, the only thing you'll get slapped with is smooth Australian Genovese coffee and speciality teas. Simple food options include homemade granola and gourmet panini. Cash only.

AH SAM COLD DRINK STALL   COCKTAIL BAR

Map p202 (☎6535 0838; www.facebook.com/ AhSamColdDrinkStall; 60A Boat Quay; ☺6pm-midnight Mon-Thu, to 3am Fri & Sat; ℳClarke Quay, Raffles Place) Get that in-the-know glow at this sneaky cocktail den, perched above the tacky Boat Quay pubs. Adorned

with vintage Hong Kong posters and feeling more like a private party than a bar, Ah Sam specialises in Asian mixology. Simply tell the bartender your preferences, and watch them twist, shake and torch up clever creations.

ALCHEMIST BEER LAB   CRAFT BEER

Map p202 (☎6543 9100; www.facebook.com/ AlchemistBeerLab; B1-16 The South Beach, 26 Beach Rd; ☺4pm-1am Sun-Thu, to 2am Fri & Sat; ℳEsplanade) Craft beer connoisseurs will be in hops heaven at this sleek new brewhouse, the brainchild of Singapore's Little Island Brewing Co. Eyes are immediately drawn to the 16 gleaming beer-infusion towers, the first in Asia. Eight of the cylinders pour draughts while the remaining towers of beer are where the flavour infusion magic happens; think marshmallow, vanilla, pineapple – whatever the brewer fancies.

Infusion flavours change regularly, so there's always something new to try. If you're peckish, order a few bites from the modern European tapas-style menu.

LEVEL 33   MICROBREWERY

Map p204 (☎6834 3133; www.level33.com. sg; Level 33, Marina Bay Financial Tower 1, 8 Marina Blvd; ☺11.30am-midnight Mon-Wed, to 2am Thu-Sat, noon-midnight Sun; ☎; ℳDowntown) In a country obsessed with unique selling points, this one takes the cake – no, keg. Laying claim to being the world's highest 'urban craft brewery', Level 33 brews its own lager, pale ale, stout, porter and wheat beer. It's all yours to slurp alfresco with a jaw-dropping view over Marina Bay. Bargain hunters, take note: beers are cheaper before 8pm.

1-ALTITUDE   BAR

Map p202 (☎6438 0410; www.1-altitude.com; Level 63, 1 Raffles Pl; admission incl 1 drink S$30, from 9pm S$35; ☺6pm-2am Sun-Tue, to 3am Thu, to 4am Wed, Fri & Sat; ℳRaffles Place) Wedged across a triangle-shaped deck 282m above street level, this is the world's highest alfresco bar, its 360-degree panorama taking in soaring towers, colonial landmarks and a ship-clogged sea. Women enjoy free entry and all-night S$10 martinis on Wednesday, while Get Busy Thursday pumps out hip-hop and R&B hits. Dress up: no shorts or open shoes, gents.

RAFFLES HOTEL   BAR

Map p202 (www.raffles.com; 1 Beach Rd; ℳCity Hall, Esplanade) Granted, the prices are ex-

DANCE TILL DAWN

Singapore may have a reputation as an all-business-no-fun city, which after a few sunset drinks largely slips into slumber; however, night owls and dance fanatics are well catered for – you just need to know where to go. Mega-club Zouk is Singapore's most famous; here you'll find the flashpack bopping to local and international DJs. Elevate your partying to new heights at **Altimate** (Map p202; ☑6438 0410; www.1-altitude.com; Level 61, 1 Raffles Pl; admission incl 1 drink S$30; ☺10pm-4am Fri & Sat; Ⓜ Raffles Place), a futuristic club with all the gadgets, including neon lighting, digital installations and virtual avatars, not to mention the knockout view. If huge clubs aren't your scene, search for the inconspicuous **Headquarters by the Council** (Map p202; ☑8125 8880; www.facebook.com/headquarters.sg; Level 2, 66 Boat Quay; entry incl 1 drink S$15; ☺10pm-3am Wed-Fri, to 4am Sat; Ⓜ Clarke Quay). There's no fancy lighting at this small shophouse nightspot – just a lone laser – but great techno and house beats to let loose to.

orbitant, but there's something undeniably fabulous about an afternoon cocktail amid whitewashed colonial architecture and thick, tropical foliage. The forever-famous Singapore Sling is churned out at the peanut littered Long Bar, but for those wanting a little more space and atmosphere, head for the fountain-graced Raffles Courtyard or sip Raj-style on the verandah at the **Bar & Billiard Room** (☑6412 1816; ☺11am-12.30am Sun-Thu, to 1.30am Fri & Sat). Check the website for opening times.

LOOF
BAR

Map p202 (☑6337 9416; www.loof.com.sg; 03-07, Odeon Towers Bldg, 331 North Bridge Rd; ☺5pm-1am Mon-Thu, to 2am Fri & Sat; ☎; Ⓜ City Hall, Bras Basah) Red neon warmly declares 'Glad you came up' at upbeat Loof, its name the Singlish mangling of the word 'roof'. Sit on the leafy rooftop deck and look out over the Raffles Hotel and Marina Bay Sands with a calamansi-spiked 'Singapore sour' in hand. The great-value weekday happy hour lasts from 5pm to 8pm, with drink prices increasing by the hour.

WINE CONNECTION
WINE BAR

Map p202 (☑6235 5466; www.wineconnection.com.sg; 01-19/20 Robertson Walk, 11 Unity St; ☺11.30am-1am Mon-Thu, to 2am Fri & Sat, to 11pm Sun; ☎; Ⓜ Fort Canning) Oenophiles love this savvy wine store and bar at Robertson Quay. The team works closely with winemakers across the world, which means no intermediary. They have an interesting wine list and very palatable prices: glasses from S$7 and bottles as low as S$30. Edibles include decent salads and tartines, not to mention top-notch cheeses from their fabulously stinky, next-door Cheese Bar.

POST BAR
BAR

Map p202 (☑6733 8388; www.fullertonhotel.com; Fullerton Hotel, 1 Fullerton Rd; ☺5pm-2am; Ⓜ Raffles Place) Retaining the original post-office ceiling, decked out with modern sculptures and some decidedly futuristic underfloor lighting, Post Bar exudes class without snobbery and mixes a classy cocktail, named after the postal codes of their creation. Check the Facebook page for theme nights – Tuesday's yesteryear swing nights are fun and quite a workout! It's worth dressing up for.

 ENTERTAINMENT

★ZOUK
CLUB

Map p202 (www.zoukclub.com; 3C River Valley Rd; women/men S$30/35 incl 2 drinks; ☺Zouk 9pm-3am Wed & Fri, to 4am Sat, Phuture 9pm-3am Wed & Fri, to 2am Thu & 4am Sat, Red Tail 6-11pm Sun-Tue, 7pm-3am Wed & Fri, to 4am Sat, Capital 9pm-2am Thu, to 3am Fri & 4am Sat; Ⓜ Clarke Quay, Fort Canning) After a massive farewell to Zouk's original location, this legendary club has settled in to its new home in pumping Clarke Quay. Drawing some of the world's biggest DJs and Singapore's seen-to-be-seen crowd, this is the place to go to if you want to let loose. Choose between the main, two-level club with pumping dance floor and insane lighting, or the hip-hop-centric, graffiti-splashed Phuture.

ATTICA
CLUB

Map p202 (☑6333 9973; www.attica.com.sg; 01-03 Clarke Quay, 3A River Valley Rd; ☺10pm-late Wed-Sat; Ⓜ Clarke Quay, Fort Canning) Attica has secured a loyal following among Singapore's fickle clubbers, modelling itself on

New York's hippest clubs but losing the attitude somewhere over the Pacific. Locals will tell you it's where the expats go to pick up on the weekends, mostly in the courtyard. Beats span chart hits, house and R&B; check the website for themed nights.

ESPLANADE –
THEATRES ON THE BAY
ARTS CENTRE

Map p202 (✐6828 8377; www.esplanade.com; 1 Esplanade Dr; ⊗box office noon-8.30pm; 🐾; Ⓜ Esplanade, City Hall) Singapore's S$600 million Esplanade – Theatres on the Bay offers a nonstop program of international and local performances, and free outdoor performances. Book tickets through **Sistic** (✐6348 5555; www.sistic.com.sg; Level 4 Concierge, ION Orchard, 2 Orchard Turn; ⒨Orchard). The controversial aluminium shades – which have been compared to flies' eyes, melting honey-comb and two upturned durians – reference Asian reed-weaving geometries and maximise natural light. Over a decade since its opening in 2002, the building has been accepted as part of the local landscape.

Performing home of the esteemed Singapore Symphony Orchestra (SSO), this architecturally striking arts centre includes an 1800-seat state-of-the-art concert hall, a 1940-seat theatre, and an action-packed program spanning music, theatre and dance from local and international ensembles. Check the website for upcoming events, which include regular free concerts, and don't miss an evening tipple at sultry rooftop bar **Orgo** (Map p202; ✐6336 9366; www.orgo.sg; ⊗6pm-1.30am).

SINGAPORE
CHINESE ORCHESTRA
CLASSICAL MUSIC

(✐6557 4034; www.sco.com.sg; Singapore Conference Hall, 7 Shenton Way; ⊗8.30am-6pm Mon-Fri; Ⓜ Tanjong Pagar, Downtown) Using traditional instruments such as the *liuqin, ruan* and *sanxian,* the SCO treats listeners to classical Chinese concerts throughout the year. Concerts are held in various venues around the city, with occasional collaborations showcasing jazz musicians.

COMEDY MASALA
COMEDY

Map p202 (✐8525 7414; www.comedymasala. com; 69 Circular Rd; adult/student S$25/15; ⊗8pm Tue; Ⓜ Raffles Place, Clarke Quay) Need a good belly laugh? Head to Hero's bar on a Tuesday night to watch comics from far

and wide. The good times keep rolling with a live band once the laughs have died down. It's usually standing room only, so if you'd like a place to park your derrière, book via the website; tickets are a few dollars cheaper too.

THEATREWORKS
THEATRE

(✐6737 7213; www.theatreworks.org.sg; 72-13 Mohamed Sultan Rd; Ⓜ Fort Canning) One of the more experimental theatre companies in Singapore, TheatreWorks is led by enigmatic artistic director Ong Keng Sen. A mix of fresh local work and international collaborations, performances are housed in the company's headquarters, a former rice warehouse just off Robertson Quay. See the website for updates.

SINGAPORE
REPERTORY THEATRE
THEATRE

Map p202 (✐6221 5585; www.srt.com.sg; KC Arts Centre, 20 Merbau Rd; Ⓜ Fort Canning) Based at the KC Arts Centre but also performing at other venues, the SRT produces international repertory standards as well as modern Singaporean plays. Check the website for upcoming productions.

CRAZY ELEPHANT
LIVE MUSIC

Map p202 (✐6337 7859; www.crazyelephant. sg; 01-03/04 3E River Valley Rd; ⊗5pm-2am Tue-Thu & Sun, to 1am Mon, to 3am Fri & Sat; Ⓜ Clarke Quay, Fort Canning) Anywhere that bills itself as 'crazy' should set the alarm bells ringing, but you won't hear them once you're inside. This touristy, graffiti-pimped rock bar is beery, blokey and loud. Music ranges from rock to deep funky blues. Happy hour runs 5pm to 9pm and the musicians hit the stage from 10pm.

SHOPPING

While the area has no shortage of malls – from high-fashion to electronics – it's also home to a handful of inspired boutiques, selling everything from local art and design to independent fashion and homewares.

KAPOK
GIFTS & SOUVENIRS

Map p202 (✐6339 7987; www.ka-pok.com; 01-05 National Design Centre, 111 Middle Rd; ⊗11am-9pm; Ⓜ Bugis, Bras Basah) Inside the National Design Centre, Kapok showcases beautifully designed products from Singapore and beyond. Restyle your world with local jewellery from Amado Gudek, fragrances from Code Deco and wristwatches from Hyper-Grand. Imports include anything from seamless Italian wallets to French tees and Nordic courier bags. When you're shopped out, recharge at the on-site cafe.

RAFFLES HOTEL ARCADE — MALL
Map p202 (www.raffles.com; 328 North Bridge Rd; City Hall, Esplanade) Part of the hotel complex, Raffles Hotel Arcade has been home to some of the world's most notable retailers. This famous shopping destination welcomes big spenders and big browsers alike. The gift shop is the place to pick up unique and good quality souvenirs, from vintage hotel posters to handcrafted silk cushions, and branded Raffles stationery, tea sets and toiletries.

BASHEER GRAPHIC BOOKS — BOOKS
Map p202 (6336 1917; www.basheergraphic. com; 04-19 Bras Basah Complex, 231 Bain St; 10am-8pm Mon-Sat, 11am-6.30pm Sun; Bugis, Bras Basah) Spruce up your coffee table at this temple to design books and magazines. Located inside Bras Basah Complex (locally dubbed 'Book City'), it has everything from fashion tomes to titles on art, architecture and urban planning. The shop also does a brisk mail-order business, so if you're mid-visit and want to have something posted to you, the staff is happy to help.

ROXY DISC HOUSE — MUSIC
Map p202 (9061 3491; www.roxydischouse. com; 03-42 The Adelphi, 1 Coleman St; 1-7pm Mon-Sat, from 2pm Sun; City Hall) Squeeze into Roxy's skinny aisles and scan the shelves of top-notch new vinyl as well as CDs. Jazz and blues make up the bulk of the offerings, with both English- and Chinese-language collectors' editions thrown into the mix. You'll find the shop on the 3rd floor of the Adelphi, a lo-fi mall dotted with audio-equipment shops.

CAT SOCRATES — GIFTS & SOUVENIRS
Map p202 (6333 0870; www.catsocrates. com.sg; 02-25 Bras Basah Complex, 231 Bain St; noon-8pm Mon-Sat, 1-7pm Sun; Bugis, Bras Basah) Can't find that retro Chinese toy car? What about Pan Am wrapping paper? Chances are you'll find them at this quirky shop, inside the bookworm heaven that is

the Bras Basah Complex. Expect anything from felt laptop sleeves and quirky totes to supercool Singapore souvenirs, such as city-themed graphic postcards and neighbourhood sketch books.

SHOPPES AT MARINA BAY SANDS — MALL
Map p204 (6688 6888; www.marinabaysands. com; 10 Bayfront Ave; 10.30am-11pm Sun-Thu, to 11.30pm Fri & Sat; Bayfront) From Miu Miu pumps and Prada frocks to Boggi Milano blazers, this sprawling temple of aspiration gives credit cards a thorough workout. Despite being one of Singapore's largest luxury malls, it's relatively thin on crowds – great if you're not a fan of the Orchard Rd pandemonium. The world's first floating Louis Vuitton store is also here, right on Marina Bay.

ROYAL SELANGOR — GIFTS & SOUVENIRS
Map p204 (6688 7167; www.royalselangor. com; B2-92 Shoppes at Marina Bay Sands, 10 Bayfront Ave; 10.30am-11pm; Bayfront) Malaysia's pewter specialists mightn't rank high on the hip list – think the kind of personalised tankards your uncle uses for his real ale – but don't discount their jewellery, some items of which might even suit painfully fashionable teens.

RAFFLES CITY — MALL
Map p202 (6318 0238; www.rafflescity.com.sg; 252 North Bridge Rd; 10am-10pm; City Hall) Atrium-graced Raffles City includes a three-level branch of fashion-savvy Robinsons department store and a string of fashionable bag and luggage retailers, including Coach, Tumi and Kate Spade. You'll find kids' boutiques on level three. For high-end art by established and emerging Asian and Western artists, drop into **Ode to Art** (Map p202; 6250 1901; www. odetoart.com; 01-36 Raffles City; 11am-9pm) gallery. Hungry? Trawl the decent basement food court.

PENINSULA PLAZA — MALL
Map p202 (www.peninsulaplaza.com.sg; 111 North Bridge Rd; 9am-9pm; City Hall) This place is almost 'little Burma', with floors crammed with Burmese grocery stores, and hole-in-the-wall Burmese eateries – our pick is **Inle Myanmar** (Map p202; 6333 5438; www.inlemyanmar.com.sg; B1-07 A/B Peninsula Plaza; dishes S$8-25; 11am-10pm;). There are moneychangers here, and Singapore's best-stocked camera store (though

not necessarily the cheapest), **Cathay Photo** (Map p202; ☑6337 4274; www.cathayphoto. com.sg; 01-11 Peninsula Plaza; ⊙10am-7pm Mon-Sat), is on the ground floor.

CITYLINK MALL
MALL

Map p202 (☑6339 9913; www.citylink.com.sg; 1 Raffles Link; ⊙10am-10pm; Ⓜ City Hall, Esplanade) Designed by New York's Kohn Pedersen Fox, this seemingly endless tunnel of retail and food outlets links City Hall MRT station with Suntec City and the Esplanade – Theatres on the Bay. It's a handy means of escaping searing sun or teeming rain, and a comfortable way of getting into the city from the Marina Bay hotels.

MARINA SQUARE
MALL

Map p202 (☑6339 8787; www.marinasquare. com.sg; 6 Raffles Blvd; ⊙10am-10pm; Ⓜ City Hall, Esplanade) Over 250 outlets, including loads of global brands like Desigual, Zara and Muji, are packed into this massive shopping space. Centrally located in the Marina Centre area, it has easy access to and from CityLink Mall, Suntec City, Millenia Walk and the Esplanade – Theatres on the Bay.

SUNTEC CITY
MALL

Map p202 (☑6266 1502; www.suntecity.com. sg; 3 Temasek Blvd; ⊙10am-10pm; Ⓜ Esplanade, Promenade) Vast, bewildering and often frustratingly inaccessible, Suntec has no shortage of retail hits, including Uniqlo, Fossil, Kiehl's and Aesop, not to mention an abundance of restaurants, cafes, food courts and a sprawling branch of supermarket Giant Hyperfresh. The star turn is the **Fountain of Wealth** (Map p202; ⊙10am-noon, 2-4pm & 6-7.30pm), declared the World's Largest Fountain (though not Most Attractive) in the *Guinness World Records*.

SPORTS & ACTIVITIES

ULTIMATE DRIVE
ADVENTURE SPORTS

Map p204 (☑6688 7997; www.ultimatedrive.com; Tower 3, 01-14 Marina Bay Sands Hotel, 10 Bayfront Ave; ride as driver/passenger from S$298/238; ⊙9am-10pm; Ⓜ Bayfront) Dress to kill, then make a show of getting into a Ferrari California (red), Lamborghini Gallardo Spyder (orange) or McLaren MP4-12 (white) before tearing out for a spin. A taste of luxury can be yours, if only for 15 to 60 minutes. One can dream, right? Rides also depart from Suntec City (p68) at the convention centre entrance (01-K27) between 10am and 8pm.

WILLOW STREAM
SPA

Map p202 (☑6431 5600; www.willowstream. com/singapore; Level 6, Fairmont Hotel, 80 Bras Basah Rd; treatments from S$148; ⊙7am-10pm, treatments from 9am; Ⓜ City Hall, Esplanade) Spoil yourself silly at this lavish spa, complete with Jacuzzis, plunge pools, rooms that puff aromatic steam and staff who will slather good stuff on your face before pushing, prodding and kneading the kinks out of your jet-lagged (or shopped-out) body. There's also an in-house salon covering everything from hair and waxing to manicures and pedicures.

GX-5 EXTREME SWING
ADVENTURE SPORTS

Map p202 (☑6338 1766; www.gmaxgx5.sg; 3E River Valley Rd; adult/student per ride S$45/35, incl G-Max Reverse Bungy S$69/50; ⊙2pm-late; Ⓜ Clarke Quay, Fort Canning) A relatively gentle high ('relatively' is the key here) is offered right next door to the **G-Max Reverse Bungy** (adult/student per ride S$45/35, incl GX-5 Extreme Swing S$69/50; ⊙2pm-late). Whereas the G-Max offers a straight-up face-peeling vertical trip, the GX-5 swings riders up and over the Singapore River with somewhat less nauseating velocity.

Chinatown, Tanjong Pagar & the CBD

CHINATOWN | TANJONG PAGAR | TIONG BAHRU

Neighbourhood Top Five

1 Chinatown Heritage Centre (p71) Visiting the evocative museum and delving into the unspeakable hardships, destructive temptations and ultimate resilience of the immigrants who gave this part of town its name.

2 Chinese Theatre Circle (p80) Meeting the stars of the show in the unusually informal teahouse.

3 Ya Kun Kaya Toast (p75) Skipping your hotel brekkie and heading to this old-school coffeeshop for a traditional morning slap-up.

4 Burnt Ends (p76) Giving the chopsticks a rest to savour show-stopping grilled meats at this mod-Oz favourite.

5 Operation Dagger (p77) Toasting, chatting and flirting the night away in this basement bar before coming up for air at Club Street, the city's bar-scene heartland.

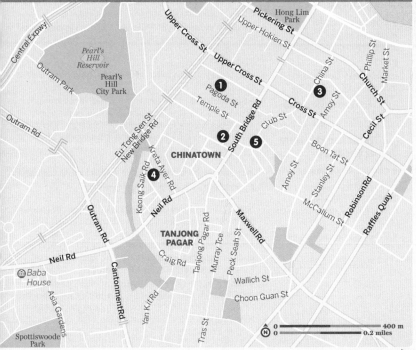

For more detail of this area see Map p206 and p209 ➡

Lonely Planet's Top Tip

As with anywhere in Singapore, it's worth taking advantage of happy hours (usually until 8pm or 9pm) at the hot bars around Chinatown. If it's still too pricey for you, neck a few beers at a hawker centre instead.

CHINATOWN, TANJONG PAGAR & THE CBD

 Best Places to Eat

➡ Burnt Ends (p76)
➡ A Noodle Story (p73)
➡ Momma Kong's (p76)
➡ Hong Kong Soya Sauce Chicken Rice & Noodle (p73)
➡ Ding Dong (p76)

For reviews, see p73.➡

 Best Places to Drink

➡ Operation Dagger (p77)
➡ Native (p82)
➡ Nylon Coffee Roasters (p77)
➡ Good Beer Company (p80)

For reviews, see p77.➡

Best for History & Culture

➡ Chinatown Heritage Centre (p71)
➡ Baba House (p72)
➡ Thian Hock Keng Temple (p72)
➡ Sri Mariamman Temple (p73)

For reviews, see p72.➡

Explore: Chinatown, Tanjong Pagar & the CBD

With the exception of the fascinating Chinatown Heritage Centre, sights here are interesting rather than must-see, but that's a good thing. It leaves more time to focus on Chinatown's star attraction – food. Start early with a traditional Singaporean breakfast in a *kopitiam* (coffee-shop). For lunch, join the crowds at one of Chinatown's bustling hawker centres. Come evening, take your pick of Singapore's hot-list eateries, serving anything from real-deal Mexican to punchy Southeast Asian.

In between meals, poke your head into an antiques shop, gallery or a handy temple or two. Savour beautifully renovated shophouses and superlative lattes on the gentrified streets of the Duxton Hill area (south of Chinatown). Once the sun's gone down, catch the breeze and the city skyline from a rooftop bar on Ann Siang Rd or Club Street.

Local Life

➡**Hawker centres** It's a wonder any of Singapore's high-end restaurants stay in business given that hawker-centre food is dirt cheap and so damn good. Chinatown is no exception. Eat at as many hawker centres as you can while you're here, but if you've only time for one, make it Maxwell Food Centre (p77).

➡**Coffee versus kopi** While hip, third-wave cafes and roasteries are making big waves in the Duxton Hill area, don't miss the chance to slurp old-school *kopi* ('koh-pee') at a traditional *kopitiam*. Try Ya Kun Kaya Toast (p75) or for a twist on the old-school brew, Coffee Break (p79).

➡**Souvenirs** Skip the tourist tat in the lanes around Trengganu St and hunt down an antiques shop or a local art gallery for a souvenir with a story. Our favourites are Tong Mern Sern Antiques (p81) and Utterly Art (p81).

Getting There & Away

➡**MRT** The heart of Chinatown is served by Chinatown MRT station, which spits you out onto Pagoda St. Telok Ayer station is handy for eateries and bars around Amoy St and Club Street. Further south, Outram Park and Tanjong Pagar stations are best for Duxton Hill. Raffles Place station is best for the CBD.

➡**Bus** From the Colonial District, hop on bus 61, 145 or 166, which take you from North Bridge Rd to South Bridge Rd. From Hill St, buses 2, 12 and 147 run down New Bridge Rd. It's easy to walk from the river and the CBD to Chinatown.

DISCOVER CHINATOWN HERITAGE CENTRE

The Chinatown Heritage Centre lifts the lid off Chinatown's chaotic, colourful and often scandalous past. Its endearing jumble of old photographs, personal anecdotes and re-created environments delivers an evocative stroll through the neighbourhood's highs and lows. Spend some time here and you'll see Chinatown's now tourist-conscious streets in a much more intriguing light.

Tailor Shop & Living Cubicles

The journey back to old Singapore begins on the ground floor with a re-created tailor shopfront, workshop and cramped living quarters of the tailor's family and apprentices. By the early 1950s, Pagoda St was heaving with tailor shops and this is an incredibly detailed replica of what was once a common neighbourhood fixture.

Re-created Cubicles

Time travel continues on the 1st floor. Faithfully designed according to the memories and stories of former residents, a row of cubicles will have you peering into the ramshackle living quarters of opium-addicted coolies, stoic Samsui women and even a family of eight! Keep your eyes peeled for the vermin (don't worry, they are fake) in every cubicle.

Early Pioneers

The top floor invites you to join the perilous journey Chinese immigrants undertook to reach Singapore, and to discover the customs, cuisine and importance of family networks when they arrived. One street you won't want to go down is Sago Lane ('Street of the Dead'), a sombre but fascinating glimpse into what occurred during a person's time of expiration.

DON'T MISS

➡ Historical anecdotes of life in Chinatown
➡ Re-created living cubicles
➡ Sago Lane
➡ The brilliant audio-tour (included)

PRACTICALITIES

➡ Map p206, D2
➡ ☏6224 3928
➡ www.chinatown heritagecentre.com.sg
➡ 48 Pagoda St
➡ adult S$15, child under 13/7yr S$11/free
➡ ⊘9am-8pm, closed 1st Mon of month
➡ Ⓜ Chinatown

◉ SIGHTS

CHINATOWN HERITAGE CENTRE   MUSEUM
See p71.

★BUDDHA TOOTH
RELIC TEMPLE   BUDDHIST TEMPLE
Map p206 (🕿6220 0220; www.btrts.org.sg; 288 South Bridge Rd; ⊙7am-7pm, relic viewing 9am-6pm; Ⓜ Chinatown) FREE Consecrated in 2008, this hulking, five-storey temple is home to what is reputedly the left canine tooth of the Buddha, recovered from his funeral pyre in Kushinagar, northern India. While its authenticity is debated, the relic enjoys VIP status inside a 420kg solid-gold stupa in a dazzlingly ornate 4th-floor room. More religious relics await at the 3rd-floor Buddhism museum, while the peaceful rooftop garden features a huge prayer wheel.

★THIAN HOCK KENG
MURAL BY YIP YEW CHONG   PUBLIC ART
Map p206 (www.yipyc.com; Amoy St, rear wall of Thian Hock Keng Temple, 158 Telok Ayer St; Ⓜ Telok Ayer) Spanning 44m, this mural, painted by Singaporean artist Yip Yew Chong (accountant by weekday, artist by weekend), tells the story of Singapore's early Hokkien immigrants. You'll find it on the outside rear wall of the Thian Hock Keng Temple (p72); start from the right end and follow the immigrants' story, from leaving China to arriving in Singapore, and the sacrifices, hardships and joys they experienced along the way. Discover the mural's hidden secrets via the LocoMole app: instructions are on the far left of the mural.

THIAN HOCK KENG TEMPLE   TAOIST TEMPLE
Map p206 (🕿6423 4616; www.thianhockkeng. com.sg; 158 Telok Ayer St; ⊙7.30am-5.30pm; Ⓜ Telok Ayer) FREE Surprisingly, Chinatown's oldest and most important Hokkien temple is often a haven of tranquillity. Built between 1839 and 1842, it's a beautiful place, and was once the favourite landing point of Chinese sailors, before land reclamation pushed the sea far down the road. Typically, the temple's design features are richly symbolic: the stone lions at the entrance ward off evil spirits, while the painted depiction of phoenixes and peonies in the central hall symbolise peace and good tidings respectively. Interestingly, the temple gates are Scottish and the tiles Dutch.

◉ TOP EXPERIENCE
TAKE A TOUR OF BABA HOUSE

A short walk west of Chinatown is Baba House, one of the best-preserved Peranakan heritage homes in Singapore. This beautiful blue three-storey building was donated to the National University of Singapore (NUS) by a member of the family that used to live here. The NUS then set about renovating it so that it best matched how it would have looked in 1928 when, according to the family, Baba House was at its most resplendent.

Step inside and you'll find a wonderful window into the life of a wealthy Peranakan family living in Singapore a century ago. Marvel at the meticulously maintained period furniture and antiques, as well as the building's intricate architectural details. Learn the stories of the house and it's former occupants, whose original family photos still grace the walls. The elaborate bedrooms on the 2nd floor are a sight to behold; keep your eyes peeled for the *tenong*, a wedding gift box, which takes pride of place.

Baba House can only be visited on a one-hour guided tour, held every Monday, Tuesday, Thursday and Saturday, but the tour is excellent and costs absolutely nothing. Call ahead – bookings are a must and, frustratingly, emails do not always receive replies.

DON'T MISS
➡ Original photos
➡ Period Peranakan furniture
➡ Ornate architectural details
➡ *Tenong*, a wedding gift box

PRACTICALITIES
➡ Map p209, A4
➡ 🕿6227 5731
➡ http://babahouse. nus.edu.sg
➡ 157 Neil Rd
➡ admission free
➡ ⊙1hr tour 2pm Mon, 2pm & 6.30pm Tue, 10am Thu, 11am Sat
➡ Ⓜ Outram Park

SINGAPORE MUSICAL BOX MUSEUM MUSEUM

Map p206 (☎6221 0102; www.singaporemusicalboxmuseum.org; 168 Telok Ayer St; 40min tour per person S$12; ⌚10am-6pm Wed-Mon; Ⓜ Telok Ayer) Walk through music history and be captivated by the exquisite melodies of antique music boxes, some more than 200 years old. Peer into the inner workings of the very first, and rather basic, boxes all the way through to cupboard-sized, multi-instrument music makers. One was even destined for the *Titanic* but missed the boat! There's something for everyone; the older generations will love the old-time tunes, and youngsters will marvel at what the first iPod looked like.

SINGAPORE CITY GALLERY MUSEUM

Map p206 (☎6321 8321; www.ura.gov.sg/citygallery; URA Centre, 45 Maxwell Rd; ⌚9am-5pm Mon-Sat; Ⓜ Chinatown, Tanjong Pagar) FREE See into Singapore's future at this interactive city-planning exhibition, which provides compelling insight into the government's resolute policies of land reclamation, high-rise housing and meticulous urban planning. The highlight is an 11m-by-11m scale model of the central city, which shows just how different Singapore will look once all the projects currently under development join the skyline.

SRI MARIAMMAN TEMPLE HINDU TEMPLE

Map p206 (☎6223 4064; www.smt.org.sg; 244 South Bridge Rd; take photos/videos S$3/6; ⌚5.30am-noon & 6-9pm; Ⓜ Chinatown) FREE Paradoxically in the middle of Chinatown, this is the oldest Hindu temple in Singapore, originally built in 1823, then rebuilt in 1843. You can't miss the fabulously animated, Technicolor 1930s *gopuram* (tower) above the entrance, the key to the temple's South Indian Dravidian style. Sacred cow sculptures grace the boundary walls, while the *gopuram* is covered in kitsch plasterwork images of Brahma the creator, Vishnu the preserver and Shiva the destroyer.

PINNACLE@DUXTON VIEWPOINT

Map p206 (☎8683 7760; www.pinnacleduxton.com.sg; Block 1G, 1 Cantonment Rd; 50th-fl skybridge S$6; ⌚9am-9.30pm; Ⓜ Outram Park) For killer city views at a bargain S$6, head to the 50th-floor rooftop of Pinnacle@Duxton. Skybridges connecting the seven towers provide a 360-degree sweep of city, port and sea. Find the 'blink or you'll miss it' ticket booth at level one, Block G, hand over your cash and register your Ez-Link transport card, before taking the lift up to the 50th floor, where you'll tap your card at the gate – stand inside the turnstile before tapping.

SENG WONG BEO TEMPLE TAOIST TEMPLE

Map p209 (☎6221 9930; 113 Peck Seah St; ⌚8am-5pm; Ⓜ Tanjong Pagar) FREE Tucked behind red gates next to the Tanjong Pagar MRT, this untouristed temple is dedicated to the Chinese City God, who is not only responsible for the well-being of the metropolis but also for guiding the souls of the dead to the underworld. It's also notable as the only temple in Singapore that still performs ghost marriages, helping parents of children who died young arrange a marriage for their deceased loved one in the afterlife.

EATING

★A NOODLE STORY NOODLES $

Map p206 (☎9027 6289; www.anoodlestorydotcom.wordpress.com; 01-39 Amoy Street Food Centre, cnr Amoy & Telok Ayer Sts; noodles S$7-9; ⌚11.15am-2.30pm & 5.30-7.30pm Mon-Fri, 10.30am-1.30pm Sat; Ⓜ Telok Ayer) With a snaking line and proffered apology that 'we may sell out earlier than stipulated timing' on the facade, this one-dish-only stall is a magnet for Singapore foodies. The object of desire is Singapore-style ramen created by two young chefs, Gwern Khoo and Ben Tham. It's Japanese ramen meets wanton *mee* (noodles): pure bliss in a bowl topped with a crispy potato-wrapped prawn.

★HONG KONG SOYA SAUCE CHICKEN RICE & NOODLE HAWKER $

Map p206 (Hawker Chan; 02-126 Chinatown Complex, 335 Smith St; dishes S$2-3; ⌚10.30am-7pm Mon, Tue, Thu & Fri, from 8.30am Sat & Sun; Ⓜ Chinatown) With its newly bestowed Michelin star, this humble hawker stall has been thrust into the culinary spotlight. The line forms hours before Mr Chan Hon Meng opens for business, and waiting times can reach three hours. Standout dishes are the tender soy sauce chicken and the caramelised *pork char siew* ordered with rice or perfectly cooked noodles. Worth the wait? You bet.

Capitalising on the stall's success, hawker Chan Hong Meng has already opened three new outlets. The closest is just outside the Chinatown Complex on Smith St, look for the bright red and blue sign. Here you'll find a larger menu, higher prices (dishes S$3 to

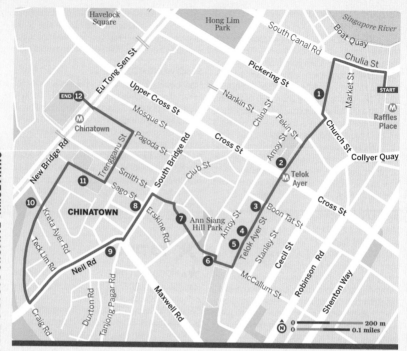

Neighbourhood Walk
Chinatown

START RAFFLES PLACE MRT STATION
END PEOPLE'S PARK COMPLEX
LENGTH 2.5KM; 2½ HOURS

From Raffles Place MRT station head west along Chulia St then south down Phillip St to ❶ **Wak Hai Cheng Bio Temple** (📞6737 9555; ⏰8am-5pm). Cross over Church St to Telok Ayer St until you reach ❷ **Ying Fo Fui Kun**, a two-storey building established in 1822 for the Ying Fo Clan Association. It serves Singapore's Hakka Chinese to this day. At the junction with Boon Tat St is the ❸ **Nagore Durgha Shrine**, a mosque built between 1828 and 1830 by Chulia Muslims from South India. A little further on is the beautifully restored ❹ **Thian Hock Keng Temple** (p72) and the ❺ **Al-Abrar Mosque**, built in the 1850s.

Turn right and walk one block to Amoy St, where at No 66 you'll see ❻ **Siang Cho Keong Temple**. Left of the entrance is a small 'dragon well' into which you can drop a coin and make a wish. Close by is a small archway marked Ann Siang Hill Park. Go

through and follow the walkway upwards to what is Chinatown's highest point and the entry to ❼ **Ann Siang Rd**. Some of the terraces here once housed Chinese guilds and clubs – note the art deco buildings at Nos 15, 17 and 21.

At the end of the street, turn left into South Bridge Rd and drop into the epic ❽ **Buddha Tooth Relic Temple** (p72). Where South Bridge Rd meets Neil Rd and Tanjong Pagar Rd is the triangular ❾ **Jinriksha station**, once the depot for hand-pulled rickshaws. Walk along Neil Rd to Keong Saik Rd, a curving street of ornate old terraces. At the junction with Kreta Ayer Rd is the Hindu ❿ **Layar Sithi Vinygar Temple**, built in 1925. The five-tier *gopuram* over the entrance was added in 2007.

Continuing along Keong Saik Rd, you'll hit the back of the ⓫ **Chinatown Complex** (p77), where you can stop for a cheap feed, or carry on through kitschy Trengganu St, turning left at Pagoda St and using the pedestrian bridge at the end to reach ⓬ **People's Park Complex** (p82) for some reflexology.

$S10) and more sterile environment – we say stick with the original.

J2 FAMOUS CRISPY CURRY PUFF HAWKER $
Map p206 (01-21 Amoy Street Food Centre, cnr Amoy & Telok Ayer Sts; puffs S$1.20-1.50; ⊙8am-4pm Mon-Sat; MTelok Ayer) The golden parcels of curried goodness are a favourite Singaporean snack, and this hawker stall serves some of the best puffs around. Our pick is the chicken curry puff, with sauce that isn't too strong and flaky, crispy pastry. The line gets long, so time your visit after the lunch rush. Puffs are best enjoyed hot.

CHOP TAI CHONG KOK BAKERY $
Map p206 (⊘6227 5701; www.taichongkok.com; 34 Sago St; pastries from S$1; ⊙9.30am-6pm Mon, to 8pm Tue-Sun; MChinatown) Pick up something sweet at Chop Tai Chong Kok, a traditional pastry shop in business since 1938. If you're undecided, opt for the speciality lotus-paste mooncakes. Once known for its sago factories and brothels, Sago St itself now peddles everything from barbecued meat to pottery.

CI YAN ORGANIC VEGETARIAN HEALTH FOOD VEGETARIAN $
Map p206 (⊘6225 9026; www.facebook.com/ciyanveg; 8-10 Smith St; mains S$4-8; ⊙noon-10pm; ⚲; MChinatown) Excellent food, a friendly manager and an informal atmosphere make this a fine choice for a no-fuss vegetarian meal in the heart of Chinatown. It tends to only have five or six dishes (when we ate here choices ranged from the delicious brown-rice set meal to wholemeal hamburgers, vegetarian Penang laksa and almond tofu), written up on a blackboard daily. Also has an interesting range of fruit drinks.

JING HUA XIAO CHI CHINESE $
Map p206 (Qun Zhong Eating House; ⊘6221 3060; www.jinghua.sg; 21 Neil Rd; dishes S$3.50-11; ⊙11.30am-3pm & 5.30-9.30pm Thu-Tue; MChinatown) Locals outnumber out-of-towners at halogen-and-laminex Jing Hua. Tuck into a limited yet satisfying repertoire of northern Chinese classics, among them plump pork dumplings, noodles with minced pork and soya-bean sauce, and red-bean-paste pancake. Skip the lacklustre *xiao long bao* for the moreish Chinese pizza, a hearty, deep-fried pastry packed with minced pork and vegetables, perfect with shredded ginger. Cash only.

YA KUN KAYA TOAST CAFE $
Map p206 (⊘6438 3638; www.yakun.com; 01-01 Far East Sq, 18 China St; kaya toast set S$4.80, kopi S$1.80; ⊙7.30am-7pm Mon-Fri, to 4.30pm Sat, 8.30am-3pm Sun; MTelok Ayer) Though it's now part of a chain, this airy, retro coffeeshop is an institution, and the best way to start the day the Singaporean way. The speciality is buttery *kaya* (coconut jam) toast, dipped in runny eggs (add white pepper and a swirl of soy sauce) and washed down with strong *kopi* (coffee). The outdoor seating is a good spot for rush-hour people watching.

FAT PRINCE TURKISH $$
Map p206 (⊘6221 3683; www.fatprincesg.com; 48 Peck Seah St; mezze S$12-14; ⊙11.30am-3pm Mon-Fri & 6pm-midnight Mon-Sat, brunch 11.30am-3pm Sat & Sun; MTanjong Pagar) Slip into this dimly lit shophouse and be seduced by its golden glinting opulence. Book ahead and smugly sink into your velvet seat, and start your meal with inspired cocktails or homemade Turkish soda. Dishes are made for sharing, and the kebabs are a standout, especially the spicy Adalar prawn.

COCONUT CLUB MALAYSIAN $$
Map p206 (⊘6635 2999; www.thecoconutclub.sg; 6 Ann Siang Hill; mains S$12.80; ⊙11am-3pm & 6-9.30pm Tue-Sat, 11am-3pm Sun; MChinatown, Telok Ayer) Not just any old *nasi lemak* joint, here they're nuts about coconuts and only a certain Malaysian West African (MAWA) hybrid will do. Chicken is super crispy, encrusted in a flavour-punching lemongrass, ginger and galangal coating. The *sambal* (sauce of fried chilli, onions and prawn paste), however, is on the mild side. Save room for the refreshing *cendol* dessert.

RED STAR CHINESE $$
Map p209 (⊘6532 5266; www.redstarrestaurant.com.sg/; Level 7, 54 Chin Swee Rd; yum cha from S$3.50-8; ⊙yum cha 8am-3pm & dinner 6-10pm; MChinatown) Armed with trolley-clutching aunties who swoop like fighter jets, classic Red Star is perfect for a Hong Kong–style yum cha. Keep your ears pricked for the pork bao and *liu sha* bao, the latter a smooth bun filled with runny salted egg yolk custard. The restaurant is tucked away on the 7th floor of a HDB block; look for red signs.

LUCHA LOCO MEXICAN $$
Map p206 (⊘6226 3938; www.facebook.com/pg/LuchaLocoSingapore; 15 Duxton Hill; tacos S$9-10,

quesadillas S$14-16; ⏰noon-3pm Tue-Fri, 5pm to late Tue-Sat; Ⓜ Tanjong Pagar) On pumping Duxton Hill, Lucha Loco keeps the crowds purring with its flirtatious barkeeps, effortlessly cool vibe and finger-licking Mexican street food. Though we adore the ceviche, *tostaditas* and addictive *elotes* (corn rolled in mayonnaise and Cotija cheese), it's the tacos generously topped with fresh, beautiful produce that leave us *loco*. If you don't have a reservation it's best to head in early or late – grab a mescal and wait.

BLUE GINGER
PERANAKAN $$

Map p206 (☑ 6222 3928; www.theblueginger. com; 97 Tanjong Pagar Rd; mains S$7-38; ⏰ noon-2.15pm & 6.30-9.45pm; Ⓜ Tanjong Pagar) Elegant Blue Ginger is one of the few places in Singapore showcasing the spicy, sour flavours of Peranakan food; a unique fusion of Chinese and Malay influences. Mouthwatering musts include *kueh pie ti* (shredded bamboo shoots and turnips garnished with shrimp in fried *pie ti* cups), *sambal terong goreng* (spicy fried eggplant) and a sublimely delicate Nonya fish-head curry. Bookings recommended.

PS CAFE
INTERNATIONAL $$

Map p206 (☑ 9797 0648; www.pscafe.com; 45 Ann Siang Rd; mains S$24-40; ⏰ 11.30am-11pm Mon-Wed, to midnight Thu, to 1am Fri, 9.30am-1am Sat, to 11pm Sun; Ⓜ Chinatown, Telok Ayer) From the ground-floor black-marble bar to the upstairs sweep of crisp linen, Chesterfield banquettes and Dior-clad women, colonial glamour is always in vogue at this leafy, heavenly scented hideaway. Compare notes on the stock market or your last holiday over vibrant, seductive bistro fare like creamy wasabi-dressed seared tuna salad, or delicate miso cod. Those with little ones in tow please note only teenagers are welcome here – bring ID to prove their age – seriously.

★ BURNT ENDS
BARBECUE $$$

Map p206 (☑ 6224 3933; www.burntends.com.sg; 20 Teck Lim Rd; dishes S$8-45; ⏰ 11.45am-2pm & 6-11pm Wed-Sat, 6-11pm Tue; Ⓜ Chinatown, Outram Park) The best seats at this mod-Oz hot spot are at the counter, which offers a prime view of chef Dave Pynt and his 4-tonne, wood-fired ovens and custom grills. The affable Aussie cut his teeth under Spanish charcoal deity Victor Arguinzoniz (Asador Etxebarri), an education echoed in pulled pork shoulder in homemade brioche, and

beef marmalade and pickles on chargrilled sourdough.

★ MOMMA KONG'S
SEAFOOD $$$

Map p206 (☑ 6225 2722; www.mommakongs. com; 34 Mosque St; crab dishes S$48, set menu for 2 from S$122; ⏰ 5-11pm Mon-Fri, from 11am Sat & Sun; Ⓜ Chinatown) Small, funky Momma Kong's is run by two young brothers and a cousin obsessed with crab. While the compact menu features numerous fingerlicking, MSG-free crab classics, opt for the phenomenal chilli crab, its kick and nongelatinous gravy unmatched in this town. One serve of crab and four giant, fresh *mantou* (Chinese bread buns) should happily feed two stomachs. Unlike many other chilli-crab joints, you'll find fixed prices, which means no unpleasant surprises when it's payment time. Book two days ahead (three days for Friday and Saturday) or take a chance and head in late.

DING DONG
SOUTHEAST ASIAN $$$

Map p206 (☑ 6557 0189; www.dingdong.com.sg; 01-02, 115 Amoy St; dishes S$16-29; ⏰ noon-3pm & 6pm-midnight Mon-Sat; Ⓜ Telok Ayer) From the kitschy vintage posters to the meticulous cocktails and modern take on Southeast Asian flavours, it's all about attention to detail at this iconic Asian fusion restaurant. Book a table and drool over zingtastic lobster tail with tom yum broth and sriracha crab cake, crispy pork trotter with spiced vinegar, or the moreish Vietnamese Scotch egg. Good-value options include a weekday two-course set lunch (S$28) and 'feed me' menus (S$80) for indecisive gourmets.

META
FRENCH $$$

Map p206 (☑ 6513 0898; www.metarestaurant. sg; 9 Keong Saik Rd; set lunch/dinner S$48/98; ⏰ noon-2pm Mon-Fri, 6-9.30pm Mon-Thu & to 10.30pm Fri & Sat; ✍; Ⓜ Chinatown, Outram Park) It's all about French food with a delicate Asian twist at this sleek eatery in trendy Keong Saik Rd. The open kitchen runs nearly the length of this very long and narrow space, with the high stools positioned so guests have front-row seats as chefs create delectable masterpieces. The evolutionary menu changes with the seasons.

BINCHO
JAPANESE $$$

(☑ 6438 4567; www.bincho.com.sg; 01-19, 78 Moh Guan Tce; lunch set from S$25, dinner sets from S$68; ⏰ noon-2.30pm & 6pm-late Tue-Sun;

HAWKER CENTRE MUSTS

If you're new to Singapore, brush up on your hawker centre etiquette, then follow your nose into one of the following for a cheap, delicious feed.

Maxwell Food Centre (cnr Maxwell & South Bridge Rds; dishes from S$2.50; ☺stall hours vary; ⓂChinatown) Chinatown's most touristy hawker centre is a good spot for the uninitiated, and best at lunch. Top choices include rice porridge from Zhen Zhen Porridge and fragrant chicken rice from Tian Tian Hainanese Chicken Rice.

Chinatown Complex (335 Smith St ; dishes from S$3; ☺stall hours vary; ⓂChinatown) Join old-timers and foodies here and make a beeline for the Michelin star–brandishing Hong Kong Soya Sauce Chicken Rice and Noodle. If the usual one-hour-plus wait puts you off, head to Lian He Ben Ji Claypot Rice for a mixed claypot rice, or a rich and nutty satay at Shi Xiang Satay. For a little TLC, opt for Ten Tonic Ginseng Chicken Soup at Bonne Soup.

Hong Lim Food Centre (Block 531A, Upper Cross St; dishes from S$3; ☺8am-8pm, stall hours vary; ⓂChinatown) Musts include *char kway teow* (stir-fried rice noodles) from Outram Park Fried Kway Teow and the *Hokkien chang* from Hiong Kee Dumplings. Seafood lovers queue at Tuck Kee Ipoh Sah Hor Fun for the crayfish and *prawn hor fun*.

Lau Pa Sat (www.laupasat.biz; 18 Raffles Quay; dishes from S$4, satay from S$0.60; ☺24hr, stall hours vary; ⓂTelok Ayer, Raffles Place) *Lau pa sat* means 'old market' in Hokkien, which is appropriate since the handsome iron structure shipped from Glasgow in 1894 remains intact. The real magic happens on the facing street, when Boon Tat St transforms into Satay Street, a KL-style sprawl of tables, beer-peddling aunties and smoky satay stalls.

ⓂTiong Bahru) In heritage heavyweight Tiong Bahru, the last thing you'd think you'd find is a sleek yakatori joint serving some of the best Japanese fare in town. The menu changes frequently and revolves around *tori* (chicken): order one of the set menus, which highlight chef Asai Masashi's impressive techniques and skills. It's hidden behind a noodleshop; enter via the car park service door.

🍷 **DRINKING &**
🍸 **NIGHTLIFE**

Club Street and adjacent Ann Siang Rd are the heart of Singapore's booming bar scene, with both streets closed to traffic from 7pm on Friday and Saturday. Just over the hill, on Amoy and Telok Ayer Sts, are many hidden watering holes, but you'll need to find them first. South of Chinatown, Tanjong Pagar and the Duxton Hill area offer an ever-expanding number of in-the-know cafes and drinking spots, while Chinatown's hawker centres are always a good standby for a no-frills beer.

★**OPERATION DAGGER**　　COCKTAIL BAR
Map p206 (✆6438 4057; www.operationdagger.com; 7 Ann Siang Hill; ☺6pm-late Tue-Sat; ⓂChinatown, Telok Ayer) From the 'cloud-like' light

sculpture to the boundary-pushing cocktails, 'extraordinary' is the keyword here. To encourage experimentation, libations are described by flavour, not spirit, the latter shelved in uniform, apothecary-like bottles. Sample the sesame-infused *gomashio,* or the textural surprise of the 'hot & cold'. Head up the hill where Club Street and Ann Siang Hill meet; a symbol shows the way.

★**TIPPLING CLUB**　　COCKTAIL BAR
Map p206 (✆6475 2217; www.tipplingclub.com; 38 Tanjong Pagar Rd; ☺noon-midnight Mon-Fri, 6pm-midnight Sat; ⓂTanjong Pagar) Tippling Club propels mixology to dizzying heights, with a technique and creativity that could turn a teetotaller into a born-again soak. The 'Sensorium' menu, created in collaboration with International Flavors and Fragrances Inc (IFF), is designed to trigger memories from scents. Select a dropper from a cocktail strainer until you find a smell that makes you swoon, and then order away. The best seats are at the bar, under a ceiling of hanging bottles. The adjoining restaurant is highly regarded, though painfully priced.

★**NYLON COFFEE ROASTERS**　　CAFE
Map p209 (✆6220 2330; www.nyloncoffee.sg; 01-40, 4 Everton Park; ☺8.30am-5.30pm Mon & Wed-Fri, 9am-6pm Sat & Sun; ⓂOutram Park, Tanjong Pagar) Hidden in the Everton Park

Local Life
A Lazy Morning in Tiong Bahru

Spend a late weekend morning in Tiong Bahru, three stops from Raffles Place on the East–West (green) MRT line. More than just hip boutiques, bars and cafes, this low-rise neighbourhood was Singapore's first public-housing estate, and its walk-up, art deco apartments now make for unexpected architectural treats.

1 To Market
The **Tiong Bahru Market & Food Centre** (83 Seng Poh Rd; dishes from S$3, stall hours vary; P; M Tiong Bahru) remains staunchly old-school, right down to its orange-hued exterior, the neighbourhood's original shade. Whet your appetite exploring the wet market, then head upstairs to the hawker centre for *shui kueh* (steamed rice cake with diced preserved radish) at **Jian Bo Shui Kueh** (02-05 Tiong Bahru Market & Food Centre, 83 Seng Poh Rd; shui kueh from S$2.50; 7am-9pm; M Tiong Bahru).

2 Book Hunting
BooksActually (6222 9195; www.books actually.com; 9 Yong Siak St; 10am-8pm Tue-Sat, to 6pm Mon & Sun; M Tiong Bahru) is one of Singapore's coolest independent bookstores, with often unexpected choices of fiction and nonfiction, including some interesting titles on Singapore. For beautiful children's books, check out **Woods in the Books** (6222 9980; www.woodsinthebooks.

sg; 3 Yong Siak St; 10am-7pm Tue-Fri, to 8pm Sat & 6pm Sun; M Tiong Bahru), three doors down.

3 A Good-Looking Bird
Originally a pop-up concept store, **Nana & Bird** (www.nanaandbird.com; 1M Yong Siak St; noon-7pm Mon-Fri, from 11am Sat & Sun; M Tiong Bahru) is a sound spot for fresh independent fashion and accessories for women, with labels including Singapore designers Aijek and Ylin Lu, and international up-and-comers like Kuwaii and Danielle Atkinson of Milk & Thistle.

4 Perfect Porridge
Join old-timers and Gen-Y nostalgics for a little Cantonese soul food at **Ah Chiang's** (6557 0084; www.facebook.com/ahchiang porridgesg; 01-38, 65 Tiong Poh Rd; porridge S$4-5; 6am-11pm; M Outram Park). The star turn at this retro corner *kopitiam* (coffee-shop) is fragrant, charcoal-fired porridge. Do not go past the raw sliced fish, delectably drizzled with sesame oil.

Tiong Bahru Market & Food Centre

⑤ A French Affair

The quintessential Frenchman, baker Gontran Cherrier has all and sundry itching for a little French lovin'. You too can get some at **Tiong Bahru Bakery** (☑6220 3430; www.tiongbahrubakery.com; 01-70, 56 Eng Hoon St; pastries S$2.50-4.60, sandwiches from S$5.30-9.50; ☺8am-8pm Sun-Thu, to 10pm Fri & Sat; ⓜTiong Bahru), his cool, contemporary bakery and cafe. Faultless pastries include flaky *kouign amanns* (Breton-style pastry), while savouries include salubrious sandwiches exploding with prime ingredients. Topping it off is luscious coffee from Common Man Roasters.

⑥ Groom Room

Especially for blokes, **We Need A Hero** (☑6222 5590; www.weneedahero.sg; 01-86, 57 Eng Hoon St; barber cut from S$55, shave from S$35; ☺11am-9pm Mon-Fri, from 10am Sat, 10am-8pm Sun; ⓜTiong Bahru) is the perfect place to plonk yourself down (in an old-school barber chair) and let the Hero team unleash their grooming superpowers. Choose from basic shaves and cuts, face masks or massages – you'll be slick in no time. Bookings are highly recommended, especially on weekends.

public housing complex, this pocket-sized, standing-room-only cafe has an epic reputation for phenomenal seasonal blends and impressive single origins. At the helm is a personable crew of coffee fanatics, chatting away with customers about their latest coffee-sourcing trip (they deal directly with the farmers), or the virtues of Frenchpress brewing. While the espresso is outstanding, try the 'clever dripper', which shows off the more subtle notes in your cup of Joe.

TEA CHAPTER   TEAHOUSE
Map p206 (☑6226 1175; www.teachapter.com; 9-11 Neil Rd; ☺teahouse 11am-10.30pm Sun-Thu, to 11pm Fri & Sat, shop 10.30am-10.30pm daily; ⓜChinatown) Queen Elizabeth and Prince Philip dropped by this tranquil teahouse in 1989, and for S$10 you can sit at the table they sipped at. A minimum charge of S$8 per person will get you a heavenly pot of loose-leaf tea, prepared with traditional precision. The selection is excellent and the adjoining shop sells tea and a selection of beautiful tea sets. Want to take your tea tasting to a new level? Book a tea appreciation package, either the 'fragrance and aroma' or 'shades of tea', and become a tea master.

COFFEE BREAK   COFFEE
Map p206 (www.facebook.com/coffeebreakamoy street; 02-78 Amoy Street Food Centre, cnr Amoy & Telok Ayer Sts; ☺7.30am-2.30pm Mon-Fri; ⓜTelok Ayer) Operated by a sister and brother team who recently took the reins from their grandfather, this humble drink stall has a menu that reads more like it's from a hipster cafe. Sea-salt caramel lattes and melon milk taneyo? Make no mistake, it's still good old Singaporean *kopi* (coffee) – with a twist. Toast spreads have also been given an overhaul – try the black sesame.

POTATO HEAD SINGAPORE   COCKTAIL BAR
Map p206 (☑6327 1939; www.pttheadfolk. com; 36 Keong Saik Rd; ☺Studio 1939 & rooftop bar 5pm to late; ☎; ⓜOutram Park) Offshoot of the legendary Bali bar, this standout, multilevel playground incorporates three spaces, all reached via a chequered stairwell pimped with creepy storybook murals and giant glowing dolls. Skip the Three Buns burger joint and head straight for the dark, plush glamour of cocktail lounge Studio 1939 or the laid-back frivolity of the rooftop tiki bar.

The latter is best for languid tropical nights, where kitschy, crafty drinks like Coco Jak (pineapple-infused Nusa Caña rum, Merlet peach liqueur, agave syrup, mint and Cachaça float) come with skyline views.

BLACK SWAN
BAR

Map p209 (☑6438 3757; www.theblackswan. com.sg; 19 Cecil St; ☺Black Swan 11.30am-11pm Mon, to midnight Tue-Thu, to 1am Fri, 5pm-midnight Sat; Powder Room 5pm-midnight Tue-Thu, to 1am Fri; 🛜; MRaffles Place, Telok Ayer) Was that Rita Hayworth? This art deco marvel is set inside a 1930s bank building. Hit the bustling ground-floor bar for happy-hour oysters (S$2) served with draught beers, house pours and wines (S$9) from 5pm to 8pm weekdays, or channel Bette Davis in the Powder Room, a decadent cocktail lounge.

JEKYLL & HYDE
COCKTAIL BAR

Map p206 (☑6222 3349; www.jekyllandhyde. sg; 49 Tras St; ☺6pm-1am Mon-Thu, to 2am Fri & Sat; MTanjong Pagar) Jekyll & Hyde splits itself into two spaces – buzzing back bar and milder-mannered front space tailored for more tranquil tête-à-têtes. Whichever you choose, expect inspired libations like the Vaping Geisha, a smoking concoction of plum-infused gin, shiso and lemon juice poured over plum sorbet, or the strangely seductive Mr Bean, made with fresh bean curd, vodka, *kaya,* butterscotch liqueur and Frangelico.

GOOD BEER COMPANY
CRAFT BEER

Map p206 (☑9430 2750; www.facebook.com/ goodbeersg; 02-58 Chinatown Complex, 335 Smith St; ☺6-10pm Mon-Sat; MChinatown) Injecting Chinatown Complex with a dose of new-school cool, this hawker-centre beer stall has an impressive booty of bottled craft suds, sourced from far-flung corners of the world. A few stalls down is the co-owned **Smith Street Taps** (Map p206; ☑9430 2750; www.facebook.com/smithstreet-taps; 02-62 Chinatown Complex; ☺6.30-10.30pm Tue-Sat), run by a friendly dude and offering a rotating selection of craft and premium beers on tap.

BITTERS & LOVE
COCKTAIL BAR

Map p206 (☑6438 1836; www.bittersandlove. com; 118 Telok Ayer St; ☺6pm-midnight Mon-Thu, to 2am Fri & Sat; MTelok Ayer) Look for the bottle-shaped lights, swing open the door and dive into this affable, loud cocktail den, home to some of the city's top barkeeps. Forget the drinks list. Simply rattle off your mood, favourite flavours or spirit base and let the team work their magic. For something local, request a rum-based, tea-infused Kaya Toast.

STRANGERS' REUNION
CAFE

Map p209 (☑6222 4869; www.facebook.com/ StrangersReunion; 33/35/37 Kampong Bahru Rd; ☺9am-10pm Wed-Mon, to midnight Fri & Sat; MOutram Park) A cafe run by Singapore's three-time (and counting) barista champion Ryan Tan equals silky smooth lattes every time you visit. The food, a selection of salads and hearty mains, looks inviting, but it is the buttermilk waffles that almost threaten to take away the limelight from the coffee. If it's hot out, grab a cold brew 'white magic' – a perfect cool kick.

☆ ENTERTAINMENT

CHINESE THEATRE CIRCLE
OPERA

Map p206 (☑6323 4862; www.ctcopera.com; 5 Smith St; show & snacks S$25, show & dinner S$40; ☺7-9pm Fri & Sat; MChinatown) Teahouse evenings organised by this nonprofit opera company are a wonderful, informal introduction to Chinese opera. Every Friday and Saturday at 8pm there is a brief talk on Chinese opera, followed by a 45-minute excerpt from an opera classic, performed by actors in full costume. You can also opt for a pre-show Chinese meal at 7pm. Book ahead.

SCREENING ROOM
CINEMA

Map p206 (☑6221 1694; www.screeningroom. com.sg; 12 Ann Siang Rd; ☺nightly Mon-Sat; MChinatown, Telok Ayer) If your idea of a good night involves sinking into a sofa and watching classic flicks, make some time for Screening Room. Expect anything from *On the Town* to *Sex, Lies and Videotape,* projected onto a pull-down screen. Flicks are screened twice a day Monday to Saturday, timings posted on its Facebook page.

TABOO
CLUB, LGBTIQ+

Map p206 (☑6225 6256; www.taboo.sg; 65 Neil Rd; ☺8pm-2am Wed & Thu, 10pm-3am Fri, 10pm-4am Sat; MOutram Park, Chinatown) Conquer the dance floor at what remains the favourite gay club in town. Expect the requisite line-up of shirtless gyrators, doting straight women and racy-themed nights. The dance floor goes ballistic from midnight and the beats bump till the wee hours of the morning.

TANTRIC BAR
BAR, LGBTIQ+

Map p206 (☑6423 9232; www.homeofthe bluespin.com; 78 Neil Rd; ☺8pm-3am Sun-Fri, 8pm-4am Sat; ⓂOutram Park, Chinatown) Two indoor bars and two alfresco palm-fringed courtyards is what you get at Singapore's best-loved gay drinking hole. Especially heaving on Friday and Saturday nights, it's a hit with preened locals and eager expats and out-of-towners, who schmooze and cruise to Kylie, Gaga and Katy Perry chart-toppers.

If you're after a touch of old-school oriental glamour, head upstairs to May Wong's Cafe, named after Anna May Wong, considered to be the first Chinese American movie star.

SHOPPING

Pagoda St and its immediate surroundings have become a byword for tourist tat, but behind and beyond the stalls crammed with souvenir T-shirts and two-minute calligraphers is a more inspiring selection of shops and galleries selling everything from contemporary local artwork, antique furniture and traditional Chinese remedies, to cognoscenti fashion labels from Singapore, Sydney and Copenhagen.

★TONG MERN SERN ANTIQUES
ANTIQUES

Map p206 (☑6223 1037; www.tmsantiques.com; 51 Craig Rd; ☺9.30am-5.30pm Mon-Sat, from 1.30pm Sun; ⓂOutram Park) An Aladdin's cave of dusty furniture, books, records, wood carvings, porcelain and other bits and bobs (we even found an old cash register), Tong Mern Sern is a curious hunting ground for Singapore nostalgia. A banner hung above the front door proclaims: 'We buy junk and sell antiques. Some fools buy. Some fools sell'. Better have your wits about you.

ANTHONY THE SPICE MAKER
SPICES

Map p206 (☑9117 7573; www.anthonythespice maker.com; B1-169 Chinatown Complex, 335 Smith St; ☺8.15am-3.30pm Tue-Sun; ⓂChinatown) If you want to re-create the aromas and tastes of Singapore at home, make a beeline for this tiny stall where little brown

airtight packets, which don't allow even the slightest whiff of the heady spices to escape, are uniformly lined up. Anthony is only too happy to help you choose, but we can personally recommend the meat *rendang* blend.

NAM'S SUPPLIES
GIFTS & SOUVENIRS

Map p206 (☑6324 5872; http://namssupplies. com; 22 Smith St; ☺8am-7pm; ⓂChinatown) The curious paper objects on sale around Chinatown – from miniature cars to computers – are offerings burned at funeral wakes to ensure the material wealth of the dead. Nam's has been peddling such offerings since 1948, when nearby Sago Lane heaved with so-called 'death houses', where dying relatives were sent to spend their final days.

EU YAN SANG
CHINESE MEDICINE

Map p206 (☑6223 6333; www.euyansang.com. sg; 269 South Bridge Rd; ☺shop 10am-10pm, clinic 8.30am-6pm Mon-Tue & Thu-Fri, from 9am Wed, 8.30am-7.30pm Sat; ⓂChinatown) Get your *qi* back in order at Singapore's most famous and user-friendly Chinese medicine store. Pick up some Monkey Bezoar powder to relieve excess phlegm, or Liu Jun Zi pills to dispel dampness. You'll find herbal teas, soups and oils, and you can consult a practitioner of Chinese medicine at the clinic next door (bring your passport).

UTTERLY ART
ART

Map p206 (☑9487 2006; www.utterlyart.com.sg; Level 3, 20B Mosque St; ☺2-8pm Mon-Sat, noon-5.30pm Sun; ⓂChinatown) Climb the stairs to this tiny, welcoming gallery for works by emerging contemporary Singaporean and Asian artists. Painting is the gallery's focus, but exhibitions dabble in sculpture, photography and ceramics occasionally; check Facebook for current and upcoming exhibitions. Opening times can be a little erratic, so always call ahead if making a special trip.

✗ SPORTS & ACTIVITIES

FOOD PLAYGROUND
COOKING

Map p206 (☑9452 3669; www.foodplayground. com.sg; 24A Sago St; 3hr class from S$119; ☺9.30am-12.30pm Mon-Fri; ⓂChinatown) You've been gorging on Singapore's famous food, so why not learn to make it? This

DON'T MISS: HIDDEN HANGS

In an area where hidden opium and gambling dens once reigned, crafty mixologists are now king. You won't find any signboards leading the way, though – you'll need to follow the clues down alleys, up staircases, even past a fortune teller. Amoy St is where to start: head up above Wanton restaurant to be seduced by the flavours of Southeast Asia at **Native** (Map p206; ☑8869 6520; www.tribenative.com; 52A Amoy St; ☺6pm-midnight Mon-Sat; ⓂTelok Ayer), where locally foraged ingredients are paired with spirits distilled from the region. Next, head across the road to hunt for the Dapper Coffee signboard and slink up to the **Spiffy Dapper** (Map p206; ☑8742 8908; www.spiffydapper.com; 73 Amoy St; ☺5pm until late Mon-Fri, from 6pm Sat & Sun; ⓂTelok Ayer) on the 2nd floor. Alternately, head further down the street towards Telok Ayer MRT and look-out for the neon pink 'pyschic' sign, behind which you'll be welcomed into **Employees Only** (Map p206; http://employeesonlysg.com; 112 Amoy St; ☺5pm-1am Sun-Fri, to 2am Sat, 6pm-1am Sun; ⓂTelok Ayer), the local outpost of the famous New York City cocktail bar.

fantastic hands-on cooking school explores Singapore's multicultural make-up and sees you cook up classic dishes like laksa, *nasi lemak* (coconut rice) and Hainanese chicken rice. Courses usually run for three hours and can be tailored for budding cooks with dietary restrictions.

NIMBLE AND KNEAD   SPA

(☑6438 3933; www.nimbleknead.com; 01-28, 66 Eng Watt St; 60min massage from S$76, 90min facials from S$169; ☺11am-10pm; ⓂTiong Bahru) When your weary body 'kneads' a massage, head to this funky spa tucked inside a shophouse. Get lost in the maze of shipping containers (it's any wonder how they got them through the door) before settling in for some serious relaxation. Nimble fingers will work out every knot, kink and ache, while the list of facial and body treatments will have you feeling like new.

KENKO WELLNESS SPA   SPA

Map p206 (☑6223 0303; www.kenko.com.sg; 199 South Bridge Rd; reflexology per 40min S$59, body massage per 60min S$120; ☺10am-11pm;

ⓂChinatown) Kenko is the McDonald's of Singapore's spas with branches throughout the city, but there's nothing drive-through about its foot reflexology, romantic couples' sessions (S$290 per 1½-hour session) or Chinese and Swedish massage (Chinese is more forceful, using pointy elbows).

PEOPLE'S PARK COMPLEX   MASSAGE

Map p206 (www.peoplesparkcomplex.sg; 1 Park Cres; ☺9am-10pm, shop hours vary; ⓂChinatown) Heady with the scent of Tiger balm, Singapore's oldest mall is well known for its cheap massage joints. Our favourite is **Mr Lim Foot Reflexology** (Map p206; ☑63274498; 03-54 & 03-78 People's Park Complex; 1hr foot reflexology S$25; ☺10.30am-10pm; ☎), where you'll queue with regulars after a robust rubdown. Feeling adventurous? Try one of the fish-pond foot spas, where schools of fish nibble the dead skin right off your feet. Rooftop bar **Lepark** (Map p206; www.lepark.co; ☺4-11pm Tue-Thu, to midnight Fri, noon-midnight Sat, to 11pm Sun) is tucked away up on the 6th-floor car park; enjoy the craft beers and street tapas, if you can find it.

Little India & Kampong Glam

LITTLE INDIA | KAMPONG GLAM | BUGIS | JALAN BESAR

Neighbourhood Top Five

1 Lagnaa Barefoot Dining (p89) Kicking off your flip-flops and braving the infamous chilli challenge at one of the tastiest nosh spots in Little India.

2 Sifr Aromatics (p93) Customising the perfect fragrance at this perfume lab, one of a string of one-off shops in eclectic Kampong Glam.

3 Tekka Centre (p87) Shopping for saris, then heading downstairs for lip-smacking street eats at Little India's liveliest hawker centre.

4 Sri Veeramakaliamman Temple (p85) Taking a back seat during *puja* (prayers) at this atmospheric Hindu temple.

5 Piedra Negra (p90) Kick-starting your night with bolshy margaritas at this Mexican place, slap bang on buzzing Haji Lane.

For more detail of this area see Map p210 ➡

Lonely Planet's Top Tip

If you want to experience Little India at its busy, sub-continental best, come on a Sunday. This is the only day off for many workers, particularly Indian labourers, and at times it feels as though you're sharing the streets with half of Mumbai.

Best Places to Eat

➡ Kilo (p91)

➡ Hill Street Tai Hwa Pork Noodle (p91)

➡ Lagnaa Barefoot Dining (p90)

➡ Sungei Road Laksa (p89)

➡ Nan Hwa Chong Fish-Head Steamboat Corner (p91)

For reviews, see p87.➡

Best Places to Shop

➡ Haji Lane (p94)

➡ Supermama (p94)

➡ Sifr Aromatics (p93)

➡ Rugged Gentlemen Shoppe (p93)

➡ Bugis Street Market (p94)

For reviews, see p93.➡

Best Places to Drink

➡ Atlas (p92)

➡ Chye Seng Huat Hardware (p88)

➡ Druggists (p88)

➡ Maison Ikkoku (p92)

➡ BluJaz Café (p92)

For reviews, see p91.➡

Explore: Little India & Kampong Glam

The heart of Little India lies in the colourful, incense-scented lanes between Serangoon Rd and Jln Besar, stretching from Campbell Lane in the south to Syed Alwi Rd in the north. The best way to take in this area's bewitching sights, smells and sounds is to simply wander the lanes on foot. Shopping and temple-hopping rank highly, but the main attraction is authentic Indian food. Arm yourself with an empty stomach and dive in.

From Malay and Middle Eastern to Italian and Chinese, scrumptious flavours also await in Kampong Glam, an area sometimes referred to as Arab St. It's an intriguing blend of the Islamic and the hipster, a place of storybook mosques, third-wave cafes and trendy boutiques dotted around brightly painted laneways. For fun drinking options, Kampong Glam is where it's at, with notable cocktail dens, live-music gigs and a bustling, back-alley vibe.

Local Life

➡**Eating with your hands** Using your fingers rather than cutlery is an integral part of the Indian dining experience. Wash your hands before and after (all Indian restaurants have sinks), and be sure to only use your right hand (the left is for toilet duties).

➡**South Indian breakfasts** You'll soon tire of toast-and-tea hotel breakfasts, so head to one of Little India's plethora of canteen restaurants and dig into a scrummy South Indian breakfast of *dosa* (paper-thin lentil-flour pancake), *idly* (fermented rice cakes) or *uttapam* (thick, savoury rice pancake).

➡**Bollywood movies** The colour and rhythm of Little India may just leave you itching to see a big Bollywood number. Head straight to the historic Rex Cinemas (p92) to catch an all-singing, all-dancing Indian blockbuster.

Getting There & Away

➡**MRT** Little India MRT station is right by the Tekka Centre. You can walk here from Rochor, Jalan Besar, Bugis and Farrer Park MRT stations. Bugis is best for Kampong Glam, and Jalan Besar is easily reached from Bendemeer, Lavender or Farrer Park.

➡**Bus** Bus 65 runs from Orchard Rd to Serangoon Rd. From the Colonial District, catch bus 131 or 147 on Stamford Rd. For Kampong Glam, take bus 7 from Orchard Rd to Victoria St (get off at Stamford Primary School, just past Arab St). From the Colonial District, buses 130, 133, 145 and 197 go up Victoria St, and bus 100 and 107 run along Beach Rd from the Raffles Hotel to Bussorah St.

◉ SIGHTS

◉ Little India

SRI VEERAMAKALIAMMAN
TEMPLE   HINDU TEMPLE
Map p210 (⏹6295 4538; www.sriveerama
kaliamman.com; 141 Serangoon Rd; ☺8am-noon
& 6.30-9pm Mon-Thu & Sat, 8am-noon & 6-9pm Fri
& Sun; Ⓜ Little India) FREE Little India's most
colourful, visually stunning temple is dedicated to the ferocious goddess Kali, depict-
ed wearing a garland of skulls, ripping out
the insides of her victims, and sharing more
tranquil family moments with her sons
Ganesh and Murugan. The bloodthirsty
consort of Shiva has always been popular in
Bengal, the birthplace of the labourers who
built the structure in 1881. The temple is at
its most evocative during each of the four
daily *puja* (prayer) sessions.

SRI VADAPATHIRA
KALIAMMAN TEMPLE   HINDU TEMPLE
(⏹6298 5053; www.srivadapathirakali.org; 555
Serangoon Rd; ☺5am-12.30pm & 4-9pm Sun-Thu,
6am-12.30pm & 4.30-9.30pm Fri & Sat; Ⓜ Farrer
Park, Bendemeer) FREE Dedicated to Kaliamman, the Destroyer of Evil, this South Indian temple began life in 1870 as a modest
shrine but underwent a significant facelift
in 1969 to transform it into the beauty
standing today. The carvings here – particularly on the *vimana* (domed structure
within the temple) – are among the best
temple artwork you'll see anywhere in Singapore.

SRI SRINIVASA
PERUMAL TEMPLE   HINDU TEMPLE
(⏹6298 5771; www.sspt.org.sg; 397 Serangoon
Rd; ☺6am-noon & 6-9pm Sun-Mon, 5.30am-
12.30pm & 5.30-9.30pm Sat; Ⓜ Farrer Park,
Bendemeer) FREE Dedicated to Vishnu, this
temple dates from 1855, but the striking,
20m-tall *gopuram* (tower) is a S$300,000
1966 add-on. Inside are statues of Vishnu,
Lakshmi and Andal, and Vishnu's bird-
mount Garuda. The temple is the starting
point for a colourful, wince-inducing street
parade during the Thaipusam festival: to
show their devotion, many participants
pierce their bodies with hooks and skewers.

LEONG SAN SEE TEMPLE   TAOIST TEMPLE
(⏹6298 9371; 371 Race Course Rd; ☺7.30am-
5pm; Ⓜ Farrer Park, Bendemeer) FREE Dating

from 1917, this relatively modest temple is
dedicated to goddess of mercy Kuan Yin
(Guan Yin). The temple's name translates
as Dragon Mountain Temple, and both its
wooden beams and tiled roof ridge are decorated with animated dragons, chimera,
flowers and human figures. To get here,
walk north up Serangoon Rd then, opposite
Beatty Rd, turn left through a decorative
yellow-and-red archway emblazoned with
the Chinese characters for the temple (寺山
龍) and you'll find it at the end of the lane.

SAKYA MUNI BUDDHA
GAYA TEMPLE   BUDDHIST TEMPLE
(Temple of 1000 Lights; 366 Race Course Rd;
☺8am-4.30pm; Ⓜ Farrer Park, Bendemeer)
FREE Dominating this temple is a 15m-tall,
300-tonne Buddha. Keeping him company is an eclectic cast of deities, including
Kuan Yin (Guan Yin; the Chinese goddess
of mercy) and, interestingly, the Hindu deities Brahma and Ganesh. The yellow tigers
flanking the entrance symbolise protection
and vitality, while the huge mother-of-pearl
Buddha footprint to your left as you enter
is reputedly a replica of the footprint on
top of Adam's Peak in Sri Lanka. The footprint's 108 auspicious marks distinguish a
Buddha foot from any other 2m-long foot.
The temple was founded by a Thai monk in
1927 and stands opposite the Taoist Leong
San See Temple.

INDIAN HERITAGE CENTRE
The S$12 million, state-of-the-art
Indian Heritage Centre (Map p210;
⏹6291 1601; www.indianheritage.org.
sg; 5 Campbell Lane; adult/child under
7yr S$4/free; ☺10am-7pm Tue-Thu, to
8pm Fri & Sat, to 4pm Sun; Ⓜ Little India,
Rochor) opened in 2015 to spotlight
the origins and heritage of Singapore's
Indian community through artefacts,
maps, archival footage and multimedia
displays (don't miss the 19th-century
Chettinad doorway). Aside from its five
themed exhibition galleries, the centre
also houses a visitor centre, a rooftop
garden and activity spaces. The building itself is a striking contemporary
statement: iridescent during the day,
its translucent facade becomes trans-
parent at night, revealing a suitably
colour-packed mural.

🏃 Neighbourhood Walk
Little India

START FARRER PARK MRT STATION
END TEKKA CENTRE
LENGTH 2.7KM; 1½ HOURS

From Farrer Park MRT, head north along Race Course Rd to **❶Sakya Muni Buddha Gaya Temple** (p85). Peek inside at its 15m-tall Buddha, then cross the street to appreciate the colourful detailing of Taoist **❷Leong San See Temple** (p85). The alleyway opposite leads to bustling Serangoon Rd. Head south along it to the striking **❸Sri Srinivasa Perumal Temple** (p85), Singapore's first temple for worshippers of Lord Vishnu (aka Perumal). Blessings give way to bargains further south at the **❹Mustafa Centre** (p93), Little India's 24-hour shopping complex. The domed **❺Angullia Mosque** (📞6295 1478 ; www.angulliamosque. com.sg ; 265 Serangoon Rd ; ⏰8.30am-5.30pm Mon-Fri, to 2pm Sat; Little India, Farrer Park) across the street is popular with Singapore's Bangladeshi foreign workers. Further south, pop into **❻Sri Veeramakaliamman Temple** (p85), Little India's main Hindu Temple, then head along Veerasamy Rd. Turn right down Kampong Kapor Rd to find the whitewashed 1929 **❼Kampong Kapor Methodist Church**, then left along Upper Weld Rd and right into Perak Rd. At Dunlop St, turn left to admire the whimsical **❽Abdul Gafoor Mosque** (📞6295 4209; 41 Dunlop St; ⏰8am-8pm Sat-Thu, 8am-noon & 2.30-8pm Fri; MRochor), a storybook fusion of Arab and Victorian architecture. Above the main entrance is a unique sundial, its 25 rays decorated with Arabic calligraphy denoting the 25 names of the prophets. Backtrack west along **❾Dunlop St** to soak up the colourful jumble of shophouses, then cross over Serangoon Rd and head down Kerbau Rd to eye up the kaleidoscopic **❿Tan House**. Pick your jaw up off the ground and walk down the side alley to Buffalo Rd, a thoroughfare lined with buxom produce, colourful garlands and the airbrushed stares of Bollywood divas. Both Buffalo Rd and Kerbau Rd (*kerbau* means 'buffalo' in Malay) echo a time when this area was awash with the cattle sheds of North Indian farmers. Weary and perhaps a little hungry, slip into the **⓫Tekka Centre** (p87) for cheap and scrumptious snacks.

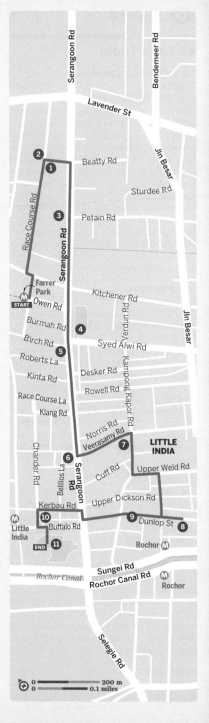

◎ Kampong Glam

★SULTAN MOSQUE MOSQUE
Map p210 (✆6293 4405; www.sultanmosque.sg;
3 Muscat St; ☉10am-noon & 2-4pm Sat-Thu, 2.30-
4pm Fri; Ⓜ Bugis) FREE Seemingly pulled
from the pages of the *Arabian Nights,* Singapore's largest mosque is nothing short
of enchanting, designed in the Saracenic
style and topped by a golden dome. It was
originally built in 1825 with the aid of a
grant from Raffles and the East India Company, after Raffles' treaty with the sultan
of Singapore allowed the Malay leader to
retain sovereignty over the area. In 1928,
the original mosque was replaced by the
present magnificent building, designed by
an Irish architect. Non-Muslims are asked
to refrain from entering the prayer hall at
any time, and all visitors are expected to be
dressed suitably (cloaks are available at the
entrance). Pointing cameras at people during prayer time is never appropriate.

MALAY HERITAGE CENTRE MUSEUM
Map p210 (✆6391 0450; www.malayheritage.
org.sg; 85 Sultan Gate; adult/child under 6yr $4/
free; ☉10am-6pm Tue-Sun; Ⓜ Bugis) The Kampong Glam area is the historic seat of Malay
royalty, resident here before the arrival of
Raffles, and the *istana* (palace) on this site
was built for the last sultan of Singapore,
Ali Iskander Shah, between 1836 and 1843.
It's now a museum, its recently revamped
galleries exploring Malay-Singaporean culture and history, from the early migration
of traders to Kampong Glam to the development of Malay-Singaporean film, theatre,
music and publishing.

**MALABAR MUSLIM
JAMA-ATH MOSQUE** MOSQUE
Map p210 (✆6294 3862; www.malabar.org.
sg; 471 Victoria St; ☉noon-1pm & 2-4pm, from
2.30pm Fri; Ⓜ Bugis, Lavender) FREE Architecture goes easy-wipe at the golden-domed
Malabar Muslim Jama-ath Mosque, a curious creation clad entirely in striking blue
geometric tiles. This is the only mosque on
the island dedicated to Malabar Muslims
from the South Indian state of Kerala, and
though the building was commenced in
1956, it wasn't officially opened until 1963
due to cash-flow problems. The better-late-
than-never motif continued with the tiling,
which was only completed in 1995.

◎ Bugis

**KWAN IM THONG
HOOD CHO TEMPLE** BUDDHIST TEMPLE
Map p210 (✆6348 0967; 178 Waterloo St; ☉6am-
6.30pm; Ⓜ Bugis) FREE Awash with the frenetic click of *chien tung* (Chinese fortune
sticks), this is one of Singapore's busiest
(and according to devotees, luckiest) temples. It's dedicated to the goddess of mercy,
Kuan Yin (Guan Yin), a much-loved be-
stower of good fortune. Flower sellers and
fortune tellers swarm around the entrance,
while, further up the street, believers rub
the belly of a large bronze Buddha Maitreya
for extra luck.

In a very Singaporean case of religious
pragmatism, worshippers also offer prayers
at the polychromatic **Sri Krishnan Temple**
(Map p210; 152 Waterloo St; ☉6am-2pm & 5.30-
9pm; Ⓜ Bugis) FREE next door.

✖ EATING

✖ Little India

TEKKA CENTRE HAWKER $
Map p210 (cnr Serangoon & Buffalo Rds; dishes
S$3-10; ☉7am-11pm, stall hours vary; ✖; Ⓜ Lit-
tle India) There's no shortage of subconti-
nental spice at this bustling hawker centre, wrapped around the sloshed guts and
hacked bones of the wet market. Queue
up for real-deal biryani, *dosa* (paper thin,
lentil-flour pancake), *roti prata* (dough-
flour pancake) and *teh tarik* (pulled tea).
Worth seeking out is **Ah-Rahman Royal
Prata** (01-248 Tekka Centre; murtabak from S$5;
☉7.30am-10pm Tue-Sun), which flips some
of Singapore's finest *murtabak* (stuffed
savoury pancake). One floor up is a rainbow-coloured sea of Indian sari and textile
stores, not to mention a small battalion of
tailors. This is probably the cheapest place
to pick up an Indian outfit, and while prices
are marked, well-mannered bargaining is
always worth a try.

GANDHI RESTAURANT SOUTH INDIAN $
Map p210 (29-31 Chander Rd; dishes S$2.50-6.50,
set meals from S$4.50; ☉11am-4pm & 6-11pm;
Ⓜ Little India) It might be a canteen-style joint
with erratic service and cheap decor, but
who cares when the food is this good? Wash
your hands by the sink at the back, and take

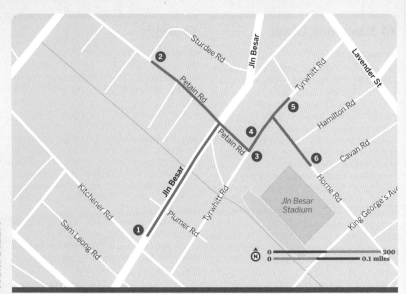

🏃 Local Life
An Afternoon in Jalan Besar

Once better known for hardware stores and boxing matches, Jalan Besar is metamorphosing into an area where heritage architecture meets new-school Singapore cool. Just northeast of Little India, this compact district, centred on Jln Besar, is studded with artisan cafes and is the perfect mix of old meets new.

① Scissor Snips

Start by fuelling up at **Beach Road Scissor Cut Curry Rice** (Map p210; 229 Jln Besar, cnr Kitchener Rd; ⊗11am-3.30am; M Lavender, Farrer Park). Choose from the glass cabinet – our pick is the pork chop – and then watch as the hawker expertly snips it up into bite-sized pieces with a pair of old-school scissors. It's then heaped on a plate with white rice and covered with sauce, and tastes much better than it looks!

② Peranakan Perfection

Between Jln Besar and Sturdee Rd is an extraordinary row of lavishly decorated double-storey **terraces** (off Map p210; Petain Rd; M Farrer Park, Bendemeer) dating back to the 1920s. It's an explosion of colour, from the floral-motif ceramic wall tiles to pillar bas-reliefs adorned with flowers, birds and trees. The hyper-ornate decoration is typical of what's known as 'late shophouse style'.

③ Cooling Dip

Pack your bathers and work off your sugar high at **Jalan Besar Swimming Complex** (Map p210; ☑6293 9058; 100 Tyrwhitt Rd; weekdays/weekends S$1.30/1.70; ⊗8am-9.30pm Thu-Tue, 2.30-9.30pm Wed; M Farrer Park, Lavender), opposite Two Bakers. The 50m pool is perfect for banging out a few laps even just saving you from the oppressive Singapore heat. Entry will only set you back a couple of bucks – and is so worth it.

④ Beer Brews

Looking at the signboard, you'd think this is the place to have your medical prescription filled, but the Chinese Druggist Association moved out long ago. Duck inside this heritage shophouse to discover what new tenant **Druggists** (Map p210; ☑6341 5967; www.facebook.com/DruggistsSG; 119 Tyrwhitt Rd; ⊗4pm-midnight Mon-Thu, to 2am Fri & Sat, 2-10pm Sun; M Bendemeer, Farrer Park, Lavender) is now dispensing. Along the back wall, 23 gleaming craft beer taps await. Check the blackboard menu and order away.

⑤ Coffee in a Hardware Shop

An art deco former hardware store provides both the setting and the name for **Chye**

Detail of shophouse architecture (p176)

Seng Huat Hardware (off Map p210; CSHH Coffee Bar; ☑6396 0609; www.cshh coffee.com; 150 Tyrwhitt Rd; ⊙9am-10pm Tue-Thu & Sun, to midnight Fri & Sat; Ⓜ Bendemeer, Farrer Park, Lavender), Singapore's hottest cafe and roastery. Slurp a glass of 'nitro black matter', a malty, cold-brew coffee infused with CO_2 and served on tap, or get your coffee geek on at one of the education sessions; see www.papapalheta.com/education/classes for details.

❻ Sweet Endings

Reward yourself for all that walking by popping into **Two Bakers** (Map p210; ☑6293 0329; www.two-bakers.com; 88 Horne Rd; pastries & cakes S$6.80-9; ⊙9am-6pm Mon, Wed, Thu & Sun, 10am-10pm Fri & Sat; Ⓜ Bendemeer, Lavender), where the masters behind the irresistible sweet treats earned their stripes at Paris' Cordon Bleu. The result? Countless broken diets. Which tart to choose: crowd favourite yuzu lemon or the decadent 'purple gold' (lavender-infused chocolate ganache, caramel ganache, caramel tuile and roasted almonds)? What the hell: order both!

a seat. A banana-leaf plate heaped with rice and condiments (set-meal thali) will appear, order extra items from the servers – chicken curry is a must – then tuck in.

SUNGEI ROAD LAKSA   MALAYSIAN **$**

Map p210 (www.sungeiroadlaksa.com.sg; 01-100, Block 27, Jln Berseh; laksa S$3; ⊙9am-6pm, closed 1st & 3rd Wed of month; Ⓜ Rochor, Jalan Besar) Get a cheap, steamy fix at Sungei Road Laksa. The fragrant, savoury coconut-base soup here enjoys a cult following, and only charcoal is used to keep the precious gravy warm. To avoid the lunchtime crowds, head in before 11.30am or after 2pm.

MOGHUL SWEETS   SWEETS **$**

Map p210 (☑6392 5797; 01-16 Little India Arcade, 48 Serangoon Rd; sweets from S$1; ⊙9.30am-9.30pm; Ⓜ Little India) If you're after a subcontinental sugar rush, tiny Moghul is the place to get it. Bite into luscious *gulab jamun* (syrup-soaked fried dough balls), harder-to-find *rasmalai* (paneer soaked in cardamom-infused clotted cream) and *barfi* (condensed milk and sugar slice) in flavours including pistachio, chocolate...and carrot.

ANANDA BHAVAN   INDIAN **$**

Map p210 (www.anandabhavan.com; 58 Serangoon Rd; dosa S$2.60-5.20, set meals S$6-10; ⊙7.30am-10pm Mon-Thu, to 10.30pm Fri-Sun; Ⓜ Little India) This super-cheap chain restaurant is a top spot to sample South Indian breakfast staples like *idly* (fermented rice cakes) and *dosa* (thin, lentil-flour pancake; spelt 'thosai' on the menu). It also does great-value set-meal thali. There are other branches around Little India, just as no-frills as this one, and all with the same commitment to dishing up tasty, healthy vegetarian food.

USMAN   PAKISTANI, INDIAN **$**

Map p210 (☑6296 8949; 238 Serangoon Rd, cnr Desker Rd; dishes S$1.60-26; ⊙noon-2am; Ⓜ Farrer Park) Cluttered with sacks of flour and onions, tiny Usman whips up seriously fine paneer (soft, unfermented cheese made from milk curd); the *pulak paneer* (paneer with a creamy spinach gravy) is especially good. Dhal is a dirt-cheap S$1.60, while the tandoori chicken bursts with flavour. Whatever you choose, mop it up with soft, freshly baked naan (tandoor-cooked flatbread).

★LAGNAA BAREFOOT DINING   INDIAN **$$**

Map p210 (☑6296 1215; www.lagnaa.com; 6 Upper Dickson Rd; dishes S$8-20; ⊙11.30am-10.30pm;

☎; Ⓜ Little India) You can choose your level of spice at friendly Lagnaa: level three denotes standard spiciness, level four significant spiciness, and anything above admirable bravery. Whatever you opt for, you're in for finger-licking-good homestyle cooking from both ends of Mother India, devoured at Western seating downstairs or on floor cushions upstairs. If you're indecisive, order chef Kaesavan's famous Threadfin fish curry.

Those who eat a level-three dish without the aid of yoghurt-based drinks or dishes get their own peg on Lagnaa's string of chilli fame. Devour a level-six dish and expect an invitation to Lagnaa's monthly Full Moon Chilli Challenge. Survive that and the meal is on the house. Cash only for bills under S$30.

MUSTARD   INDIAN $$

Map p210 (✉6297 8422; www.mustardsingapore. com; 32 Race Course Rd; mains S$6.90-19.90; ⏱11.30am-3pm & 6-10.45pm Sun-Fri, 11.30am-4pm & 6-10.45pm Sat; Ⓜ Little India) One of the most refined of the more upmarket Indian restaurants that line this end of Race Course Rd, this small restaurant with excellent service offers dishes – all cooked in mustard oil – hailing mostly from Bengal and Punjab. Kebabs are the speciality, but there are several good curries and biryanis on offer too.

✖ Kampong Glam

★ ZAM ZAM   MALAYSIAN $

Map p210 (✉6298 6320; 697-699 North Bridge Rd; murtabak from S$5; ⏱7am-11pm; Ⓜ Bugis) These guys have been here since 1908, so they know what they're doing. Tenure hasn't bred complacency, though – the touts still try to herd customers in off the street, while frenetic chefs inside whip up delicious *murtabak,* the restaurant's speciality savoury pancakes, filled with succulent mutton, chicken, beef, venison or even sardines. Servings are epic, so order a medium between two.

WARONG NASI
PARIAMAN   MALAYSIAN, INDONESIAN $

Map p210 (✉6292 2374; www.pariaman.com.sg; 736-738 North Bridge Rd; dishes from S$4.50; ⏱7am-6pm; Ⓜ Bugis) This no-frills corner *nasi padang* (rice with curries) stall is the stuff of legend. Top choices include the

delicate *rendang* beef, *ayam bakar* (grilled chicken with coconut sauce) and spicy sambal goreng (long beans, tempeh and fried beancurd). Get here by 11am to avoid the lunch hordes and by 5pm for the dinner queue.

And be warned: most of it sells out well before closing time.

★ CICHETI   ITALIAN $$

Map p210 (✉6292 5012; www.cicheti.com; 52 Kandahar St; pizzas S$18-28, mains S$29-39; ⏱noon-2.30pm & 6.30-10.30pm Mon-Fri, 6-10.30pm Sat; Ⓜ Bugis, Nicoll Hwy) Cool-kid Cicheti is a slick, friendly, buzzing scene of young-gun pizzaioli, trendy diners and seductive, contemporary Italian dishes made with hand-picked market produce. Tuck into beautifully charred woodfired pizzas, made-from-scratch pasta and evening standouts like *polpette di carne grana* (slow-cooked meatballs topped with shaved Grana Padana). Book early in the week if heading in on a Friday or Saturday night.

PIEDRA NEGRA   MEXICAN $$

Map p210 (✉6291 1297; www.facebook.com/ Piedra.Negra.Haji.Lane; cnr Beach Rd & Haji Lane; mains S$8.90-21.90; ⏱noon-1am Mon-Sat; ☎; Ⓜ Bugis) Sexy Latin beats, bombastic murals and tables right on free-spirited Haji Lane: this electric Mexican joint is a brilliant spot for cheapish cocktails and a little evening people watching. Frozen or shaken, the margaritas pack a punch, and the joint's burritos, quesadillas, tacos and other Tex-Mex staples are filling and delish.

MRS PHO   VIETNAMESE $$

Map p210 (✉6292 0018; www.mrspho.com; 349 Beach Rd; mains S$8.90-9.90; ⏱11am-9.30pm; Ⓜ Bugis, Nicoll Hwy) Stepping inside this shophouse feels like being transported to a back alley in Vietnam, complete with exposed wiring, concrete walls, tiny metal tables with even tinier stools. Pho is king here; however, the *bun thit nuong cha gio* (dry vermicelli salad with barbecue pork and fried spring roll) delivers a perfect balance of crunch with sweet-and-sour flavours.

Wash it down with a glass of strangely addictive tangy Saigon salty lemonade.

NAN HWA CHONG FISH-HEAD
STEAMBOAT CORNER   CHINESE $$

Map p210 (✉6297 9319; www.facebook.com/ nanhwachong; 812-816 North Bridge Rd; fish

STAR HAWKERS

When the *Michelin Guide* launched in Singapore in 2016, two humble Singaporean hawkers were bestowed with the honour of receiving one shiny star each. Chinatown's Hong Kong Soya Sauce Chicken Rice & Noodle (p73) also boasts the accolade of being the world's cheapest Michelin-star meal – at just S$2, hawker Chan Hong Meng's delicately flavoured chicken and rice has always been popular with locals, but now it's known worldwide. Quick to build on his success, he's opened another three outlets (and counting!) and has plans to export his famous recipes overseas. The new shops have a more McDonald's-esque vibe, so we recommend sticking to the Chinatown Complex original if you've got time to wait in the snaking queue.

The other line you'll want to join is at **Hill Street Tai Hwa Pork Noodle** (Map p210; www.taihwa.com.sg; 01-12, Block 466, Crawford Lane; noodles S$5-10; ⊙9.30am-9pm; ⓂLavender). It's a little further out of the way, about a 10-minute walk from the Lavender MRT station, but the queue here is shorter (though you can still expect a lengthy wait, especially at lunchtime). The object of desire? Teochew-style *bak chor mee* (minced pork noodles), springy noodles, tender pork and liver slices, crispy flat fish and a punch-packing vinegary chilli sauce. This second-generation hawker stall has been at it since 1932, so it's safe to say they know what they're doing.

steamboats from S$20; ⊙4pm-1am; ⓂBugis, Lavender) If you only try fish-head steamboat once, do it at this noisy, open-fronted veteran. Cooked on charcoal, the large pot of fish heads is brought to you in a steaming broth spiked with *tee po* (dried flat sole fish). One pot is enough for three or four people, and can stretch to more with rice and side dishes. There are several fish types to choose from; the grouper is the most popular with locals.

★KILO   FUSION $$$
(✎after 4pm 6467 3987; www.kilokitchen.com; 66 Kampong Bugis; sharing plates S$18-34, mains S$28-38; ⊙6-10.15pm Mon-Sat; ⓂLavender) Despite Singapore's cut-throat restaurant scene, gastro geeks remain loyal to this ode to fusion cooking. Expect the unexpected, from beef-tongue tacos with apple-miso slaw to goat-cheese and ricotta gnocchi with *maitake* mushrooms, brown-miso butter and *shiso* (a mintlike Asian herb). Slightly tricky to find, the restaurant occupies the 2nd floor of a lone industrial building on the Kallang River; take a taxi.

✘ **Bugis**

QS269 FOOD HOUSE   HAWKER $
Map p210 (Block 269B, Queen St; dishes from S$3; ⊙stall hours vary; ⓂBugis) This is not so much a 'food house' as a loud, crowded undercover laneway lined with cult-status stalls. Work up a sweat with a bowl of

award-winning coconut-curry noodle soup from **Ah Heng** (Map p210; www.facebook.com/AhHengChickenCurryNoodles; 01-236 QS269 Food House; dishes from S$4; ⊙8am-4.30pm Sat-Thu) or join the queue at **New Rong Liang Ge** (Map p210; 01-235 QS269 Food House; dishes from S$3; ⊙9am-8pm), with succulent roast-duck dishes that draw foodies from across the city. The laneway is down the side of the building.

🍺 DRINKING & NIGHTLIFE

When it comes to knocking back a few, Kampong Glam trumps Little India. The scene is focused on and around pedestrianised Haji Lane, with everything from hipster boltholes serving single-origin brews to band-jamming bars and the odd bespoke-cocktail den. For a cheap, no-frills swill, you can always grab a beer at one of the hawker centres.

🍺 Little India

PRINCE OF WALES   PUB
Map p210 (✎6299 0130; www.pow.com.sg; 101 Dunlop St; ⊙5pm-midnight Mon, to 1am Tue-Thu, 3pm-2am Fri & Sat, to midnight Sun; ⓂRochor) The closest thing to a pub in Little India, this grungy Aussie hang-out is an affable, popular spot, with a small beer garden, a pool table and sports screens. Weekly

staples include Wednesday quiz night (from 8pm) and live bands every Tuesday, Thursday, Friday and Sunday nights. Plenty of good drink deals to keep the good times rolling.

Kampong Glam

★ATLAS
BAR

Map p210 (☑6396 4466; www.atlasbar.sg; Lobby, Parkview Sq, 600 North Bridge Rd; ☺10am-1am Mon-Thu, to 2am Fri, 3pm-2am Sat; ⓂBugis) Straight out of 1920s Manhattan, this cocktail lounge is an art deco–inspired extravaganza, adorned with ornate bronze ceilings and low-lit plush lounge seating, and a drinks menu filled with decadent Champagnes, curated cocktails and some mean martinis. However, it's the 12m-high gin wall, displaying over 1000 labels, that really makes a statement – make sure you ask for a tour. Bookings are a good idea later in the week. Doors open in the morning for coffees, and European-inspired bites are served throughout the day and well into the night.

MAISON IKKOKU
COCKTAIL BAR

Map p210 (☑6294 0078; www.maison-ikkoku. net; 20 Kandahar St; ☺cafe 9am-9pm Mon-Thu, to 11pm Fri & Sat, to 7pm Sun, bar 4pm-1am Sun-Thu, to 2am Fri & Sat; ☏; ⓂBugis) Pimped with suspended dressers, Maison Ikkoku's cafe flies the flag for third-wave coffee, with options including Chemex, syphon, cold drip, V60, woodneck, AeroPress and French press. The real magic happens in the upstairs cocktail bar, where a request for something sour might land you a tart, hot combo of spicy gin, grape, lemon and Japanese-chilli threads. Not cheap but worth it.

HEAP SENG LEONG
COFFEESHOP
COFFEE

Map p210 (01-5109, Block 10, North Bridge Rd; ☺4am-7pm; ⓂLavender) Have you joined the new bulletproof coffee craze? Where health nuts are adding butter to their coffee? Well, in Singapore they've been doing it for decades. Called *kopi gu you* (coffee with butter), this smooth and caramely brew is served in this old-school coffeeshop by an elderly uncle. For just over S$1, the brew is a coffee lover's bargain.

ENTERTAINMENT

This being Little India, Bollywood blockbusters are the hot ticket at Rex Cinemas. If live music is more your jam, you'll find plenty of it here – especially jazz.

★SINGAPORE
DANCE THEATRE
DANCE

Map p210 (☑6338 0611; www.singaporedance theatre.com; Level 7, Bugis+, 201 Victoria St; ☺10am-8pm Mon-Fri, to 4pm Sat & Sun; ⓂBugis) This is the headquarters of Singapore's premier dance company, which keeps fans swooning with its repertoire of classic ballets and contemporary works, many of which are performed at Esplanade – Theatres on the Bay (p66). The true highlight is the group's Ballet under the Stars season at Fort Canning Park (p56), which usually runs midyear. See the website for program details.

REX CINEMAS
CINEMA

Map p210 (☑6337 6607; www.rexcinemas.com. sg; 2 Mackenzie Rd; tickets S$12; ⓂLittle India) Where can you catch the Bollywood blockbusters advertised all over Little India? Why, at the Rex, of course. This historic theatre screens films from around the subcontinent, most subtitled in English.

WILD RICE
THEATRE

Map p210 (☑6292 2695; www.wildrice.com.sg; 65 Kerbau Rd; ⓂLittle India) Singapore's sexiest theatre group is based in Kerbau Rd but performs shows elsewhere in the city (as well as abroad). A mix of homegrown and foreign work, productions range from farce to serious politics, fearlessly wading into issues not commonly on the agenda in Singapore.

BLUJAZ CAFÉ
LIVE MUSIC

Map p210 (☑6292 3800; www.blujazcafe.net; 11 Bali Lane; ☺noon-1am Mon-Thu, to 2am Fri, 3pm-2am Sat; ☏; ⓂBugis) Bohemian pub BluJaz is one of the best options in town for live music, with regular jazz jams, and other acts playing anything from blues to rockabilly. Check the website for the list of events, which includes DJ-spun funk, R&B and retro nights, as well as 'Talk Cock' open-mic comedy nights on Wednesday and Thursday. Cover charge for some shows.

BANKSY, ASIAN-STYLE

Malaysia's answer to Banksy is street artist Ernest Zacharevic (www.ernestzacharevic. com). From Stavanger to Singapore, his murals often incorporate real-life props, whether old bicycles, wooden chairs or even the moss growing out of cracks. In one small work opposite the Malabar Muslim Jama-ath Mosque, two exhilarated kids freewheel it on a pair of 3D supermarket trolleys. To the right, a young boy somersaults out of a box, while further south, on the corner of Victoria St and Jln Pisang, a giant girl caresses a snoozing lion cub. These three Zacharevic creations are not the only ones in town either. Head to the corner of Joo Chiat Tce and Everitt Rd in the eastern neighbourhood of Katong and you'll stumble upon his Jousting Painters (p107), a giant mural featuring two very real-looking boys prepared for battle on brightly painted horses.

HOOD
LIVE MUSIC

Map p210 (☑6221 8846; www.hoodbarandcafe. com; 05-07 Bugis+, 201 Victoria St; ⓘ5pm-1am Sun-Wed, to 3am Thu-Sat; ⓜBugis) Inside the Bugis+ mall, Hood's street-art interior sets a youthful scene for nightly music jams with acts such as Rush Hour and Smells Like Last Friday. If it's undiscovered talent you're after, head in for the weekly 'Saturday Original Sessions', a showcase for budding musos itching to share their singer-songwriter skills.

 # SHOPPING

🔒 Little India

Little India's streets are a browser's delight, laced with art, antiques, textiles, food and music. Quieter and more relaxed, Kampong Glam is even more eclectic – head to Arab St for textiles, rugs and bespoke perfumes, or Haji and Bali Lanes for independent fashion and hipster-approved accessories.

MUSTAFA CENTRE
DEPARTMENT STORE

Map p210 (☑6295 5855; www.mustafa.com.sg; 145 Syed Alwi Rd; ⓘ24hr; ⓜFarrer Park) Little India's bustling Mustafa Centre is a magnet for budget shoppers, most of them from the subcontinent. It's a sprawling place, selling everything from electronics and garish gold jewellery to shoes, bags, luggage and beauty products. There's also a large supermarket with a great range of Indian foodstuffs. If you can't handle crowds, avoid the place on Sunday.

RUGGED GENTLEMEN
SHOPPE
FASHION & ACCESSORIES

Map p210 (☑6396 4568; www.tuckshopsundry supplies.com; 8 Perak Rd; ⓘnoon-8pm Mon-Sat, by appt Sun; ⓜRochor) A vintage-inspired ode to American working-class culture, this little menswear store offers a clued-in selection of rugged threads and accessories, including Red Wing boots, grooming products and made-in-house leather goods. Stock up on plaid shirts, sweat tops and harder-to-find denim from brands like Japan's Iron Heart and China's Red Cloud.

SIM LIM SQUARE
ELECTRONICS, MALL

Map p210 (☑6338 3859; www.simlimsquare.com. sg; 1 Rochor Canal Rd; ⓘ10.30am-9pm; ⓜRochor) A byword for all that is cut price and geeky, Sim Lim is jammed with stalls selling laptops, cameras, soundcards and games consoles. If you know what you're doing, there are deals to be had, but the untutored are likely to be out of their depth. Bargain hard (yet politely) and always check that the warranty is valid in your home country.

🔒 Kampong Glam

SIFR AROMATICS
PERFUME

Map p210 (☑6392 1966; www.sifr.sg; 42 Arab St; ⓘ11am-8pm Mon-Sat, to 5pm Sun; ⓜBugis, Nicoll Hwy) This Zen-like perfume laboratory belongs to third-generation perfumer Johari Kazura, whose exquisite creations include the heady East (30mL S$135), a blend of oud, rose absolute, amber and neroli. The focus is on custom-made fragrances (consider calling ahead to arrange an appointment), with other heavenly offerings including affordable, high-quality body balms, scented candles and vintage perfume bottles.

HAJI LANE HIP

Running parallel to old-school Arab St, narrow, pastel **Haji Lane** (Map p210 Ⓜ Bugis) is a go-to for one-off boutiques, bolthole cafes and people watching. Although Haji Lane's shops can be a little hit or miss, **Dulcetfig** (Map p210; ☑6396 5648; www.dulcet fig.com; 41 Haji Lane; ☺11am-9pm Mon-Sat, to 8pm Sun) is a sure bet for cool frocks. Raid the racks for local and foreign brands, paired with an eclectic mix of vintage bling, bags and more. Late afternoon is the best time to visit Haji Lane: the streets are cooler and the restaurants and bars starting to buzz. For a cold craft brew, squeeze into tiny **Good Luck Beerhouse** (Map p210; ☑8742 4809; www.facebook.com/GoodLuck Beerhouse; 9 Haji Lane; ☺4pm-midnight Mon-Thu, from noon Fri-Sun), there are eight beers on tap and more than 50 labels in the fridge.

Pop around the corner onto Beach Rd and you'll discover designer-cool homeware and gift shops **Supermama** (Map p210; ☑6291 1946; www.supermama.sg; 265 Beach Rd; ☺11am-8pm) and **Scene Shang** (Map p210; ☑6291 9629; http://shop.sceneshang.com; 263 Beach Rd; ☺11am-8pm Sun-Thu, to 9.30pm Fri & Sat), both definitely worth a browse.

LITTLE SHOPHOUSE   ARTS & CRAFTS
Map p210 (☑6295 2328; 43 Bussorah St; ☺10am-5pm; Ⓜ Bugis) Traditional Peranakan beadwork is a dying art, but it's kept very much alive in this shop and workshop. The shop's colourful slippers are designed by craftsman Robert Sng and hand-beaded by himself and his sister, Irene. While they're not cheap (approximately S$1000), each pair takes a painstaking 100 hours to complete. You'll also find Peranakan-style tea sets, crockery, vases, handbags and jewellery.

Robert runs one-on-one beading workshops, lasting five hours and costing from S$350; book one week ahead.

🏠 Bugis

BUGIS STREET MARKET   MARKET
Map p210 (☑6338 9513; www.bugisstreet.com. sg; 3 New Bugis St; ☺11am-10pm; Ⓜ Bugis) What was once Singapore's most infamous sleaze pit – packed with foreign service-men on R&R and gambling dens – is now its most famous undercover street market, crammed with cheap clothes, shoes, accessories and manicurists, and especially popular with teens and 20-somethings. In a nod to its past, there's even a sex shop.

🏃 SPORTS & ACTIVITIES

KSB AYURVEDIC CENTRE   MASSAGE
Map p210 (☑6635 2339; www.ayurvedaksb.sg; 11 Upper Dickson Rd; 30min massage from S$35; ☺9am-9pm Mon-Sat, to 3pm Sun; Ⓜ Little India) If Little India's hyperactive energy leaves you frazzled, revive the Indian way with an Ayurvedic (traditional Indian medicine) massage at this modest, friendly place. Treatments include the highly popular Abhyangam (synchronised massage using medicated oils) and the deeply relaxing Shirodhara (warm oil poured over the forehead). Yoga classes are also on offer.

Orchard Road

Neighbourhood Top Five

1 ION Orchard Mall (p101) Shopping the new-millennium way at Singapore's sleekest, sharpest, mega mall, and the epitome of retail escapism.

2 Tanglin Shopping Centre (p102) Hunting for antiques, bartering for an oriental rug or poring over ancient maps of Asia in this culturally savvy shopping centre.

3 Emerald Hill Road (p97) Pacing your shopping spree with a leisurely stroll along this heritage-packed area, steps from Orchard Road.

4 Iggy's (p99) Treating your palate to a tasting menu at one of Singapore's most exalted restaurants.

5 Killiney Kopitiam (p97) Coming back down to earth with a traditional Singaporean breakfast of *kaya* (coconut jam) toast and *kopi* (coffee) at the original locals' coffeeshop.

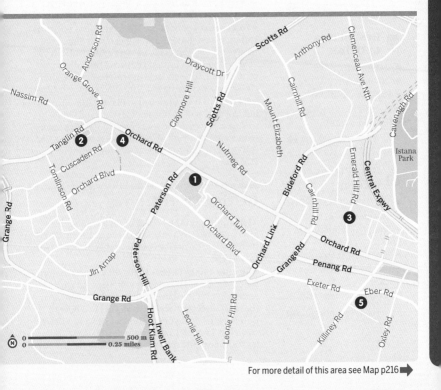

For more detail of this area see Map p216 ➡

Lonely Planet's Top Tip

It's hard to believe it as you walk from mall to mall, but there is a rainforest within 2km of Orchard Rd, inside the grounds of the wonderful Botanic Gardens (p123). So, if you fancy a green escape from the concrete jungle, hop on bus 7 or 174 from the Orchard MRT exit on Orchard Blvd, and you'll be there in 10 to 20 minutes.

✖ Best Places to Eat

➡ Iggy's (p99)

➡ Takashimaya Food Village (p98)

➡ Buona Terra (p99)

➡ StraitsKitchen (p99)

➡ Fish and Chicks (p98)

➡ Paradise Dynasty (p98)

For reviews, see p97.➡

☐ Best Places to Drink

➡ Manhattan (p99)

➡ Other Room (p100)

➡ Bar Canary (p100)

➡ Horse's Mouth (p100)

➡ Providore (p99)

For reviews, see p99.➡

☐ Best Places to Shop

➡ ION Orchard Mall (p101)

➡ Paragon (p102)

➡ Antiques of the Orient (p102)

➡ Pedder On Scotts (p101)

➡ Tanglin Shopping Centre (p102)

➡ In Good Company (p101)

For reviews, see p101.➡

ORCHARD ROAD

Explore: Orchard Road

You would need the best part of a week to explore every floor of every mall in **Orchard Rd** (Map p216; Orchard Rd; MOrchard, Somerset, Dhoby Ghaut) area, so do some shopping-mall homework before you go – keep reading.

Most malls don't open until 10am, but if you arrive early, fear not: you have the perfect excuse to charge up with breakfast and a powerful cup of coffee, either the old-school, Singaporean way at Killiney Kopitiam (p97), or the trendy, new-school way at the Providore (p99) or Wild Honey (p99).

Whichever malls you trawl, it won't be long before your pins yearn for a well-earned break. Spoil them with a quick foot rub at Lucky Plaza (p101) or go all out with some luxe pampering at one of the area's top-tier hotel spas.

Come 5pm, it's time to toast to your purchases with cut-price, happy-hour drinks – on Orchard Rd itself or just off it on historic beauty Emerald Hill Rd (p97).

Local Life

➡**Crowds** Shopping is Singapore's national sport, and the malls on Orchard Rd can get exceedingly busy. That can be half the fun, but if you prefer your shopping *sans* the hordes, head in as they open (usually around 10am) and browse bustle-free for about an hour or so.

➡**Food courts** Shopping-mall food courts might be culinary wastelands back home, but in Singapore they're fantastic spots to eat fresh, authentic grub at very digestible prices. They're practically hawker centres with air-con, offering no shortage of local classics, as well as flavours from across the continent.

➡**Fresh air** Air-conditioned malls are all well and good, but the time will come for a blast of good old-fashioned fresh air. So when the shopping is done, kick back with a cooling drink above the madness at Bar Canary (p100), or mingle with the post-work crowd on Emerald Hill Rd.

Getting There & Away

➡**MRT** Orchard Rd is served by no less than three MRT stations: Orchard, Somerset and Dhoby Ghaut, so there's really no need to use any other form of transport to get here.

➡**Bus** Bus 7 links Orchard Rd with Victoria St (for Kampong Glam), bus 65 links Orchard Rd with Serangoon Rd (for Little India), while bus 190 is the most direct service between Orchard Rd and Chinatown. For Dempsey Hill and Holland Village, catch bus 7 or 106 from Penang Rd, Somerset Rd or Orchard Blvd just south of Orchard Rd.

⊙ SIGHTS

★ION SKY
VIEWPOINT

Map p216 (☑6238 8228; www.ionorchard.com/
en/ion-sky.html; Level 56, ION Orchard, 2 Orchard
Turn; ☺3-6pm; ⓂOrchard) FREE Observation
deck on Level 56 of the ION Orchard complex. Last entry 5.30pm.

ISTANA
PALACE

Map p216 (www.istana.gov.sg; Orchard Rd;
ⓂDhoby Ghaut) The grand, whitewashed,
neoclassical home of Singapore's president,
set in 16 hectares of grounds, was built by
the British between 1867 and 1869 as Government House, and is open to visitors five
times a year (8.30am to 6pm; grounds/
palace S$2/4): on Labour Day (1 May), a
chosen date before National Day (7 August),
Chinese New Year (January or February),
Diwali (October or November) and Hari
Raya Puasa (or Eid-ul Fitr, the festival
marking the end of Ramadan; dates vary).
Check website to confirm.

Only on these days will you get the
chance to stroll past the nine-hole golf
course, through the beautiful terraced gardens and into some of the reception rooms.
Bring your passport and get here early, the
queue builds quickly. The rest of the time,
the closest you'll get are the heavily guarded gates on Orchard Rd.

EMERALD HILL ROAD
ARCHITECTURE

Map p216 (Emerald Hill Rd; ⓂSomerset) Take
time out from your shopping to wander
up frangipani-scented Emerald Hill Rd,
graced with some of Singapore's finest
terrace houses. Special mentions go to
No 56 (one of the earliest buildings here,
built in 1902), No 39 to 45 (unusually wide
frontages and a grand Chinese-style entrance gate), and No 120 to 130 (art deco
features dating from around 1925). At the
Orchard Rd end of the hill is a cluster of
popular bars housed in fetching shophouse
renovations.

ISTANA HERITAGE GALLERY
MUSEUM

Map p216 (☑6904 4289; www.istana.gov.sg;
Istana Park, 35 Orchard Rd; ☺10am-6pm Thu-
Tue; ⓂDhoby Ghaut) FREE If your visit to Singapore doesn't coincide with one of the five
days per year the Istana opens to the public (or you don't have time to spend hours
queuing on one of those days), you can now
take a peek behind the formidable gates
at this informative museum. Discover the
building's history, peruse the guest book,

ORCHARD ROAD'S LAST BUILDING BLOCK

With new shopping malls being shoe-
horned into every available space on
Orchard Rd, why, many visitors ask,
does the Thai embassy occupy such
a large, prominent grounds in an area
of staggeringly expensive real estate?
Back in the 1990s, the Thai government was reportedly offered S$139
million for the site, but they turned it
down because selling the land, bought
by Thailand for S$9000 in 1983 by the
revered King Chulalongkorn (Rama
V), would be seen as an affront to his
memory. And so, it remains, drooled
over by frustrated developers.

marvel at opulent state gifts and even sit
for a picture-perfect moment in front of a
life-sized backdrop of the East Drawing
Room.

CATHAY GALLERY
MUSEUM

Map p216 (www.thecathaygallery.com.sg; 02-16
The Cathay, 2 Handy Rd; ☺11am-7pm Mon-Sat;
☎; ⓂDhoby Ghaut) FREE Film and nostalgia buffs will appreciate this pocket-sized
silver-screen museum, housed in Singapore's first high-rise building. The displays
trace the history of the Loke family, early
pioneers in film production and distribu-
tion in Singapore and founders of the Cathay Organisation. Highlights include old
movie posters, cameras and programs that
capture the golden age of local cinema.

✕ EATING

**Between its plethora of shops, Orchard
Rd boasts almost as many places to
satisfy your hunger. Choose from high-
end culinary heavyweights, international
chain restaurants and bustling indoor
hawker food courts. Everyone's taste
and budget is catered for.**

KILLINEY KOPITIAM
CAFE $

Map p216 (☑6734 3910; www.killiney-kopitiam.
com; 67 Killiney Rd; dishes S$1-7; ☺6am-11pm
Mon & Wed-Sat, to 6pm Tue & Sun; ⓂSomerset)
Start the day the old-school way at this veteran coffee joint, pimped with endearingly
lame laminated jokes. Order a strong *kopi*

(coffee), a serve of *kaya* (coconut jam) toast and a side of soft-boiled egg. Crack open the egg, add a dash of soy sauce and white pepper, then dip your *kaya* toast in it.

Post-breakfast, chow down on bargain staples like chicken curry, laksa or *nasi lemak* (coconut rice, dried anchovies and spices wrapped in a banana leaf).

★PARADISE DYNASTY   CHINESE $$
Map p216 (www.paradisegroup.com.sg; 04-12A ION Orchard, 2 Orchard Turn; dishes S$5-20; ⊙11am-10pm; Ⓜ️Orchard) Preened staffers in headsets whisk you into this svelte dumpling den, passing a glassed-in kitchen where Chinese chefs stretch their noodles and steam their buns. Skip the novelty-flavoured *xiao long bao* (soup dumplings) for the original version, which arguably beat those of legendary competitor Din Tai Fung. Beyond these, standouts include *la mian* (hand-pulled noodles) with buttery, braised pork belly.

FISH AND CHICKS   FISH & CHIPS $$
Map p216 (✆9828 3490; www.facebook.com/fishnchicksg; B1-01, Cathay Cineleisure, 8 Grange Rd; mains S$6.90-11.80; ⊙11am-10pm; Ⓜ️Somerset) Dishing up seriously good fish and chicken dishes (geddit?), these two young hawkers are famous for their Singaporean twist on fish 'n' chips. Choose from either chilli crab or salted egg yolk sauce, which is generously slathered over the super crunchy battered fish. Can't decide? Order 'best of both worlds', double the fish and both sauces!

TAMBUAH MAS   INDONESIAN $$
Map p216 (✆6733 2220; www.tambuahmas.com.sg; B1-44 Paragon, 290 Orchard Rd; mains S$8-29; ⊙11am-10pm; 🛜; Ⓜ️Somerset) Hiding shyly in a corner of Paragon's food-packed basement, Tambuah Mas is where Indonesian expats head for a taste of home. Bright, modern and good value for Orchard Rd, it proudly makes much of what it serves from scratch, a fact evident in what could possibly be Singapore's best beef *rendang*. No reservations, so arrive early if dining Thursday to Saturday.

WASABI TEI   JAPANESE $$
Map p216 (05-70 Far East Plaza, 14 Scotts Rd; mains S$10-35; ⊙noon-3pm & 5.30-9.30pm Mon-Fri, noon-4.30pm & 5.30-9.30pm Sat; Ⓜ️Orchard) Channelling 1972 with its Laminex countertop and wood-panelled walls, this tiny, cash-only sushi bar feels like a scrumptious local secret. Nab a spot at the counter and watch the Chinese chef prove that you don't have to be Japanese to make raw fish sing with flavour. Note: the newer sibling restaurant next door is no substitute for the original.

DIN TAI FUNG   CHINESE $$
Map p216 (✆6836 8336; www.dintaifung.com.sg; B1-03 Paragon, 290 Orchard Rd; buns from S$1.60,

FOOD COURT FAVOURITES

Food courts offer up a glorious mix of stalls selling cheap, freshly cooked dishes from all over the world. Here are three of the best:

Takashimaya Food Village (Map p216; ✆6506 0458; www.takashimaya.com.sg; B2 Takashimaya Department Store, Ngee Ann City, 391 Orchard Rd; dishes S$4-17; ⊙10am-9.30pm; Ⓜ️Orchard) Slick, sprawling and heavenly scented, Takashimaya's basement food hall serves up a *Who's Who* of Japanese, Korean and other Asian culinary classics. Look out for *soon kueh* (steamed dumplings stuffed with bamboo shoots, *bang-kwang*, dried mushroom, carrot and dried prawn), and don't miss a fragrant bowl of noodles from the Tsuru-koshi stand.

Food Republic (Map p216; ✆6737 9881; www.foodrepublic.com.sg; Level 4, Wisma Atria, 435 Orchard Rd; dishes S$5-15; ⊙10am-10pm; 🛜; Ⓜ️Orchard) The same great formula: lip-smacking food, a plethora of choices and democratic prices. Food Republic offers traditional hawker classics, as well as Korean, Japanese, Indian, Thai and Indonesian. Muck in with the rest of the crowd for seats before joining the longest queues. Roving 'aunties' push around trolleys filled with drinks and dim sum.

Newton Food Centre (500 Clemenceau Ave Nth; dishes from S$2; ⊙9am-2am, stall hours vary; 🚇Newton) Opened in 1971, this famous hawker centre still has a great, at times smoky, atmosphere and you could eat here for a whole year and never get bored. Well-known stalls include Alliance seafood (01-27), Hup Kee Fried Oyster Omelette (01-73) and Kwee Heng (01-13). Touts can be overly eager, but just ignore them.

dumplings from S$8.50; ☺11am-10pm Mon-Fri, 10am-10pm Sat & Sun; Ⓜ Somerset) This outlet of the prolific Taiwanese chain was the first to open in Singapore. Years later, its mere mention still leaves dumpling diehards in a drooling mess. Scan the menu and tick your choices, which should include the cult-status *xiao long bao* (soup dumplings) and the shrimp and pork wonton soup.

WILD HONEY   CAFE **$$**
Map p216 (☑6235 3900; www.wildhoney.com. sg; 03-02 Mandarin Gallery, 333A Orchard Rd; dishes S$12-35; ☺9am-9.30pm Sun-Thu, to 10.30pm Fri & Sat; ☑; Ⓜ Somerset) Industrial-style windows, concrete floors and plush designer furniture: airy, contemporary Wild Honey serves scrumptious all-day breakfasts from around the world, from the smoked-salmon-laced Norwegian to the Tunisian *shakshuka* (eggs poached in a spicy tomato sauce). Other options include muesli, gourmet sandwiches and freshly roasted coffee. Consider booking a day in advance if heading in on weekends.

PROVIDORE   CAFE **$$**
Map p216 (☑6732 1565; www.theprovidore.com; 02-05 Mandarin Gallery, 333A Orchard Rd; dishes S$13-30; ☺9am-10.30pm; ☎; Ⓜ Somerset) Waiting at the top of Mandarin Gallery's outdoor escalator is Providore, a cool, up-beat cafe pimped with white tiles, industrial details and shelves neatly stocked with gourmet pantry fillers. Sip a full-bodied latte or scan the menu for an all-bases list of options, from breakfast-friendly organic muesli and pancakes, to gourmet salads and sandwiches, to a carbalicious lobster mac and cheese.

★IGGY'S   FUSION **$$$**
Map p216 (☑6732 2234; www.iggys.com.sg; Level 3, Hilton Hotel, 581 Orchard Rd; set lunch/dinner from S$85/175; ☺seating 7-9.30pm Mon-Wed, noon-1.30pm & 7-9.30pm Thu-Sat; ☑; Ⓜ Orchard) Iggy's refined, sleek design promises something special, and with a large picture window drawing your eye to the magic happening in the kitchen, you can take a peek. Head chef Aitor Jeronimo Orive delivers with his creative fusion dishes – the 'bomba mellow rice' with lobster, sakura ebi and squid is a standout. Superlatives extend to the wine list, one of the city's finest.

There is no à la carte menu, but a number of extra dishes are served in between ordered courses.

★BUONA TERRA   ITALIAN **$$$**
Map p216 (☑6733 0209; www.buonaterra.com. sg; 29 Scotts Rd; 3-/4-course set lunch S$48/68, 4-/5-/6-course dinner S$128/148/168; ☺noon-2.30pm & 6.30-10.30pm Mon-Fri, 6.30-10.30pm Sat; ☎; Ⓜ Newton) This intimate, linen-lined Italian is one of Singapore's unsung glories. In the kitchen is young Lombard chef Denis Lucchi, who turns exceptional ingredients into elegant, modern dishes, like seared duck liver with poached peach, amaretti crumble and Vin Santo ice cream. Lucchi's right-hand man is Emilian sommelier Gabriele Rizzardi, whose wine list, though expensive, is extraordinary.

STRAITSKITCHEN   BUFFET **$$$**
Map p216 (☑6738 1234; www.singapore.grand. hyattrestaurants.com/straitskitchen; Grand Hyatt, 10 Scotts Rd; buffet lunch/dinner S$52/62; ☺noon-2.30pm & 6.30-10.30pm; Ⓜ Orchard) Better value at lunch than dinner, buffet-style StraitsKitchen is the Grand Hyatt's upmarket take on the hawker centre, serving up scrumptious regional classics from satay, laksa and fried carrot cake to *rendang* and *murtabak* (hallal; paper-thin dough filled with egg and minced mutton and lightly grilled with oil). Come early and hungry, book ahead for dinner later in the week.

🍷 DRINKING & NIGHTLIFE

Shopping is thirsty work. Thankfully, there's a string of places on or near Orchard Rd in which to refuel. You won't find (many) bargain beer prices, but you will find cool cafes and some good happy hour deals. Of course, you can always grab a cheap beer at many of the shopping mall food courts.

MANHATTAN   BAR
Map p216 (☑6725 3377; www.regenthotels.com/ en/Singapore; Level 2, Regent, 1 Cuscaden Rd; ☺5pm-1am Sun-Thu, to 2am Fri & Sat, 11.30am-3.30pm Sun; Ⓜ Orchard) Step back in time to the golden age of fine drinking at this handsome *Mad Men*–esque bar, where long-forgotten cocktails come back to life. Grouped by New York neighbourhoods, the drinks menu is ever changing; however, waistcoated bartenders are only too happy to guide you. Sunday brings freshly shucked

DRINKS ON THE HILL
••

Car-free Emerald Hill Rd offers a refreshing antidote to the mega malls and chains of Orchard Rd. Its cluster of bars – housed in century-old Peranakan shophouses – are popular with the after-work crowd, who kick back with beers and vino at atmospheric, alfresco tables.

While we love **Que Pasa** (Map p216; ☑6235 6626; www.quepasa.com.sg; 7 Emerald Hill Rd; ⊙1.30pm-2am Mon-Sat, 5.30pm-2am Sun; ⓂSomerset) for its Iberian vibe, tapas and wine list, top billing goes to neon-pimped **Ice Cold Beer** (Map p216; ☑6735 9929; www.ice-cold-beer.com; 9 Emerald Hill Rd; ⊙5pm-2am, to 3am Fri & Sat; ⓂSomerset), a raucous, boozy dive bar with dart boards, pool table and tongue-in-cheek soft-core pin-ups on the wall. It's a come-as-you-are kind of place where you don't have to be 20- or 30-something to have a rocking good time. Happy-hour deals run from 5pm to 9pm, and it's especially kicking on Friday nights.

oysters, and an adults-only cocktail brunch (S$150) during which you can make your own bloody Marys. Number 11 on the World's 50 Best Bars 2016 list, this is not one to miss.

OTHER ROOM
BAR

Map p216 (☑6100 7778; www.theotherroom.com.sg; 01-05 Singapore Marriott, 320 Orchard Rd; ⊙6pm-3am Mon-Thu, to 4am Fri-Sun; ⓂOrchard) You'll find this secret drinking house, a throwback to a bygone era, hidden behind a velvet curtain in the Singapore Marriott (p162) lobby. Admire the brass Boston cocktail shaker centrepiece, light the torch shaped like a handgun and peruse the 50-page drinks menu. Award-winning mixologist Dario Knox takes spirits seriously; the American oak-barrel-aged spirits in different finishings are where to begin.

HORSE'S MOUTH
BAR

Map p216 (☑8188 0900; www.horsesmouthbar.com; B1-39 Forum Shopping Mall, 583 Orchard Rd; ⊙6pm-midnight Mon-Thu, to 1am Fri & Sat; ⓂOrchard) As discreet as bars come, this hidden Japanese izakaya-inspired watering hole is accessed through a ground floor black door or via the better-lit Uma Uma Ramen restaurant above (01-41). Inside, discover slick, inventive cocktails and a long list of sake and whiskey. Perch at the bar, chat with the friendly bartenders and watch delectable concoctions come to fruition.

The Japanese fare is also top-notch; soulful bowls of steaming ramen are delivered from the restaurant above.

BAR CANARY
BAR

Map p216 (☑6603 8855; www.parkhotelgroup.com/orchard; Level 4, Park Hotel Orchard, 270 Orchard Rd, entry on Bideford Rd; ⊙noon-1am Sun-Thu, to 2am Fri & Sat; ☎; ⓂSomerset) Canary-yellow beanbags, artificial turf and the sound of humming traffic and screeching birds – this alfresco bar hovers high above frenetic Orchard Rd. It's fab for an evening tipple, with well-positioned fans. Book at least a week ahead for its Wednesday Girls' Night Out: S$50, plus tax, for free-flow champagne, house wines, spirits and signature cocktails from 7pm to 9pm (S$100 for guys).

CUSCADEN PATIO
BAR

Map p216 (☑6887 3319; B1-11 Ming Arcade, 21 Cuscaden Rd; ⊙3pm-1am Mon, Wed & Thu, to 2am Tue, to 3am Fri & Sat; ⓂOrchard) This rundown basement bar with a small, open-air patio shouldn't be any good, but extra-friendly staff and extra-cheap drinks ensure it's as popular as any of the shiny bars around Orchard Rd. On Tuesday nights, jugs of beer are yours for S$14. Bargain. Soak up the savings with a serve of the disturbingly good chicken wings.

TWG TEA
TEAHOUSE

Map p216 (☑6735 1837; www.twgtea.com; 02-21 ION Orchard, 2 Orchard Rd; ⊙10am-10pm; ☎; ⓂOrchard) Posh tea purveyor TWG sells more than 800 single-estate teas and blends from around the world, from English breakfast to Rolls Royce varieties such as 24-carat-gold-coated Grand Golden Yin Zhen. Edibles include tea-infused macarons (the *bain de roses* is divine), ice cream and sorbet. It also has an all-day dining menu available.

SHOPPING

If you want to shop 'til you drop, well you've come to the right place. Heaving retail malls sit shoulder to shoulder all the way along this 2.2km stretch of road, each bigger and flashier than the one before. The second a new plot of land becomes available you can hear the bulldozers start up, ready to build another monument to the gods of retail.

ION ORCHARD MALL   MALL
Map p216 (☑6238 8228; www.ionorchard.com; 2 Orchard Turn; ☺10am-10pm; ☎; ⓂOrchard) Rising directly above Orchard MRT station, futuristic ION is the cream of Orchard Rd malls. Basement floors focus on mere-mortal high-street labels like Zara and Uniqlo, while upper-floor tenants read like the index of *Vogue*. Dining options range from food-court bites to posher nosh, and the attached 56-storey tower offers a top-floor viewing gallery, ION Sky (p97).

IN GOOD COMPANY   CLOTHING
Map p216 (☑6509 4786; www.ingoodcompany. asia; B1-06 ION Orchard, 2 Orchard Turn; ☺10am-9.30pm; ⓂOrchard) One of Singapore's most lauded home-grown fashion labels has experienced a spectacular rise, just three years since the design house opened its flagship store in Orchard Rd's swanky ION mall. All white interiors with industrial black racks, light woods, granite and polished concrete create a serene canvas to display the label's geometric modern aesthetic that also includes lust-worthy statement necklaces.

PEDDER ON SCOTTS   SHOES
Map p216 (☑6244 2883; www.pedderonscotts. com; Level 2, Scotts Sq, 6 Scotts Rd; ☺10am-9pm; ⓂOrchard) Even if you're not in the market for high-end heels and bags, Pedder On Scotts thrills with its creative, whimsical items. The store hand picks only the most unique pieces from leading designers, and displays them in separate 'zones' – each more creative than the next. Accessories include statement jewellery fit for a modern

POST-SHOP PAMPERING

When the relentless crowds, hulking carry bags and buyer's remorse get too much, de-stress at one of the area's top pampering retreats. High-end spas recommend booking a few days in advance, though it's always worth trying your luck if you're already in the area.

→ For cheap(ish) and cheerful, head straight to **Tomi Foot Reflexology** (Map p216; ☑6736 4249; 01-94 Lucky Plaza, 304 Orchard Rd; 30min reflexology/massage S$30/50; ☺10am-10pm; ⓂOrchard), in the 1980s throwback mall Lucky Plaza. Techniques include acupressure and shiatsu, all approved by Jesus and Mary, hanging on the wall.

→ Up several notches is **Spa Esprit** (Map p216; ☑6836 0500; www.spa-esprit.com; 05-10 Paragon, 290 Orchard Rd; massage from S$59; ☺10am-9pm; ⓂSomerset), a hip apothecary-spa inside Paragon. Freshly picked ingredients and Certified Pure Therapeutic Grade (CPTG) essential oils feature in treatments like the sublime 'back to balance' body massage (S$235).

→ Around the corner from Orchard Rd at the St Regis Hotel, **Remède Spa** (Map p216; ☑6506 6896; www.remedespasingapore.com; St Regis Hotel, 29 Tanglin Rd; massage from S$180; ☺9am-11pm; ⓂOrchard) is reputed to have the best masseurs in town. The wet lounge – a marbled wonderland of steam room, sauna, ice fountains and Jacuzzis – makes for a perfect prelude to standout treatments like the warm jade stone massage (S$290).

→ 'Ladies who lunch' swear by the facials at the Grand Hyatt's **Damai Spa** (Map p216; ☑6416 7156; www.singapore.grand.hyatt.com/hyatt/pure/spas; Grand Hyatt, 10 Scotts Rd; 30min facial from S$160, 1hr massage from S$195; ☺10am-10pm; ⓂOrchard). Choose from custom treatments based on skin type (from S$160), the opulence facial (S$350) or celebrity-standard anti-ageing options using high-tech serums and oxygen (from S$350).

ORCHARD ROAD SHOPPING

gallery. In-house label **Pedder Red** (Map p216; ✆6735 5735; www.pedderred.com; 03-04 Ngee Ann City, 391 Orchard Rd; ⏰10am-9.30pm; Ⓜ Somerset) has a branch at Ngee Ann City, opposite.

TANGLIN SHOPPING CENTRE MALL
Map p216 (✆6737 0849; www.tanglinsc.com; 19 Tanglin Rd; ⏰10am-10pm; Ⓜ Orchard) This retro mall specialises in Asian art and is the place to come to for quality rugs, carvings, ornaments, jewellery, paintings, furniture and the like. Top billing goes to **Antiques of the Orient** (Map p216; ✆6734 9351; www.aoto.com.sg; 02-40 Tanglin Shopping Centre; ⏰10am-5.30pm Mon-Sat, 11am-3.30pm Sun; Ⓜ Orchard), with original and reproduction prints, photographs, and maps of Singapore and Asia. Especially beautiful are the richly coloured botanical drawings commissioned by British colonist William Farquhar.

PARAGON MALL
Map p216 (✆6738 5535; www.paragon.com.sg; 290 Orchard Rd; ⏰10am-10pm; ☎; Ⓜ Somerset) Even if you don't have a Black Amex, strike a pose inside this Maserati of Orchard Rd malls. Status labels include Burberry, Prada, Jimmy Choo and Gucci. High-street brands include Banana Republic and G-Star Raw. In the basement you'll find a large Cold Storage supermarket and dumpling king Din Tai Fung (p98).

NGEE ANN CITY MALL
Map p216 (✆6506 0461; www.ngeeanncity.com.sg; 391 Orchard Rd; ⏰10am-9.30pm, restaurants till 11pm; Ⓜ Somerset) It might look like a forbidding mausoleum, but this marble-and-granite behemoth promises retail giddiness on its seven floors. International luxury brands compete for space with sprawling bookworm nirvana **Kinokuniya** (Map

MALL GUIDE 101

Which malls should you raid? That depends on what you're looking for. Scan the following quick-glance guide for an overview of which malls are best for you.

SHOPPING FOCUS	BEST MALLS
High-End Fashion	**Hilton Shopping Gallery** (Map p216; ✆6737 2233; www.hiltonshoppinggallery.com; 581 Orchard Rd; ⏰10am-7.30pm Mon-Sat, 10.30am-6pm Sun; Ⓜ Orchard), ION Orchard (p101), Paragon (p102), Ngee Ann City (p102)
High-Street Fashion	**313@Somerset** (Map p216; ✆6496 9313; www.313somerset.com.sg; 313 Orchard Rd; ⏰10am-10pm Sun-Thu, to 11pm Fri & Sat; ☎; Ⓜ Somerset), **Wisma Atria** (Map p216; ✆6235 2103; www.wismaonline.com; 435 Orchard Rd; ⏰10am-10pm; ☎; Ⓜ Orchard), ION Orchard (p101), Orchard-gateway (p103)
Youth Fashion	**Cathay Cineleisure Orchard** (Map p216; ✆6738 7477; www.cineleisure.com.sg; 8 Grange Rd; ⏰10am-10pm; ☎; Ⓜ Somerset), **The Cathay** (Map p216; ✆6732 7332; www.thecathay.com.sg; 2 Handy Rd; ⏰11am-10pm; ☎; Ⓜ Dhoby Ghaut), **Orchard Central** (Map p216; ✆6238 1051; www.orchardcentral.com.sg; 181 Orchard Rd; ⏰11am-10pm; ☎; Ⓜ Somerset), **Far East Plaza** (Map p216; ✆6734 2325; www.fareastplaza.com.sg; 14 Scotts Rd; ⏰10am-10pm; Ⓜ Orchard), 313@Somerset
Kidswear	**Forum** (Map p216; ✆6732 2469; www.forumtheshoppingmall.com.sg; 583 Orchard Rd; ⏰10am-9pm; Ⓜ Orchard), Paragon (p102)
Shoes	**Scotts Square** (Map p216; ✆6636 3633; www.scottssquareretail.com; 6 Scotts Rd; ⏰10am-10pm; Ⓜ Orchard), Wisma Atria, Far East Plaza
Beauty & Grooming	Ngee Ann City (p102), ION Orchard (p101), Far East Plaza
Jewellery & Watches	ION Orchard (p101), Mandarin Gallery (p103), Wisma Atria, Paragon (p102)
Antiques, Crafts & Furnishings	**Tanglin Mall** (Map p216; ✆6736 4922; www.tanglinmall.com.sg; 163 Tanglin Rd; ⏰10am-10pm; Ⓜ Orchard), Tanglin Shopping Centre (p102)
Books	Ngee Ann City (p102)

p216; ☑6737 5021; www.kinokuniya.com.sg; 04-20/21 Ngee Ann City; ⊙10am-9.30pm; Ⓜ Orchard) and upmarket Japanese department store **Takashimaya** (Map p216; ☑6506 0458; www.takashimaya.com.sg; ⊙10am-9.30pm; 🛜; ⓂSomerset), home to Takashimaya Food Village, one of the strip's best food courts.

EXOTIC TATTOO   TATTOOS
Map p216 (☑6834 0558; www.exoticpiercing. tattoo; 04-11 Far East Plaza, 14 Scotts Rd; ⊙noon-8pm Mon-Sat, to 6pm Sun; ⓂOrchard) Visitors looking for a tattoo shop with a definite pedigree should know about this place, for it's here that you'll be able to get exquisite work from Sumithra Debi (aka Su). One of the few female tattoo artists in Singapore, Sumithra is the granddaughter of Johnny Two-Thumbs, arguably Singapore's most legendary tattoo artist.

ORCHARDGATEWAY   MALL
Map p216 (☑6513 4633; www.orchardgateway. sg; 277 & 218 Orchard Rd; ⊙10.30am-10.30pm; ⓂSomerset) Occupying a position on both sides of Orchard Rd, conveniently linked by an underground and above-ground walkway, this mall is home to boundary-pushing fashion stores **Sects Shop** (Map p216; ☑9754 7355; www.sectsshop.com; 04-14 Orchardgateway, 218 Orchard Rd; ⊙noon-10pm) and **i.t** (Map p216; ☑6702 7186; www.itlabels.

com.sg; B1-13 & 01-18 Orchardgateway, 277 Orchard Rd; ⊙11am-9pm Sun-Thu, to 10pm Fri & Sat). Fellas head to level four, where you'll find unique fashion and accessories tailored to discerning gentlemen.

MANDARIN GALLERY   MALL
Map p216 (☑6831 6363; www.mandaringallery. com.sg; 333A Orchard Rd; ⊙11am-10pm; 🛜; ⓂSomerset) Rehabilitate your wardrobe at this tranquil, high-end mall. Fashion savvy females shouldn't miss local womenswear label **Beyond The Vines** (Map p216; ☑8157 0577; www.beyondthevines.com; 02-21 Mandarin Gallery; ⊙10am-9pm; ⓂSomerset), where minimalism drives chic yet playful creations. On the same floor, trendy cafe Providore (p99) is a feast of pantry filling goodies and bites to eat.

ROBINSONS THE HEEREN   DEPARTMENT STORE
Map p216 (☑6735 8838; www.robinsons.com.sg; 260 Orchard Rd; ⊙10.30am-10pm; ⓂSomerset) The flagship for Singapore's top department store offers sharp fashion edits, pairing well-known 'It' labels like Ted Baker and See by Chloé with street-smart cognoscenti brands, such as Sass and Bide and Saturdays NYC. Clothes and kicks aside, you'll find anything from Tocco Toscano leathergoods to Skandinavisk home fragrances.

ORCHARD ROAD SHOPPING

Eastern Singapore

GEYLANG | JOO CHIAT (KATONG) | EAST COAST PARK | CHANGI & PASIR RIS

Neighbourhood Top Five

1 East Coast Park (p108) Riding a bicycle or roller-blading along East Coast Park before plonking yourself down to rest, watch the ships in the strait, and soak up the atmosphere.

2 Peranakan Terrace Houses (p107) Eyeing-up the exuberant architec-

tural candy of Joo Chiat (Katong), with its pastel-pretty exteriors and intricate stucco work, on Koon Seng Rd, just off Joo Chiat Rd.

3 328 Katong Laksa (p109) Licking to the bottom of the bowl at this cult-status laksa shop.

4 Katong Antique House (p107) Delving into rich Peranakan culture.

5 No Signboard Seafood (p109) Indulging in night-time white-pepper crab and people-watching at Geylang's iconic seafood restaurant.

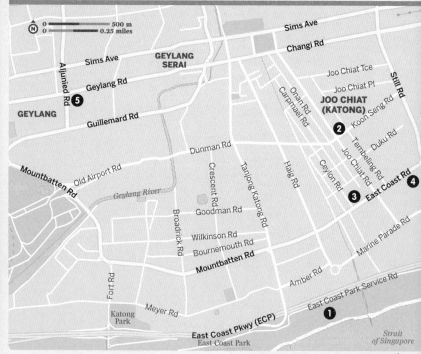

For more detail of this area see Map p214 ➡

Explore: Eastern Singapore

Though comprising a fair swathe of the island, the neighbourhoods of the east receive far less attention from tourists than those of the city centre. It's a shame, really, because these neighbourhoods are vibrant, alive and, on the whole, more reflective of Singapore culture. Closest to the city is the Geylang district, at once notorious as a red-light district, yet spiritual with myriad temples and mosques. The staggering amount of food outlets here is also a big draw.

Further east is Joo Chiat (also known as Katong), a picturesque neighbourhood of restored multicoloured shophouses that in recent years has come into its own as the spiritual heartland of Singapore's Peranakan people. Bordering Joo Chiat (Katong), and stretching for several kilometres along the seafront from the city right up to Tanah Merah, is East Coast Park.

Don't discount a visit to Changi and Pasir Ris, the city's easternmost regions. Here's where you'll find the moving Changi Museum & Chapel, a water theme park for kids, and the launching point for bumboats to the bucolic, bike-friendly oasis that is Pulau Ubin.

Local Life

➡**Food where it counts** Joo Chiat (Katong) is Singapore's culinary heart, with everything from Singaporean laksa, to Vietnamese, Mexican and even American barbecue. Locals also raise their chopsticks in Geylang, a neighbourhood famed for its frog porridge.

➡**People watching people** Locals flock to Geylang for its fantastic food, true, but just as many go there to gawk at the sex workers trawling the streets. A swirl of neon and screaming scooters, it's Singapore's wilder side.

➡**East Coast Park** This is the East Coasters' communal backyard. Join them for beachside barbecues, cycling, sea sports and (more) great food under the coconut palms.

Getting There & Away

➡**MRT** The east isn't well served by the MRT. Aljunied is Geylang's closest station; Paya Lebar and Eunos take you to the north end of Joo Chiat. Pasir Ris has its own station.

➡**Bus** Buses 33 and 16 go to the centre of Joo Chiat, passing through Geylang; bus 14 goes from Orchard Rd to East Coast Rd. Bus 12 goes to East Coast Rd from Victoria St; bus 36 gets there from Bras Basah Rd. Bus 2 from Tanah Merah MRT goes to Changi Village.

➡**Taxi** Best for East Coast Park.

Lonely Planet's Top Tip

Although there are shops here worth browsing during the day, this area really comes to life at night. Spend an afternoon wandering the streets of Joo Chiat (Katong), then head to bustling Geylang for local culinary treats and some colourful people-watching.

◉ Best Sights

➡ Changi Museum & Chapel (p106)
➡ Peranakan Terrace Houses (p107)
➡ Sri Senpaga Vinayagar Temple (p107)
➡ Katong Antique House (p107)

For reviews, see p107. ➡

✕ Best Places to Eat

➡ No Signboard Seafood (p109)
➡ Smokey's BBQ (p110)
➡ East Coast Lagoon Food Village (p111)
➡ Long Phung (p110)
➡ Chin Mee Chin Confectionery (p110)

For reviews, see p109. ➡

🔒 Best Places to Shop

➡ Rumah Bebe (p113)
➡ Isan Gallery (p113)
➡ Cat Socrates (p113)
➡ 112 Katong (p113)
➡ Kim Choo Kueh Chang (p113)

For reviews, see p112. ➡

EASTERN SINGAPORE

UNDERSTAND CHANGI MUSEUM & CHAPEL

Although shifted from the original Changi Prison site in 2001, the Changi Museum & Chapel remains a powerful ode to the WWII Allied prisoners-of-war (POWs) who suffered horrifically at the hands of the invading Japanese. Stories are told through photographs, letters, drawings and other fascinating artefacts. The tattered shoes of a civilian prisoner prove unexpectedly moving, while a tiny Morse-code transmitter hidden inside a matchbox is a testament to the prisoners' ingenuity.

The museum is home to full-sized replicas of the famous Changi Murals painted by POW Stanley Warren in the old POW hospital, the originals of which are off limits in Block 151 of the nearby Changi Army Camp. At the time of research, both the museum and the chapel were closed for renovations; they have since reopened.

DON'T MISS

➡ Audio guide
➡ Historic artefacts
➡ Changi Murals
➡ Replica chapel

PRACTICALITIES

➡ Map p213, C2
➡ ☎6214 2451
➡ www.changi museum.sg
➡ 1000 Upper Changi Rd N
➡ audio guide adult/child S$8/4
➡ ⊘9.30am-5pm, last entry 4.30pm
➡ ◻2

⊙ SIGHTS

⊙ Geylang

SRI SIVAN TEMPLE   HINDU TEMPLE
Map p214 (☑6743 4566; www.sst.org.sg; 24 Geylang East Ave 2; ☺6am-noon & 6-9pm; Ⓜ Paya Lebar) **FREE** Built on Orchard Rd in the 1850s, the whimsically ornate Sri Sivan Temple was moved to Serangoon Rd in the 1980s before coming to its current location in 1993. The Hindu temple is especially unique for its fusion of both north and south Indian architectural influences, melding beautifully in this grandly ornate octagonal structure.

AMITABHA BUDDHIST
CENTRE   BUDDHIST SITE
(☑6745 8547; www.fpmtabc.org; 44 Lorong 25A; ☺10.30am-6pm Tue-Sat, 10am-6pm Sun; Ⓜ Aljunied) Seek inner peace at this seven-storey Tibetan Buddhist centre, which holds classes on dharma and meditation (check the website), as well as events during religious festivals. The prayer hall on level four, decorated with colourful *thangkas* (Tibetan Buddhist paintings), statues and offerings, is open to the public. Adjoining it is a small store selling prayer flags, Buddhist literature and other spiritual items.

⊙ Joo Chiat (Katong)

★PERANAKAN TERRACE HOUSES   AREA
Map p214 (Koon Seng Rd and Joo Chiat Pl; 🚍10, 14, 16, 32) Just off Joo Chiat Rd, Koon Seng Rd (between Joo Chiat and Tembeling Rds) and Joo Chiat Pl (between Everitt and Man-gis Rds) feature Singapore's most extraordinary Peranakan terrace houses, joyously decorated with stucco dragons, birds, crabs and brilliantly glazed tiles. *Pintu pagar* (swinging doors) at the front of the houses are a typical feature, allowing cross breezes while retaining privacy.

SRI SENPAGA
VINAYAGAR TEMPLE   HINDU TEMPLE
Map p214 (☑6345 8176; www.senpaga.org.sg; 19 Ceylon Rd; ☺6am-12.30pm & 5.30-11pm; 🚍10, 12, 14, 32) **FREE** Easily among the most beautiful Hindu temples in Singapore, Sri Senpaga Vinayagar's interior is adorned with wonderfully colourful devotional art, all labelled in various languages. Another feature is the temple's *kamala paatham*, a specially sculpted granite footstone found in certain ancient Hindu temples. Topping it all off, literally, is the roof of the inner *sanctum sanctorum*, lavishly covered in gold.

KATONG ANTIQUE HOUSE   MUSEUM
Map p214 (☑6345 8541; 208 East Coast Rd; 45min tour $15; ☺by appointment; 🚍10, 12, 14, 32, 40) Part shop, part museum, this place is a labour of love for owner Peter Wee, a fourth-generation Baba Peranakan. A noted expert on Peranakan history and culture, Peter will happily regale yo u with tales as you browse an intriguing collection of Peranakan antiques, artefacts and other objets d'art.

JOUSTING PAINTERS MURAL
BY ERNEST ZACHAREVIC   PUBLIC ART
Map p214 (cnr Everitt Rd & Joo Chiat Tce; Ⓜ Paya Lebar) Street artist Ernest Zacharevic (www.ernestzacharevic.com) has been dubbed the

---

GEYLANG: RED LIGHTS, SACRED SIGHTS
••

All those rumours about Geylang being an open-air meat market packed with brothels, girly bars and alleys lined with sex workers are absolutely true. Yet strange as it may seem, Geylang is also one of the Lion City's spiritual hubs, with huge temples and mosques, and picturesque alleys dotted with religious schools, shrines and temples. A daytime stroll through the *lorongs* (alleys) that run north to south between Sims Ave and Geylang Rd offers unexpected charm for those who take the time to look.

Several fetching side streets well worth checking out include tree-lined Lorong 27, a small street chock-a-block with colourful shrines and temples. Chanting is a common sound on Lorong 24A – many of its renovated shophouses are home to smaller Buddhist associations. Gorgeous Lorong 34 boasts both restored and unrestored shophouses painted in varying hues, as well as a number of colourful shrines and braziers for burning incense.

Geylang's other blessing is its food scene. Both Geylang Rd and Sims Ave heave with cheap, tasty, unceremonious local eateries, so round off your wander with the sort of local steam your mother would approve of.

Malaysian Banksy. Born in Lithuania and based in Penang, the 20-something artist has a global following for his fantastically playful, interactive street art. This giant mural features two very real-looking boys prepared for battle on brightly painted horses.

KUAN IM TNG TEMPLE BUDDHIST TEMPLE

Map p214 (☑6348 0967; www.kuanimtng.org.sg; cnr Tembeling Rd & Joo Chiat Lane; ☺5am-6pm; ⓂPaya Lebar) Dedicated to Kuan Yin, goddess of mercy, this beautiful Buddhist temple is home to many festivals throughout the year. Of particular interest to temple lovers are the ornate roof ridges, adorned with dancing dragons and other symbols important to worshippers of the goddess.

GEYLANG SERAI NEW MARKET MARKET

Map p214 (1 Geylang Serai; ☺8am-10pm; ⓂPaya Lebar) Suitably inspired by *kampong* architecture, this bustling market lies at the heart of Singapore's Malay community. The ground floor is crammed with stalls selling everything from tropical fruits and spices to halal meats and Malay CDs. Upstairs, cheap, colourful Islamic fashion hobnobs with a popular hawker centre. Lined with great Malay and Indian stalls, the hawker centre is a good spot for a fix of *pisang goreng* (banana fritters) and *bandung* (milk with rose-cordial syrup).

⊚ East Coast Park

EAST COAST PARK PARK

Map p214 (☑1800 471 7300; www.nparks.gov.sg; ☐36, 43, 48, 196, 197, 401) This 15km stretch of seafront park is where Singaporeans come to swim, windsurf, wakeboard, kayak, picnic, bicycle, in-line skate, skateboard, and – of course – eat. You'll find swaying coconut palms, patches of bushland, a lagoon, seasports clubs, and some excellent eateries.

Renting a bike, enjoying the sea breezes, watching the veritable city of container ships out in the strait, and capping it all off with a beachfront meal is one of the most pleasant ways to spend a Singapore afternoon.

East Coast Park starts at the end of Tanjong Katong Rd in Joo Chiat (Katong) and ends at the National Sailing Centre in Bedok, which is actually closer to the Tanah Merah MRT station. It's connected to Changi Beach Park by the Coastal Park Connector Network (PCN), an 8km park connector running along Changi Coast Rd, beside the airport runway. At the western end of the park, the bicycle track continues right through to Joo Chiat, ending at the Kallang River.

From central Singapore, catch bus 36 or 48 to Marine Parade Rd, then walk south one block to East Coast Parkway (ECP), crossing it to East Coast Park via one of the pedestrian underpasses.

⊙ Changi, Pasir Ris & Punggol

PASIR RIS PARK PARK

Map p213 (☑1800 471 7300; www.nparks.gov.sg; Pasir Ris Dr 3; ☺24hr; ⓂPasir Ris) Stretching a couple of kilometres along the northeast coast, a short walk from Pasir Ris MRT station, this peaceful, 70-hectare waterside park has no shortage of family-friendly activities. Rent a bike to get around, or hoof it and explore the 6-hectare mangrove boardwalk – go during low tide to see little crabs scurrying in the mud. There are 65 barbecue pits, bookable and payable (S$12 to S$20) on the website, which makes it one of Singapore's most popular picnic spots.

Flanking the eastern side of the park, **Downtown East** (Map p213; ☑6589 1688; www.downtowneast.com.sg; cnr Pasir Ris Dr 3 & Pasir Ris Close; ☺10am-10pm; ⓂPasir Ris) mall is a handy spot to grab a bite. Alternatively, look out for the several bars within the park.

CONEY ISLAND ISLAND

(☑1800 471 7300; www.nparks.gov.sg; Beside Punggol Promenade Nature Walk; ☺7am-7pm; ☐84) Opened to the public by two pedestrian roads in 2015, this nature reserve is perfect for escaping the city. There's a wide variety of flora and fauna (birdwatchers will love the three bird hides), and a variety of habitats, from mangroves to grasslands. Enter via the west entrance about 500m from Punggol Settlement; while here, use the bathrooms (there's only one on the island's east side) and stock up on water. You can also hire a bike (S$8 per hour) here.

Come early to spot lots of animals; a family of otters loves to bask on the beaches here. Besides all the lush vegetation, there is also an abandoned mansion – built by the famous Haw Par brothers of Tiger Balm fame – but it is located in the mangroves, so if you'd like to see it, you must join one of the free guided tours offered by the National Parks Board; check the website for details.

DURIAN: THE KING OF (SMELLY) FRUITS

Durians get a bad rap in Singapore. They're banned from pretty much all forms of public transport, few hotels will allow you to bring one through their front doors, and shopping malls enforce a 'no durians' policy. Why? It's simple: they stink. Even before the formidable thorn-covered husk is removed, they stink. And once you've opened it: pooh-whee! And yet durians are known throughout Southeast Asia as the King of Fruits (largely because of their enormous size and those crown-like thorns) and are still loved by many Singaporeans. Aficionados say the flavour of the soft, mushy flesh is like custard with a hint of almond. Others are less complimentary. If the smell of durian lingers on your hands, try soaking your fingers in a glass of Coca-Cola: apparently it conquers the stench.

You can buy durians from markets and street stalls, but if you're looking for somewhere to eat the thing too, drop into the flagship store of **Durian Culture** (☑6744 5232; www.durianculture.com; 77 Sims Ave; durian from S$5; ⊘24hr; ⓂAljunied). Located in Geylang, the sellers will happily advise you on what to pick and how to eat it, then laugh as you take your first bite.

LOYANG TUA PEK KONG TEMPLE TEMPLE
Map p213 (☑6363 6336; www.lytpk.org.sg; 20 Loyang Way; ⊘24hr; ⓺6, 9, 19, 59, 89, 109) Adorned with large wooden carvings, swirling dragons, and hundreds of colourful effigies of deities, gods and saints, this modern temple embodies the Singaporean approach to spirituality, hosting three religions – Hinduism, Buddhism and Taoism – under one vast roof. There's even a shrine devoted to Datuk Kung, a saint of Malay mysticism and Chinese Taoist practices. Off the beaten path, it's worth the trip if you're en route to Changi Village. Get off bus 9 at the Loyang Valley condominium and walk in.

✖ EATING

Eastern Singapore is not only rich in history, culture and architecture, it's home to some exceptional food, from the multicultural delights of Joo Chiat (Katong) to the superb seafood along the East Coast. Hardier souls might brave the nightly, never-sleeping sleaze of Geylang, where some great food lurks among the prostitutes and punters. Look out for durian stalls along the way.

✖ Geylang

126 EATING HOUSE CHINESE $
(126 Sims Ave; dishes S$2-15; ⊘24hr; ⓂAljunied) Plastic stools, '70s wall tiles and thumping beats from the girlie bar next door: this round-the-clock classic is the quintessential Geylang experience. While the menu

can be a little hit-and-miss, solid choices include the dumplings, fried carrot cake, prawn *chee chong fan* (rice noodle roll) and pork belly buns. The sweet-toothed should try the coconut or pineapple tarts.

GEYLANG LOR 9 FRESH FROG PORRIDGE CHINESE $
(www.geylanglor9.com; 235 Geylang Rd; frog porridge from S$8.50; ⊘3pm-3.30am; ⓂKallang) This hawker-style corner joint is one of the best spots to tuck into classic frog porridge. The Cantonese-style porridge is beautifully smooth and gooey, and the trademark *kung bao* sauce is richly flavoured. For the slightly less adventurous, the sambal barbecue stingray here is among the city's best.

★**NO SIGNBOARD SEAFOOD** SEAFOOD $$
(☑6842 3415; www.nosignboardseafood.com; 414 Geylang Rd; dishes S$15-60, crab per kg from S$80; ⊘11am-1am; ⓂAljunied) Madam Ong Kim Hoi famously started out with an unnamed hawker stall (hence 'No Signboard'), but the popularity of her seafood made her a rich woman, with four restaurants and counting. Principally famous for its white-pepper crab, No Signboard also dishes up delightful lobster, abalone and less familiar dishes such as bullfrog.

✖ Joo Chiat (Katong)

328 KATONG LAKSA MALAYSIAN $
Map p214 (51 East Coast Rd; laksa S$5-8; ⊘10am-10pm Mon-Fri, from 9am Sat & Sun; ⓺10, 12, 14, 32) For a bargain foodie high, hit this cult-status corner shop. The star is the namesake laksa:

thin rice noodles in a light curry broth made with coconut milk and Vietnamese coriander, and topped with shrimps and cockles. Order a side of *otak-otak* (spiced mackerel cake grilled in a banana leaf) and wash it down with a cooling glass of lime juice.

CHIN MEE CHIN CONFECTIONERY BAKERY $

Map p214 (☑6345 0419; 204 East Coast Rd; kaya toast & coffee from S$2; ☉8.30am-4pm Tue-Sun; ☐10, 12, 14, 32) A nostalgia trip for many older Singaporeans, old-style bakeries such as Chin Mee Chin are a dying breed, with their geometric floors, wooden chairs and industrious aunties pouring *kopi* (coffee). One of the few Singaporean breakfast joints that still makes its own *kaya* (coconut jam), it's also a good spot to pick up some pastries to go.

LE CHASSEUR CHINESE $

Map p214 (☑6337 7677; Block 27, Eunos Rd 2; dishes from S$5, claypot rice from S$11; ☉11.30am-3pm & 5.30-10.30pm; ☐Eunos) Think you're in for escargot? Think again. Set inside an airy, super-local hawker centre, low-frills Le Chasseur is one of Singapore's best bets for claypot chicken rice. Its version has a beautiful smokiness, weight and texture, and no added MSG, preservatives or pigment. Claypot rice aside, other winners include crispy pork knuckle and succulent barbecue cuttlefish.

Head out of Exit B at Eunos MRT station, then north up Eunos Cres and turn left at Eunos Ave 5. Turn left on Eunos Rd 2 and the hawker centre is 80m to your right. Alternatively, cut straight through the Eunos Court housing complex on Eunos Cres.

BIRDS OF PARADISE GELATO $

Map p214 (☑9678 6092; www.facebook.com/bopgelato; 01-05, 63 East Coast Rd; s/d S$5/8; ☉noon-10pm Sun-Thu, to 10.30pm Fri & Sat; ☐10, 14, 16, 32) Not your run-of-the-mill ice-cream shop, this is more a high-end boutique stocked with artisinal gelatos. Taking flavour cues from nature, think white chrysanthemum and strawberry basil, even the cone (S$1 extra) gets the botanical touch, infused with a subtle thyme fragrance. In homage to Singapore's heritage, there are also local flavours – try the heady Marsala spice, if available.

★SMOKEY'S BBQ AMERICAN $$

Map p214 (☑6345 6914; www.smokeysbbq.com.sg; 73 Joo Chiat Pl; mains S$20-70; ☉3-11pm Mon-Thu, to midnight Fri, 11am-11pm Sat & Sun; ☎; ☐Paya Lebar) You'll be longing for sweet home Alabama at this breezy, all-American barbecue legend. Californian owner Rob makes all the dry rubs using secret recipes and the meats are smoked using hickory and mesquite woodchips straight from the USA. Start with the spicy buffalo wings with blue-cheese dipping sauce, then stick to slow-roasted, smoked meats such as ridiculously tender, fall-off-the-bone ribs. Portions are typically huge, so come hungry. You'll also find a solid selection of interesting beers and ciders. Book ahead for dinner on weekends.

LONG PHUNG VIETNAMESE $$

Map p214 (☑9105 8519; 159 Joo Chiat Rd; dishes S$7-23; ☉noon-10pm; ☐Paya Lebar) Yellow plastic chairs, easy-wipe tables and staff shouting out orders: down-to-earth Long Phung serves up some of Singapore's best Vietnamese food. The *pho* (noodle soup) is simply gorgeous, its fragrant broth featuring just the right amount of sweetness. There's also a mouth-watering choice of real-deal classics, including mango salad and the popular *sò huyết xào sate* (cockles with satay).

ROLAND RESTAURANT SEAFOOD $$

Map p214 (☑6440 8205; www.rolandrestaurant.com.sg; 06-750 Block 89, Marine Parade Central, Deck J, multistorey carpark; dishes from S$10-50, crab per kg from S$68; ☉11.30am-2.15pm & 6-10.15pm Mon-Sat, from 11am Sun; ☐36, 48, 196, 197) According to Roland, it was his mum, Mrs Lim, who invented Singapore's iconic chilli crab back in the 1950s.

The Lims emigrated to New Zealand in the 1960s, but Roland returned to Singapore to find his mum's dish a huge hit. He opened his own restaurant in 1985, and since moving to its present location along Marine Pde in 2000. The 1300-seater place has built up a solid reputation, with a chilli crab that lures former prime minister Goh Chok Tong on National Day. The crabs are fleshy and sweet and the gravy milder than many of its competitors: good news if you're not a big spice fan.

Kick start your meal with an order of the delicious steamed golden bean curd – tender bean curd filled with crab and shrimp paste and topped with salted egg yolk. The restaurant is tucked away at the top of a car park.

WORTH A DETOUR

FAR EAST: CHANGI VILLAGE

On the far northeast coast, **Changi Village** (Map p143; Changi Village Rd; ☐2) is a refreshing escape from the hubbub of the city. A wander around the area offers a window into a more relaxed side of Singapore. The atmosphere is almost village-like and a browse around the area will turn up cheap clothes, batik, Indian textiles and electronics.

Getting here is relatively easy. You can catch the East West MRT to Tanah Merah station, where bus 2 will whisk you right into the heart of Changi Village, and terminating beside the lively, renowned Changi Village Hawker Centre (p111). Alternatively, grab a bike from one of the rental kiosks in East Coast Park and peddle the flat 18km route, which will take you east through tranquil coastal parkland, north along Changi Coast Rd (heaven for plane spotters), and finally west along Changi Beach, where thousands of Singaporean civilians were executed during WWII.

Changi Beach is lapped by the polluted waters of the Straits of Johor and is lousy for swimming, but there's a good stretch of sand for a romantic stroll. It's popular for weekend picnics and barbecues, but almost deserted during the week.

Next to the bus terminal and just up from Changi Beach is the Changi Point Ferry Terminal (p183), where you can catch bumboats to nostalgic Pulau Ubin – Singapore's most outstanding day trip. Just beyond the ferry terminal is the starting point for the Changi Point Coastal Walk, a relaxing, 2.2km-long boardwalk that straddles mangroves, a sandy beach and the verdant grounds of government holiday villas. The walk leads to the private Changi Sailing Club, whose public **Coachman Inn** (Map p143; ☑6214 9600; www.csc.org.sg; Changi Sailing Club, 32 Netheravon Rd; ⊙10am-10pm; ☐29) restaurant-bar is a wonderful spot to polish off a couple of beers while gazing at bobbing yachts and Pulau Ubin. From the sailing club, it's a 750m up Netheravon Rd to Coastal Settlement (p112), with its great coffee, food and lush garden locale.

If riding, a return trip from **Bike Stop** (Coast Leisure; Map p213; ☑6443 3489; www.coastlineleisure.com.sg; East Coast Park Area E; bike hire per hr S$12; ⊙24hr; ☐36, 43, 47, 48, 196, 197, 401) in East Coast Park to Changi Village, with a lazy lunch thrown in, will take around four hours.

LOWER EAST SIDE
MEXICAN **$$**

Map p214 (☑6348 1302; www.hiddendoorconcepts.com; 19 East Coast Rd; quesadillas & burritos S$10-15, three tacos S$18; ⊙4.30pm-2am Mon-Fri, from 11.30am Sat, 11.30am-11pm Sun; ☐10, 12, 14, 32) Chairs hanging from the ceiling, recycled timber tables and sexy Latino beats: this cool, casual taco shack packs in a diverse crowd, all here for a little south-of-the-border action. Dig into flavour packed tacos such as the standout *tilapia* (fish fillet, tomato, onion, coriander, red peppers and caper berries) or opt for firm, juicy burritos. Happy hour deals run until 8pm.

✗ East Coast Park

EAST COAST LAGOON FOOD VILLAGE
HAWKER **$**

Map p213 (1220 East Coast Parkway; dishes from S$3; ⊙10.30am-11pm; ☐36, 43, 47, 48, 196, 197, 401) There are few hawker centres with a better location. Tramp barefoot off the beach, find a table (note the table number for when you order), then trawl the stalls for staples such as satay, laksa, stingray and the uniquely Singaporean *satay bee hoon* (rice noodles in a chilli-based peanut sauce). Not all stalls are open during the day – it's best to visit between 5pm and 8pm.

✗ Changi & Pasir Ris

CHANGI VILLAGE HAWKER CENTRE
HAWKER **$**

Map p143 (2 Changi Village Rd; dishes from S$3; ⊙6am-midnight; ☐2) Located in chilled-out Changi Village, this is the most Malay of Singapore's food centres, with locals heading here for one thing: the *nasi lemak* (fragrant coconut rice topped with fried chicken or fish, fried anchovies and sambal chilli). While food bloggers never cease arguing about which stall does it best, the original **International Nasi Lemak** (stall 01-03;

nasi lemak from S$3.50; ⊘9.30am-1.30pm & 6pm-midnight Mon-Fri, 9am-7.30pm Sat, 9am-midnight Sun) gets the most loving.

End on a sweet note at **Mei Xiang Goreng Pisang** (www.facebook.com/pg/Meixiang GorengPisang; stall 01-51; snacks from S$0.80; ⊘11am-9pm Wed-Mon), famed for its beautifully crisp, golden bana na fritters. Catch the MTR to Tanah Merah MRT station and then take bus 2.

MAKAN MELAKA   DESSERTS $

Map p143 (www.facebook.com/pg/MakanAtMelaka; 01-2046, 1 Changi Village Rd; cendol S$2; ⊘8am-10pm; 🚇2) Overcome the feeling you're about to eat a bowl full of luminous green worms, because once you've tasted the sweet, subtle, pandan flavour of cendol, a wiggly noodle dessert, you'll be diving in for more. This refreshing treat is comprised of crushed ice, fresh coconut milk, noodles and *gula melaka* (palm sugar), which is specially sourced from Malacca. If you're feeling adventurous, add some durian or red bean paste.

DRINKING & NIGHTLIFE

High-brow cocktail bars have yet to move into this area, but it's just a matter of time. That doesn't mean you can't get a drink here, though! Hawker centres are plentiful and serve cheap, cold brews. For something a little more upmarket, try the craft beer bars around Joo Chiat (Katong). Further afield in Changi, you'll find local spots perfect for sinking a few rounds.

LITTLE ISLAND BREWING CO.   BREWERY

Map p143 (🖉6543 9100; www.libc.co; 01-01/02, 6 Changi Village Rd; ⊘noon-11pm Sun-Thu, to midnight Fri, 11am-11pm Sat & Sun; 🛜; 🚇2) A perfect spot to perch up after a trip to Pulau Ubin. This rustic, shed-like, microbrewery serves six in-house brews as well as international craft beers and even wines on tap. Purchase a top-up card at the counter, then use it to dispense the exact amount of beer you'd like – well, to the card's value at least.

Leave a little room in your tank for the tasty pub grub – our picks are the tender 15-hour smoked wagyu beef brisket and the crispy fish and chips.

COASTAL SETTLEMENT   BAR

Map p143 (🖉6475 0200; www.thecoastal settlement.com; 200 Netheravon Rd; ⊘10.30am-11pm Tue-Thu & Sun, to midnight Fri & Sat; 🚇29) In a black-and-white colonial bungalow on verdant grounds, this cafe-bar-restaurant is ideal for unhurried idling. It's like a hipster op shop, packed with modernist furniture, the odd Vespa and cabinets filled with retro gizmos. The fresh juices are delicious and the coffee is top notch; food options cover most bases, from pastas and pizzas to a wagyu-beef cheeseburger.

CIDER PIT   BAR

Map p214 (🖉6440 0504; www.eastofavalon-wines.com; 328 Joo Chiat Rd; ⊘3pm-1am Mon-Fri, 1pm-1am Sat & Sun; 🛜; Ⓜ Paya Lebar) Wedged in a nondescript concrete structure, Cider Pit is easy to miss. Don't. The watering hole offers an extensive range of draught ciders, and speciality beers such as Australia's Little Creatures. It's a refreshingly casual, unfussy kind of place, ideal for a drinking sessions among expats in shorts, tees and flip-flops.

ENTERTAINMENT

NECESSARY STAGE   THEATRE

Map p214 (🖉6440 8115; www.necessary.org; B1-02 Marine Parade Community Bldg, 278 Marine Parade Rd; 🚇12, 16, 36, 196) Since the theatre's inception in 1987, artistic director Alvin Tan has collaborated with resident playwright Haresh Sharma to produce over 60 original works. Innovative, indigenous and often controversial, the Necessary Stage is one of Singapore's best-known theatre groups. Productions are performed at the Necessary Stage Black Box and other venues; check the website for current shows and purchase tickets through Sistic (p66).

SHOPPING

The narrow lanes of shophouses and affluent residential suburbs of eastern Singapore are more renowned for their food than their shopping, and rightly so. Indeed, some of the better shopping options in the area are food related, though there are a couple of decent malls to divert the mind from its culinary pursuits.

★RUMAH BEBE
CLOTHING, HANDICRAFTS

Map p214 (☑6247 8781; www.rumahbebe.com; 113 East Coast Rd; ☺9.30am-6.30pm Tue-Sun; ☑10, 14, 16, 32) Bebe Seet is the owner of this 1928 shophouse and purveyor of all things Peranakan. She sells traditional *kebayas* (Nonya-style blouses with decorative lace) with contemporary twists and beautifully beaded shoes. If you've got time and the inclination, you can take one of Bebe's beading classes. Tours of the shophouse are also available, check the website for details

KIM CHOO KUEH CHANG
FOOD, HANDICRAFTS

Map p214 (☑6741 2125; www.kimchoo.com; 109 East Coast Rd; ☺10am-10pm; ☑10, 14, 16, 32) Joo Chiat (Katong) is stuffed with bakeries and dessert shops, but few equal old-school Kim Choo. Pick up traditional pineapple tarts and other brightly coloured Peranakan *kueh* (bite-sized snacks), and stop by the adjoining boutique for colourful Peranakan ceramics, clothing and accessories. Fashion designer Raymond Wong runs Peranakan-beading workshops (S$65, 1½ hours).

CAT SOCRATES
GIFTS & SOUVENIRS

Map p214 (☑6348 0863; www.catsocrates.wix.com/catsocrates; 448 Joo Chiat Rd; ☺12.30-9.30pm Tue-Sun; ☑10, 14, 16, 32) Complete with friendly feline 'assistant shopkeeper', this eclectic boutique is filled with wares from independent local and foreign designers. Creatives flock here for the mix of whimsical stationery, lo-fi cameras, on-trend homewares, stylish jewellery and indie books. Souvenir hunters will love the range of Singapore-inspired curios, most notably the Peranakan-themed notebooks and tiles.

ISAN GALLERY
ARTS & CRAFTS

Map p213 (☑6442 4278; www.isangallery.com.sg; 42 Jln Kembangan; ☺by appointment; Ⓜ Kembangan) The home gallery of Percy Vatsaloo showcases exquisite hand-picked antiques from places such as Myanmar, Cambodia, Laos and Thailand. The intricately crafted textiles are made by tribal craftspeople from Esarn in northeast Thailand. Percy works closely with the people themselves, through 'Weaving Village', a socially responsibly project which ensures fair payment to workers.

112 KATONG
MALL

Map p214 (☑6636 2112; www.112katong.com.sg; 112 East Coast Rd; ☺10am-10pm; ☑10, 14, 16, 32) This contemporary mall is home to a branch of the excellent Food Republic, where you can chow down on hawker clas-

WORTH A DETOUR

JEWEL AT CHANGI

If you're arriving or departing from Changi airport, make sure to set aside time to explore **Jewel** (www.jewelchangiairport.com; ☺24, most stores 10am-10pm). Directly connected to Terminals 1, 2 and 3, this 'multidimensional lifestyle destination' is packed with everything you could possibly want at an airport. However, it's the 40m-high HSBC Rain Vortex (the world's largest indoor waterfall) that will honestly take your breath away. In the evening the water becomes a screen for a dazzling light-and-sound show.

sics. Kids will love the water playground on the 4th floor.

SPORTS & ACTIVITIES

SINGAPORE WAKE PARK
WATER SPORTS

Map p213 (☑6636 4266; www.singaporewakepark.com; 1206A East Coast Parkway; weekday/weekend 1hr from S$32/42; ☺10am-10pm Mon-Fri, from 9am Sat & Sun; ☑31, 36, 43, 47, 48, 196, 197, 401) What better way to cool off than by strapping on a wakeboard, a kneeboard or waterskis and getting dragged around a lagoon on the end of a cable? It's best to visit weekday mornings, when there's hardly anyone there. There's also a breezy on-site cafe, which serves decent meals and cold beers. From central Singapore, catch bus 196 to Marina Parade Rd, then walk south one block to East Coast Parkway (ECP), crossing to East Coast Park via one of the pedestrian underpasses.

WILD WILD WET
AMUSEMENT PARK

Map p213 (☑6581 9128; www.wildwildwet.com; 1 Pasir Ris Close; adult/child/family from S$20/14/62; ☺1-7pm Mon-Fri, 10am-7pm Sat & Sun; Ⓜ Pasir Ris) Get splash happy at this water-themed fun park. Its eight 'rides' include twisting water slides, a wave pool and a giant, giddy water ramp. If you're after a serious thrill, hit the Torpedo, which will hurtle you from an 18m-high capsule for a free fall you won't forget in a hurry. Thankfully, there's a Jacuzzi to sooth frazzled nerves. Prices rise at weekends and during school and public holidays.

Northern & Central Singapore

Neighbourhood Top Five

1 **Bukit Timah Nature Reserve** (p118) Trekking through Singapore's steamy heart of darkness in this listed Asean Heritage Park, home to one of the largest surviving tracts of primary rainforest on the island.

2 **Singapore Zoo** (p116) Treating your kids to break-fast with orang-utans at this lush, engaging zoo.

3 **Night Safari** (p117) Spotting leopards and dodging bats as you give the tram tour the slip and roam around this nocturnal animal park.

4 **MacRitchie Reservoir** (p118) Seeing the forest from a dizzying new angle on the 25m-high Treetop Walk at this soul-tonic patch of greenery.

5 **Lorong Buangkok** (p120) Travelling back to humbler island days at Singapore's last surviving *kampong* (village).

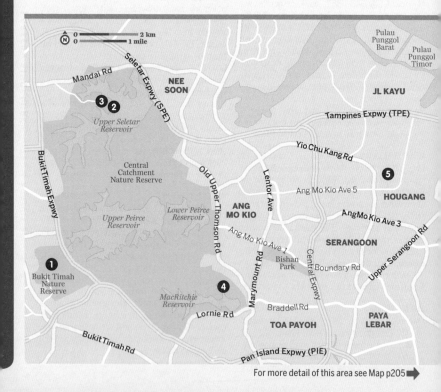

For more detail of this area see Map p205 ➡

Explore: Northern & Central Singapore

This wonderfully wild and gloriously green part of Singapore is packed with sights and activities that take time to see and do, so unless you're here for an extended stay you're going to have to pick and choose carefully among the main attractions.

If you fancy taking advantage of the excellent walking trails, try to get your hiking done early in the morning. The weather will be cooler, and it will leave you most of the rest of the day to do other sightseeing.

The Singapore Zoo (p116) and the Night Safari (p117) are both crammed with restaurants and cafes, but if you're visiting the other local sights, you might have to do some planning around meal times. Eat before you set off, bring some food with you – especially if you're planning to trek round MacRitchie Reservoir (p118) – or grab something to eat at one of the MRT stations you'll be passing through.

Local Life

➡**Into the wild** Join local joggers, nature enthusiasts, foragers and curious monkeys on the trails through the lush jungle of MacRitchie Reservoir, the Treetop Walk (p118) is a must for those not squeamish about heights.

➡**Suburban feasts** Get sticky fingers in Singapore's heartlands (internal suburban areas), packed with in-the-know, cult-status local eateries. One of the best is Mellben Seafood (p120), famed for its spicy, eggy chilli crab and locals love to queue for tiny, crispy coin pratas (mini fried flatheads) from Sin Ming Roti Prata (p120).

Getting There & Away

➡**MRT** Northern and central Singapore is encircled by the North South Line, and the Downtown Line services a few areas to the northwest. Bukit Timah Nature Reserve is easily accessible from Beauty City MRT station. Unfortunately, the rest of the areas are still a fair distance from MRT stations; however, they are close enough to limit your taxi costs or shorten your bus rides.

➡**Bus** Bus 170 goes from Queen St terminal to Bukit Timah in around 50 minutes. Other buses depart from the hubs at Toa Payoh or Ang Mo Kio MRT stations.

➡**Train** Woodlands Train Checkpoint (p183) is the Singapore terminus for the shuttle train service to Johor Bahru in Malaysia.

Lonely Planet's Top Tip

Places like Bukit Timah Nature Reserve (p118), Chestnut Park (p119) and MacRitchie Reservoir (p118) are by no means remote, but they can get exceedingly hot and humid, and once you're out on those walking trails there's nowhere to buy anything. So as well as remembering to don a hat and slap on some mosquito repellent, make sure you carry plenty of water, and perhaps a few snacks to keep you going.

 ## Best Places for Kids

➡ Singapore Zoo (p116)
➡ Night Safari (p117)
➡ River Safari (p119)
➡ MacRitchie Reservoir (p118)

For reviews, see p118.

Best Places for Adventure

➡ Bukit Timah Nature Reserve (p118)
➡ MacRitchie Reservoir (p118)
➡ Jungle Breakfast with Wildlife (p116)
➡ Chestnut Park (p119)

For reviews, see p118.

Best for History

➡ Former Ford Factory (p118)
➡ Lorong Buangkok (p120)
➡ Lian Shan Shuang Lin Monastery (p118)

For reviews, see p118.

GO WILD AT SINGAPORE ZOO

Singapore Zoo is a verdant, tropical wonderland of spacious, naturalistic enclosures, freely roaming animals and interactive attractions. Then there's the setting: 26 soothing hectares on a lush peninsula jutting out onto the waters of the Upper Seletar Reservoir. A Singapore must visit.

Animal Encounters

Orang-utans are the zoo's celebrity residents and you can devour a scrumptious breakfast buffet in their company at **Jungle Breakfast with Wildlife** (adult/child 6-12yr S$35/25; ☺9-10.30am), or get your photo taken with them during the feeding sessions at 11am and 3.30pm.

Further close encounters await at the Fragile Forest, a giant bio-dome that replicates the stratas of a rainforest. Cross paths with free-roaming butterflies and colourful lories, swooping Malayan flying foxes and unperturbed ring-tailed lemurs. The pathway leads up to the forest canopy and the dome's most chilled-out locals, the two-toed sloths.

Complete with cliffs and a waterfall, the evocative Great Rift Valley exhibit is home to Hamadryas baboons, Nubian ibexes, banded mongooses, black-backed jackals and rock hyraxes. You'll also find replica Ethiopian villages, which offers an insight into the area's harsh living conditions.

Fun for the Kids

Let your own little critters go wild at **Rainforest Kidzworld** (carousel/pony rides per person S$4/6; ☺9am-6pm), a Technicolor play area complete with slides, swings, pulling boats and a carousel. Kids can also ride ponies, feed farmyard animals and squeal to their heart's content in the wet-play area. Swimwear is available for purchase on-site.

DON'T MISS

→ The orang-utans
→ Fragile Forest
→ Great Rift Valley
→ Rainforest Kidzworld

PRACTICALITIES

→ Map p205, A2
→ ☎6269 3411
→ www.zoo.com.sg
→ 80 Mandai Lake Rd
→ adult/child under 13yr S$33/22
→ ☺8.30am-6pm
→ ☎
→ ☐138

STAY UP LATE ON THE NIGHT SAFARI

Next door to the zoo, but completely separate, Singapore's acclaimed Night Safari offers a very different type of nightlife. Home to more than 130 species of animals, the park's barriers melt away in the darkness, giving you the feeling of travelling through a jungle filled with the likes of lions, leopards and elephants.

Trams & Trails

Almost everyone heads to the tram queue as they enter. These open-sided shuttle trams quietly cart you around on a 45-minute commentated introductory tour of the park's animals and different habitats. If possible, opt for the second or third cars as they offer the best views.

Sections of the park can only be explored on foot via atmospheric walking trails. Get centimetres away from wild spotted felines on the Leopard Trail, also home to the thrilling Giant Flying Squirrel walk-through aviary. While the outstanding East Lodge Trail awaits with highly endangered babirusas and elegant Malay tigers.

Creatures of the Night

If you have kids in tow, consider checking out **Creatures of the Night** (⊘7.15pm, 8.30pm, 9.30pm, plus 10.30pm Fri & Sat), an interactive 20-minute show with stars that include otters, owls and a hyena. Seating is unassigned, so arrive a little early to secure a good vantage point. Animal performances have been criticised by animal-welfare groups, who say that captivity is debilitating and stressful for animals, and that this is exacerbated by human interaction. Note that shows may be cancelled in case of wet weather. You'll need to catch a bus at around 10.45pm to make the last MRT train from Ang Mo Kio at 11.30pm. Otherwise, the taxis out front will set you back about S$25 for a ride to the CBD. Night Safari tickets purchased online are subject to a 5% discount.

DON'T MISS

➜ Electric tram tour
➜ East Lodge Walking Trail
➜ Giant flying squirrel's walk-through habitat on the Leopard Trail

PRACTICALITIES

➜ Map p205, A2
➜ ☑6269 3411
➜ www.nightsafari.com.sg
➜ 80 Mandai Lake Rd
➜ adult/child under 13yr S$45/30
➜ ⊘7.15pm-midnight
➜ 🔊
➜ 🚌138

⊙ SIGHTS

SINGAPORE ZOO ZOO
See p116.

NIGHT SAFARI ZOO
See p117.

★**MACRITCHIE RESERVOIR** NATURE RESERVE
Map p205 (✆1800 471 7300; www.nparks.gov.sg; Lornie Rd; ☒162, 166, 167, 980) MacRitchie Reservoir makes for a calming, evocative jungle escape. Walking trails skirt the water's edge and snake through the mature secondary rainforest spotted with long-tailed macaques and huge monitor lizards.

You can rent kayaks at the **Paddle Lodge** (Map p205; ✆6258 0057; www.scf.org.sg; per hr from S$15; ⊙9am-noon & 2-6pm), but the highlight is the excellent 11km walking trail – and its various well-signposted offshoots. Aim for the **TreeTop Walk** (Map p205; ✆1800 471 7300; www.nparks.gov.sg; ⊙9am-5pm Tue-Fri, 8.30am-5pm Sat & Sun), the highlight of which is traversing a 250m-long suspension bridge, perched 25m up in the forest canopy.

Trails then continue through the forest and around the reservoir, sometimes on dirt tracks, sometimes on wooden boardwalks. It takes three to four hours to complete the main circuit. From the service centre (which has changing facilities and a small cafe), near where the bus drops you off, start walking off to your right (anticlockwise around the lake) and you'll soon reach the Paddle Lodge. TreeTop Walk is about 3km or 4km beyond this.

★**FORMER FORD FACTORY** MUSEUM
Map p205 (✆6462 6724; www.nas.gov.sg; 351 Upper Bukit Timah Rd; adult/child under 6yr S$3/free; ⊙9am-5.30pm Mon-Sat, from noon Sun; ℙ; ☒67, 75, 170, 961) The former Ford Motors assembly plant is best remembered as the place where the British surrendered Singapore to the Japanese on 15 February 1942. It's now home to an exhibition that charts Singapore's descent into war, the three dark years of Japanese occupation and Singapore's recovery and path to independence. This sombre story is told through audio interviews, news reels and clippings, photographs, diaries and harrowing personal accounts.

LIAN SHAN SHUANG LIN MONASTERY TEMPLE
Map p205 (Siong Lim Temple; ✆6259 5292; www.shuanglin.sg; 184 Jln Toa Payoh; ⊙8am-5pm; Ⓜ Toa Payoh) FREE This breathtaking monastery was established in 1898 and inspired by the Xi Chang Shi temple in Fuzhou, China. Two majestic gates frame the entrance, while further to the right is a seven-storey pagoda adorned with carvings. Inside

---

BUKIT TIMAH NATURE RESERVE

Once teeming with tigers, **Bukit Timah Nature Reserve** (Map p205; ✆1800 471 7300; www.nparks.gov.sg; 177 Hindhede Dr; ⊙7am-7pm Sat & Sun; Ⓜ Beauty World) is a tiny pocket of primary rainforest a short MRT ride from Singapore's centre and provides the ultimate urban jungle antidote. The last tiger was shot here in the 1920s, but you'll still find plenty of monkeys (long-tailed macaques), plus dozens of bird species.

The 163-hectare sprawl offers five well-established walking trails (35 minutes to two hours return), plus a popular 6km mountain-bike trail. You'll find a bike-rental shop as you enter Hindhede Dr (bikes and helmets from S$40). Maps of all the colour-coded routes can be found on signboards.

The quickest, most popular hike is the one leading straight up to the summit of Bukit Timah (163m), Singapore's highest peak. The reserve's official entrance is on Hindhede Dr, where you'll find a visitor centre with restrooms, water fountains, and an exhibition on the forest's flora and fauna.

The fastest way here is to catch the MRT to Beauty World station, depart via exit A and continue onwards along Upper Bukit Timah Road. Cross the second pedestrian overhead bridge and the street on your right is Hindhede Rd, which becomes Hindhede Dr

Also, keep in mind that the steep paths are sweaty work, so take plenty of water, smother yourself in mosquito repellent, and don't feed the monkeys no matter how politely they ask.

the complex, shaded pathways lead from bonsai-filled courtyards to the monastery's three main halls, of which the Mahavira Hall is the most spectacular.

To the left of the monastery stands the weathered **Cheng Huang Temple** (Map p205; ☑6259 5292; www.shuanglin.sg; ☺9am-5pm) FREE, dedicated to the Town God, administrator of justice in the netherworld. The main hall was built in 1912, its thick beams stained from decades of incense smoke. The monastery and temple are about a 1km walk east of Toa Payoh MRT station.

CHESTNUT PARK   PARK

Map p205 (☑1800 471 7300; www.nparks.gov.sg; Chestnut Ave; ☺7am-7pm; ☒700, 966) Mountain bikers of Singapore have been gearing up for this park to open. Set over 81 hectares, making it Singapore's largest nature park, it has 8.2km of bike trails ranging from beginner to hell-bent crazy. Two skill parks are also available for bikers to practise their moves; those who prefer to use their feet are also catered for with designated hiking trails – running adjacent to the bike trails, they're separated from them by a barrier. Bring water, sunscreen and mosquito repellent.

With the closest bus stop 2km away, it's not the easiest place to get to. A taxi from the city will cost approx S$15. Mountain bikes can be hired at the entrance (per hour S$15).

RIVER SAFARI   ZOO

Map p205 (☑6269 3411; www.riversafari.com.sg; 80 Mandai Lake Rd; adult/child under 13yr S$30/20; ☺10am-7pm; ☎; ☒138) This wildlife park re-creates the habitats of numerous world-famous rivers, including the Yangtze, Nile and Congo. While most are underwhelming, the Mekong River and Amazon Flooded Forest exhibits are impressive, their epic aquariums rippling with giant catfish and stingrays, electric eels, red-bellied piranhas, manatees and sea cows. Another highlight is the Giant Panda Forest enclosure, home to rare red pandas and the park's famous black-and-whiters, KaiKai and JiaJia.

Young kids (must be at least 1.06cm tall) will enjoy the 10-minute **Amazon River Quest Boat Ride** (adult/child S$5/3), a tranquil, theme park–style tour past roaming monkeys, wild cats and exotic birdlife. The

ⓘ COMBO TICKETS

If you plan on visiting the Singapore Zoo, Night Safari, River Safari or Jurong Bird Park, save money by buying one of the 'Park Hopper' combo tickets. Of the four attractions, the best two by far are the Singapore Zoo and Night Safari, for which a combined ticket costs S$69 for adults and S$49 for children. Tickets are valid for seven days from the date of the first park visit. Book online to avoid the queues.

ride begins with a big splash, so if you're sitting in the front row, keep feet and bags off the floor. Boat-ride time slots often fill by 1pm, so go early. River Safari tickets purchased online are subject to a 10% discount.

To get here catch bus 138 from the Ang Mo Kio MRT station.

SUN YAT SEN NANYANG
MEMORIAL HALL   MUSEUM

Map p205 (☑6256 7377; www.sysnmh.org.sg; 12 Tai Gin Rd; adult/child S$6/4; ☺10am-5pm Tue-Sun; Ⓜ Toa Payoh) Built in the 1880s, this national monument was the headquarters of Dr Sun Yat Sen's Chinese Revolutionary Alliance in Southeast Asia, which led to the overthrow of the Qing dynasty and the creation of the first Chinese republic. Dr Sun Yat Sen briefly stayed in the house while touring Asia to whip up support for the cause. It's a fine example of a colonial Victorian villa and houses a museum with items pertaining to Dr Sun's life and work.

Next door is the **Sasanaramsi Burmese Buddhist Temple** (Map p205; ☑6251 1717; www.burmesebuddhisttemple.org.sg; 14 Tai Gin Rd; ☺6.30am-9pm) FREE, a towering building guarded by two *chinthes* (lion-like figures) and housing a beautiful white-marble Buddha statue, decorated somewhat bizarrely with a 'halo' of different-coloured LED lights.

✕ EATING

Foodies happy to travel will be rewarded by traditional delights found in these outer areas of Singapore. Here it's all about local hawker centres, decades

WORTH A DETOUR

SINGAPORE'S LAST KAMPONG

It might be an effort to get to, but the wonderfully ramshackle *kampong* (village) of **Lorong Buangkok** (Map p205; Lorong Buangkok; 🚌88) seems willed into existence from an old black-and-white photograph. Chickens roam past colourful wooden houses, crickets hum in the background, and the occupants of the 26 remaining dwellings seem to have carefree sensibilities uncommon in the general populace (the S$10 per month rent probably helps).

This is mainland Singapore's last blip of resistance against the tide of modern development, and an evocative way to experience what life was like for many Singaporeans before independence. Although the area is slated for redevelopment, the bulldozers have so far stayed away.

Expect to spend around 30 minutes here as the area is quite small. You can catch a taxi (best ask the driver to wait for you), or take bus 88 from Ang Mo Kio MRT station in the direction of Pasir Ris and get off on Ang Mo Kio Ave 5 (10 minutes), just after Yio Chu Kang Rd. Walk north up Yio Chu Kang Rd and, after about 50m, turn right onto Gerald Dr. After about 200m, turn right into Lorong Buangkok; 50m later you'll see a dirt track on your left that leads to the village.

old bakeries tucked in quaint shophouses and bustling family restaurants ensconced beneath HDB buildings.

SIN MING ROTI PRATA INDIAN $
Map p205 (01-51, 24 Sin Ming Rd; six prata S$3.50; ⊙6am-7pm; 🚌130, 162, 166, 167, 980) There's a hidden treasure to be found in this small, neighbourhood *kopitiam* (coffeeshop), small, crispy, can't-stop-at-one coin *prata* (mini fried flatbreads). It's run by two third-generation hawkers (still under the watchful eye of their father) and the dough is made the traditional way – hand kneaded and well rested – before being shaped. The result? Join the queue to find out.

MELLBEN SEAFOOD SEAFOOD $$
Map p205 (✆6285 6762; 01-1222, 232 Ang Mo Kio Ave 3; dishes from S$16-22, crab per kg from S$65; ⊙5-10pm; Ⓜ️Braddell) When it comes to chart-topping crab, no shortage of locals will direct you to Mellben, a modern, hawker-style set-up at the bottom of a nondescript block. Signature dishes are claypot crab *bee hoon* (rice vermicelli noodles), butter crab and the ever-famous chilli crab. The crabs here yield gorgeous chunks of sweet, fresh meat; order a male unless you like roe.

Arrive before 5.30pm or after 8.30pm to avoid the longest queues; midweek is also quieter. Service can sometimes be slow, so come with a little patience. Prices are not written on the menu, so check as you order.

 # DRINKING & NIGHTLIFE

WILDSEED CAFE, BAR
Map p205 (✆6262 1063; www.thesummerhouse. sg; 3 Park Lane; ⊙cafe 10am-7pm, bar 5-11pm; 🚌117) Sitting pretty on the lower floor of a revamped heritage bungalow, Wildseed is a quaint cafe by day, languid drinking spot by night. Previously part of Seletar Airbase (now the Oval), it's the perfect spot if you feel like getting away from the city. Good coffee by Nomad The Gallant and inspired cocktails – the refreshing 'beetroot hibiscus sling' is a must-try. Upstairs you'll find the Summerhouse, a fine-dining restaurant that's popular with the dating set.

MIDDLE ROCK BAR
Map p205 (✆9113 4666; www.middlerock.com. sg; Bishan Park 2, 1382 Ang Mo Kio Ave 1; ⊙5pm-1am, to 2am Sat; Ⓜ️Ang Mo Kio) Swaying palms, flickering tea lights, and no shortage of snug nooks and gazebos – no, you're not in Phuket, you're at one of Singapore's best-kept secrets, a languid garden bar right in Bishan Park. It's a grown-up, relaxing hideout, with music soft enough for audible conversation and a generous happy hour that runs from 5pm to 8pm Sunday to Thursday.

Holland Village, Dempsey Hill & the Botanic Gardens

HOLLAND VILLAGE | DEMPSEY HILL | BOTANIC GARDENS

Neighbourhood Top Four

1 Singapore Botanic Gardens (p123) Taking deep, blissful breaths of air in Singapore's lush and velvety retreat, picnicking on the lawns, slipping into ancient rainforest and exploring a string of tranquil themed gardens.

2 National Orchid Garden (p123) Marvelling at the beauty, diversity and sheer quantity of varieties on display at this orchid showcase set snugly in the Botanic Gardens.

3 Dempsey Hill antique shops & galleries (p126) Shopping for unique homewares in relaxed boutiques.

4 Candlenut (p125) Joining Singaporeans and those they're out to impress at this Michelin-starred Peranakan restaurant in colonial Dempsey Hill.

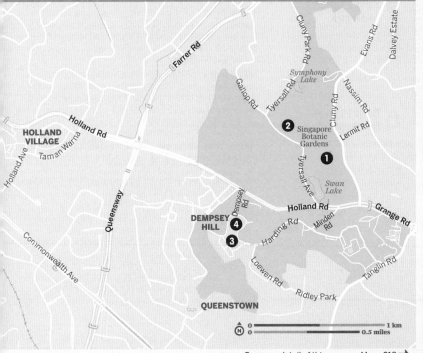

For more detail of this area see Map p218 ➡

Lonely Planet's Top Tip

Check the Singapore Botanic Gardens website (www.sbg.org.sg) for details of upcoming concerts, which are staged for free by Symphony Lake. Also keep an eye out for free guided tours of the gardens. At the time of writing they were running on Saturday morning, but always check for updates.

 Best Places to Eat

➡ Chopsuey (p125)

➡ Blu Kouzina (p125)

➡ Candlenut (p125)

➡ Dempsey Cookhouse & Bar (p124)

➡ 2am Dessert Bar (p124)

For reviews, see p124.➡

 Best Places to Drink

➡ Atlas Coffeehouse (p126)

➡ Wala Wala Café Bar (p126)

For reviews, see p126.➡

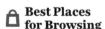 **Best Places for Browsing**

➡ Dempsey Hill Antique Shops (p126)

➡ Bynd Artisan (p127)

➡ Bungalow 55 (p127)

➡ Em Gallery (p127)

➡ Ong Shunmugam (p127)

For reviews, see p127.➡

Explore: Holland Village, Dempsey Hill & the Botanic Gardens

The must-see sight here is the Singapore Botanic Gardens (p123) and you'd do well to set aside half a day to fully soak up its charms.

Making a picnic out of your visit can be fun, especially if you have kids in tow. Stock up on picnic goodies at the gourmet delis in upmarket Holland Village or leafy Dempsey Hill. Alternatively, browse for antiques in Dempsey Hill and lunch there as well, at either Candlenut (p125), Chopsuey (p125) or PS Cafe (p124), before heading across to the Botanic Gardens. For a dirt-cheap hawker feed by the gardens, make a beeline for leafy Food Canopy (p125).

Come evening, head to lively Holland Village to wine and dine with what tends to be a well-heeled expat crowd.

Local Life

➡**Jogging** If you've brought a pair of trainers with you on your travels, do as many Singapore residents do and work that city smog out of your lungs with a brisk jog around the Singapore Botanic Gardens. Early morning is best, when the air is still cool, or else just before sunset.

➡**Shopping** If the high-energy, same-same shopping malls of nearby Orchard Rd begin to bore you, shift down a gear or two and amble over to Dempsey Hill or Holland Village and their booty of small, independent shops and boutiques.

➡**Gourmet** It's not just the expats who lap up the international food offerings in Holland Village and Dempsey Hill. Follow moneyed Singaporeans through the doors of cute cafes and well-stocked delicatessens to get your fix of comfort food.

Getting There & Away

➡**MRT** Singapore Botanic Gardens and Holland Village both have their own MRT stations.

➡**Bus** Dempsey Hill isn't connected to the MRT. You can walk here from the Singapore Botanic Gardens, or else catch a bus (7, 75, 77, 105, 106, 123 or 174) from behind Orchard MRT, on Orchard Blvd. Get off two stops after the Singapore Botanic Gardens, then walk up to your left. Buses 75 and 106 are two of several linking Holland Village with Dempsey Hill. It's just under 2km to walk between the two, but the walk is an unpleasant one along busy Holland Rd.

STROLL IN SINGAPORE BOTANIC GARDENS

At the tail end of Orchard Rd, Singapore's most famous sprawl of greenery offers more than just picnic-friendly lawns and lakes. It's home to ancient rainforest, themed gardens, rare orchids, free concerts and tasty nosh spots.

Orchid & Ginger Gardens

Orchid breeding here began in 1928 and you can get the low-down at the **National Orchid Garden** (adult/child under 12yr S$5/free; ⊙8.30am-7pm), pictured. Its 3 hectares are home to over 1000 species and 2000 hybrids, around 600 of which are on display – the largest showcase of tropical orchids on Earth. Located next to the National Orchid Garden, the 1-hectare **Ginger Garden** (⊙5am-midnight) contains more than 250 members of the Zingiberaceae family. It's also where you'll find ginger-centric restaurant Halia (p126), which offers some of Singapore's most memorable dining moments.

The Forests

Hit the elevated walkways and boardwalks of the Learning Forest, the Garden's newest habitat to explore. Those needing a break can lay back in the canopy web, a spider-like web built into the elevated walkway, and listen to the sounds of the forest. Then step back in time and head to primeval **rainforest** (⊙5am-midnight) older than the Botanic Gardens themselves. Of the rainforest's 314 species of vegetation, over half are considered rare in Singapore.

Jacob Ballas Children's Garden

For those with little ones head to this kidcentric **garden** (⊙8am-7pm Tue-Sun, last entry 6.30pm) with interactive zones, including a sensory garden and 'Magic of Photosynthesis' (process in which plants make food). Burn off some energy exploring the tree house or cooling waterplay feature.

DON'T MISS

➡ National Orchid Garden

➡ Canopy web in the Learning Forest

➡ Free concerts at the Symphony Stage

➡ Primeval rainforest boardwalk

PRACTICALITIES

➡ Map p218, H3

➡ ☑64717361

➡ www.sbg.org.sg

➡ 1 Cluny Rd

➡ admission free

➡ ⊙5am midnight

➡ ☐7, 75, 77, 105, 106, 123, 174, Ⓜ Botanic Gardens

SIGHTS

SINGAPORE BOTANIC GARDENS
GARDENS

See p123.

SWAN LAKE
LAKE

Map p218 (✆6471 7361; www.sbg.org.sg; 1 Cluny Rd, Singapore Botanic Gardens; ⊗5am-midnight; ☐7, 75, 77, 105, 106, 123, 174) One of three lakes in the Botanic Gardens, Swan Lake boasts a large bronze sculpture of a flock of swans taking flight and a tiny island cluttered with nibong palms. Look out for the real mute swans, imported from Amsterdam.

✕ EATING

Expat-heavy Holland Village is home to a host of restaurants and cafes serving predominantly Western food. Over in fellow expat staple Dempsey Hill, the location is less city residential and more colonial hill station – this was once an army barracks, after all.

✕ Holland Village

HOLLAND VILLAGE MARKET & FOOD CENTRE
HAWKER $

Map p218 (1 Lor Mambong; dishes from S$3; ⊗6am-midnight; ⓜHolland Village) Avoid the run-of-the-mill restaurants across the street and join the locals for cheap, scrumptious Singapore grub. A small clutch of stalls sell chicken rice, prawn noodles and other hawker staples. For those new to the hawker food scene, there's a handy signboard outside that gives the low-down on the most popular dishes.

SUNDAY FOLKS
DESSERTS $$

Map p218 (✆6479 9166; www.sundayfolks.com; 01-52, 44 Jln Merah Saga; waffles S$9-17; ⊗1-10pm Tue-Thu, to 11pm Fri, noon-11pm Sat, noon-10pm Sun; ⓜHolland Village) A sugar rush is a given at this airy, industrial-style dessert cafe where every delectable treat is handmade. Folks flock here for the fluffy waffles crowned with a towering swirl of decadent soft-serve ice-cream. Choose one of six ice-cream flavours – our pick is the sweet-and-savoury sea-salt *gula melaka* (palm sugar) – and then go nuts with toppings. Cash only.

2AM DESSERT BAR
DESSERTS $$

Map p218 (✆6291 9727; www.2amdessertbar.com; 21A Lorong Liput; dishes S$15-24; ⊗3pm-2am Tue-Fri, 2pm-2am Sat & Sun; ⓜHolland Village) Posh desserts with wine and cocktail pairings is the deal at this swanky hideout. While the menu includes savoury grub like pork sliders and mac and cheese, you're here for Janice Wong's sweet showstoppers, from chocolate tart to cassis plum bombe with elderflower yoghurt foam, Choya (Japanese plum liqueur) granita, yuzu (Japanese citrus fruit) pearls and yuzu rubies. Book ahead if heading here Thursday to Saturday night.

ORIGINAL SIN
VEGETARIAN $$

Map p218 (✆6475 5605; www.originalsin.com.sg; 01-62, 43 Jln Merah Saga; mains S$24-32; ⊗11.30am-2.30pm & 6-10.30pm; ✎; ⓜHolland Village) Vibrant textiles, crisp linen and beautiful stemware set a smart, upbeat scene for sophisticated, flesh-free dishes like spicy, quinoa-stuffed roasted capsicum, and chargrilled eggplant moussaka. The restaurant is on a residential street dotted with eateries; book an outdoor table if possible.

✕ Dempsey Hill

DEMPSEY COOKHOUSE & BAR
BISTRO $$

Map p218 (✆1800 304 5588; www.como dempsey.sg/the-dempsey-cookhouse-and-bar; Block 17D, Dempsey Rd; mains $19-70; ⊗noon-2.30pm & 6-10pm, to 11pm Fri & Sat; ☐7, 75, 77, 105, 106, 123, 174) Visually stunning with a white-and-black colour scheme, a soaring ceiling dotted with oversized lantern lights, and touches of tropical greenery, there is a definite buzz in this new restaurant opened by one of New York's most celebrated chefs, Jean-Georges Vongerichten. Skip the signature egg caviar and opt for the creamy burrata (Italian semi-soft cheese) with lemon jam, followed by the spice-crusted snapper. Desserts should not be overlooked, the raspberry frangipani tart with raspberry swirl ice cream is sublime. Arrive a little early to enjoy a drink at the stunning bar.

PS CAFE
INTERNATIONAL $$

Map p218 (✆9070 8782; www.pscafe.com; 28B Harding Rd; mains S$26-54; ⊗8am-11pm, till 1am Fri & Sat; ✎; ☐7, 75, 77, 105, 106, 123, 174) A chic, light-filled oasis of wooden floor-

HIGH ON DEMPSEY HILL

One of the first barracks constructed in Singapore, Tanglin Barracks (now known as Dempsey Hill) made its debut in 1861. The original buildings were spacious, elevated wooden structures topped with thatched attap (sugar-palm) roofs and able to house 50 men. Among the barracks' amenities were hospital wards, wash houses, kitchens, a library, a reading room and a school, as well as office quarters. Extensive renovation between 1934 and 1936 saw the airy verandahs make way for more interior space, though the French-tiled roofs – which had replaced the original thatched ones – were, thankfully, preserved. Home to the British military for over a century, the barracks served as the headquarters of the Ministry of Defence between 1972 and 1989, before their current reinvention as an upmarket lunch hang-out.

boards, floor-to-ceiling windows and patio tables facing thick tropical foliage. From brunch to dinner, edibles are beautiful and healthy, whether it's fish-croquette Benedict or a 'Morocco miracle stack' of roasted portobello mushroom, grilled vegetables, smoked eggplant and couscous. No bookings taken for weekend brunch; head in before 9am to avoid the longest queues.

SAMY'S CURRY RESTAURANT INDIAN $$
Map p218 (☑6472 2080; info@samyscurry.com; Block 25, Dempsey Rd; mains S$5-21; ☺11am-3pm & 6-10pm Wed-Mon; ☑; ☑7, 75, 77, 105, 106, 123, 174) A Dempsey institution, Samy's opened in 1950 and has been in this particular spot since the 1980s. Its location is charming and the food is as outstanding as it has always been, plus this is one of the least pretentious restaurants in Dempsey.

★CHOPSUEY CHINESE $$$
Map p218 (☑9224 6611; www.chopsueycafe.com; 01-23, Block 10, Dempsey Rd; dumplings S$7-12, mains S$18-46; ☺11.30am-11pm Mon-Fri, from 10.30am Sat & Sun; ☑7, 75, 77, 105, 106, 123, 174) Swirling ceiling fans, crackly 1930s tunes and ladies on rattan chairs – Chopsuey has colonial chic down pat. It serves revamped versions of retro American-Chinese dishes, but the real highlight is the lunchtime yum cha; standouts include Sichuan pepperchilli tofu, pumpkin and cod dumplings, and *san choy pau* (minced meat in lettuce cups). The marble bar is perfect for solo diners.

Last order for lunch 4pm, last order for dinner 10.30pm and last bar order 11pm.

BLU KOUZINA GREEK $$$
Map p218 (☑6875 0872; www.blukouzina.com/SG; 01-21, Block 10, Dempsey Rd; dishes S$14-46, sharing platters from S$95; ☺noon-2.30pm

& 6-10pm; ☑7, 75, 77, 105, 106, 123, 174) Opa! Stepping into this large, bustling restaurant, you'll feel like you've joined a large and very festive gathering. Plates of succulent meats, grilled seafood and flavourful salads are shared among guests at cosy and family-sized tables. Take a seat and get ordering – don't miss the *saganaki* (cheese) with figs, which you can wash down with decent Greek wine. For a quieter spot, ask for a table in the back room, which has stunning views of the lush greenery during the day.

CANDLENUT PERANAKAN $$$
Map p218 (☑in Singapore 1800 304 2288; www.comodempsey.sg/candlenut; Block 17A, Dempsey Rd; mains S$16-32; ☺noon-2.30pm & 6-9.30pm, to 10.30pm Fri & Sat; ☑7, 75, 77, 105, 106, 123, 174) The first and only Peranakan restaurant with a Michelin star, Candlenut is where Singaporeans head to impress out-of-towners. Chef Malcolm Lee does not churn out any old Straits Chinese dishes, instead elevates them to new culinary heights. Most are amazing, but some are a little lost in translation. The jury is still out on whether Nonya would approve.

✖ Botanic Gardens

FOOD CANOPY HAWKER $
Map p218 (www.foodcanopy.com.sg; 1J Cluny Rd; dishes from S$3; ☺7am-8pm; ☑7, 75, 77, 105, 106, 123, 174, Ⓜ Botanic Gardens) ✔ You'll find this breezy collection of hawker stalls outside the Botanic Gardens' Healing Garden. There's no shortage of favourites, from *kaya* (coconut jam) toast and *kopi* (coffee) to roasted duck, *ban mian* (handmade noodles) and Indian *roti prata* (mini flatbread). It's next to the Raffles Building.

CASA VERDE
ITALIAN $$

Map p218 (☑6467 7326; www.casaverde.com.
sg; 1 Cluny Rd, Singapore Botanic Gardens; lunch
S$10-20, pizza S$24, dinner mains S$18-35;
⊙7.30am-11pm; 🚻; 🚌7, 75, 77, 105, 106, 123,
174, MBotanic Gardens) The most acces-
sible restaurant in the Botanic Gardens,
'Green House' serves acceptable Italian
grub – pasta, salads, sandwiches – plus
wood-fired pizzas (not for pizza snobs) and
a few Sing-aporean and Western dishes;
last orders 9.30pm. It's family friendly,
with plenty of space and a kids' menu. For
a special experience, order a Picnic Set
(S$30; from 11.30am) and set up wherever
you please.

HALIA
FUSION $$$

Map p218 (☑8444 1148; www.halia.com.sg; 1
Cluny Rd, Singapore Botanic Gardens; mains
S$26-68; ⊙noon-9.30pm Mon-Fri, from 10am
Sat & Sun; 🅿🚻; 🚌7, 75, 77, 105, 106, 123, 174,
MBotanic Gardens) Atmospheric Halia is
surrounded by the Botanic Gardens' ginger plants, a fact echoed in several unusual ginger-based dishes. Menus are a
competent, fusion affair (think chilli-crab
spaghettini), and the weekday set lunch
(two/three courses S$28/32) is especially
good value. There's a vegetarian and a
kids' menu, and at weekends you can also
do brunch (10am to 5pm); no reservations
taken. No alcohol is served, but they do refreshing fruit mocktails.

🍷 DRINKING & NIGHTLIFE

Lorong Mambong in Holland Village
is pedestrianised in the evenings and
transforms into a throng of bars and
eateries. Discerning drinkers have since
moved on to the new wave of bars in
Chinatown and Tanjong Pagar, so the only
real reason to head here is for the good
after-work happy-hour deals. In contrast,
Dempsey is more upmarket and sedate,
and better for supping than sipping.

ATLAS COFFEEHOUSE
COFFEE

(☑6314 2674; www.facebook.com/atlascoffee-
house; 6 Duke's Rd; ⊙8am-7pm Tue-Sun; MBotanic Gardens) This airy industrial-styled
coffeehouse has caffeine lovers lining up
for the in-house Guatemalan and Brazilian
bean blend by Two Degrees North Coffee
Co. Like your coffee served cold? Try the
Black Bird, a taste flight of cold brew, nitro
brew and iced black, perfect for a hot day.
Check out the all-day brunch menu; the
pancakes, and the creamy mushrooms on
sourdough, are highlights.

WALA WALA CAFÉ BAR
BAR

Map p218 (☑6462 4288; www.walawala.sg; 31
Lorong Mambong; ⊙4pm-1am Mon-Thu, till 2am
Fri, 3pm-2am Sat, 3pm-1am Sun; MHolland Village) Perennially packed at weekends (and
most evenings, in fact), Wala Wala has live
music on the 2nd floor, with warm-up acts
Monday to Friday from 7pm and main acts

DEMPSEY HILL ANTIQUES

Many parts of Dempsey Hill's former British Army barracks are home to long-
established **art and antique shops** (Map p218; www.dempseyhill.com; Dempsey Rd; 🚌7,
75, 77, 105, 106, 123, 174), selling anything from teak furniture to landscaping ornaments
and ancient temple artefacts. Beyond the places listed here, there are more than a
dozen similar shops, most open daily from around 10am to 6pm. See www.dempsey
hill.com for a complete rundown.

Shang Antique (☑6388 8838; www.shangantique.com.sg; 01-03, Block 26, Dempsey Rd;
⊙10am-9pm) Specialises in Southeast Asian objects, some of them around 2000 years
old, with price tags to match. Those with more style than savings can pick up anything
from old bronze gongs to beautiful Thai silk scarves for under S$50.

Pasardina Fine Living (☑6472 0228; www.pasardina.com; 01-10, Block 13, Demspey Rd;
⊙9.30am-6.30pm Mon-Fri, 11am-7pm Sat & Sun) Has just about everything decorative and
Asian for the home.

Asiatique Collections (☑6471 3146; www.asiatiquecollections.com; Block 14A, Dempsey Rd;
⊙11am-7pm Tue-Sun) Stocks unique, statement furniture, some made using petrified wood.

nightly from 9.30pm. Downstairs it pulls in football fans with its large sports screens. As at most nearby places, tables spill out onto the street in the evenings.

 SHOPPING

★ BYND ARTISAN ARTS & CRAFTS
Map p218 (☑6475 1680; www.byndartisan.com; 01-54, 44 Jln Merah Saga; ⊘noon-9pm Mon-Fri, from 10am Sat & Sun; Ⓜ Holland Village) Connoisseurs of bespoke stationery and leather will love this sublime store that prides itself on artisanal excellence. Select from the range of handmade journals or spend time customising your own, don't forget to de-boss your name. Other items include leather travel accessories and jewellery pieces. For the complete artist experience, sign up for a course (from S$88) in bookbinding, modern calligraphy or watercolour brushwork.

BUNGALOW 55 HOMEWARES
(☑6463 3831; www.thebungalow55.com; 01-05A, Cluny Court, 501 Bukit Timah Rd; ⊘10am-7pm Mon-Sat, to 6pm Sun; Ⓜ Botanic Gardens) Colonial chic hits overdrive in this beautifully curated store brimming with Chinoiserie lamps, tropical scented candles, overstuffed cushions and everything a Singapore-based hostess-with-the-mostest would need in her life. Wander around and imagine relaxing on the verandah sipping G&Ts from your well-stocked cane bar cart – don't forget a Panama hat for the complete experience.

ONG SHUNMUGAM CLOTHING
Map p218 (☑6252 2612; www.ongshunmugam. com; 01-76, 43 Jln Merah Saga; ⊘noon-2pm Mon-Fri, to 7pm Sat; Ⓜ Holland Village) The gallery-esqe shop of Priscilla Shunmugam, one of Singapore's top up-and-coming designers, is just as stunning as her modern interpretations on Asian dresses. Walk-in times are limited (she's in demand with the couture crowd), but if you're after something special, make it a point to stop by. Ready-to-wear garments start from S$500 and custom items will set you back S$1500-plus.

The workshop, where the magic happens, can be viewed through a large picture window at the back of the store.

EM GALLERY FASHION, HOMEWARES
Map p218 (☑6475 6941; www.emtradedesign. com; 01-04/05, Block 16, Dempsey Rd; ⊘10am-7pm Mon-Fri, from 11am Sat & Sun; ☑7, 75, 77, 105, 106, 123, 174) Singapore-based Japanese designer Emiko Nakamura keeps Dempsey's society women looking whimsically chic in her light, sculptural creations. Emiko also collaborates with hill tribes in northern Laos to create naturally dyed hand-woven handicrafts, such as bags and cushions. Other homewares might include limited-edition (and reasonably priced) Khmer pottery from Cambodia.

LIM'S HOLLAND VILLAGE HOMEWARES
Map p218 (☑6466 3188; www.facebook.com/ limshollandvillage; 02-01, Holland Road Shopping Centre, 211 Holland Ave; ⊘10am-8pm; Ⓜ Holland Village) Targeting the expat crowd, Lim's is overflowing with Asian inspired homewares and furniture pieces, from Chinese wedding cabinets in every colour of the rainbow to fashionable ginger jar lamps. Most items are new (no antiques here) and the majority is well-priced. Great if you're looking to add an Oriental touch to your home decor.

HOLLAND ROAD SHOPPING CENTRE MALL
Map p218 (211 Holland Ave; ⊘10am-8.30pm; Ⓜ Holland Village) Holland Road Shopping Centre remains a magnet for expats seeking art, handicrafts, homewares and off-beat fashion. Dive into Lim's for some good Asian-inspired find. Shopped out? Hit the nail spas or massage parlours, which are dotted over the two levels.

 ACTIVITIES

PALATE SENSATIONS COOKING SCHOOL COOKING
Map p218 (☑6589 8843; www.palatesensations. com; 01-03 Chromos, 10 Biopolis Rd; courses from S$100; ⊘by appointment; Ⓜ Buona Vista) Novices and serious foodies head here to hone their skills with top-notch chefs. Standard courses run for three hours and are wonderfully hands-on, with everything anything from Thai favourites to North Indian cuisine and French designer eclairs. For a true Singaporean culinary adventure, sign up for the tourist class to learn how to perfect local favourites like chicken rice and laksa.

West & Southwest Singapore

Neighbourhood Top Five

1 Southern Ridges (p134) Stretching your legs for a park-to-park walk along the Southern Ridges to Mt Faber, then hop onto the cable car for gob-smacking views of the city, port and Sentosa Island.

2 Gillman Barracks (p130) Immersing yourself in culture, art and food while wandering around colonial Gillman Barracks.

3 Jurong Bird Park (p131) Landing a peckish, rainbow-coloured parrot on your arm at family-friendly Jurong Bird Park.

4 Sungei Buloh Wetland Reserve (p131) Joining serious twitchers for a spot of birdwatching in the mangroves.

5 Haw Par Villa (p130) Reliving a little 1950s tourism at this wonderfully quirky and offbeat theme park.

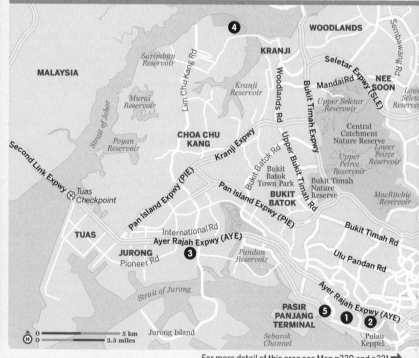

For more detail of this area see Map p220 and p221 ➡

Explore: West & Southwest Singapore

This vast area is packed with sights that together would take a number of days to see. But you don't need to visit them all – none are absolute must-see attractions, most are quirky or somewhat specialist – so pick and choose what best suits you to plan your foray into western Singapore without wasting too much travel time.

Bundling sights together into one trip makes sense. The Science Centre (p131), Omni-Theatre (p133) and Snow City (p134) stand side by side, while a number of sights in the northwest are accessed via Kranji MRT station.

Consider timing your visit to Mt Faber Park (p130) to coincide with sunset, so as the sun goes down you can either be on the cable car or at a restaurant or bar on the summit. It's then easy to get back to your hotel via the HarbourFront MRT station.

Local Life

→**Deals** Look into the combined ticket deals for the Science Centre, Omni-Theatre and Snow City. Likewise, Jurong Bird Park (p131) is part of a three-in-one ticket deal with Singapore Zoo (p116) and the Night Safari (p117). You can also get various Sentosa Island deals if you're travelling there by cable car.

→**University treasures** Western Singapore's universities harbour some lesser-known cultural diversions. The National University of Singapore (NUS) is home to three museums (p130) in one, as well as the visually stunning Lee Kong Chian Natural History Museum (p130). Further afield you'll find the Chinese Heritage Centre (p131), a tranquil museum exploring the Chinese diaspora at Nanyang Technological University.

→**Sun-kissed** The west and southwest are full of parks, hills and nature reserves. They're wonderful places for strolling around, but don't underestimate the strength of the Singapore sun. Slop on the sunscreen, slap on a hat, and pack those water bottles.

Getting There & Away

→**MRT** This vast area is actually served pretty well by the MRT. Some attractions have namesake stations. HarbourFront, Jurong East, Boon Lay, Chinese Garden, Pioneer and Kranji are all useful stations that are either walking distance to sights or have bus connections to them.

→**Bus** For the more out-of-the-way sights you'll need to combine MRT trips with a bus ride. The Kranji Express is a handy minibus service you can use to visit the farms in the northwest.

Lonely Planet's Top Tip

Each Friday night the Science Centre (p131) offers free stargazing at the Observatory in the Omni-Theatre building (p133). Visitors take turns peeking through the telescopes at the starry sky above. Additional talks and slide shows are often conducted; visit www.science.edu.sg for schedules.

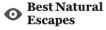 **Best Places to Eat**

➡ Tamarind Hill (p132)
➡ Timbre+ (p132)
➡ Naked Finn (p130)

For reviews, see p132.➡

 Best Natural Escapes

➡ Southern Ridges (p134)
➡ Sungei Buloh Wetland Reserve (p131)
➡ Kranji farms (p133)

For reviews, see p130.➡

 Best For Kids

➡ Jurong Bird Park (p131)
➡ Science Centre Singapore (p131)
➡ Snow City (p134)

For reviews, see p130.➡

WEST & SOUTHWEST SINGAPORE

⊙ SIGHTS

⊙ Southwest Singapore

MT FABER PARK — PARK
Map p220 (☑1800 471 7300; www.nparks.gov. sg; Mt Faber Rd; ⊙24hr; Ⓟ; ⓅMt Faber) The eponymous mountain (105m) is the centrepiece of Mt Faber Park and the climax to the Southern Ridges (p134) nature walk. The most spectacular (and exorbitantly expensive) way to get here (or to get away) is via the cable car, which connects Mt Faber to HarbourFront and Sentosa Island.

NUS MUSEUM — MUSEUM
Map p221 (☑6516 8817; www.museum.nus.edu. sg; National University of Singapore, 50 Kent Ridge Cres; ⊙10am-6pm Tue-Sat; Ⓟ; ⓺96) FREE Located on the verdant campus of the NUS, this museum is one of the city's lesser-known cultural delights. Ancient Chinese ceramics and bronzes, as well as archaeological fragments found in Singapore, dominate the ground-floor Lee Kong Chian Collection; one floor up, the South and Southeast Asian Gallery showcases paintings, sculpture and textiles from the region. The Ng Eng Teng Collection is dedicated to Ng Eng Teng (1934–2001), Singapore's foremost modern artist, best known for his figurative sculptures.

LEE KONG CHIAN
NATURAL HISTORY MUSEUM — MUSEUM
Map p221 (☑6601 3333; http://lkcnhm.nus.edu. sg; 2 Conservatory Dr; adult/child under 13yr S$21/12; ⊙10am-7pm Tue-Sun; Ⓟ; ⓺96) What looks like a giant rock bursting with greenery is actually Singapore's high-tech, child-friendly natural history museum. The main Biodiversity Gallery delves into the origin of life using a stimulating combo of fossils, taxidermy and interactive displays. Hard to miss are Prince, Apollonia and Twinky: three 150-million-year-old Diplodocid sauropod dinosaur skeletons, two with their original skulls. Upstairs, the Heritage Gallery explores the collection's 19th-century origins, with an interesting section on Singapore's geology to boot.

There are three entry sessions per day: 10am to 1pm, 1pm to 4pm and 4pm to 7pm.

HAW PAR VILLA — MUSEUM, PARK
Map p220 (☑6773 0103; www.hawparvilla. sg; 262 Pasir Panjang Rd; ⊙9am-10pm; Ⓟ; ⓂHaw Par Villa) FREE The refreshingly

---

WORTH A DETOUR

GILLMAN BARRACKS

Where soldiers once stomped, curators now roam. Built in 1936 as a British military encampment, **Gillman Barracks** (Map p220; www.gillmanbarracks.com; 9 Lock Rd; ⊙11am-7pm Tue-Sun; Ⓟ) FREE is now a rambling art outpost with 11 commercial galleries studding the verdant grounds. It's a civilised way to spend a few hours, browsing free temporary exhibitions of painting, sculpture and photography from some of the world's most coveted creatives.

Among the galleries is New York's **Sundaram Tagore** (Map p220; ☑6694 3378; www. sundaramtagore.com; 01-05, 5 Lock Rd; ⊙11am-7pm Tue-Sat, to 6pm Sun), whose stable of artists includes award-winning photographers Edward Burtynsky and Annie Leibovitz. Across the street, Italy's **Partners & Mucciaccia** (Map p220; ☑6694 3777; www. partnersandmucciaccia.net; 02-10, 6 Lock Rd; ⊙10am-8pm Tue-Sat, from 3pm Mon) profiles mostly modern and contemporary Italian artists, with the odd retrospective featuring the likes of Marc Chagall and Pablo Picasso. Next door, **Chan + Hori Contemporary** (Map p220; ☑6338 1962; www.chanhori.com; 02-09, Block 6, Lock Rd; ⊙11am-7pm Tue-Sun) showcases mostly contemporary, emerging Singaporean talent.

Plan ahead and book a table at Gillman's **Naked Finn** (Map p220; ☑6694 0807; www. nakedfinn.com; 39 Malan Rd, Gillman Barracks; mains S$25-78; ⊙noon-2.30pm & 6-9pm Tue-Sat), a hip eatery and cocktail joint with an ever-changing menu of phenomenally fresh seafood (if you're there for lunch don't pass up the lobster roll). If you don't have a booking, try your luck – walk-ins are welcome, but space is limited.

If heading there on the MRT, alight at Labrador Park station and walk north up Alexandra Rd for 800m; the entry to Gillman Barracks is on your right. A one-way taxi fare from the CBD is around S$12.

weird and kitsch Haw Par Villa was the brainchild of Aw Boon Haw, the creator of the medicinal salve Tiger Balm. After Aw Boon Haw built a villa here in 1937 for his beloved brother and business partner, Aw Boon Par, the siblings began building a Chinese-mythology theme park within the grounds. Top billing goes to the Ten Courts of Hell (last entry 9.15pm), a walk-through exhibit depicting the gruesome torments awaiting sinners in the underworld.

CHINESE HERITAGE CENTRE   MUSEUM
Map p221 (🗗6790 6176; http://chc.ntu.edu.sg; Nanyang Technological University, 12 Nanyang Dr; S$4; ◷9.30am-5pm Mon-Fri, 10am-5pm Sat; 🅿; 🚍179) It's no must-see, but this small museum at Nanyang Technological University is worth a visit if you're seeking some off-the-radar culture. Of its three exhibitions, 'Chinese More or Less' is the most interesting. The central theme focuses on the Chinese diaspora, including representations of Chinese people in popular Western culture. Catch the bus from Pioneer MRT station.

◉ West Singapore

JURONG BIRD PARK   BIRD SANCTUARY
Map p221 (🗗6269 3411; www.birdpark.com.sg; 2 Jurong Hill; adult/child under 13yr S$29/19; ◷8.30am-6pm; 🅿 🚼; 🚍194) Home to some 400 species of feathered friends – including spectacular macaws – Jurong is a great place for young kids. Highlights include the wonderful Lory Loft forest enclosure, where you can feed colourful lories and lorikeets, and the interactive High Flyers (11am and 3pm) and Kings of the Skies (10am and 4pm). We must note, however, that some birds are made to perform for humans, which is discouraged by animal-welfare groups. The park is set to relocate to Mandai by 2022.

SUNGEI BULOH
WETLAND RESERVE   WILDLIFE RESERVE
Map p221 (🗗6794 1401; www.nparks.gov.sg; 301 Neo Tiew Cres; ◷7am-7pm; 🅿; 🚍925) Sungei Buloh's 202 hectares of mangroves, mudflats, ponds and secondary rainforest are a birdwatcher's paradise, with migratory birds including egrets, sandpipers and plovers joining locals such as herons, bitterns, coucals and kingfishers. The reserve is also a good spot to see monitor lizards, mud-

skippers, crabs and – if you're very lucky – an estuarine crocodile. Free guided tours run every Saturday at 9.30am; registration required via the website.

KRANJI WAR MEMORIAL   MEMORIAL
Map p221 (🗗6269 6158; www.cwgc.org; 9 Woodlands Rd; ◷8am-6.30pm; 🅿; 🚍160, 170, 178, 925, 960, 961) ꜰʀᴇᴇ The austere white structures and rolling hillside of the Kranji War Memorial contain the WWII graves of thousands of Allied troops. Headstones, many of which are inscribed simply with the words 'a soldier of the 1939–1945 war', are lined in neat rows across manicured lawns. Walls are inscribed with the names of over 24,000 men and women who lost their lives in Southeast Asia, and registers are available for inspection. There is no wheelchair access.

SCIENCE CENTRE SINGAPORE   MUSEUM
Map p221 (🗗6425 2500; www.science.edu.sg; 15 Science Centre Rd; adult/child under 13yr S$12/8; ◷10am-6pm; 🅿; Ⓜ Jurong East) Packed with all types of push-pull-twist-and-turn gadgets, Singapore's endearingly geeky science museum electrifies curious little minds. It's as absorbing as it is educational, covering subjects as varied as the human body, climate change, optical illusions and fire. To reach it, alight at Jurong East MRT station, turn left along the covered walkway, cross the road and continue past a covered row of stalls before crossing Jurong Town Hall Rd.

TIGER BREWERY   BREWERY
Map p221 (🗗6860 3005; www.tigerbrewery tour.com.sg; 459 Jln Ahmad Ibrahim; adult/child S$18/12; ◷1-5pm Mon-Sat; 🅿; Ⓜ Tuas West Rd) You've been drinking its beers all holiday, so you might as well see how they make them. Visits to the Tiger Brewery are divided into two parts: the first is a 45-minute tour of the place, including the brewhouse and the packaging hall; the second is the real highlight – 45 minutes of tree beer tasting in the wood-and-leather Tiger Tavern. Tours must be booked in advance.

CHINESE GARDEN   PARK
Map p221 (🗗1800 471 7300; www.nparks.gov. sg; 1 Chinese Garden Rd; ◷5.30am-11pm; 🅿; Ⓜ Chinese Garden) Flanking Jurong Lake, the Chinese Garden offers 13.5 hectares of landscaped tranquillity – perfect for an afternoon stroll and popular with photographers. The garden features numerous

Chinese-style pavilions, a seven-storey pagoda (open 8am to 7pm), an impressive display of *penjing* (Chinese bonsai; open 9am to 5pm), and a lantern-studded Japanese Garden (5.30am to 7pm). During Chinese New Year and the Mid-Autumn Festival the gardens are lit by hundreds of fairy lights and paper lanterns.

THOW KWANG POTTERY JUNGLE GALLERY
Map p221 (🗹6265 5808; www.thowkwang.com.sg; 85 Lorong Tawas; ⊙9am-5pm; ℗; 🚆199) 🔳 You could spend hours perusing the overflowing shelves of brightly coloured ceramics (most imported from overseas) for sale in this pottery shop's labyrinth of rooms, but it's the 70-year-old dragon kiln that makes the trek here especially worth it. Just one of two remaining in Singapore, the kiln is fired up only three to four times a year, but tours and pottery classes are run year-round.

EATING

Many of the bigger attractions in this part of Singapore have their own dining facilities. Jurong East MRT station is connected to two major malls with fantastic food options, and Kranji MRT station also has some eateries. Newly opened Timbre+ houses traditional and new-age hawkers stalls, but with the addition of live music, craft beers and graffiti artwork.

⭐**TIMBRE+** HAWKER $
Map p220 (🗹6252 2545; www.timbreplus.sg; JTC LaunchPad@one-north, 73A Ayer Rajah Cres; dishes from S$3; ⊙6am-midnight Mon-Thu, to 1am Fri & Sat; Ⓜ️One North) Welcome to the new generation of hawker centres. With over 30 food outlets, Timbre+ has it all: artwork-covered shipping containers, Airstream trailer food trucks, craft beer, live music Monday to Saturdays (from 8pm), and the list goes on. But it's the food that draws the crowds: a mixture of traditional and new age. Head here in the late afternoon before the old-school hawker stalls shut at 6pm.

⭐**TAMARIND HILL** THAI $$$
Map p220 (🗹6278 6364; www.tamarindrestaurants.com; 30 Labrador Villa Rd; mains S$18-59; ⊙noon-2.30pm & 6.30-10.30pm; 🐾; Ⓜ️Labrador Park) In a colonial bungalow in Labrador Park, Tamarind Hill sets an elegant scene

for exceptional Thai. The highlight is the Sunday brunch (S$60; noon to 3pm), a buffet of beautiful cold dishes and salads plus as many dishes from the à la carte menu as you like (the sautéed squid is sublime). Book ahead.

🍷 DRINKING & NIGHTLIFE

The nightlife is a little quiet in this part of town, though it's worth stopping in at Colbar for its 1950s throwback feel, or at biker hangout Handlebar for its laid-back vibe and cheapish drinks.

COLBAR BAR
Map p220 (🗹6779 4859; 9A Whitchurch Rd; ⊙11.30am-midnight Tue-Sun; 🚆191) Raffish Colbar is an evocative colonial throwback, a former British officers' mess turned languid drinking spot. It's still 1930-something here, a place where money is kept in a drawer, football team photos hang on the wall and locals linger with beers and well-priced ciders on the spacious verandah. It is still run by Mr and Mrs Lim, who opened the doors in 1953.

HANDLEBAR PUB
Map p220 (🗹6268 5550; www.handlebaroriginal.com; Block 10, Lock Rd, Gillman Barracks; ⊙noon-midnight Tue-Thu & Sun, to 1am Fri & Sat; Ⓜ️Labrador Park) You might not expect to find a biker bar sitting alongside fancy art galleries and top-notch restaurants, but here Handlebar is. You'll typically find more families here than motorheads, and it makes a lovely place to perch up and enjoy a few drinks in the cool of the afternoon. The daiquiris made in blenders fashioned out of petrol engines go down a treat.

☆ ENTERTAINMENT

SINGAPORE TURF CLUB HORSE RACING
Map p221 (🗹6879 1008; www.turfclub.com.sg; 1 Turf Club Ave; from S$6; Ⓜ️Kranji) Although not quite as manic as the Hong Kong races, a trip to Singapore Turf Club is a hugely popular day out. Race times vary, but usually run on Friday evening and Sunday afternoon, and a dress code is enforced; see the website for details. Bring photo ID; over 18s only. Owners' Lounge entry costs S$30.

VISITING SINGAPORE'S KRANJI FARMS

Few visitors to Singapore realise that there's a small but thriving farming industry alive and well in northwest Singapore. We're not talking rolling fields of grazing cows here; in Singapore, limited space calls for the type of farm that specialises in organic vegetables, goat's milk, or plants, flowers and herbs. But they offer a refreshingly different take on Singaporean life.

The Kranji Countryside Association is a farm collective helping to promote the industry. It runs a daily minibus service, the **Kranji Express** (Map p221; www.kranji countryside.com; Kranji MRT Station; per round trip S$3; ⊙8.30am-5.45pm; ⓂKranji) that does a loop from the Kranji MRT Station, visiting many of the best farms en route, including ones where you can buy goat's milk, sample frog meat, see fish, grab a coffee, have lunch or even spend the night. You can hop off the bus whenever you see a farm you like the look of, then hop back on again when the bus next comes around. The scheduled stops change from time to time, but usually include the following:

D'Kranji Farm Resort (Map p221; ☑6862 9717; www.dkranji.com.sg; 10 Neo Tiew Lane 2; r from S$120; Ⓟ❉🛏) Smart villa-style accommodation, plus a restaurant and beer garden.

Bollywood Veggies (Map p221; ☑6898 5001; www.bollywoodveggies.com; 100 Neo Tiew Rd; ⊙8am-6.30pm Wed-Sun; Ⓟ) FREE A very popular place to stop and amble through the rustic farm with its cashew, papaya and starfruit trees, and nosh on beautiful, healthy grub at the bistro.

Hay Dairies Goat Farm (Map p221; ☑6792 0931; www.haydairies.com.sg; 3 Lim Chu Kang Lane 4; ⊙9am-4pm Wed-Mon; Ⓟ) FREE A goat farm where you can buy fresh goat's milk and other snacks.

Jurong Frog Farm (Map p221; ☑9763 9077; www.jurongfrogfarm.com.sg; 51 Lim Chu Kang Lane 6; tour S$12; ⊙by appointment Tue-Fri, 9am-5.30pm Sat & Sun; Ⓟ🛏) FREE A bit run down, but visitors can sample frog meat here.

OMNI-THEATRE CINEMA

Map p221 (☑6425 2500; www.omnitheatre.com. sg; 21 Jurong Town Hall Rd; tickets S$14; ⊙usually noon-6pm; 🛏; ⓂJurong East) Next door to the Science Centre (p131) and Snow City (p134), this Imax cinema is home to Asia's largest seamless dome screen (23m diameter) and shows stunning 45-minute documentary films.

SHOPPING

You'll find large shopping centres near major MRT stations, which offer good eating options as well as shopping.

JEM MALL

Map p221 (☑6225 5536; www.jem.sg; 50 Jurong Gateway Rd; ⊙10am-10pm; 🛏; ⓂJurong East) Jem is located in booming Jurong East, an area planned to become a major shopping hub. Tenants include Uniqlo and H&M, excellent Japanese bookstore chain Kinokunya, and local department store Robinsons. There's a booty of kids' clothing stores on level four, state-of-the-art cinemas on level five, and a funky food court in between.

Jem is attached to fellow newcomer **Westgate** (Map p221; ☑6908 3737; www. westgate.com.sg; 3 Gateway Dr; ⊙10am-10pm; 🛏; ⓂJurong East), home to Japanese department store Isetan and its fantastic basement food hall.

VIVOCITY MALL

Map p220 (☑6377 6860; www.vivocity.com.sg; 1 HarbourFront Walk; ⊙10am-10pm; 🛏; ⓂHarbourFront, 🚝Sentosa Express) More than just Singapore's largest shopping mall, Vivo-City offers that rare commodity: open space. There's an outdoor kids' playground on level two and a rooftop 'skypark' where little ones can splash about in free-to-use paddling pools. The retail mix is predominantly midrange, and there's a large Golden Village cineplex.

WALKING THE SOUTHERN RIDGES

Mt Faber is connected to Kent Ridge Park via a series of parks and hills known as the **Southern Ridges** (Map p220; ☑1800 471 7300; www.nparks.gov.sg; ☺24hr; P; MPasir Panjang). It's a wonderfully accessible area to walk in, and much less testing than the hikes around Bukit Timah (p118) or MacRitchie Reservoir (p118). The entire network of trails stretches for 9km, though the direct route from Kent Ridge Park to Mt Faber is a manageable 4km. And while the walking itself isn't tough, Singapore's hot, humid weather makes it important to pack plenty of water.

Start at **Kent Ridge Park** (Map p220; Vigilante Dr; ☺24hr; P; MPasir Panjang), located a brief walk beyond wartime-museum Reflections at Bukit Chandu. Hit the short canopy walk, before strolling downhill to **HortPark** (Map p220; 33 Hyderabad Rd; ☺24hr; P; MPasir Panjang), which includes a children's playground and themed gardens with winding pathways and stepping stones crossing trickling streams. The prototype glasshouses, not open to the public, were used to test building materials, cooling systems, temperatures and humidity for the giant conservatories at Gardens by the Bay (p53).

From HortPark, a leaf-like bridge crosses over Alexandra Rd to the stunning Forest Walk, which offers eye-level views of the jungle canopy blanketing Telok Blangah Hill. The walkway eventually leads to **Telok Blangah Hill Park** (Map p220; Telok Blangah Green; ☺24hr; P; ☐120, 124, 131, 145, 408) with its flower-filled Terrace Garden, and further along to Henderson Waves, an undulating sculptural pedestrian walkway suspended 36m above the forest floor. The shard-like towers soaring in the distance are part of Reflections at Keppel Bay, a residential development designed by star architect Daniel Libeskind.

The final 500m to the summit of Mt Faber is a short but reasonably steep climb that's rewarded with fine views, restaurants and the option of a **cable-car ride** (☑6377 9688; www.singaporecablecar.com.sg; adult/child return S$29/18; ☺8.45am-9.30pm) back down the hill to HarbourFront mall and MRT station, or further on to Sentosa Island. It's easy to walk down to HarbourFront from here, on a pathway that descends the forested hillside.

To get to Kent Ridge Park, take the MRT to Pasir Panjang, cross the main road then walk about 15 minutes up Pepys Rd to museum **Reflections at Bukit Chandu** (Map p220; ☑6375 2510; www.nhb.gov.sg; 31K Pepys Rd; ☺9am-5.30pm Tue-Sun; P; MPasir Panjang) FREE. If you go this way, you can grab a bite to eat at **Eng Lock Koo** (Map p220; 114 Pasir Panjang Rd, cnr Pepys Rd; mains from S$3; ☺5am-3pm; MPasir Panjang).

SPORTS & ACTIVITIES

RINK   SKATING
Map p221 (☑6684 2374; www.therink.sg; Level 3, JCube, 2 Jurong East Central 1; adult/child S$14/12, with hire of skate boots, gloves & socks S$22/19.50; ☺varies; MJurong East) Singapore's first Olympic-sized ice rink is located in youthful mall JCube. Between 9.45pm and 11.45pm on Fridays and Saturdays, disco bunnies get their skates on for the weekly 'Disco on Ice'. Check the website for public skating hours.

SNOW CITY   SNOW SPORTS
Map p221 (☑6560 2306; www.snowcity.com.sg; 21 Jurong Town Hall Rd; adult/child under 13yr from S$18/12; ☺10am-6pm, last entry 5pm; MJurong East) A hangar-sized deep freeze chilled to a numbing -5°C, Snow City features a slope three-storeys high and 60m long. It's best suited to children as it's more of a village than a city. No photography is allowed inside – you have to pay for professional shots. Visitors must wear long trousers (which can be rented) and socks (which can be bought). Ski jackets and boots are provided. Discounted entry is available if you've bought tickets to another attraction at the Science Centre (p131) on the same day.

Sentosa Island

Neighbourhood Top Three

① Universal Studios (p137) Indulging your inner child at Singapore's blockbuster theme park, home to warrior mummies, bad-tempered dinosaurs and the world's tallest duelling roller coasters.

② SEA Aquarium (p138) Visiting the adorable, the curious and the deadly at the world's largest aquarium.

③ Tanjong Beach Club (p139) Feeling the sand between your toes and the breeze on your face as you toast the sunset with the party set.

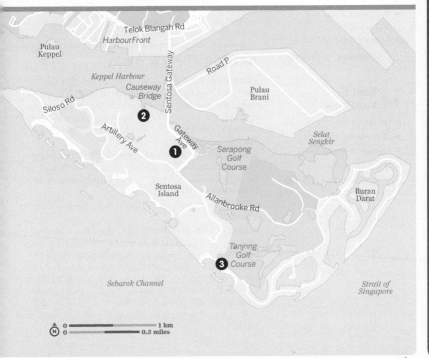

For more detail of this area see Map p222 ➡

Lonely Planet's Top Tip

Sentosa can get oppressively busy at weekends and on public holidays. Queues and waiting times are generally shorter earlier in the week. Where possible, purchase tickets online to save time. And be sure to pick up the handy *Sentosa Island* map-leaflet, available at booths as you enter the island.

Best Thrills

➡ iFly (p140)
➡ MegaZip (p140)

For reviews, see p140.➡

Best Places to Eat

➡ Mykonos on the Bay (p138)
➡ Malaysian Food Street (p138)
➡ Knolls (p139)

For reviews, see p138.➡

Best for Families

➡ Universal Studios (p137)
➡ SEA Aquarium (p138)
➡ Images of Singapore Live (p138)

For reviews, see p138.➡

SENTOSA ISLAND

Explore Sentosa Island

Epitomised by its star attraction, Universal Studios (p137), Sentosa is essentially one giant theme park – and, as such, kids love it. It's packed with rides, activities and shows, most of which cost extra, so it's very easy for a family to rack up a huge bill in one day spent here (and that's not counting visits to the casino). The beaches are completely free and very popular with locals and tourists alike.

You'll need at least a full day (and a well-stocked wallet) to experience everything Sentosa has to offer, but it's also possible to come here for just a morning or afternoon on the beach. In fact, some people come here purely to have a drink in the evening. There are certainly worse ways to watch the sunset than at a beach bar on Sentosa, pina colada in hand.

Local Life

➡**Enjoy weekend brunch** Join clued-up locals and expats for a see-and-be-seen weekend brunch at Sentosa Cove, an upmarket residential and restaurant precinct in Sentosa's far east.

➡**Attend a pool party** Join the beautiful people at W Singapore hotel's to-die-for pool, and chill out at its popular pool party, Endless Summer (p139). Check the website for dates.

Getting There & Away

➡**Cable car** Ride to Sentosa from Mt Faber or the HarbourFront Centre. (On the island itself, a separate **cable-car line** (☎6377 9688; www.singaporecablecar.com.sg; S\$13/8; ⊗8.45am-9.30pm; 🚠Sentosa Station, 🚠Imbiah Station) stops at Imbiah Lookout, Merlion and Siloso Point.)

➡**Monorail** The **Sentosa Express** (⊗7am-midnight) goes from VivoCity to three stations on Sentosa: Waterfront, Imbiah and Beach. VivoCity is directly connected to HarbourFront MRT station.

➡**Walk** Simply walk across the Sentosa Boardwalk from VivoCity.

➡**Bus** On Sentosa, a 'beach tram' (an electric bus) shuttles the length of all three beaches, running from 9am to 10.30pm Sunday to Friday, and from 9am to midnight Saturday. Three colour-coded bus routes link the main attractions. Bus 1 runs from 7am to 10.30pm, bus 2 runs 9am to 10.30pm and bus 3 runs from 8am to 10.30pm. All routes depart from the bus stop just east of Beach monorail station. The monorail, tram and buses are free.

GET YOUR THRILLS AT UNIVERSAL STUDIOS

The top attraction at Resorts World, Universal Studios offers a booty of rides, shows, shops and restaurants, all neatly packaged into fantasy-world themes based on your favourite Hollywood films. Attractions span the toddler friendly to the seriously gut wrenching.

Rides & Roller Coasters

Transformers the Ride, an exhilarating, next-generation motion thrill ride, deploys high-definition 3D animation to transport you to a dark, urban other-world where you'll be battling giant robots, engaging in high-speed chases, and even plunging off the edge of a soaring skyscraper. It's an incredibly realistic, adrenaline-pumping experience.

If you're a hard-core thrill seeker, strap yourself into Battlestar Galactica, which consists of the world's tallest duelling roller coasters. Choose between the sit-down Human roller coaster and the Cylon, an inverted roller coaster with multiple loops and flips. If you can pull your attention away from the screaming, be sure to enjoy the bird's-eye view.

Roller-coaster thrills of the indoor kind are what you'll get on Revenge of the Mummy. The main attraction of the park's Ancient Egypt section, the ride will have you twisting, dipping and hopping in darkness in your search for the Book of the Living. Contrary to Hollywood convention, your journey will end with a surprising, fiery twist.

WaterWorld

Gripping stunts, fiery explosions and ridiculously fit eye-candy is what you get at Water-World, a spectacular live show based on the Kevin Costner flick. Head here at least 20 minutes before show time if you want a decent seat. Those wanting a drenching should sit in the soak zone, right at the front.

DON'T MISS

➤ Transformers the Ride

➤ Battlestar Galactica

➤ Revenge of the Mummy

➤ WaterWorld

PRACTICALITIES

➤ Map p222, C3

➤ ☑ 6577 8888

➤ www.rwsentosa.com

➤ Resorts World, 8 Sentosa Gateway

➤ adult/child under 13yr S$76/56

➤ ⏰ 10am 6pm

➤ 🛜

➤ 🚇 Waterfront

◉ SIGHTS

UNIVERSAL STUDIOS   AMUSEMENT PARK
See p137.

★SEA AQUARIUM   AQUARIUM
Map p222 (☑6577 8888; www.rwsentosa.com; Resorts World, 8 Sentosa Gateway; adult/child under 13yr S$34/24; ☺10am-7pm; P; ⬛Waterfront) You'll be gawking at more than 800 species of aquatic creature at Singapore's impressive, sprawling aquarium. The state-of-the-art complex recreates 49 aquatic habitats found between Southeast Asia, Australia and Africa. The Open Ocean habitat is especially spectacular, its 36m-long, 8.3m-high viewing panel one of the world's largest. The complex is also home to an interactive, family-friendly exhibition exploring the history of the maritime Silk Route.

FORT SILOSO   MUSEUM
Map p222 (☑6736 8672; www.sentosa.com.sg; Siloso Point, Siloso Rd; ☺10am-6pm; 🚗; ⬛Beach) **FREE** Dating from the 1880s, when Sentosa was called Pulau Blakang Mati (Malay for 'the island behind which lies death'), this British coastal fort was famously useless during the Japanese invasion of 1942.

Documentaries, artefacts, animatronics and re-created historical scenes take visitors through the fort's history, and the underground tunnels are fun to explore. The Surrender Chambers bring to life two pivotal moments in Singapore's history: the surrender of the British to the Japanese in 1942, and then the reverse in 1945. Designed to repel a maritime assault from the south, Siloso's heavy guns had to be turned around when the Japanese invaded from the Malaya mainland in WWII. The British surrender soon followed, with the fort later used as a POW camp by the Japanese.

ℹ SENTOSA ISLAND ENTRANCE FEE

Sentosa Island charges a small entry fee, based on the form of transport you take. If you walk across from VivoCity, you pay nothing. If you ride the Sentosa Express monorail, it's S$4, which you can pay using cash or your EZ Link card. Ride the cable car and the entrance fee is included in the price of your cable-car ticket.

Connected to Fort Siloso is the new (and free) Fort Siloso Skywalk, an 11-storey-high walking trail above the canopy treetops.

IMAGES OF SINGAPORE LIVE   MUSEUM
Map p222 (☑6715 4000; www.imagesofsingaporelive.com; 40 Imbiah Rd; adult/child under 13yr S$39/29; ☺10am-6pm Mon-Fri, to 7.30pm Sat & Sun; ⬛Imbiah) Using actors, immersive exhibitions and dramatic light-and-sound effects, Images of Singapore Live resuscitates the nation's history, from humble Malay fishing village to bustling colonial port and beyond. Young kids will especially love the Spirit of Singapore Boat Ride, a trippy, high-tech journey that feels just a little *Avatar*. Tickets are S$10 cheaper when purchased online.

EATING

In addition to the regular eating options across the island, the beach bars here offer food as well as drinks. And there are dozens of restaurants and cafes in Resorts World (www.rwsentosa.com); most attractions have at least a snack stall by the entrance, if not a full-blown cafe-restaurant.

MALAYSIAN FOOD STREET   HAWKER $
Map p222 (www.rwsentosa.com; Level 1, Waterfront, Resorts World, 8 Sentosa Gateway; dishes from S$5; ☺11am-9pm Mon, Tue & Thu, 9am-10pm Fri & Sat, 9am-9pm Sun; ⬛Waterfront) With its faux-Malaysian streetscape, this indoor hawker centre beside Universal Studios feels a bit Disney. Thankfully, there's nothing fake about the food, cooked by some of Malaysia's best hawker vendors.

MYKONOS ON THE BAY   GREEK $$
Map p222 (☑6334 3818; www.mykonosonthebay.com; 01-10 Quayside Isle, 31 Ocean Way; tapas S$9-26, mains S$24-43; ☺6-10.30pm Mon-Wed, noon-2.30pm & 6-10.30pm Thu & Fri, noon-10.30pm Sat & Sun; 🖉; ⬛3) At Sentosa Cove, this slick, marina-flanking taverna serves up Hellenic flavours that could make your *papou* weep. Sit alfresco and tuck into perfectly charred, marinated octopus, pan-fried Graviera cheese and house-made *giaourtlou* (spicy lamb sausage). Happy hour buzzes from 6pm to 8pm Monday to Friday and from 3pm Saturday and Sunday. Book ahead if you plan to come later in the week.

KNOLLS
EUROPEAN $$$

Map p222 (65915046; www.capellahotels.com/singapore; Capella, 1 The Knolls; mains S$24-49, Sun brunch S$148; ⊙7am-11pm; 🚌3) Free-flowing-alcohol Sunday brunch is huge in Singapore, and this posh, secluded spot – complete with peacocks and roaming band – serves one of the best (12.30pm to 3pm). Style up and join the fabulous for scrumptious buffet fare like freshly shucked oysters, sizzling skewers straight from the live grills, fine-cut meats, mountains of cheese and don't forget to leave room for the delectable dessert bites..

DRINKING & NIGHTLIFE

With its easily accessible beaches and cooling sea breeze, Sentosa is popular with the Singapore party set. The beach bars dotted along the coast are perfect for letting your hair down; weekends are particularly festive.

TANJONG BEACH CLUB
BAR

Map p222 (6270 1355; www.tanjongbeachclub.com; 120 Tanjong Beach Walk; ⊙11am-10pm Tue-Fri, from 10am Sat, 10am-11pm Sun; 🚌Tanjong Beach) Generally cooler than the bars on Siloso Beach, Tanjong Beach Club is an evocative spot, with striped deckchairs on the sand, a small, stylish pool for guests, and a sultry music soundtrack. The restaurant serves trendy beachside fare, and a kick-ass weekend-brunch menu. Some of the island's hottest parties happen on this shore.

WOOBAR
BAR

Map p222 (6808 7258; www.wsingaporesentosacove.com; W Singapore, 21 Ocean Way; ⊙11.30am-1am Mon-Fri, 9am-1am Sat & Sun; 🛜; 🚌3) The W Singapore's hotel bar is glam and camp, with suspended egg-shaped pods, gold footrests and floor-to-ceiling windows looking out at palms and pool. The afternoon 'high tea' (from S$65/75 for two weekdays/weekends) is served in dainty birdcages, while the Wednesday Ladies' Night (from S$36) comes with free-pour bubbly between 7.30pm and 9pm, followed by half-price drinks until midnight.

OLA BEACH CLUB
BAR

Map p222 (6250 6978; www.olabeachclub.com; 46 Siloso Beach Walk; ⊙10am-10pm Mon-

 TOP TIP

Sentosa can get oppressively busy at weekends and on public holidays. Queues and waiting times are generally shorter earlier in the week. Where possible, purchase tickets online to save time. And be sure to pick up the handy Sentosa Island map-leaflet, available at booths as you enter the island.

Fri, from 9am Sat & Sun; 🚌Beach) It's a bit of a stretch to compare Siloso Beach to Waikiki, but after a few cocktails at this beach club's Hawaiian bar, served in fabulously kitschy tiki glasses, you could imagine you're in Oahu. Grab a cabana, sun lounger, beach swing or a spot by the pool and make a day of it, ideally on a Sunday, when DJs pump the tunes.

COASTES
BAR

Map p222 (6631 8938; www.coastes.com; 01-05, 50 Siloso Beach Walk; ⊙9am-11pm Sun-Thu, to 1am Fri & Sat; 🚌Beach) More family friendly than many of the other beach venues, Coastes has picnic tables on the palm-studded sand and sun loungers (S$20) by the water. If you're peckish, there's a comprehensive menu of standard offerings, including burgers, pasta and salads.

☆ ENTERTAINMENT

WINGS OF TIME
THEATRE

Map p222 (6736 8672; www.wingsoftime.com.sg; Siloso Beach; standard/premium seats S$18/23; ⊙shows 7.40pm & 8.40pm; 🚌Beach) Set above the ocean, this ambitious show fuses Lloyd Webber–esque theatricality with an awe-inspiring sound, light and laser extravaganza. Prepare to gasp, swoon and (occasionally) cringe.

ENDLESS SUMMER
LIVE MUSIC

Map p222 (68087258; www.wsingaporesentosacove.com; W Singapore, 21 Ocean Way; incl 1 drink S$35; ⊙dates vary; 🚌3) Hang with Singapore's sun-kissed party people at Endless Summer, W Singapore hotel's popular pool party. It's a fun, chilled-out session with no shortage of eye candy downing drinks, scanning the crowd and cooling off in the hotel's to-die-for pool. Beats are provided by international DJs and there's a host of beach-themed games to play. Check the website for upcoming dates.

SPORTS & ACTIVITIES

Sentosa is Singapore's activity central. Whatever you're into — from indoor skydiving to zip-lining to luge racing — you can find it here. But it'll cost you. Sentosa's beaches, however, are free.

KIDZANIA
AMUSEMENT PARK

Map p222 (⌨1800 653 6888; www.kidzania. com.sg; 01-01/02 Palawan Kidz City, 31 Beach View; adult/child under 18yr S\$58/35; ⊙10am-5pm Sun-Thu, to 8pm Fri & Sat; ⊠Beach) Young ones get to be the grown-ups in this huge, indoor, kid-sized city. Comprising different 'workplaces', kids can try out their dream jobs, from pilot to crime-scene investigator. Parents can only watch, which means waiting around, but it's worth it to see your kid become a firefighter. Weekends are particularly busy.

IFLY
ADVENTURE SPORTS

Map p222 (⌨6571 0000; www.iflysingapore. com; 43 Siloso Beach Walk; 1/2/4 skydives S\$89/119/199; ⊙9am-9.30pm Thu-Tue, from 11am Wed; ⊠Beach) If you fancy free-falling from 3660m to 914m without leaping out of a plane, leap into this indoor-skydiving centre. The price includes an hour's instruction followed by a short but thrilling skydive in a vertical wind chamber. Divers must be at least seven years old. Tickets purchased two days in advance for off-peak times are significantly cheaper. See the website for details.

ADVENTURE COVE WATERPARK
WATER PARK

Map p222 (⌨6577 8888; www.rwsentosa.com; Resorts World, 8 Sentosa Gateway; adult/child under 13yr S\$38/30; ⊙10am-6pm; ☎; ⊠Waterfront) Despite its rides being better suited to kids and families, adult thrill-seekers will appreciate the Riptide Rocket (Southeast Asia's first hydro-magnetic coaster), Pipeline Plunge and Bluwater Bay, a wave pool

with serious gusto. Dolphin Island, charged separately, allows visitors to interact with Indo-Pacific dolphins in a pool. Captive-dolphin swims have been criticised by animal-welfare groups, who say that captivity is debilitating and stressful for the animals, and that this is exacerbated by human interaction.

MEGAZIP
ADVENTURE SPORTS

Map p222 (www.sg.megaadventure.com; Imbiah Hill Rd; zip-line ride S\$45; ⊙11am-7pm; ⊠Beach) Part of the MegaAdventure playground, this 450m-long, 75m-tall zip-line runs from Imbiah Lookout to a tiny island off Siloso Beach. Alternatively, you can conquer the 15m drop in the MegaJump or head up instead of down on MegaWall, the 15m climbing wall. There's also a high-ropes adventure course, which will have you feeling like Tarzan, but with a harness.

GOGREEN SEGWAY ECO ADVENTURE
TOURS

Map p222 (⌨9825 4066; www.segway-sentosa. com; Beach Station, Sentosa; from S\$17; ⊙10am-7.30pm; ⊠Beach) Hop aboard for a 10-minute 'fun ride' (S\$17) or explore the beachfront on a guided Eco Adventure trip (from S\$40). Really keen riders can book on a 2½-hour tour of the island (S\$140), which includes Fort Siloso (p138) and the Merlion. Eco Adventure riders must be at least 10 years old and Sentosa Tour riders at least 15 years old. There's a second outlet at Siloso Beach, opposite Bikini Bar.

SKYLINE LUGE SENTOSA
ADVENTURE SPORTS

Map p222 (⌨6274 0472; www.skylineluge.com; 45 Siloso Beach Walk; luge & skyride combo from S\$18; ⊙10am-9.30pm; ⊠Beach) Take the cable-car from Siloso Beach to Imbiah Lookout, then hop onto your luge (think go-cart meets toboggan) and race family and friends around hairpin bends and along bone-shaking straights carved through the forest (mandatory helmets are provided). Young kids will love this. Those with heart conditions or bad backs won't.

Islands & Day Trips from Singapore

Pulau Ubin p142
An unkempt jungle of an island, Pulau Ubin offers a forest full of weird and wonderful creatures, dusty village streets and, best of all, the chance to explore it all by bicycle.

Southern Islands p144
Located just off the southeast coast of Sentosa, the three Southern Islands – Kusu, Lazarus and St John's – are tailor-made for beachside picnics and lazy tropical lounging. Head across for a quick, soothing getaway.

Pulau Bintan p146
Expats and moneyed Singaporeans lap up the all-inclusive resorts in the north, but exploring Bintan's south offers an altogether more authentic taste for Indonesian island life.

Johor Bahru p149
Just under an hour away by bus from Singapore, the Malaysian city of Johor Bahru, or JB, is popular for cheap food, cheap-ish shopping, lively streets and a Lego theme park.

Pulau Ubin

Explore

It may be just a 10-minute bumboat (motorised sampan) ride from Changi Village, but Ubin seems worlds from mainland Singapore and is the perfect city getaway for those who love the outdoors, particularly cycling.

Singaporeans like to wax nostalgic about Ubin's *kampong* (village) atmosphere, and it remains a rural, unkempt expanse of jungle full of fast-moving lizards, strange shrines and a cacophony of birdlife. Tin-roofed buildings bake in the sun, chickens squawk and panting dogs slump in the dust, while in the forest, families of wild pigs run for cover as visitors pedal past on squeaky rented bicycles. Set aside a full day if you can. It takes a couple of hours just to get here and, once you arrive, you won't want to be rushed.

The Best...

➡ **Sight** Chek Jawa Wetlands

➡ **Place to Eat** Pulau Ubin Village

➡ **Activity** Cycling (p144)

Top Tip

As you depart the jetty you'll see a large signboard map of the island; take a picture for reference as it is much better than the one they give out at the National Parks office at **Ubin & HSBC Volunteer Hub** (Map p143; ☑6542 4181; 61 Pulau Ubin; ⊘8.30am-5pm).

Getting There & Away

Getting to Pulau Ubin is half the fun!

➡ **MRT** Catch the East West Line to Tanah Merah MRT Station, where you'll then need to hop on a bus.

➡ **Bus** Hop on bus 2 from Tanah Merah MRT Station (30 minutes) to the terminus bus stop at Changi Point Ferry Terminal (p183).

➡ **Boat** From the Changi Point Ferry Terminal, it's a 10-minute chug-along bumboat ride (motorised sampan) to Pulau Ubin Ferry Terminal (one-way S$3, bicycle surcharge S$2). The small wooden boats seat 12 passengers, and only leave when full, but you rarely have to wait long. No tickets are issued. You just pay the boat-hand once you're on board.

◉ SIGHTS

PULAU UBIN VILLAGE   VILLAGE

(Map p143) Although not really a tourist sight, Pulau Ubin's only village of note is a ramshackle time capsule of Singapore's past and an interesting place to wander around. Fish traps and the skeletal remains of abandoned jetties poke out of the muddy water, stray cats prowl for birds, and docile dogs laze around on the sleepy streets. It's also the gateway to the island and home to the ferry terminal, bike-hire shops and the island's only restaurants.

CHEK JAWA WETLANDS   NATURE RESERVE

Map p143 (☑1800 471 7300; www.nparks.gov. sg; ⊘8.30am-6pm) **FREE** If you only have time for one part of Pulau Ubin, make it this part. Skirting the island's southeast, Chek Jawa Wetlands features a 1km coastal boardwalk that will have you strolling over the sea and through a protected mangrove swamp to the 20m-high **Jejawi Tower** (Map p143). Climb it for sweeping coastal and jungle views. You can't bring your bike into the reserve, so rent one with a lock and secure it to the bike stands at the entrance.

GERMAN GIRL SHRINE   TAOIST TEMPLE

Map p143 (near Ketam Quarry) Housed in a wooden hut beside an Assam tree, this shrine is one of the island's quirkier sights. Legend has it that the young daughter of a German coffee plantation manager was running away from British troops who had come to arrest her parents during WWI and fell fatally into the quarry behind her house. Somewhere along the way, this daughter of a Roman Catholic family became a Taoist deity, whose help some Chinese believers seek for good health and lottery numbers.

The shrine is now filled with all manner of trinkets, including many bottles of nail polish. One hopes the little girl approves; her ghost is said to haunt the area to this day.

WEI TUO FA GONG TEMPLE   BUDDHIST TEMPLE

(Map p143) Sitting on a small hillock overlooking a pond filled with carp and turtles, this 80-year-old temple decorated with thousands of prayer flags, contains a number of shrines surrounded by a huge variety of statuettes and iconography. Be greeted by the large golden Buddha as you enter. Take the first right after the Jelutong Bridge on Jln Jelutong.

 # EATING & DRINKING

The only place to have a meal is in Pulau Ubin Village. Get off the boat and turn left. There are half a dozen or so places here, most housed in *kampong* (village) huts with tin roofs. They all serve similar fare, with noodles and rice dishes featuring alongside lots of seafood (naturally). Chilli crab is a favourite – expect to pay around S$30 per person. Wash it down with a Tiger beer – what else?

There are a couple of drinks stalls along Jln Endul Senin, where you can also buy snacks.

Pulau Ubin

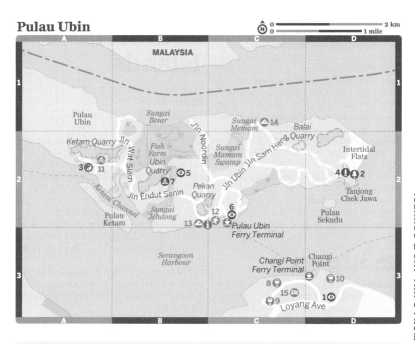

Pulau Ubin

◎ Sights
1 Changi Village.. D3
2 Chek Jawa Wetlands D2
3 German Girl Shrine................................... A2
4 Jejawi Tower.. D2
5 Pulau Ubin.. B2
6 Pulau Ubin Village.................................... C2
7 Wei Tuo Fa Gong Temple........................ B2

☻ Eating
Changi Village Hawker Centre .... (see 1)
International Nasi Lemak............... (see 1)
Makan Melaka .... (see 1)
Mei Xiang Goreng Pisang............... (see 1)

◔ Drinking & Nightlife
8 Coachman Inn.. C3
9 Coastal Settlement.................................. C3
10 Little Island Brewing Co......................... D3

◉ Sports & Activities
11 Ketam Mountain Bike Park A2
12 Ubin Adventure... C2

▣ Sleeping
13 Jelutong... B2
14 Mamam Beach... C1
15 Village Hotel Changi............................... C3

SPORTS & ACTIVITIES

KETAM MOUNTAIN BIKE PARK   CYCLING

(Map p143) A series of trails of varying difficulty leads around Ketam Quarry and through some of the surrounding area. While it's not the most hardcore bike park on the planet, you really need to be more than just a beginner to deal with the steep slopes, sharp corners and relatively poor traction at various points on most of the trails. Make sure you smoother yourself in mosquito repellent and sunscreen and carry plenty of water. There's a small bike-skills zone off to your left as you enter the area.

UBIN ADVENTURE   OUTDOORS

Map p143 (☑6733 2282; http://adventures.asian detours.com; 34 Pulau Ubin; tours adult/child 7-12yr from S$80/59) This adventure group offers kayaking and bike tours around the island. It runs three kayak adventures: a two-hour paddle through the mangroves for beginners, the more advanced four-hour, 8.27km paddle from the north to the south of the island, and a full open-sea 3½-hour adventure. The three-hour bike tour takes in lesser-known scenic areas, bird-watching spots and historical sights. Bookings are required at least two days in advance.

SLEEPING

The only way to stay overnight on Ubin is to camp – and you'll need to bring your own tent and drinking water. This is a popular option with locals.

JELUTONG   CAMPGROUND

(Map p143) **FREE** One of the two free campsites on Pulau Ubin – the other is at Mamam Beach – Jelutong is closest to the main town on the south coast. It's not particularly idyllic, but does have toilets and nonpotable running water (BYO drinking water); no showers. Register with the National Parks office at Ubin & HSBC Volunteer Hub (p142) or via email (NParks_Public_Affairs@nparks.gov.sg) before camping.

Southern Islands

Explore

Popular for local escapes, bite-sized St John's (p145), Lazarus (p145) and Kusu (p145) are scattered just south of Sentosa. They're ideal for fishing, swimming, having a picnic or simply kicking back on the sand and living out the tropical dream. While mildly crowded on weekends, they're almost deserted on weekdays – unless your visit coincides with a school camp.

The beach at Lazarus is the nicest; however, the ferry timetable will see you arrive there in the middle of the day, so it can get very hot.

Facilities are almost nonexistent but there are toilets on St John's and Kusu. Staying overnight in a bungalow is possible on St John's.

CYCLING AROUND UBIN

Cycling is the best way to get around Ubin. There are plenty of places in Pulau Ubin Village that rent perfectly adequate bikes for the day. The bikes are pretty much identical, although some vendors seem to change prices on a whim. Cheapest and fairest of the lot is Shop 31, which rents bikes for S$6 to S$12, and helmets for S$2. Uncle also has a number of fancier bikes for the more serious peddler for S$35. Vendors should throw in a basket and a bike lock if you ask. Most offer a range of tandems, as well as bikes with child seats. Those heading for the Ketam Mountain Bike Park tend to bring their own better-quality bikes with them, however a few bike stalls have started offering a small number for hire.

Maps are found on signboards dotted around the place; take a picture on your phone for instant access. Because of the large swamp area in the central northern region of the island, you can't do a complete loop, so if you want to explore the east and the west (note: the far west is off limits) you'll have to do a bit of back-tracking; but distances here are small so it hardly matters.

The Best...

➡ **Sight** Kusu Kramats
➡ **Place for a picnic** Kusu Island
➡ **Activity** Beach bumming on Lazarus Island

Top Tip

Consider visiting on a Sunday, when the ferry service operates longer hours. Make sure you stock up on food and drinks before going as there are no shops or eateries on the islands. You'll find a provisions shop and small eatery at Marina South Pier.

Getting There & Away

➡ **Boat** Sailing first to St John's (a 30-minute journey) and then on to Kusu (15 minutes), **Singapore Island Cruise** (Map p204; ☑6534 9339; www.islandcruise.com.sg; 01-04 Marina South Pier, 31 Marina Coastal Dr; Southern Islands return adult/child under 13yr S$18/12) returns to Marina South Pier. Hop off at St John's, go exploring, and then catch the next ferry to Kusu. Note that there aren't many services (two on weekdays, four on Saturday, five on Sunday), so watch the clock. The last ferry leaves Kusu at 4pm Monday to Friday, at 4.30pm on Saturday and at 6.15pm on Sunday. Always check the schedule on the ferry company website before heading to the terminal.

➡ To get to the ferry terminal, take the MRT to Marina South Pier.

◉ SIGHTS & ACTIVITIES

KUSU ISLAND   ISLAND

(☑6323 9829; www.sla.gov.sg/Islands; ⬧Singapore Island Cruises) By far the smallest of the three Southern Islands, Kusu is also the most pleasant. Step off the boat and into an area of picnic-friendly landscaped gardens, home to a small turtle sanctuary and the colourful Taoist Tua Pek Kong Temple. Further on is the beach, its shallow water ideal for young kids. All of this, though, is on reclaimed flat land, which surrounds the original piece of Kusu – a forest-covered rock topped by

the Kusu Kramats, three 19th-century Malay shrines.

You can visit the shrines, all painted a bright canary yellow, by climbing the 152 steps up through the trees to the top.

The island is generally quiet, except during the Kusu pilgrimage during the ninth lunar month (sometime between September and November), when thousands of devotees arrive to pay homage at the temples. Tea, coffee and cold drinks are sometimes available at Tua Pek Kong Temple, but don't count on it.

ST JOHN'S ISLAND   ISLAND

(☑6323 9829; www.sla.gov.sg/Islands; ⬧Singapore Island Cruises) Spooky St John's has a chequered past: it was a quarantine station for immigrants in the 1930s before becoming a political prison and later a rehabilitation centre for opium addicts. A prison feel still lingers – barbed-wire fences and watchtowers dot the landscape and you'll see plenty of 'do not enter' signs. There's a small beach that some families use for picnicking, and a tiny tin-roofed mosque used by maintenance workers, but most visitors head here for a spot of fishing.

If you plan to travel here during the Kusu pilgrimage (during the ninth lunar month sometime between September and November), check the ferry has not cancelled its stop at St John's – as it sometimes does.

LAZARUS ISLAND   ISLAND

(☑6323 9829; www.sla.gov.sg/Islands; ⬧Singapore Island Cruises) Almost entirely undeveloped, with little more than a bit of jungle and a sweeping beach, Lazarus Island is connected to nearby St John's Island via a concrete walkway (approximately 20 minutes to cross). The beach is a gorgeous, sandy affair – dotted with the odd yacht and (unfortunately) rubbish swept up by the tides. That said, it's as perfect a beach as you can expect in Singapore, and a fabulous spot to roll out your towel and soak up some rays.

🛏 SLEEPING

The one and only accommodation option on these islands is the bungalow on St John's Island (p146). Public camping is not allowed on St John's, although some people occasionally flout the rules.

ST JOHN'S
HOLIDAY BUNGALOW BUNGALOW **$**

(☎6323 9829; www.sla.gov.sg/Islands; St John's Island; 3 nights Tue-Thu $53.50, Fri-Sun $107; 🚢Singapore Island Cruises) This three-bedroom bungalow accommodates up to 10 people and comes with a basic kitchen and cooking utensils. You must book it in person at the SLA Service Counter (Level 12, Revenue House, 55 Newton Rd); reservations are only available between two weeks and two months in advance of your intended visit. Rates double during the school holidays.

Keep in mind that there are no dining or retail outlets on the island, so you'll need to bring all of your own food and drinks.

Pulau Bintan

Explore

While the all-inclusive resorts in Bintan's north are a popular quick escape from Singapore, few venture to the island's rawer south. It's here that you'll find Bintan's cultural heart and biggest town, Tanjung Pinang – a gritty, ramshackle place of noisy, dusty, potholed streets that are utterly Indonesian. Dodge mopeds and rickshaws as you fight through the busy back-alleys to a local coffeeshop to get your bearings.

Rested, explore the market alleyways at the northeastern end of Jln Merdeka (between Jln Plantar and Jln Gambir), then head to the small jetties where you can board bumboats to either Senggarang (home to a Chinatown on stilts) or Penyengat, a small, rural island with royal tombs, palaces and a beautiful mosque.

The Best...

➡**Sight** Masjid Raya Sultan Riao
➡**Dish** *Ikan bakar* (barbecued fish) at Penyengat (p148)
➡**Place to Eat** Pinang Citywalk (p148)

Top Tip

It's cheaper and far less hassle to change money at moneychangers than in a bank. There are loads on Jln Merdeka (turn left out of the ferry terminal).

Getting There & Away

➡**Boat** Ferries leave for Tanjung Pinang (1½ hours) from Singapore's Tanah Merah Ferry Terminal (bus 35 from Tanah Merah MRT station). Many nationalities are granted a free 30-day tourist visa, while others are eligible for a visa on arrival (US$15 for a seven day tourist visa) or will need to obtain one prior to arrival – make sure you check before travelling. The 55,000Rp departure tax must be paid in local currency when you leave.

Ferry companies include the following:

Sindo Ferry (☎+65 6331 4122; www.sindo ferry.com.sg; Sri Bintan Pura Ferry Terminal)

Majestic Fast Ferry (☎0771-450 0199; www.majesticfastferry.com.sg; Sri Bintan Pura Ferry Terminal)

Need to Know

➡**Area Code** ☎0771
➡**Location** 60km from Singapore

⊙ SIGHTS

⊙ Tanjung Pinang

Bintan's capital Tanjung Pinang is a historic port town and trade centre with a still-thriving market culture and plenty of hustle and bustle. Touts swarm as you get off the ferry, but the town is easy to navigate without their persistent 'assistance'. Few travellers linger long here, but there are a couple of worthwhile attractions if you're curious.

CETIYA BODHI SASANA BUDDHIST TEMPLE

(Jln Plantar 2) This small Chinese temple down by the docks can actually be seen from the water as you leave on boats to Senggarang. There's a small open-air stage in front of it, where Chinese opera performances are sometimes held. Frenetic dragon-boat races start here every year during the Dragon Boat Festival (the fifth day of the fifth lunar month).

To get here, turn left out of the ferry terminal, walk about 500m down the main road, then turn left – opposite the temple Vihara Bhatra Sasana – down Jln Plantar 2. Just before you reach the water, turn left

SLEEPING ON BINTAN

Tanjung Pinang is best tackled as a day trip from Singapore. The town's hotels range from spartan to utterly depressing. If you do end up staying overnight, book one of the better-quality resorts in the island's north.

There are five direct services each way with **Bintan Resort Ferries** (Map p213; ☑6542 4369; www.brf.com.sg; 01-21 Tanah Merah Ferry Terminal, 50 Tanah Merah Ferry Rd; ⏰7am-8pm Mon-Fri, 6.30am-8pm Sat & Sun; Ⓜ Tanah Merah, then bus 35) between Tanah Merah Ferry terminal and Bandar Bentan Telani on the north coast (six to seven each way on weekends). Most resorts organise shuttle services to/from the harbour as part of the package price.

Beyond these two slumber options, you'll find a comprehensive list of resorts at www.bintan-resorts.com.

Trikora Beach Club (☑0811-7700 898; www.trikorabeachclub.com; Desa Teluk Bakau; d from 2,000,000Rp; ❉ ▨) Rustic whitewashed beach huts and a white sandy beach make this spot perfect for relaxing. The gorgeous blue-tiled pool is perfect for a cooling dip, as is the clear ocean, where you can try your hand at snorkelling and numerous water sports.

Banyan Tree Bintan (☑0770-693 100; www.banyantree.com; Jln Teluk Berembang; d from 6,250,000Rp; ❉ 🛜 ▨) The lush and privileged Banyan Tree has famed spa facilities, a long beach and airy, elevated guest villas with traditional Indonesian accents and private relaxation pools.

---

to the temple. The area here is a fascinating maze of alleyways and market stalls.

VIHARA BHATRA SASANA   BUDDHIST TEMPLE
(Jln Merdeka) Dragons adorn the beautifully painted upturned eaves on the roof of this Chinese temple. A statue of Kuan Yin (Guanyin), the goddess of mercy, stands at the central altar. To get here, turn left out of the ferry terminal and keep walking to the end of the road. The temple is on your right, on the corner with Jln Ketapang.

⊙ Penyengat

⭐ PULAU PENYENGAT   ISLAND
Pulau Penyengat, reached by frequent boats (7000Rp) from the Tanjung Pinang pier, was once the capital of the Riau rajahs. The ruins of the old palace of Rajah Ali and the tombs and graveyards of Rajah Jaafar and Rajah Ali are signposted inland. The most impressive site is the sulphur-coloured mosque, with its many domes and minarets.

The beautiful fairy-tale castle of a mosque that is the Masjid Raya Sultan Riau was built in 1832 and is painted in pastels of yellow and green. Its minarets are topped with tall conical spires and are almost Gothic Revival in style. This is an active mosque and although visitors are welcomed, appropriate clothing should be

worn; cover yourself up, or else admire the building from afar.

Penyengat was the royal capital of the Riao-Johor sultanate, and the island is dotted with the ruins of the palaces and tombs of these Malay rulers. Ones to look out for on your wanders include the ruined palace Astana Kantor, straight on from the mosque, and the tomb of Raja Hamidah, off to the left of the mosque. There are many others that you'll stumble across as you walk around the island.

At the far west of the island are the ruins of an impressive stone fort, built by the sultan Raja Haji in the 18th century to fend off Dutch attacks. Ironically, the cannons you see here are Dutch made. Raja Haji, incidentally, was the author of the first Malay grammar book, a reminder that this island was once a hotbed of intellectual and religious minds, and at one time was home to more than 9000 people.

The best way to get around the island is by motorised tricycle; expect to pay between 30,000Rp and 50,000Rp for a day trip.

⊙ Sennggarang

This predominantly Chinese village, on the other side of the bay from Tanjung Pinang, is easily reached by a quick 10-minute boat ride. The main attractions of this area are the floating stilt Chinese village and a Buddhist temple, which has been basically swallowed by a banyan tree. Plan to spend approximately 1½ hours here.

CHINATOWN AREA

(Chinese Water Village) Unless you ask to dock at the temples, your boat from Tanjung Pinang will drop you at the jetties at Senggarang's so-called Chinatown. This residential village sits propped up over the ocean on stilts – some dwellings are a little precarious-looking. Spend some time wandering the rustic laneways. Most of the house doors are open so you can have a peek inside; you'll usually spot a religious shrine. The community is believed to have been here since the 18th century, and is predominantly Teochew Chinese.

VIHARA DHARMA SASANA BUDDHIST TEMPLE

This well-maintained temple complex, looking out to sea, is accessed through a beautifully decorative Chinese archway and contains three main temples. The oldest two, and the first ones you approach after walking through the archway, are thought to be between 200 and 300 years old, although they have been repainted and repaired many times. Their roof carvings are particularly ornate. Behind them is a more modern temple and two huge and very colourful Buddha statues.

To get to the temples, either tell your Tanjung Pinang boatman to take you directly to the temple jetty or go to the usual Senggarang jetty (6000Rp to 8000Rp). Once you've made your way to dry land, you can easily spot the archway entrance to the complex.

BANYAN TREE TEMPLE BUDDHIST TEMPLE

This particularly unusual temple is housed in a building dating from the early 19th century. Originally owned by a wealthy Chinese man, believed to be buried here, the building has, over the years, been swallowed up by the roots of a large banyan tree. It's only in recent decades that the site has become a shrine, as locals and devotees from further afield began to come here to give offerings and ask for blessings.

You can get back to the jetty from here without returning to the Vihara Dharma Sasana temple complex; just take the first left on your way back.

EATING

Food options in Bintan's resort are limited to all-you-can-eat buffets and fine dining, however, in Tanjung Pinang you'll get excellent local food at roadside food stalls.

If you're planning to catch an early morning ferry from Singapore, Tanah Merah Ferry Terminal has a branch of the excellent coffeeshop chain Killiney Kopitiam, where you can enjoy a Singaporean breakfast of *kaya* (coconut jam) toast, runny eggs and *kopi* (coffee). They do plenty of main dishes too and, if you don't like *kopi*, they also do fresh Western-style coffee.

Tanjung Pinang

Turn left out of the ferry terminal and you'll soon find a few *kedai kopi* (local coffeeshops), where you can grab a drink, a snack or a bowl of *goreng* (noodles). In the evening, you'll find several food stalls scattered around town selling *mie bangka*, a Hakkastyle dumpling soup. Other delicacies to look out for include *gong gong* (snails eaten with a toothpick) and *otak-otak* (small fishcakes barbecued in strips of banana leaves).

The colourful pasar buah (fruit market) is at the northern end of Jl Merdeka. There are a few Western fast-food chains too if you're after a taste of home.

PINANG CITYWALK HAWKER $

(Jln Teuku Umar; dishes 5000-15,000Rp; ☺7am-2am, individual stalls hours vary) Pinang Citywalk is a good place for eating (as well as a spot of local clothing and snack shopping), with an array of hawker stalls available.

One of the cleaner places to eat in town is this modern, airy hawker centre, complete with a stage for bands. The large selection of stalls sell everything from fresh seafood, to *ayam penyat* (smashed fried chicken with spicy sambal) and *nasi lemak* (coconut rice). The beer here is refrigerated, which means there's no need for dodgy ice.

Pinang Citwalk is located behind the Vihara Bhatra Sasana temple. Enter from Jln Teuku Umar or Jln Ketapang.

Penyengat

The jetty you walk along as you arrive on the island has a few small restaurants with outdoor seating. Look out for *ikan bakar*, delicious barbecued fish eaten with a side salad, a sweet-chilli dip and plain rice. Expect to pay around 38,000Rp per serving. Do as the locals do and eat it with your fingers. The teapots on the table are hand-washing water.

✗ Senggarang

Some locals open up the front of their stilt houses as small restaurants. Expect only the most basic of dishes, and little choice. Otherwise, you can grab snacks at small shops in the village near the Banyan Tree Temple.

Johor Bahru

Explore

Easy to visit in a day from Singapore, JB (no one calls it Johor Bahru) is determined to shake off its 'Wild West' reputation. New developments such as Puteri Harbour and Legoland to the west of the centre offer a glimpse of the region's shiny future, while central JB itself continues

to offer a raffish antidote to Singapore's near-perfection.

Legoland aside, JB isn't known for any major tourist attractions. The main reason to visit is to experience a city more laid-back and gritty than its southern cousin.

Arrive in the morning and head to a coffeeshop like Restoran Huamui in the Heritage District for a leisurely breakfast. Wander the colourful lanes nearby, see a couple of the area's temples and the quaint Chinese Heritage Museum, then catch a bus or taxi to Johor Premium Outlets for a dose of cheap-ish shopping.

Head back to the Heritage District for a bite and a drink in a funky back-alley bar before making your way back across the border.

The Best...

➜**Sight** Heritage District (p151)
➜**Place to Eat** Kam Long Fishhead Curry (p151)
➜**Place to Drink** Chaiwalla & Co (p152)

Top Tip

Immigration checkpoints, for people coming back into Singapore, can be hellishly

SLEEPING IN & AROUND JOHOR BAHRU

The main cheap and low-bracket midrange hotels cluster on and around the relatively ambient Jln Meldrum, in the centre of town, or just to the east. More midrange, boutique and business-oriented hotels hover in the lively area around KSL Mall, where you'll also find tons of good eating options and shopping. Many hotels inflate prices on Friday, Saturday and Sunday by about 10%.

Hilton DoubleTree (☑07-268 6868; www.doubletree3.hilton.com; 12 Jln Ngee Heng; d RM400; P 🌢 @ 🛜 🌊) While it lacks the intimacy of the small boutiques in town, the DoubleTree does deliver business-class comfort with well-tailored ample rooms, several restaurants and a 13th-floor pool and bar terrace that gives you a bird's-eye view of the city. There are big savings online. A word of warning: the lighting system in the rooms is confusing as hell.

Citrus Hotel (Map p150; ☑07-222 2888; www.citrushoteljb.com; 16 Jln Station; d/tr RM129/390; 🌢 @ 🛜) Rooms are small but clean with white walls and bright accents of green and orange – citrusy indeed. Breakfasts are tasty, staff are helpful and the location, just next to Johor Bahru City Square (p152), couldn't be better.

Legoland Hotel (☑07-597 8888; www.legoland.com.my/Hotel; 7 Jln Legoland, Bandar Medini Iskandar; r RM850; P 🌢 🛜 🌊 🍴; 🚍LM1) Complete your Legoland (p152) experience by spending a night or two at this Lego-tastic hotel. From the giant Lego playground in the lobby, to the themed rooms (choose from Pirate, Kingdom, Adventure and the recently added Ninjago), the fun is in the detail – from figurine swapping with staff, to the in-room treasure hunt. Rooms sleep up to five people.

Johor Bahru

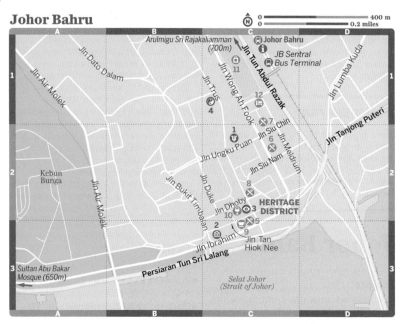

Johor Bahru

busy in the evenings, especially on weekends and public holidays. Try to avoid coming back at this time if you can.

Getting There & Away

➡ **Bus** Getting to JB by bus takes about an hour. The easiest way is to catch the **Causeway Link** (www.causewaylink.com. my). There are several routes, of which CW2 (departing from Queen Street Bus Terminal) and CW5 (departing from the Newton Food Centre car park on Clemenceau Ave N) are the most convenient. Buy your ticket at the bus stop using the correct change. You will need to disembark at the Singapore immigration checkpoint to clear immigration, then reboard any Causeway Link bus route across to JB (don't lose your ticket!), where you will need to clear Malaysian immigration. The Malaysian immigration checkpoint is in the heart of JB, and buses to KSL City Mall (bus IM17), Puteri Harbour (bus LM1) and Legoland (bus LM1) depart from the adjoining JB Sentral bus station at street level. If heading to Legoland, ignore the uniformed touts at the bus station; buy your bus ticket (one way RM4.60) on the bus, and your Legoland ticket online or at the park itself.

➡ **Taxi** A taxi from central Singapore to central JB will cost you around S$48. You can also pay for a seat in a shared taxi from Queen Street Bus Terminal for S$12 per person. Shared taxis leave when full.

⦿ SIGHTS

HERITAGE DISTRICT   ARCHITECTURE
(Map p150) Wandering around the heritage area between Jln Ibrahim and Jln Ungku Puan is a real highlight of Johor Bahru. Walk past colourful old shophouses filled with barbers, Ayurvedic salons, sari shops, gorgeous temples, a few modern-art galleries and old-style eateries.

ROUFO GUMIAO   TAOIST TEMPLE
Map p150 (Old Chinese Temple; Jln Trus; ⊘7am-5pm) FREE Once the centre of JB's Chinese immigrant community, and used by five different ethnic groups to worship five different Chinese gods, this small but atmospheric temple is more than 130 years old. Little remains of its original masonry after major renovations in 1995, but it does house some genuine antiques.

CHINESE HERITAGE MUSEUM   MUSEUM
Map p150 (☑07-224 9633; 42 Jln Ibrahim; adult/child RM6/3; ⊘9am-5pm Tue-Sun) Well-laid-out exhibits chronicling the history of Chinese immigrants in this part of the Malay peninsula are the highlight of this three-storey museum. Learn how the Cantonese brought their carpentry skills to this area, while the Hakkas traded in Chinese medicines and the Hainanese kick-started a trend in coffeeshops, which lasts to this day. There's good English signage.

ARULMIGU SRI RAJAKALIAMMAN   HINDU TEMPLE
(Glass Temple; 22 Lorong 1; RM10; ⊘1-5pm) FREE Step through the looking glass into this wonderland of a temple built from mirrors, glass and metal – not a single inch of the vaulted roof or wall has been left unadorned. The temple is dedicated to Kali, known as the goddess of time, change, power and destruction.

ARULMIGU RAJAMARIAMMAN DEVASTHANAM   HINDU TEMPLE
Map p150 (☑07-2233989; www.rajamariammanjb.com; 1A Jln Ungku Puan; ⊘7am-9pm) FREE This beautiful Hindu temple, with ornate carvings, devotional artwork and a tall, brightly painted *gopuram* (tower) entrance way, is the heart of JB's Hindu community. Photos are allowed, but be respectful of devotees.

SULTAN ABU BAKAR MOSQUE   MOSQUE
(Jln Gertak Merah) FREE The stunning white-washed walls and blue-tiled roof of this Victorian-inspired mosque speak of a mix of architectural influences. Built between 1892 and 1900, it is quite rightly hailed as one of the most magnificent mosques in the area. At the time of research it was undergoing renovations with no confirmed completion date.

✖ EATING & DRINKING

KAM LONG FISHHEAD CURRY   SEAFOOD $
Map p150 (74 Jln Wong Ah Fook; curry from RM19; ⊘8am-4pm) The lunch line snakes up the sidewalk so if you want to get a taste of this seriously addictive, mildly spicy fish curry, get here before 11am. There's only one dish on the menu, but you can choose from fish head or tail; the head is best, dished up with bean-curd skin, ladyfingers, tomatoes and cabbage.

HIAP JOO BAKERY & BISCUIT FACTORY   BAKERY $
Map p150 (13 Jln Tan Hiok Nee; buns/cake from RM3.50/5; ⊘7am-5.30pm) For over 80 years this little bakery has prepared delicious buns, cakes and biscuits in a charcoal oven just as the founder had done in his native Hainan, China. Join the queue spilling out the bright blue door for the famous spongy banana cake – not too sweet and slightly smoky – sold in lots of five or 10 (RM5/10).

The coconut buns are also a winner.

RESTORAN HUA MUI   MALAYSIAN $
Map p150 (☑07-224 7364; 131 Jln Trus; mains RM6-31; ⊘8am-6pm) This airy, old-schooled coffeeshop with delightful mosaic-tiled

ⓘ MALAYSIAN VISAS
Most foreigners do not need a Malaysian visa for short-term stays, but check before you leave. Border formalities are pretty straightforward, although weekends can get very busy. Don't forget your passport!

ISLANDS & DAY TRIPS FROM SINGAPORE JOHOR BAHRU

ISKANDAR MALAYSIA: BACK TO THE FUTURE

Peninsular Malaysia's southernmost city has some very ambitious plans. Upon completion in 2025, Iskandar Malaysia – a development region that includes Johor Bahru and stretches from Pasir Gudang in the east to Tanjung Pelepas in the west – is set to radically transform the area into a cutting-edge metropolis and liberal trading port.

Its new, Moorish-inspired administrative centre, Kota Iskandar, has been built from scratch, 33km west of central Johor Bahru, in Nusajaya. This district is also home to Puteri Harbour, a burgeoning marina district that's home to the luxe **Hotel Jen** (⏱07-560 8888; www.hoteljen.com/johor/puteriharbour; Persiaran Puteri Selatan; d RM480; 🅿❄@🛜🏊; 🖳LM1), shops, cafes and waterfront restaurants.

Four kilometres west of Puteri Harbour is Iskandar's first theme park, **Legoland Malaysia Resort** (⏱07-597 8888; www.legoland.com.my; Medini, Nusajaya; adult/child RM195/155; ⏲10am-6pm; ♿). The resort incorporates the rides, roller coasters and giant Lego replicas of Legoland, the waterslides and pools of Legoland Water Park, as well as the Legoland Hotel (p149), which makes for a fun one-night base if you're travelling with young kids. If you don't have kids, neither of the parks is really worth going out of your way for.

Bus LM1 connects JB Sentral to Puteri Harbour (35 minutes) and Legoland (45 minutes) via the Larkin Bus Terminal. A taxi from central Johor Bahru to Legoland will cost around RM70 to RM80 – use only the trusted blue-coloured 'Executive Taxis'.

flooring is very popular with locals and tourists alike. Take a seat under the whirling fans and order from the menu that offers a mix of Malay, Indonesian and Chinese dishes. We loved the *kampong* fried rice, and the grilled *kaya* toast and runny eggs are perfect for breakfast.

MEDAN SELERA
MELDRUM WALK   HAWKER $
Map p150 (Meldrum Walk; meals from RM3; ⏲5pm-late) Every late afternoon, the little food stalls crammed along this alley (parallel to Jln Meldrum) start frying up everything from *ikan bakar* (grilled fish) to laksa. Wash down your meal with fresh sugar-cane juice or a Chinese herbal jelly drink. Nothing here is excellent, but it's all good.

CHAIWALLA & CO.   CAFE
Map p150 (⏱12-735 3572; www.facebook.com/chaiwalla.co; Lot 2810, Jln Tan Hiok Nee; ⏲11am-midnight Sun-Wed, to 1am Thu-Sat; 🛜) Elevating the usual *chai walla* (tea seller) stall, this drinks cafe has made its home in a trendy, all-black, double-storey shipping container, with industrial-styled interiors and lush hanging-garden wall. You can grab a decent cup of hot coffee; however, the speciality of the house is iced beverages, including Vietnamese coffee, Thai milk tea, and build-your-own smoothies.

ROOST JUICE BAR   BAR
Map p150 (9 Jln Dhoby; ⏲1pm-midnight; 🛜) A trendy back-alley bar with retro furniture and laid-back staff, this is the coolest hangout in the colonial district. Beer is half the price you'd pay in Singapore, and the fresh-fruit smoothies are delicious.

 # SHOPPING

JOHOR PREMIUM OUTLETS   MALL
(⏱07-661 8888; www.premiumoutlets.com.my; Indahpura, Kulai; ⏲10am-10pm) Home to 130 stores, including Aigner, Bally, Burberry, Calvin Klein, Coach, Ermenegildo Zegna, Furla, Michael Kors, Nike, Polo Ralph Lauren and Salvatore Ferragamo. To get here, catch bus JPO1 from the JB Sentral Bus Terminal: travel time is one hour. From Puteri Harbour or Legoland, catch JPO2.

JOHOR BAHRU CITY SQUARE   MALL
Map p150 (www.citysqjb.com; 108 Jln Wong Ah Fook; ⏲10am-10pm) A flashy mall with affordable designer shops, cinema and a great food court.

KSL CITY MALL   MALL
(⏱07-288 2930; www.kslcity.com.my; 33 Jln Seladang; ⏲10am-10pm) A large shopping mall with stores, cafes, restaurants and bars. The main drawcard here is the Tesco supermarket, although it pales in comparison to the UK original.

Sleeping

Staying in Singapore is expensive. Budget travellers can stay in hostel rooms for S$25 a night. Newer midrange hotels are lifting the game with better facilities and good, regular online deals. Luxury digs are expensive but plentiful and among the world's best, with options from colonial and romantic to architecturally cutting-edge.

Hostels
A recent wave of 'flashpacker' and pod hostels in and around Chinatown and Little India have smartened up the budget slumber scene. Dorms may still be on the smaller side, but new bunks, coupled with stylish communal bathrooms and lounge areas are making for an altogether more appealing scenario. Note that hostels tend to get booked up on weekends, especially the (limited) private rooms, so book in advance. Little India remains the place with the most budget beds.

Hotels
Singapore offers a thrilling collection of hotels, from luxe colonial digs such as the Raffles Hotel (p156) and Fullerton Hotel (p157), to hip, idiosyncratic boutique spots such as Naumi (p157) and the Warehouse (p157). Standards are high, but then so are the prices – check web offers for bargains. Central business hotels such as **Carlton City** (Map p209; ☑6632 8888; www.carltoncity.sg; 1 Gopeng St; r from S$290; ✳@🛜☒; Ⓜ️Tanjong Pagar) can be great value on weekends, while other midrange options like Ramada Singapore at Zhongshan Park (p163) counter their not-so-central location with lower prices and top-notch facilities.

Serviced Apartments
For medium- to long-term stays, Singapore has a number of serviced apartments. It is also possible to rent rooms in private flats or whole private apartments. Rents are high, regardless of how near or far from the city centre you are.

Probably the best place to start looking for long-term rental in Singapore is **Singapore Expats** (www.singaporeexpats.com), which has detailed information on the different districts, outlines the whole rental procedure and has an apartment search engine. The Singapore section of www.craigslist.org is also a good place to look.

Actual Prices May Vary
In Singapore's midrange and top-end hotels, room rates are about supply and demand, fluctuating daily. Travellers arranging a trip to Singapore need to keep this in mind, especially if you're planning to come here during a major event. For example, room prices triple during the Formula One night race.

Be aware that top hotels usually add a 'plus plus' (++) after the rate they quote you. Ignore this at your peril. The two pluses are a service charge and GST, which together amount to a breezy 17% on top of your bill.

Accommodation Websites
Apart from booking directly via the hotel websites listed in our reviews, you can also book rooms on these websites.

Lonely Planet (lonelyplanet.com/singapore/hotels) Book rooms on Lonely Planet's website.

LateRooms (www.laterooms.com) Great deals on rooms; book now then pay when you stay.

StayinSingapore (www.stayinsingapore.com) Hotel-booking website dedicated to Singapore, managed by the Singapore Hotel Association.

NEED TO KNOW

Prices
(Double room including taxes.)

$ less than S$150

$$ S$150–S$350

$$$ more than S$350

Reservations
Book in advance during peak periods, including for the Formula One race and Chinese New Year. Even average hostels can be booked up over weekends.

Tipping
Tipping isn't expected in hostels; it's good form to tip hotel porters and cleaning staff a dollar or two.

Checking In & Out
Check-in time is usually 2pm with check-out at 11am. If the hotel isn't at full occupancy, you can usually extend these times by an hour or two if you ask politely. If not, you should be able to leave your luggage at the hotel until your room is ready.

Breakfast
Hostels usually include a simple breakfast (toast with spreads and coffee/tea). Midrange and top-end hotels may or may not include breakfast. This is usually indicated when booking online. If breakfast isn't included in the price, it's usually offered as an add-on purchase.

Air-Conditioning
Air-conditioning is standard in most hotels and hostels. In reviews, the air-con icon indicates properties with air-conditioning.

Lonely Planet's Top Choices

Fullerton Bay Hotel (p156) What's not to love about a luxe hotel where every handsome room is waterside?

Parkroyal on Pickering (p159) A lush, vertical jungle designed by one of Singapore's hottest architect studios.

Raffles Hotel (p156) Legend and romance still linger at Singapore's most famous slumber pad.

W Singapore – Sentosa Cove (p163) Luxury meets youthful verve at this chic, playful retreat on hedonistic Sentosa Island.

Best by Budget

$

Adler Hostel (p157) This self-proclaimed 'poshtel' just near the Chinatown MRT comes with Chinese antiques.

COO (p157) A new-school hostel with neon lighting and a hip location in Tiong Bahru.

Bunc@Radius (p159) Delivers cheap chic in the backpacker heartland of Little India.

$$

Lloyd's Inn (p161) Minimalist boutique hotel a short stroll from Orchard Rd.

Hotel Indigo (p162) Peranakan-inspired hotel bursting with nostalgic memorabilia, steps from heritage-heavy Joo Chiat Rd.

$$$

Fullerton Bay Hotel (p156) Elegant, light-filled luxury perched right on Marina Bay.

Parkroyal on Pickering (p159) A striking architectural statement, with hanging gardens and a stunning infinity pool.

Capella Singapore (p163) Cascading pools, lush jungle gardens and svelte, chic interiors on Sentosa.

Best for History

Raffles Hotel (p156) A rambling colonial icon with a long list of illustrious guests.

Fullerton Hotel (p157) Soaring columns and historical anecdotes grace Singapore's former GPO.

Hotel Fort Canning (p157) An elegant, park-fringed oasis where officers once stood to attention.

Goodwood Park Hotel (p161) Story-book Teutonic architecture within walking distance of Orchard Rd.

Best Views

Marina Bay Sands (p157) Ego-boosting views of downtown skyscrapers or sci-fi Gardens by the Bay.

Fullerton Hotel (p157) Romantic river panoramas and unobstructed views of Marina Bay Sands' light-and-laser spectacular.

Ritz-Carlton Millenia Singapore (p156) Survey the burgeoning skyline and Marina Bay from this uberluxe retreat.

Best for Kids

Marina Bay Sands (p157) Home to the world's most celebrated rooftop pool.

Shangri-La's Rasa Sentosa Resort & Spa (p164) Kid-centric poolside fun surrounded by Sentosa's theme parks and attractions.

W Singapore – Sentosa Cove (p163) Playful, spacious rooms and an epic pool at Sentosa's discerning end.

Where to Stay

NEIGHBOURHOOD	FOR	AGAINST
Colonial District, Marina Bay & the Quays	Very central, good transport options. Variety of accommodation – flashpacker hostels to iconic luxury hotels.	Cheap hotels are generally of poor to average quality and usually in noisy areas.
Chinatown, Tanjong Pagar & the CBD	A stone's throw from great eateries, bars and nightlife. Culturally rich, good transport links and an excellent range of accommodation, many in restored shophouses.	Too touristy for some; noise can be an issue.
Little India & Kampong Glam	Backpacker central, with Singapore's largest choice of cheap accommodation. Some lovely higher-end boutique hotels; unique atmosphere unlike any other district; fabulous food and good transport links.	Too grotty for some. Streets can get very noisy in the evenings, especially at weekends.
Orchard Road	On the doorstep of Singapore's shopping mecca. Fine choice of quality hotels, including top-name international chains.	Slim pickings for budget travellers. Hot-spot eateries and bars thin on the ground.
Eastern Singapore	Quiet (a relative concept in Singapore). Close to the cooling breeze of East Coast Park, and the airport.	MRT service doesn't run to this area. Sights in the east are quite spread out so there's no real central location to stay in.
Holland Village, Dempsey Hill & the Botanic Gardens	Home to the Singapore Botanic Gardens, fancy cafes and shopping boutiques, just out of the hustle and bustle of Orchard Rd.	Although serviced by MRT, the route is not direct. Dempsey Hill restaurants and shops are quite spread out – a hassle if walking.
Northern & Central Singapore	Packed with outdoor adventure areas and nature attractions.	Some distance from the city centre; best accessed via taxi.
Sentosa Island	Ideal for families, with a resort-like vibe and easy access to kid-friendly attractions, beaches and sporting activities.	Synthetic Sentosa lacks character; getting into the city centre is a slight hassle.
Pulau Ubin	Laid-back island lifestyle a 10-minute bumboat ride from the mainland.	MRT doesn't run to the bumboat terminal so it's a long bus ride unless you take a cab.
Southern Islands	Singapore's quietest and cleanest beaches, with a great view back to the mainland.	Islands are very basic; no food outlets or shops. Your day will be dictated by the limited ferry times.
West & Southwest Singapore	Filled with museums, nature reserves and quirky attractions.	A vast area where some attractions are accessible by MRT, but for most, taxi will be best.

🛏 Colonial District, Marina Bay & the Quays

PORT BY QUARTERS HOSTEL
HOSTEL $

Map p202 (☎6816 6960; www.stayquarters.com; 50A Boat Quay; single/queen capsules from S$35/85; ✳@🛜; Ⓜ Clarke Quay, Raffles Place) Smack bang on the Singapore River, the Port by Quarters Hostel has raised the bar for capsule hostels in Singapore. The sleek single and queen capsules offer under-bed storage, folding workstation, power points and roll-down privacy screen. The best bit, however, is the views – straight over to Parliament and the skyline beyond.

There is a female-only dorm available.

5FOOTWAY.INN PROJECT BOAT QUAY
HOSTEL $

Map p202 (www.5footwayinn.com; 76 Boat Quay; dm from S$28, tw from S$80; ✳@🛜; Ⓜ Clarke Quay, Raffles Place) Right on Boat Quay, the whitewashed dorms come in one-, two-, three- and four-bed configurations, and though rooms are small (superior rooms have windows), they're modern and comfortable, with wooden bunks and handy bedside power sockets and lights. Bathrooms are modern, reception operates round-the-clock, and the chic breakfast lounge comes with an amazing river view.

There's a tiny communal kitchen, though Chinatown's cheap eats are an MRT stop away.

HOLIDAY INN EXPRESS CLARKE QUAY
HOTEL $$

Map p202 (☎6589 8000; www.hiexpress.com; 2 Magazine Rd; r from S$200; P✳@🛜; Ⓜ Clarke Quay) This smart hotel delivers modern, earthy-hued rooms with high ceilings, massive floor-to-ceiling windows and comfortable beds with both soft and firm pillows. Small bathrooms come with decent-size showers. Best of all is the rooftop garden, home to a tiny gym and impressive glass-sided pool with spectacular city views. The hotel's self-service laundry room is a handy touch.

Discounted online rates can see rooms offered for under S$200.

PARK REGIS
HOTEL $$

Map p209 (☎6818 8888; www.parkregis singapore.com; 23 Merchant Rd; r from S$260; ✳@🛜💺; Ⓜ Clarke Quay, Chinatown) This newish, affable place has light-filled rooms that are smallish but modern, with window seating and warm, amber accents. The gym is petite but adequate, and overlooks the hotel's fabulous terrace pool, which comes with a cascading waterfall feature and semi-submerged sun-loungers. Staff are wonderfully helpful, and the hotel is an easy walk from both the quays and Chinatown.

⭐ RAFFLES HOTEL
HISTORIC HOTEL $$$

Map p202 (☎6337 1886; www.raffleshotel.com; 1 Beach Rd; r from S$985; ✳@🛜💺; Ⓜ City Hall, Esplanade) The grand old dame of Singapore has seen many a famous visitor in her time, from Somerset Maugham to Queen Elizabeth II. It's a beautiful place of white colonial architecture, lush pockets of green and historic bars. The most recent upgrade, completed in 2019, has seen the property meticulously revamped with all the finest modern comforts but without losing one iota of charm. Then there's the location, right in the heart of the Colonial District and within easy reach of most must-see neighbourhoods.

⭐ FULLERTON BAY HOTEL
HOTEL $$$

Map p202 (☎6333 8388; www.fullertonbayhotel.com; 80 Collyer Quay; r from S$600; P✳@🛜💺; Ⓜ Raffles Place) The Fullerton Hotel's (p157) contemporary sibling flanks Marina Bay. It's a light-filled, heavenly scented, deco-inspired number. Rooms are suitably plush, with high ceilings, wood and marble flooring, and warm, subdued hues. Recharge courtesy of the in-room Nespresso machine and lather up with Bottega Veneta toiletries; glass panels in the marble bathrooms look into the room and at Marina Bay and beyond.

The hotel's rooftop bar Lantern (p64) and pool are simply stunning, while the afternoon high tea at Landing Point (p62) is the finest in town. Note: some rooms face Customs House, so be sure to request one facing Marina Bay directly.

⭐ RITZ-CARLTON MILLENIA SINGAPORE
HOTEL $$$

Map p204 (☎6337 8888; www.ritzcarlton.com/singapore; 7 Raffles Ave; r from S$550; P✳@🛜💺; Ⓜ Promenade) No expense was spared, no feng shui geomancer went unconsulted and no animals were harmed in the building of this luxe establishment. Its spacious rooms are light, plush and beige, with good-sized work spaces, high-end linen and unimpaired city or Marina Bay views. The hotel's multimillion-dollar art collection features works by Hockney, Warhol, Stella and Chihuly; collect a guide from the concierge desk.

★ **WAREHOUSE**   BOUTIQUE HOTEL **$$$**
(☑6828 0000; www.thewarehousehotel.com; 320 Havelock Rd; r from S$350; 🅿🕸🛜❄; 🚌51, 64, 123, 186, Ⓜ Fort Canning) If the location on the main road makes you think twice about booking this hotel, stop thinking and just book! Touted as one of the hottest openings in Singapore in years, the Warehouse quietly screams super trendy. With its industrial-chic interiors, the river-view infinity pool and its luxurious, muted-toned hotel rooms, you might never want to leave.

Rooms come in a number of layouts – our pick is the mezzanine with reading library. If you like plenty of light, choose a loft.

NAUMI   BOUTIQUE HOTEL **$$$**
Map p202 (☑6403 6000; www.naumihotel.com; 41 Seah St; r from S$400; 🕸@🛜❄; Ⓜ City Hall, Esplanade) Slinky Naumi comes with commissioned artwork, playful quotes and a rooftop infinity pool with skyline views. Standard rooms are relatively small but cleverly configured, with 400-thread-count Egyptian-cotton bed linen, Nespresso machine and complimentary minibar. Shower panels turn opaque at the flick of a switch, with a dramatically lit, stand-alone 'beauty bar' (bathroom counter) in the room itself. Ninth-floor rooms have city views.

Suites are decadent and utterly extraordinary. Choose from a classic Coco Chanel–inspired design or a bold, colourful Andy Warhol number, the latter with a round tub slap bang in the middle of your room.

HOTEL FORT CANNING   HOTEL **$$$**
Map p202 (☑6559 6795; www.hfcsingapore.com; 11 Canning Walk; r from S$350; 🅿🕸@🛜❄; Ⓜ Dhoby Ghaut) What was once British military headquarters is now a luxury hideaway surrounded by Fort Canning Park. While we love the mineral-water-filled swimming pools, exceptional gym and complimentary evening aperitifs and canapés, the rooms are the star attraction. These gorgeous retreats are graced with high ceilings, parquetry flooring, soothing botanical colours, Nespresso coffee machine and Jim Thompson silk bedhead.

Original French windows and see-through glass separate room and bathroom, the latter a white-marble wonder with soaking tub and a large window looking out over the park or city. Check the website for special offers.

MARINA BAY SANDS   HOTEL **$$$**
Map p204 (☑6688 8888; www.marinabaysands. com; 10 Bayfront Ave; r from S$480; 🅿🕸@🛜❄; Ⓜ Bayfront) Part of the ambitious Marina Bay Sands casino-retail complex (p55), the Sands hotel is famed for its extraordinary rooftop infinity pool, which straddles the roofs of the three hotel skyscrapers. Rooms are modern and comfortable, though generic, and the lobby can sometimes feel like rush hour at Grand Central Station. A good choice for fans of casinos and high-end shopping sprees.

FULLERTON HOTEL   HOTEL **$$$**
Map p202 (☑6733 8388; www.fullertonhotel. com; 1 Fullerton Sq; r from S$420; 🅿🕸@🛜❄; Ⓜ Raffles Place) Occupying what was once Singapore's magnificent, Palladian-style general post office, the grand old Fullerton offers classically elegant rooms in muted tones. Entry-level rooms look 'out' into the inner atrium, so consider upgrading to one of the much more inspiring river- or bay-view rooms. A river-and-skyline backdrop awaits at the 25m terrace pool, the hotel's alfresco jewel.

🛏 Chinatown, Tanjong Pagar & the CBD

★ **ADLER HOSTEL**   HOSTEL **$**
Map p206 (☑6226 0173; www.adlerhostel.com; 259 South Bridge Rd; cabin s/d S$40/80; 🕸@🛜; Ⓜ Chinatown) Hostelling reaches sophisticated new heights at this self-proclaimed 'poshtel'. Chinese antiques grace the tranquil lobby lounge, and fresh towels and feather down duvets and pillows the beds. Airy, air-con dorms consist of custom-made cabins, each with lockable storage and curtains that can be drawn for privacy. Some even feature king-size beds for couples. Book around three weeks ahead for the best rates.

★ **COO**   HOSTEL **$**
Map p209 (☑6221 5060; www.staycoo.com; 259 Outram Rd; dm from S$44; 🕸@🛜; Ⓜ Outram Park) Looking more like a funky dance club

with its graphic artwork, neon lighting and cage walls, this self-proclaimed 'sociatel' is all about everything social – social media, socialising – you get the drift. A great place to make new friends and Snapchat about it, dorms come in four-, six- or eight-bed configurations. Super-clean and super-comfy, there's a bistro on-site and free bike rental.

Female-only dorms are available, and all dorms come with handy lockers in your sleeping space.

WINK HOSTEL   HOSTEL $

Map p206 (☑6222 2940; www.winkhostel.com; 8A Mosque St; pod s/d S$40/72; ✳@⚡; ⓂChinatown) Located in a restored shophouse in the heart of Chinatown, flashbacker favourite Wink merges hostel and capsule-hotel concepts. Instead of bunks, dorms feature private, soundproof 'pods', each with comfortable mattress, coloured mood lighting, adjacent locker and enough room to sit up in. Communal bathrooms feature rain shower heads, while the in-house kitchenette, laundry and lounge areas crank up the homey factor.

FERNLOFT   HOSTEL $

Map p206 (☑6323 3221; www.fernloft.com; 02-92, Block 5, Banda St; dm from S$18; ☺9am-11.30pm; ✳@⚡; ⓂChinatown) Located in a housing block overlooking the Buddha Tooth Relic Temple, this compact hostel is just steps from Chinatown and Tanjong Pagar's booming restaurant and bar scenes. As with many hostels in Singapore, the dorms (which include a female-only room) are windowless, though everything is kept clean and tidy.

★AMOY   BOUTIQUE HOTEL $$

Map p206 (☑6580 2888; www.stayfareast.com; 76 Telok Ayer St; s/d S$270/325; ✳@⚡; ⓂTelok Ayer) Not many hotels are accessed through a historic Chinese temple, but the Amoy is no ordinary slumber pad. History inspires this contemporary belle, from the lobby feature wall displaying old Singaporean Chinese surnames to custom-made opium beds in the cleverly configured 'Cosy Single' rooms. Plush doubles include Ming-style porcelain basins, and all rooms please with designer bathroom, Nespresso machine and complimentary minibar.

If you've got large bags with you, it's best to enter via the flat walkway beside the Dean & Deluca food store.

★WANGZ   BOUTIQUE HOTEL $$

Map p209 (☑6595 1388; www.wangzhotel.com; 231 Outram Rd; r from S$260; P✳@⚡; ⓂOutram Park) Curvaceous, metallic Wangz is a winner. A quick walk from Tiong Bahru's heritage architecture and hipster hangouts, its 41 rooms are smart and modern, accented with contemporary local art, sublimely comfortable beds, iPod docking stations and sleek bathrooms. Further perks include complimentary nonalcoholic minibar beverages, in-house gym, handy smartphone and a rooftop lounge serving well-mixed drinks, all topped off with sterling service.

HOTEL MONO   BOUTIQUE HOTEL $$

Map p206 (☑6326 0430; www.hotelmono.com; 01-04, 18 Mosque St; r from $200; ✳⚡; ⓂChinatown) After all the sights, sounds and hustle of Chinatown, it may take a while for your senses to adjust to the calming interior of this monochromatic hotel – pretty much everything is black and white. Retaining its heritage facade and spread over six shophouses, this 46 no-room-the-same boutique pad boasts heavenly beds, gel pillows, sleek

---

BOOKING ON THE FLY

If you arrive in Singapore without a hotel booking, don't despair. The efficient **Singapore Hotel Association** (www.stayinsingapore.com) has hotel reservation desks at each of Changi Airport's terminal arrival halls.

There are dozens of hotels on its lists, ranging from budget options right up to the Raffles Hotel. There's no charge for the service, and promotional or discounted rates, when available, are passed on to you. You can also book the hotels online via the association's website.

If you've made it as far as Orchard Rd and still don't have a hotel room (and don't fancy sleeping in the park), **Singapore Visitors Centre @ Orchard** (Map p216; ☑1800 736 2000; www.yoursingapore.com; 216 Orchard Rd; ☺8.30am-9.30pm; ⚡; ⓂSomerset) works with hotels in the local area and can help visitors get the best available rates.

bathrooms with rain shower heads, and a knockout location.

Not all rooms have windows; request one away from the road if you're a light sleeper.

SCARLET
BOUTIQUE HOTEL **$$**

Map p206 (☑6511 3333; www.thescarlethotel. com; 33 Erskine Rd; r from S$240; ✳@🛜; Ⓜ Chinatown, Telok Ayer) Dark, luscious Scarlet offers great service and svelte rooms just around the corner from drinking hot spots Ann Siang Rd and Club Street. In opulent jewel colour schemes, think sapphire blues and ruby reds, the chic rooms feature silky wallpaper and dark Oriental furniture. There are also five plush suites to tempt you;, the 'lavish' boasts a Hästens bed valued at S$38,500!

Although rooms on the 1st floor don't have windows, high ceilings and skylights render them far from gloomy. Check the hotel website, as discounts are common.

HOTEL 1929
BOUTIQUE HOTEL **$$**

Map p206 (☑6347 1929; www.hotel1929.com; 50 Keong Saik Rd; r from S$160; ✳🛜; Ⓜ Outram Park, Chinatown) Occupying a whitewashed heritage building, Hotel 1929 sits on up-and-coming Keong Saik Rd. Rooms are tight, but good use is made of limited space, and interiors are cheerily festooned with vintage designer furniture (look out for reproduction Eames and Jacobsen pieces) and Technicolor mosaic bathrooms. Rooftop suites spice things up with private, clawed-foot bathtub-graced verandahs.

★ PARKROYAL
ON PICKERING
HOTEL **$$$**

Map p209 (☑6809 8888; www.parkroyal hotels.com; 3 Upper Pickering St; r from S$400; ✳@🛜🏊; Ⓜ Chinatown) Dramatic, cascading gardens, bird-cage cabanas right on the infinity pool, and a striking design evocative of terraced paddy fields: this outstanding hotel is the work of local architecture firm Woha, which designed everything down to the wastepaper baskets. Rooms are light, crisp and contemporary, with natural wood and soothing green hues, high ceilings and heavenly mattresses.

Desks are generously sized, and stylish bathrooms feature sliding panels and amenities from the on-site St Gregory Spa. Online deals can see room rates slide below S$350.

🛏 Little India & Kampong Glam

★ BUNC@RADIUS
HOSTEL **$**

Map p210 (☑6262 2862; www.bunchostel.com; 15 Upper Weld Rd; dm from S$28, d S$85; ✳@🛜; Ⓜ Rochor) Fresh, clean, new-school Bunc@ Radius is the coolest flashpacker hostel in town. A concrete floor, art installations and monochromatic colour scheme give the spacious lobby a hip, boutique feel. Dorms – in four-, six-, eight-, 12- and 16-bed configurations – offer both single and double beds, with each thick mattress wrapped in a hygiene cover (no bed bugs!).

There are female-only dorms, private rooms with flat-screen TV and an outdoor movie deck with beanbags, not to mention a fabulous, semi-alfresco kitchen that will make you want to cook.

POD
HOSTEL **$**

Map p210 (☑6298 8505; www.thepod.sg; 289 Beach Rd; pod s/d from S$58/112, pod suite s/d from S$80/138; ✳@🛜; Ⓜ Bugis, Nicoll Hwy) Riding the new wave of capsule hotels, the Pod offers sleek accommodation steps from vibrant Kampong Glam. Dorms are modern and sleep 10 to 12 in single or queen pods; privacy comes in the form of roll-down screens. These new pods give you your own space; however, they're not soundproof. A free Nespresso coffee, hot breakfast and laundry service cement its popularity.

Female- and male-only dorms available, as well as private shower rooms with toilets in the shared bathroom.

FIVE STONES HOSTEL
HOSTEL **$**

Map p210 (☑6535 5607; www.fivestoneshostel. com; 285 Beach Rd; dm from S$28, tw/d S$95/105; ✳@🛜; Ⓜ Bugis, Nicoll Hwy) This upbeat, no-shoes hostel comes with polished-concrete floors and both Wii and DVDs in the common lounge, plus complimentary use of washing machines and dryers. While not all dorms have windows, all feature steel-frame bunks, personal power sockets and lamps, and bright, mood-lifting murals depicting local themes. There's an all-female floor, plus private rooms with bunks or a queen-size bed.

KAM LENG HOTEL
BOUTIQUE HOTEL **$**

(☑6239 9399; www.kamleng.com; 383 Jln Besar; r from S$85; ✳🛜; 🚌65, 145, 857, Ⓜ Bendemeer,

Farrer Park, Lavender) Hipster meets heritage at Kam Leng, a revamped retro hotel in the up-and-coming Jalan Besar district. Common areas are studiously raw, with distressed walls, faded Chinese signage, colourful wall tiles and modernist furniture. Rooms are tiny and simple yet cool, with old-school terrazzo flooring and pastel accents. A word of warning: rooms facing Jln Besar can get rather noisy.

SHOPHOUSE THE
SOCIAL HOSTEL   HOSTEL $
Map p210 (☑6298 8721; www.shophousehostel. com; 48 Arab St; dm S$18-25, tw S$70-75; ❄@중; ⓂBugis, Nicholl Hwy) A well-located, well-designed hostel, Shophouse has a fantastic rooftop lounge and terrace with great views!. Rooms feature dark-wood bunks and industrial elements such as raw-concrete floors. There's a women-only floor, and guests enjoy a 20% discount at Working Title, the indie cafe on the ground floor.

FISHER BNB   HOSTEL $
Map p210 (☑6297 8258; www.fisherbnb.com; 127 Tyrwhitt Rd; dm from S$36; ❄@중; ⓂBendemeer, Lavender, Farrer Park) With simple, industrial interiors, this squeaky-clean hostel in heritage neighbourhood Jalan Besar is a great bet for a good night's sleep. The mixed dorm sleeps 16 in metal bunk beds and the female-only dorm fits 12 – the pink walls are a fun touch. Lockers are huge and the owner James is a wealth of information.

HANGOUT@MT.EMILY   HOSTEL $
(☑6438 5588; www.hangouthotels.com; 10A Upper Wilkie Rd; dm/s/d/tr/q/quin from S$35/ 105/120/150/180/210; ❄@중; ⓂLittle India, Dhoby Ghaut) Some of Singapore's nicest dorms are located slightly out of the way atop leafy Mt Emily, making this place a quiet retreat rather than a handy hang-out. Decorated in vibrant colours, with murals by local art students, the unisex and mixed dorms and private rooms are immaculate, as are the bathrooms. There's also a rooftop terrace, a cafe, free internet and cosy lounging areas.

INNCROWD   HOSTEL $
Map p210 (☑6296 9169; www.the-inncrowd.com; 73 Dunlop St; dm from S$17; ❄@중; ⓂRochor) Wildly popular, the InnCrowd is ground zero for Singapore's backpackers. Located

HISTORIC HOTELS
....

It's not just Raffles Hotel (p156) that has an illustrious past. Goodwood Park Hotel (p161), dating from 1900 and designed to resemble a Rhine castle, served as the base for the Teutonia Club, a social club for Singapore's German community, until 1914 when it was seized by the government as part of 'enemy property'. In 1918 the building was auctioned off and renamed Club Goodwood Hall, before it morphed again into the Goodwood Park Hotel in 1929, and fast became one of the finest hotels in Asia.

During WWII it accommodated the Japanese high command, some of whom returned here at the war's end to be tried for war crimes in a tent erected in the hotel grounds. By 1947 the hotel was back in business, with a S$2.5-million renovation program bringing it back to its former glory by the early 1960s. Further improvements in the 1970s have left the hotel as it is today.

The Fullerton Hotel (p157) occupies the magnificent colonnaded Fullerton Building, named after Robert Fullerton, the first governor of the Straits Settlements. Upon opening in 1928, the S$4-million building was the largest in Singapore. The General Post Office, which occupied three floors, was said to have the longest counter (100m) in the world at the time. Above the GPO was the exclusive Singapore Club, in which Governor Sir Shenton Thomas and General Percival discussed surrendering Singapore to the Japanese.

In 1958 a revolving lighthouse beacon was added to the roof; its beams could be seen up to 29km away. By 1996 the GPO had moved out and the building underwent a multimillion-dollar renovation, reopening in 2001 to general acclaim and receiving the prestigious Urban Redevelopment Authority Architectural Heritage Award the same year.

right in the heart of Little India, the highlight of this hostel is the free kick-scooter city tours (6pm Tuesday, Thursday and Sunday), a social and fun way to discover Singapore. Staff are very helpful and there' are board games, DVDs and a laundry. Balcony rooms get noisy – request a room without one.

IBIS SINGAPORE
ON BENCOOLEN   HOTEL $$
Map p210 (⏺6593 2888; www.ibishotel.com; 170 Bencoolen St; r from S$150; ✳@🛜; MBugis) Ibis offers sensible, low-frills comfort, from a generic lobby spiffed up with colourful modular furniture to smallish, spotless, cookie-cutter rooms with crisp sheets, light wood and peachy hues. Bathrooms are small, clean and modern. Thoughtful extras include complimentary bikes and access to a nearby gym. See the website for regular discounts.

VILLAGE HOTEL
ALBERT COURT   HOTEL $$
Map p210 (⏺6339 3939; www.stayfareast.com; 180 Albert St; r from S$220; ✳@🛜; MRochor, Little India) A short walk south of Little India is this colonial-era hotel, in a shophouse redevelopment that now shoots up eight storeys. Rooms are classic and spacious, with carved wooden furniture, smallish but spotless bathrooms, and a choice of fan or air-con. Service is top notch and there's wi-fi throughout. You'll find the best deals online.

🛏 Orchard Road

★LLOYD'S INN   BOUTIQUE HOTEL $$
Map p216 (⏺6737 7309; www.lloydinn.com; 2 Lloyd Rd; r from S$180; ✳🛜; MSomerset) A short stroll from Orchard Rd is where you'll find this spread-out, minimalist boutique hotel. Eight types of rooms each engage with nature in different ways, and higher-end rooms have outdoor bathtubs. Guests can cool down in the dipping pool (not deep enough for a proper swim) or enjoy dusk on the rooftop terrace. It's insanely popular so book early.

The giant neighbourhood wall map in the lobby, paired with the downloadable walking guide, will have you navigating the streets like a local in no time.

RENDEZVOUS HOTEL   HOTEL $$
Map p216 (⏺6336 0220; www.stayfareast.com; 9 Bras Basah Rd; r from S$340; P✳@🛜; MBras Basah, Dhoby Ghaut) A good option near Orchard Rd, the Rendezvous features dramatic sculptures in its svelte lobby, a nod to its ambition to become an 'art hotel'. Admittedly, the beige-and-brown rooms aren't quite as sexy, although all are clean and comfortable, with firm mattresses and marble bathrooms with rain shower heads. Both the gym and pool are small, though the latter is nonetheless inviting.

The website offers good discounts, you can often book rooms for around S$250.

YORK HOTEL   HOTEL $$
Map p216 (⏺6737 0511; www.yorkhotel.com. sg; 21 Mount Elizabeth Rd; r from S$200; P✳@🛜; MOrchard) This big, bustling hotel comes with a gleaming lobby, sprawling restaurant and variations on white and beige. Rooms are pleasant and classically furnished, their smallish, clean bathrooms equipped with small bathtubs. Its selling point is the spaciousness of the rooms, and the proximity to Orchard Rd. Hotel facilities include a small gym, and a palm-fringed outdoor pool and Jacuzzi that screams 1980s resort.

★GOODWOOD
PARK HOTEL   HOTEL $$$
Map p216 (⏺6737 7411; www.goodwoodpark hotel.com; 22 Scotts Rd; r from S$360; P✳@🛜🚶; MOrchard) Dating back to 1900, this wonderful heritage hotel with gracious service feels like an elegant, old-world retreat: the kind of place you just want to hang out in, sinking into a plush sofa with a good book. Deluxe rooms in the main building are impressively spacious; rooms in the newer wing are renovated but smaller. There are two beautiful swimming pools.

ST REGIS   HOTEL $$$
Map p216 (⏺6506 6888; www.stregissingapore. com; 29 Tanglin Rd; d from S$520; P✳@🛜; MOrchard) One of the newer additions to Orchard Rd's five-star hotel scene, St Regis doesn't disappoint: from its striking facade to its classic, French-inspired decadence and impeccable service. Rooms are enormous, with lavish textiles, tasteful art and marble bathrooms with free-standing soaking tubs. Each room comes with 24-hour butler service to boot.

The in-house Remède Spa (p101) is one of the city's best, and the hotel also offers an indoor tennis court (for an additional fee).

QUINCY
BOUTIQUE HOTEL $$$

Map p216 (☑6738 5888; www.stayfareast. com; 22 Mount Elizabeth Rd; r from S$350; P❋@🛜🏊; MOrchard) Smart, slimline Quincy offers svelte, Armani-chic rooms, with light-grey walls and high ceilings with fetching back-lighting. TVs are flat, mattresses soft, and charcoal-tiled bathrooms stocked with fancy Le Labo Santal 33 toiletries. Minibars are complimentary, breakfast is included, as are the all-day light refreshments and evening cocktails; you might never want to leave. The glass-enclosed balcony pool is utterly inviting.

SINGAPORE MARRIOTT
HOTEL $$$

Map p216 (☑6735 5800; www.singapore marriott.com; 320 Orchard Rd; r from S$400; P❋@🛜🏊; MOrchard) A fabulously central location makes this a popular high-end choice. Rooms are stylish and well sized, with marble-topped writing desk, sofa and marble bathroom with spacious shower. Poolside rooms come with a terrace overlooking the hotel's gorgeous pool, though these can get noisy during the day.

Keep your eyes peeled for the Other Room (p100), a secret bar hidden behind a velvet curtain in the lobby.

HOTEL JEN TANGLIN
HOTEL $$$

Map p216 (☑6738 2222; www.hoteljen.com/ tanglin; 1A Cuscaden Rd; r from S$340; P❋@🛜🏊; MOrchard) Hipster chic underscores Jen's 565 rooms, from the sculptural furniture pieces and funky wallpaper to the mood lighting that makes the ridiculously comfortable beds appear to levitate. Club Rooms are small but cleverly designed (we love the bedside USB ports), while the much larger Deluxe Suites come with separate tub and shower. Other perks include pool, gym, spa and self-service laundry.

Check online for discounted rates, which can fall below S$300 per night.

SHANGRI-LA HOTEL
HOTEL $$$

Map p216 (☑6737 3644; www.shangri-la.com/ singapore; 22 Orange Grove Rd; r from S$550; P❋@🛜🏊; MOrchard) Announced by the most grand of lobbies, this vast, opulent hotel nestles in the leafy lanes surrounding the west end of Orchard Rd. Six hectares of tropical gardens set a lush, soothing mood, with the low-rise, bougainvillea-laced Garden Wing radiating an almost resort-like vibe. Rooms are spacious and elegant; those in the Tower Wing have just recently enjoyed a swanky refresh.

On-site highlights include a high-end spa and huge, curvaceous pool.

🛏 Eastern Singapore

VENUE HOTEL
HOTEL $

Map p214 (☑6346 3131; www.venuehotel.sg; 305 Joo Chiat Rd; r from $90; ❋@🛜; MPaya Lebar) Right in the heart of Joo Chiat (Katong), low-cost Venue makes a striking first impression with its dark, slinky, sculptural lobby. Rooms are small, simple and modern, with boldly coloured feature walls, contemporary bathrooms and a choice of standard or low-rise beds. Premium rooms come with a decadent soaking tub at the foot of the bed. There's no breakfast, pool or gym, but with rates like these, who's complaining?

BETEL BOX
HOSTEL $

Map p214 (☑6247 7340; www.betelbox.com; 200 Joo Chiat Rd; dm S$20-25, d S$80; @🛜; MPaya Lebar) Although somewhat cramped, Betel Box has its perks – among them, walking access to Joo Chiat's (Katong's) plethora of top local eateries and reasonably easy access to East Coast Park. The air-conditioned communal area features cheap beer, TV, video games, computers and a pool table, as well as a book-exchange and tons of travel guides. The hostel also hosts some fantastic cultural and eating tours (p31).

★HOTEL INDIGO
HOTEL $$

Map p214 (☑6723 7001; www.hotelindigo.com; 86 East Coast Rd; r from $240; P❋@🛜🏊; 🚌10, 14, 16, 32) If it's all in the detail, then this Peranakan-inspired hotel has nailed it. Taking inspiration from the traditional Singaporean neighbourhood that surrounds it, each nook and cranny is bursting with nostalgic memorabilia: from street scene murals to old-school sweets, Peranakan-inspired tiles to carrom-board coffee tables – the list is endless. Book a premier room with bathtub and enjoy your soak with a view.

Don't miss taking a dip in the 25m-long infinity pool with a panoramic vista of the Joo Chiat (Katong) and beyond.

VILLAGE HOTEL CHANGI HOTEL **$$**
Map p143 (☑6379 7111; www.stayfareast.com; 1 Netheravon Rd; r from $200; ✴@🛜🛗; 🖵29) With its free shuttle, this smart (if somewhat generic) hotel is a great choice if you want to be near Changi Airport. It's nestled among gorgeous gardens, with superb views across to Malaysia and Pulau Ubin from its beautiful rooftop pool. Close to the Changi Golf Course, the sailing club, beach park and gentle pace of Changi Village, it offers a chilled-out slice of Singapore life.

🛏 West & Southwest Singapore

VILLA SAMADHI BOUTIQUE HOTEL **$$$**
Map p220 (☑6274 5674; www.villasamadhi.com.sg; 20 Labrador Villa Rd; r from $380, villas from $920; 🅼Labrador Park) Hankering for a dose of old-world nostalgia and glamour? Villa Samadhi, housed in a tastefully restored former British officers' quarters, gives guests the ultimate colonial Singaporean experience. Surrounded by lush jungle, the hotel's lofty ceilings, teak furnishings, mood lighting and creaking floorboards add to the charm, but its the luxurious touches, including cocktail hour at Tamarind Hill (p132), that seal the deal.

Those wanting to take their nostalgic experience to the max should book the Luxe Sarang villa. In a separate building with private plunge pool, it's the epitome of colonial decadence.

🛏 Northern & Central Singapore

RAMADA SINGAPORE AT ZHONGSHAN PARK HOTEL **$$**
Map p205 (☑6808 6888; www.ramadasingapore.com; 16 Ah Hood Rd; r from S$180; 🅿✴@🛜🛗; 🅼Novena) This slick Ramada makes up for its slighty inconvenient location with great rates. In reality, it's well-serviced by buses and an easy 1km walk from Novena MRT station, from where Orchard Rd is two stops away. Rooms are simple yet sophisticated, with warm earthy hues, Singapore-themed artwork, comfortable beds and modern bathrooms. The light-filled gym features modern equipment and the pool is contemporary and stunning.

DAYS HOTEL SINGAPORE AT ZHONGSHAN PARK HOTEL **$$**
Map p205 (☑6808 6868; www.dayshotel singapore.com; 1 Jln Rajah; r from S$160; 🅿✴@🛜; 🅼Novena) This three-star hotel delivers small, comfortable rooms, each painted in bright, bold colours, with funky carpets, LED TVs and small but modern bathrooms. There's a small 24/7 gym, and communal areas that are sharp and of the moment. Buses on Balestier Rd offer easy access to Little India and the Colonial District, a complimentary shuttle runs to Novena MRT and Orchard Rd.

Check online for deals, which sometimes see room rates drop to around S$150 per night.

🛏 Sentosa Island

★W SINGAPORE – SENTOSA COVE HOTEL **$$$**
Map p222 (☑6808 7288; www.wsingapore sentosacove.com; 21 Ocean Way; r/ste from S$480/965; 🅿✴@🛜🛗; 🖵3) At one of Singapore's hottest slumber spots, rooms are playful, whimsical and spacious, with a choice of mood lighting, botanical motifs and good-size bathrooms. Of the 10 room categories, the spa-themed Away Rooms are especially fabulous, each with its own private plunge pool. The hotel's huge, 24-hour pool is one of Singapore's best, complete with wet bar and underwater speakers.

Extra perks include a state-of-the-art gym and a high-tech luxury spa. Get the best deals on rooms by booking a few months in advance via the website.

★CAPELLA SINGAPORE RESORT **$$$**
Map p222 (☑6377 8888; www.capellahotels.com/singapore; 1 The Knolls; r/villas from S$860/1270; 🅿✴@🛜🛗; 🖵Imbiah) Capella is one of Singapore's A-list slumber numbers,

MORE OPTIONS ON SENTOSA

The garish Resorts World complex (www.rwsentosa.com) on Sentosa Island has six hotels and suite complexes to choose from. They're handy to fall back on if accommodation elsewhere on the island is full.

STUCK AT THE AIRPORT

If you're only in Singapore for a short time or have a long wait between connections, try the **Ambassador Transit Hotel** (Map p213; ☑Terminal 2 6542 8122, Terminal 3 6507 9788; www.harilelahospitality.com; Terminal 2 & 3 Departures, Changi Airport; s/d/tr S$90/110/135; ❄ @ 🛜; Ⓜ Changi Airport). Rates are for the first six hours and each additional hour block thereafter is around S$20; rooms don't have windows and there are budget singles (S$55, each subsequent hour S$20) with shared bathrooms. Both branches offer gym access for an extra S$28 charge.

The only swish option at Changi Airport is the **Crowne Plaza** (Map p213; ☑6823 5300; www.ihg.com; 75 Airport Blvd; r from S$300; ❄ @ 🛜 ☒; Ⓜ Changi Airport). It's a svelte, business-oriented place with an in-house spa and lush, palm-studded pool. A skybridge connects the hotel to Terminal 3, with Terminals 1 and 2 accessible by SkyTrain. Unfortunately, the lack of competition means hiked-up prices; always check online for deals.

a seductive melange of colonial and contemporary architecture, an elegant spa, restaurants, a bar and three cascading swimming pools in lush, landscaped gardens. The beautifully appointed rooms are spacious and chic, with king-size beds, earthy, subdued hues, and striking contemporary bathrooms. The villas are even more decadent: each has its own private plunge pool.

And, as you'd expect from Sentosa's star resort, service is stellar. See the website for special deals and packages.

SHANGRI-LA'S RASA
SENTOSA RESORT & SPA   RESORT $$$

Map p222 (☑6275 0100; www.shangri-la.com; 101 Siloso Rd; r from S$450; Ⓟ ❄ @ 🛜 ☒; 🚌Beach) Singapore's only true beachfront resort is ideal for a short family break. Rooms are light, chic and tropical, in calming hues of cream and pistachio green. Service is top notch, and the huge kid-friendly pool area, which has children's water slides and leads down towards Siloso Beach, is extremely inviting.

The resort has no fewer than five restaurants, and the free shuttle bus into central Singapore is especially handy.

Understand Singapore

History

Having celebrated 50 years of independence in 2015, the Lion City is the quintessential success story. In less than an average human lifespan, Asia's Little Red Dot has metamorphosed from a dusty, developing nation into one of the world's most stable, safe and prosperous countries. The story of Singapore is one of vision, planning and unrelenting determination.

Precolonial Singapore

In 1703 English trader Andrew Hamilton described the island as a place where 'the soil is black and fat, and the woods abound in good masts for shipping, and timber for building'. The Sultan of Johor, Abdu'l Jajlil Ri'ayat Shah, had offered Hamilton the island, but he refused.

Pretty much every museum you'll see in Singapore is devoted to post-colonial history, simply because there is not a great deal of undisputed pre-colonial history. Malay legend has it that long ago a Sumatran prince visiting the island of Temasek saw a strange animal he believed to be a lion. The good omen prompted the prince to found a city on the spot of the sighting. He called it Singapura (Lion City).

Chinese traders en route to India had plied the waters around what is now Singapore from at least the 5th century CE, though the records of Chinese sailors as early as the 3rd century refer to an island called Pu Luo Chung, which may have been Singapore, while others claim there was a settlement in the 2nd century.

Between the 7th and 10th centuries, Srivijaya, a seafaring Buddhist kingdom centred on Palembang in Sumatra, held sway over the Strait of Malacca (now Melaka). Raids by rival kingdoms and the arrival of Islam brought the eclipse of Srivijaya by the 13th century. Based mainly on the thriving pirate trade, the sultanate of Melaka quickly acquired the commercial power that was once wielded by Srivijaya.

The Portuguese took Melaka in 1511, sparking off a wave of colonialism. The Dutch founded Batavia (now Jakarta) to undermine Melaka's position, finally wresting the city from their European competitors in 1641. In the late 18th century the British began looking for a harbour in the Strait of Melaka to secure lines of trade between China, the Malay world and their own interests in India. Renewed war in Europe led, in 1795, to the French annexation of Holland, which prompted the British to seize Dutch possessions in Southeast Asia, including Melaka.

TIMELINE	CE 300	1200s	1390s
	Chinese seafarers mark the island on maps, labelling it Pu Luo Chung, believed to have come from the Malay name Pulau Ujong, meaning 'island at the end'.	A Sumatran Srivijayan prince founds a settlement on the island and calls it Singapura (Lion City), having reputedly seen a lion there. Later named Temasek (Sea Town).	Srivijayan prince Parameswara flees Sumatra to Temasek after being deposed. He later founds the Sultanate of Malacca, under which Temasek is an important trading post.

After the end of the Napoleonic Wars, the British agreed to restore Dutch possessions in 1818, but there were those who were bitterly disappointed at the failure of the dream of British imperial expansion in Southeast Asia. One such figure was Sir Stamford Raffles, lieutenant-governor of Java.

The Raffles Era

For someone who spent a limited amount of time in Singapore, Sir Stamford Raffles had an extraordinary influence on its development. His name appears everywhere in the modern city – Raffles Pl in the CBD, Stamford Rd, Raffles Hotel, the Raffles City shopping mall, the prestigious Raffles Institution (where Lee Kuan Yew went to school) – but his impact extends far beyond civic commemoration.

The streets you walk along in the city centre still largely follow the original plans Raffles drew. The ethnic districts still evident today, particularly in the case of Little India, were demarcated by him. Even the classic shophouse design has been attributed to him. More importantly, Singapore's very existence as one of the world's great ports is a direct consequence of Raffles' vision of creating a British-controlled entrepôt to counter Dutch power in the region.

When Raffles landed at Singapore in early 1819, the empire of Johor was divided. When the old sultan had died in 1812, his younger son's accession to power had been engineered while an elder son, Hussein, was away. The Dutch had a treaty with the young sultan, but Raffles threw his support behind Hussein, proclaiming him sultan and installing him in residence in Singapore.

In Raffles' plans the sultan wielded no actual power but did serve to legitimise British claims on the island. Raffles also signed a treaty with the more eminent *temenggong* (senior judge) of Johor and set him up with an estate on the Singapore River. Thus, Raffles acquired the use of Singapore in exchange for modest annual allowances to Sultan Hussein and the *temenggong*. This exchange ended with a cash buyouts in 1824 and the transfer of Singapore's ownership to Britain's East India Company.

Along with Penang and Melaka, Singapore formed a triumvirate of powerful trading stations known as the Straits Settlements, which were controlled by the East India Company in Calcutta but administered from Singapore.

Raffles had hit upon the idea of turning a sparsely populated, tiger-infested malarial swamp with few natural resources into an economic powerhouse by luring in the ambitious and allowing them to unleash their entrepreneurial zeal. While it was to be many decades before Singapore's somewhat anarchic social conditions were brought under control, the essential Rafflesian spirit still underpins the city's drive to succeed.

1613	1823	1826	1867
Portuguese attack the town on the island and burn it to the ground. Singapura never regains its former importance while the Portuguese rule Malacca, and it slides into obscurity.	Raffles signs a treaty with the Sultan and *temenggong* (senior judge) hand control of most of the island to the British. Raffles returns to Britain and never sees Singapore again.	Penang, Melaka and Singapore combine to form the Straits Settlements. Large waves of immigration wash over Singapore's free ports as merchants seek to avoid Dutch tariffs.	Discontent at ineffectual administration persuades the British to declare the Straits Settlements a separate crown colony, no longer run from India.

Colonisation & Occupation

Singapore Under the British

Raffles' first and second visits to Singapore in 1819 were brief and he left instructions and operational authority with Colonel William Farquhar, former Resident (the chief British representative) in Melaka. When Raffles returned three years later, he found the colony thriving but chaotic.

It was then that he drew up his town plan, which remains today, levelling one hill to form a new commercial district (now Raffles Pl) and erecting government buildings around another prominence called Forbidden Hill (now called Fort Canning Hill).

His plan also embraced the colonial practice, still in evidence, of administering the population according to neat racial categories. The city's trades, races and dialect groups were divided into zones: Europeans were granted land to the northeast of the government offices (today's Colonial District), though many soon moved out to sequestered garden estates in the western suburbs. The Chinese predominated around the mouth and the area southwest of the Singapore River, though many Indians lived there too (hence the large Hindu temple on South Bridge Rd). Hindu Indians were, and still are, largely resident in Kampong Kapor and Serangoon Rd; Gujarati and other Muslim merchants were housed in the Arab St area; Tamil Muslim traders and small businesses operated in the Market St area; and the Malay population mainly lived on the swampy northern fringes of the city. In time, of course, these zones became less well defined, as people decanted into other parts of the island.

Despite its wealth, the colony was a dissolute place, beset by crime, clan violence, appalling sanitation, opium addiction, rats, mosquitoes and tigers. Life for the majority was extremely harsh; the Chinatown Heritage Centre is probably the best place to appreciate just how harsh.

Raffles sought to cooperate with the various *kongsi* – clan organisations for mutual assistance, known variously as secret societies, triads and heaven-man-earth societies. (Many of them had their headquarters on Club St, and a couple still hold out against the area's rapid gentrification.) Labour and dialect-based *kongsi* would become increasingly important to Singapore's success in the 19th century, as overseas demand for Chinese-harvested products such as pepper, tin and rubber – all routed through Singapore from the Malay peninsula – grew enormously. Singapore's access to *kongsi*-based economies in the region, however, depended largely on revenues from an East India Company product that came from India and was bound for China – opium.

Farquhar had established Singapore's first opium farm for domestic consumption, and by the 1830s excise and sales revenues of opium accounted for nearly half the administration's income, a situation that continued for a century after Raffles' arrival.

Colonel William Farquhar was Singapore's first official resident and a keen naturalist. He commissioned local Chinese artists to paint a series of 477 startlingly vibrant images of local flora and fauna.

1939	1942	1942–45	1945–59
Britain completes a huge naval base for around $500 million, boasting the world's largest dry dock and enough fuel to run the British Navy for months. Dubbed 'Fortress Singapore'.	Fortress Singapore is cruelly exposed when incomplete preparations for a northern invasion mean Japanese forces overrun the island. Allies surrender on 15 February.	Singapore is renamed Syonan by the Japanese. Chinese are massacred, Allied prisoners are incarcerated at Changi or shipped off to the Death Railway. Economy collapses.	British resume control. Straits Settlements is wound up in 1946. Until 1955 Singapore is run by part-elected legislative councils, then a semi-autonomous government.

In the 19th century, women were rarely permitted to leave China. Thus, Chinese men who headed for the Straits Settlements often married local women, eventually spawning a new, hybrid culture now known in Singapore as Peranakan.

Despite a massive fall in rubber prices in 1920, prosperity continued, immigration soared and millionaires were made almost overnight. In the 1930s and early '40s, politics dominated the intellectual scene. Indians looked to the subcontinent for signs of the end of colonial rule, while Kuomintang (Nationalist) and Communist Party struggles in the disintegrating Republic of China attracted passionate attention. Opposition to Japan's 1931 and 1937 invasions of China was near universal in Singapore.

Singapore Under the Japanese

When General Yamashita Tomoyuki pushed his thinly stretched army into Singapore on 15 February 1942, it began a period Singapore regards as the blackest of its history. For the British, who had set up a naval base near the city in the 1920s, surrender was sudden and humiliating – and some historians have pinpointed the fall of Singapore as the moment when the myth of British impregnability was blown apart and the empire began its final decline.

The impact of the Japanese occupation on the collective political and social memory of Singapore cannot be underestimated, and it has partly inspired Singapore's modern preoccupation with security. Japanese rule was harsh. Yamashita had the Europeans and Allied POWs herded onto the Padang, from there they were marched away for internment. Many of them were taken to the infamous Changi prison, while others were herded up to Siam (Thailand) to work on the horrific Death Railway.

The Japanese also launched Operation Sook Ching to eliminate Chinese opposition. Chinese Singaporeans were driven out of their homes, 'screened', then either given a 'chop' (a mark on the forehead meaning they had been cleared for release) or driven away to be imprisoned or executed (there's a memorial to one massacre at Changi Beach). Estimates of the number of Chinese killed vary – some sources put the number at 6000, others at more than 45,000.

The Japanese renamed the island 'Syonan' (Light of the South), changed signs into Japanese, put clocks forward to Tokyo time and introduced a Japanese currency (known by contemptuous locals as 'banana money').

The war ended suddenly with Japan's surrender on 14 August 1945, and Singapore was passed back into British control. While the returning British troops were welcomed, the occupation had eroded the innate trust in the empire's protective embrace. New political forces were at work and the road to independence was paved.

In WWII the British expected the Japanese to attack Singapore south from the sea. Instead they blitzed Singapore from the north, coming from Malaysia on foot and bicycle.

HISTORY COLONISATION & OCCUPATION

WWII Sites
....
Fort Siloso (Sentosa Island)
....
Battlebox (Colonial District)
....
Images of Singapore (Sentosa Island)
....
Reflections at Bukit Chandu (Southwest Singapore)
....
Former Ford Factory (Central Singapore)
....
Kranji War Memorial (West Singapore)
....

1959	1963	1965	1971
First full legislative elections held. People's Action Party (PAP), led by Lee Kuan Yew, wins. Aggressive economic development and social programs are launched.	After strong campaigning from Lee Kuan Yew, Singapore joins Sabah and Sarawak in combining with Malaya to form the single state of Malaysia.	Singapore is expelled from federation after unanimous vote in the Malaysian Parliament in Kuala Lumpur. Lee Kuan Yew cries as he announces the news. The Republic of Singapore is born.	British forces withdraw, sparking economic crisis. PAP mounts an election to win a mandate for tough laws curbing unions, luring foreign investment.

The Lee Dynasty

If one person can be considered responsible for the position Singapore finds itself in today, it is Lee Kuan Yew.

Born in 1923, this third-generation Straits-born Chinese was named Harry Lee, and brought up to be, in his own words, 'the equal of any Englishman'. His education at the Raffles Institution and Cambridge University equipped him well to deal with both colonial power and political opposition when Singapore took control of its own destiny in the 1960s.

The early years were not easy. Race riots in 1964 and ejection from the Malay Federation in 1965 made Lee's task even harder. Lee used tax incentives and strict new labour laws to attract foreign investment. This, combined with huge resources poured into developing an English-language education system that churned out a competent workforce, saw Singapore's economy rapidly industrialise.

Under Lee's rigidly paternal control, his People's Action Party (PAP) also set about eliminating any viable political opposition, banning critical publications and moulding the city into a disciplined, functional society built along Confucian ideals, which value the maintenance of hierarchy and social order above all things.

Lee's rapid industrialisation filled government coffers and enabled the PAP to pursue massive infrastructure, defence, health, education, pension and housing schemes, giving Singaporeans a level of prosperity and security that remains the envy of many countries in the region and around the world. Housing and urban renovation, in particular, have been key to the PAP's success. By the mid-1990s, Singapore had achieved the world's highest rate of home ownership.

Despite resigning as prime minister in 1990 after 31 years in the job, and handing over to the more avuncular but no less determined Goh Chok Tong, Lee still kept an eye on proceedings and his comments on various issues frequently flag future government policy.

Lee Kuan Yew passed away at the Singapore General Hospital on 23 March 2015, after being admitted the previous month for severe pneumonia. A week-long period of national mourning was declared. Lee lay in state at Parliament House for four days to allow Singaporeans to pay their respects. The queues were so long that the opening hours were extended to round-the-clock, and wait times stretched to eight hours. Over 445,000 filed past Mr Lee, and 100,000 lined the streets in the pouring rain on the way to his funeral service.

Lee Kuan Yew famously cried on national television in 1965 after Singapore separated from Malaysia. The event (separation, not the tears) marked the birth of modern Singapore.

Recent Past & Impending Future

Lee Kuan Yew's son, Lee Hsien Loong, who was deputy Prime Minister and Defence Minister under Goh Chok Tong, took over the top job unopposed in 2004.

1975	1981	1990	2004
Singapore becomes world's third-busiest port and third-largest oil refiner, as well as a rig- and drilling-platform manufacturer and a huge oil-storage centre.	Changi Airport opens, replacing Paya Lebar, handling eight million passengers in its first year. By 2013 passenger traffic hits 53.7 million and Changi is named the world's best airport.	Lee Kuan Yew steps down as Prime Minister, handing over the reins to Goh Chok Tong. Lee becomes Senior Minister and retains oversight of government policy.	Prime Minister Goh Chok Tong steps down, and is replaced by Lee Kuan Yew's son, Lee Hsien Loong, who builds two casinos, reversing decades of government policy on casino gambling.

The challenges he has faced to date have been as great as those faced by his father, among them the Asian financial crisis starting in 1997, the SARS outbreak in 2003 and the global financial crisis of 2007, all of which had a major impact on the country's economy and its sense of vulnerability to forces beyond its control. These factors, coupled with migration of its manufacturing base to cheaper competitors such as Vietnam and China, have forced the government to embark on a radical makeover of the country in an attempt to ensure its success extends into the future.

Challenges have also presented themselves in the form of growing opposition to the ruling PAP. While the party won the expected majority in a landslide victory in 2006, its actual votes fell by 8.69%.

In the lead-up to the 2011 election, the political landscape reflected the expected appetite for change. The election had the highest proportion of contested seats (94.3%) since Singapore achieved its independence in 1965. Local media, often accused of being mouthpieces of the government, appeared to give more even coverage to the PAP and opposition parties. Social media, once banned in campaigning, played a huge part in the dissemination of information. Even Prime Minister Lee Hsien Loong participated in an online chat (his first). Attendances at opposition rallies were off the charts.

The election results were telling. The PAP lost a further 6.46% of the electorate, winning 60.14% of the votes and 81 out of 87 seats. The biggest gains went to the Workers' Party, with a political agenda that focused on the everyday concerns of Singaporeans, from wages, the cost of living and healthcare, to housing affordability, public transport and the disproportionately high salaries of ministers. The election would prove to be a sobering wake-up call for the PAP. Post-election, a review of ministerial salaries was immediately mooted, and Senior Minister Goh Chok Tong and Minister Mentor Lee Kuan Yew both tendered their resignations.

The 2015 elections were the most fiercely contested yet; for the first time in history the opposition parties contested every seat. Hot topics included the failing economy, overcrowded and 'worsening' public transport, the high cost of living and immigration issues. Mr Lee called the election a year early, possibly in the hope of capitalising on the national pride stirred up during the nation's 50th birthday celebrations. This also coincided with the death of Singapore's founding father, and Mr Lee's own father, Lee Kuan Yew, in March. The election was a landslide win for the PAP, who gained 70% of the votes. The following 2020 general elections were held amid the COVID-19 pandemic and saw the opposition party take out 10 of the 93 parliament seats – the highest number since elections began in 1965. With vote share dropping to just a smidge above 61%, Mr Lee now has until 2025 to deal with the nation's concerns before the ballot boxes open again.

Singapore's first national campaign was launched in August 1958, shortly after the People's Action Party (PAP) took power in the city council elections. The campaign aimed to curb spitting in public, a prevalent social habit at the time.

'Majulah Singapura' (Onward Singapore) is Singapore's national anthem. Its lyrics entirely in Bahasa Malay, the anthem was created in 1958 by Indonesian-born composer Zubir Said, who took a year to complete the music and lyrics.

2011	2015	2017	2020
Watershed general election results see the ruling PAP party face its worst result ever, winning 60.14% of the vote, down 6.46% from 2006.	In March, Lee Kuan Yew, Singapore's founding Prime Minister, dies at the age of 91, throwing Singapore into a one-week period of mourning.	The country's first female president, Halimah Yacob, is elected as the eighth President of Singapore.	Singapore hawker culture is added to the Unesco Representative List of the Intangible Cultural Heritage of Humanity.

Singapore's Melting Pot

Singapore is the ultimate melting pot. With no less than four official languages, it's a place where mosques sidle up to Hindu and Taoist temples, where European chefs experiment with Chinese spices, and where local English is peppered with Hokkien, Tamil and Malay words. Since Sir Stamford Raffles set up a free trading port on the island in 1819, the Little Red Dot has been defined and redefined by its wave of migrants, from early Chinese workers to modern-day expats seeking their corporate fortunes.

Chinese

With the majority of the literate population being bilingual, English and Mandarin are the most commonly used languages in daily life. English is the main language taught in schools, but children also learn the language of their parentage to ensure they stay in touch with their traditional roots.

A scarcity of farmland, as well as political and social unrest, drove many mainland Chinese to seek their fortunes elsewhere in the 19th century, including Raffles' fledgling settlement. By 1840, 50% of Singapore's population was Chinese, made up mainly of Hokkien, Teochew, Hainanese, Cantonese and Hakka Chinese from China's southeast provinces.

Raffles' demarcation of Chinatown based on ethnic lines merely reinforced the segregation of these different dialect groups, and each would become known for a particular set of skills in the colony. The Hokkien and Teochew were commonly associated with trade and agriculture, the Cantonese and Hakka with handicrafts and construction, and the Hainanese with cooking. That Hainanese chicken rice is Singapore's best-loved dish is a lasting legacy of this culinary reputation.

While Chinese dialects are still widely spoken in the Lion City, especially among older Chinese, the government's long-standing campaign to promote Mandarin, the main nondialectal Chinese language, has been very successful and an increasing number of Singaporean Chinese now speak it at home.

Since 1921, Chinese have made up around three-quarters of the island's headcount, and their influence on Singaporean culture is dominant, from the influence of feng shui in the design of buildings such as Marina Bay Sands and Suntec City, to the Confucian principles underlying Singapore's paternalist system of government, a formula of benevolent sovereign and respectful subjects.

Malays

They may only count for 13% of the population, but the Malays – the island's original inhabitants – are Singapore's second-biggest ethnic group. From Singapore's national anthem, to the name of Singaporean streets, neighbourhoods, reserves and islands, Malay culture has played a significant role in defining the modern nation.

While the majority of Malay Singaporeans originate from the Malay peninsula, the community is heterogeneous, with others tracing their roots back to the Riau Islands, Java, Sumatra and Sulawesi. A small number are the descendants of mixed marriages between local Malay women and Arab or Indian Muslim men, the latter migrating to Singapore in the late 19th and 20th centuries.

Language and faith unify Malay Singaporeans. Most are practicing Sunni Muslims, a fact made evident by the number of bustling mosques in Malay enclaves such as Geylang Serai, not to mention the popularity of the *tudung* (head scarf) or the traditional *baju kurung* (a long-sleeved tunic worn over a sarong) among Malay-Singaporean women.

The community's historic heart is Kampong Glam, a district still packed with halal eateries serving Malay classics such as *nasi lemak* (a coconut rice dish) and *asam laksa* (a sour, spicy fish noodle dish), meals that also define the greater Singaporean food repertoire. It's here that you'll also find the Malay Cultural Centre and iconic Sultan Mosque.

Despite its cultural influence, this minority has faced challenges over the years, including an over-representation at the lower end of the educational scale, negative stereotypes in the employment sector and under-representation in senior government, military and judicial positions.

Peranakans

In Singapore, Peranakan (locally born) people are descendants of immigrants who married local women who were mostly of Malay origin. The result of hundreds of years of immersion and the meeting of foreign and local customs has resulted in an intriguing hybrid culture that's recently experienced a revival.

It's acknowledged that the Peranakan fall into three broad categories: the Chitty Melaka and Jawi Peranakan are descended from early migrants from India, while the Straits Chinese Peranakan are of mainland Chinese origin. No matter which group, there's a fierce sense of roots and traditions within.

In Singapore, the largest group is the Straits Chinese, a reflection of the population breakdown at large. The term 'Straits Chinese' originated within communities in the former colonial Straits Settlements of Singapore, Penang and Melaka.

These days, Chinese and Peranakan culture tend to overlap and it's sometimes hard to distinguish between the two. Peranakan men, called Babas, and the women, Nonya, primarily speak a patois that mixes Bahasa Malay, Hokkien dialect and English, though that's changed over

A traditional Peranakan wedding is an elaborate 12-day affair, heavily steeped in Chinese traditions from the Fujian province in China, mixed with some Malay customs. These days, such elaborate affairs are few and far between, though they have made a comeback, albeit in a severely truncated one-day form.

EXPATS

Nonpermanent residents make up just under 30% of Singapore's population of 5.6 million residents, up from around 25% in 2000.

While many are low-paid construction and service-industry workers from China and South and Southeast Asia, a huge number are highly skilled professionals working in areas as diverse as finance, oil and gas, IT, biomedical science and academia, as well as tourism and hospitality. Indeed, one in four skilled workers in Singapore is foreign.

There are over 40,000 British nationals in Singapore alone, with other large communities including Australians, Americans, French and Japanese. Popular expat neighbourhoods include Orchard, Tanglin, Novena, Holland Village, Bukit Timah and the east coast.

It's a thriving, vibrant scene, with no shortage of social and sporting clubs, international schools and expat magazines and websites. For many, Singapore's appeal is obvious: low crime, lower taxes, world-class healthcare and education, affordable domestic help and superlative international connections. Increasingly less appealing, however, is the soaring cost of living, made worse by the increasing number of companies moving away from all-inclusive expat packages to less-lucrative local contracts.

time, along with the education system in Singapore. Most of the current Peranakans speak English and Mandarin. Visually, Peranakan are indistinguishable from people of Han Chinese descent, but traditional families still cling to their customs and traditions and are proud of their heritage, evocatively showcased at both Singapore's Peranakan Museum and Baba House.

Must Read

A Peranakan Legacy: The Heritage of the Straits Chinese (Peter Wee)

The Shrimp People (Rex Shelley)

Kebaya Tales: Of Matriarchs, Maidens, Mistresses and Matchmakers (Lee Su Kim)

Indians

At just under 10% of the population, Indians are the third-largest ethnic group in Singapore. It might be a relatively small group in Singapore, but it's one of the biggest outside India, and its fidelity to the motherland's customs and traditions shines through in Little India's street life and the fervent celebration of Hindu festivals such as Thaipusam and Deepavali.

A number of Indians worked as *sepoys* (soldiers) for the British army, and Indian convict labour played a vital role in the early settlement's development, clearing jungle, filling swamps and constructing buildings that included St Andrew's Cathedral, the Istana palace and Sri Mariamman Temple. Upon completing their sentences, many stayed on in Singapore, finding work as labourers or setting up small businesses. Some became *dhobis* (laundrymen), a fact echoed in the name of Dhoby Ghaut MRT station. Many South Indians became well known as *chettiars* (moneylenders).

More than half of today's Indian Singaporeans are Tamils, hailing from the area now known as Tamil Nadu, a corner of South India where Hindu traditions are strong. The remainder are mainly Muslim or Christian, with a minority of Sikhs, Jains, Buddhists and Zoroastrians. While a small, English-educated Indian elite has always played a prominent role in Singaporean society, a large percentage of the community remains working class.

Eurasians

If you meet a Singaporean whose surname is Clarke, de Souza or Hendricks, chances are they are Eurasian, a term used to describe people of mixed Asian and European descent. In the early colonial days, the majority of Eurasian migrants arrived from the Malaysian trading port of Malacca (Melaka), which alongside Goa, Macau and Ceylon (modern Sri Lanka) claimed notable mixed-race communities, a legacy of Portuguese, Dutch and British colonisers marrying local women.

Each Housing Development Board (HDB) public-housing complex is subject to ethnic-based quotas that accurately reflect Singapore's own demographic mix. These quotas are in place to help prevent the formation of 'ethnic enclaves'.

Shared Christian beliefs and shared cultural traditions created a firm bond between Singapore's British ruling class and the island's Eurasian community, and many Eurasians enjoyed privileged posts in the civil service. The bond would erode after the opening of the Suez Canal, when an increase in European arrivals saw the 'half Europeans' sidelined. Ironically, Eurasians suffered great persecution during Singapore's Japanese occupation in WWII, in which they were branded 'British sympathisers'.

These days, Singapore is home to around 15,000 Eurasians, and the group features prominently in the media and entertainment industries. The Eurasians' mixed-race appearance is especially appealing to advertisers, who see it as conveniently encompassing Singapore's multiracial make-up. The majority of modern Singaporean Eurasians are of British descent, with English as their first language.

Architectural Wonders

Singapore is an architectural chocolate box, its assortment of treats ranging from sugar-white colonial churches and Technicolor shophouses to gobsmacking contemporary icons. Despite the wrecking-ball rampage of the 1960s and '70s, the island nation managed to retain significant swaths of heritage buildings, and their contrast against an ever-evolving skyline is delicious and dramatic.

Colonial

Not long after the East India Company set up its trading port at the mouth of the Singapore River, migrants from across Asia began leaving their architectural mark. The Chinese built seaside temples such as Thian Hock Keng Temple (p72), Indian Hindus added colour with the likes of Sri Mariamman Temple (p73), and Chulia Muslims from India's south erected shrines such as Nagore Durgha. For the most part, these early structures faithfully reflected the architectural styles of each group's homeland.

Distant influences also underscored the work of the European colonisers. Irishman George Drumgoole Coleman – considered Singapore's pre-eminent colonial architect – found inspiration in the classical aesthetics of the Palladian style developed by 16th-century Italian architect Andrea Palladio. Coleman was a skilful adapter of the style, seamlessly pairing its proclivity for Doric columns, porticoes and rotundas with wide verandahs and overhanging eaves better suited to Singapore's tropical climate. The Colonial District is home to many of his works, among them Caldwell House in Chijmes and Old Parliament House (p59). His finest creation is arguably the Armenian Church (p59), modelled after St Gregory's Church in Echmiadzin, the mother church in northern Armenia.

Coleman, who became Singapore's town surveyor and superintendent of public works in 1826, set a fine example for other colonial architects. Among these were Brother Lothaire and Father Charles Benedict Nain, who together designed the elegant St Joseph's Institution, now better known as the Singapore Art Museum (p57). Nain would go on to design the chapel at Chijimes, a sublimely elegant, Anglo-French Gothic affair.

As Singapore's wealth and importance increased during the 19th century, so did the grandeur of its buildings. Some of the finest are the work of Major John Frederick Adolphus McNair, among them the Empress Place Building, home to the Asian Civilisations Museum (p50), and Singapore's former Government House, Istana (p97), just off Orchard Rd. The popularity of all things classical held sway well into the first few decades of the 20th century, a fact reflected in buildings such as the Fullerton Hotel (p157) and the old Supreme Court, the latter being the last example of British colonial architecture in Singapore. City Hall and the old Supreme Court building reopened in 2015 as the National Gallery Singapore (p52), the sombre-looking buildings now connected by a striking yet harmonious glass-and-steel roof structure. The structure and gallery are the work of France's Studio Milou Architecture and Singapore's CPG Consultants.

Shophouses

Before Housing Development Board (HDB) flats, the definitive Singaporean building was the shophouse. Its long, narrow design was also a distinctive feature of other port cities such as Penang and Melaka.

Shophouses were designed to have a shop or business on the lower floor and accommodation upstairs. Often projecting over the footpath is a solid canopy, known as a five-foot way. The canopy was in use in southern China and parts of Southeast Asia and was mandated by Sir Stamford Raffles in 1822, when in a set of ordinances he stated that 'all houses constructed of brick or tiles have a common type of front each having an arcade of a certain depth open to all sides as a continuous and open passage'.

A considerate Raffles wanted to ensure pedestrians were protected from the sun and rain. But shopkeepers had other ideas and before long they all became extensions of the shops inside. Most five-foot ways are now clear of commerce, but walk along Buffalo Rd in Little India, or the northern end of Telok Ayer St in Chinatown, and you'll get an idea of how difficult it became for pedestrians to negotiate these passageways.

The load-bearing walls separating the buildings are heavy masonry, which was a departure from the traditional timber, and not only provided strength and privacy from neighbours, but also deterred the spread of fire.

The first shophouses dating from 1840 are plain, squat, two-storey buildings. These Early shophouses, in the vernacular, were followed by First Transitional, Late, Second Transitional and art deco style. Classical elements such as columns are often used on the facades, along with beautiful tiles and bright paint – the Chinese, Peranakans and Malays all favoured lively colours. Some of the finest surviving examples grace Koon Seng Rd and Joo Chiat Pl in Katong, as well as Pertain Rd (between Jalan Besar and Sturdee Rd) near Little India.

Shophouses typically featured a central courtyard, which was often open to the sky, allowing natural light to penetrate the building and, in the early days, acting as a useful water-collection method (the courtyards usually had open cisterns). In some designs, a high rear wall acted as a kind of wind deflector, diverting breezes downwards and channelling them through the house.

A peculiarly Singaporean variation was the 'chophouse' – recreated examples of which can be seen at the Chinatown Heritage Centre (p71). Built to the same basic design as the shophouse, they were constructed to hold many dozens, sometimes hundreds of residents. Floors were divided into tiny, dark, miserable cubicles and the high concentration of people meant conditions were squalid in the extreme. A few chophouses remain in Little India, along Desker Rd for example, but most of them have been torn down.

Housing Development Board Flats

Only in Singapore could you walk safely through a tower-block estate at night and find a drink vending machine full, working and unvandalised. While public high-rise housing estates are being torn down elsewhere, in Singapore they work. They have to: land is limited, so the government had little choice but to build upwards. The state-run Housing Development Board (HDB) is locked into a mammoth construction project, erecting areas of well-built, well-maintained and affordable housing. So far, it's built over a million units.

HDB 'towns' such as Toa Payoh, Pasir Ris and Tampines provide homes for around 85% of the population. HDB developments have markets, schools, playgrounds, shops and hawker centres incorporated into

The term 'shophouse' is a literal translation from Chinese ('tiam chu' in Hokkien, 'dian wu' in Mandarin). The most decorative of the various styles is the 'Late' shophouse style, in which even the wall space is commonly cut back by the presence of richly decorated windows, pilasters and other detailing.

Feng shui influences the design of many buildings in Singapore, including Suntec City. Its five office towers symbolise the fingers of a left hand, including one squat tower as the thumb. In the hand lies the Fountain of Wealth, its water flowing downwards into the complex, accumulating positive *qi* (energy) and prosperity.

them. The older ones (from the 1960s and '70s) have mature trees keeping them shady and (relatively) attractive. Many blocks also have 'void decks', empty areas on the ground floor that allow a breeze to circulate, and where elderly men play chess in the shade.

Singapore's most striking HDB complex is the mammoth Pinnacle@Duxton (p73), completed in 2009. Located on the corner of Cantonment Rd and Neil St, just south of Chinatown, the project consists of seven 50-storey apartment towers connected by two levels of sky bridges housing gardens and a jogging track. Height and scale aside, the complex is unique in that it offered residents an unprecedented choice of exterior facade treatments, from planter boxes to bay windows and balconies. The result is a highly differentiated facade that is one of modern Singapore's most eclectic.

The HDB has a continuous renovation and upgrading program, even though the majority of the flats are privately owned, making them perhaps unique among the world's public housing projects. Every few years, they get licks of paint and new features added.

The MRT system makes it simple to visit the HDB heartlands. Just jump on a train and pop up somewhere like Toa Payoh. You won't see stunning architecture, but you will get a glimpse of what life is like for most Singaporeans.

One of Singapore's most eclectic buildings is the granite-clad Parkview Square (2002) at 600 North Bridge Rd. Designed by American James Adam and local firm DP Architects, it's known as the 'Gotham Building' for its over-the-top art deco–inspired motifs and ornamentation. Inside you'll find Atlas (p92), the swanky art deco champagne and gin bar.

Modern & Contemporary

The Pinnacle@Duxton (p73) is one of an ever-growing number of bold architectural statements, many of them designed by world-renowned architects. Among the earliest and most iconic is the 52-level OCBC Centre in the central business district (CBD). Designed by Chinese-American IM Pei and completed in 1976, it's a striking brutalist statement, its curved concrete core embedded with three panels of windows. The windows' keypad-like appearance and the building's slimline profile are behind its local nickname, 'the calculator'.

Israeli-Canadian Moshe Safdie, best known for his modular housing complex Habitat 67 in Montreal, is the creative force behind Marina Bay Sands (p55), an integrated resort fronting Marina Bay. Completed in 2010, its three-tower hotel, topped by a curved, 340m-long cantilever, has arguably become Singapore's most internationally recognisable building. Safdie is also the powerhouse behind Jewel, a S$1.7-billion multi-dimensional lifestyle destination connected to Changi Airport. The five-storey domed shell is constructed with over 9600 pieces of glass, and tapers in the centre to form the mouth of a jaw-dropping 40m waterfall surrounded by a mythical garden.

Marina Bay, itself a functioning reservoir, is home to several outstanding examples of contemporary design. At its northern end is Esplanade – Theatres on the Bay (p66), designed by Singapore's DP Architects and London-based Michael Wilford and Partners. The complex is most famous for the aluminium sunshades that clad its bulbous theatre and concert hall buildings. Their appearance has led to comparisons with durians and the eyes of flies. Behind Marina Bay Sands are Singapore's newest botanic gardens, Gardens by the Bay (p53). The project's two giant glass-and-steel conservatories, designed by Wilkinson Eyre Architects, are the largest climate-controlled glasshouses in the world.

West of Marina Bay and the CBD is Polish-American architect Daniel Libeskind's award-winning Reflections at Keppel Bay, a high-end residential complex with undulating towers that offer constantly shifting perspectives.

BUNGALOWS: THE BLACK & WHITES

Unlike the single-storey retirement homes of the West, Singapore's bungalows are named after Bangalore-style houses and are usually two storeys high, with large verandahs on the upper floor.

Most were built in the style now locally known as 'black and whites', after the mock-Tudor, exposed-beam look adopted between the late 19th century and WWII. The design itself was greatly influenced by the Arts and Craft movement. Originating in England in the 1860s, the movement placed renewed value on craftsmanship, a counter reaction to England's rapid industrialisation. By the 1930s, the mock-Tudor style made way for the so-called 'tropical art deco' style, which favoured flat roofs, curved corners and a strong, streamlined horizontal design.

These 'black and whites' are much sought after by expatriates chasing colonialism's glory days of three generations ago, and you'll find many of them lurking in leafy residential areas off Orchard Rd, such as Nassim Rd and the stretch of Scotts Rd near the Sheraton Towers hotel. They also cluster in exclusive areas such as Alexandra Park and Ridley Park, where you can practically taste the gin slings and elegantly discreet liaisons.

Down at Mountbatten Rd in Kallang are examples of both the highly decorative Victorian bungalow and the concrete art deco bungalows dating from the 1920s and '30s.

French architect Jean Nouvel's newer Nouvel 18 is no less dramatic. Located directly opposite the Shangri-La Hotel, its towers are embedded with eight sky gardens, which break up the glass facades in a case of Jenga meets jungle.

It's a concept echoed in Foster + Partners' brand-new South Beach development. A striking mixed-use office, hotel and residential project opposite Raffles Hotel, its two curving towers are sliced with densely planted sky gardens. It's a change of style for Sir Norman Foster's firm, whose Supreme Court building and Expo MRT are famed for their UFO-like discs.

This 'building as garden' concept drives the ParkRoyal on Pickering (p159), a stunning 12-storey hotel where the lush hanging gardens, laced with gullies and waterfalls, seem to draw Hong Lim Park, located across the street, right up the building. Behind the project is Woha, whose latest project is the Oasia Hotel Downtown in Tanjong Pagar. The 30-storey building features a living green facade of creepers and flowering plants that will be one of the world's tallest vertical gardens. Foliage continues to sprout at Marina One, which contains a large landscaped garden complete with a three-storey waterfall. The building is designed by German firm Ingenhoven Architects, with its sides evoking rice paddies, terraced into steep hillsides, and the gardens evolve as you travel upwards just as they would if you were climbing a mountain.

One of Singapore's quirkier architectural feats is the Interlace, a suspended 31-block apartment development plonked on a hill near the Southern Ridges walking trail. Here, six-storey blocks are seemingly precariously placed beside and on top of each other in a hexagonal arrangement, resulting in what looks like something a three-year-old may have put together. That said, the architects, OMA/Ole Scheeren, won the top gong at the 2015 World Architecture Festival in the completed housing building category.

Singlish: A Primer

Want to go to Chinatown see see walk walk? You sit this bus. Welcome to the colourful, sometimes confusing world of Singlish, the Singaporeans' very unique take on English. A local patois spiked with borrowed words from Hokkien, Tamil and Malay, it's the direct product of the island's multiracial, multilingual history. Love it or loathe it, knowing the basics can help avoid those lost-in-translation moments. So don't pray pray ah! Get into the Singlish swing.

Singlish

While there isn't a Singlish grammar as such, there are definite characteristics. Verb tenses tend to be nonexistent. Past, present and future are indicated instead by time indicators, so in Singlish it's 'I go tomorrow' or 'I go yesterday'. Long stress is placed on the last syllable of phrases, so that the standard English 'government' becomes 'guvva-men'.

Words ending in consonants are often syncopated and vowels are often distorted. A Chinese-speaking taxi driver might not immediately understand that you want to go to Perak Rd, since they know it as 'Pera Roh'.

A typical exchange might – confusingly – go something like this: '*Eh, this Sunday you going cheong* (party) *anot*? No *ah*? Why like that? Don't be so boring *lah*!' Prepositions and pronouns are dropped, word order is flipped, phrases are clipped short and stress and cadence are unconventional, to say the least.

The particle 'lah' is often tagged onto the end of sentences for emphasis, as in 'No good lah'. Requests or questions may be marked with a tag ending, since direct questioning can be rude. As a result, questions that are formed to be more polite often come across to Westerners as rude. 'Would you like a beer?' becomes 'You wan beer or not?'

For more, check out the Coxford Singlish Dictionary on the satirical website Talking Cock (www.talkingcock.com).

While most Singaporeans love Singlish, the government does not. In 2000 it even launched a 'Speak Good English' campaign (www.goodenglish.org.sg) to improve the standard of English. The campaign includes its own downloadable app, 'Say It Right'.

Slanging Like a Local

a bit the	very; as in '*Wah! Your car a bit the slow one*'
ah beng	every country has them – boys with spiky gelled hair, loud clothes, the latest mobile phones and a choice line in gutter phrases
ahlian	the female version of the *ah beng* – large, moussed hair, garish outfits, armed with a vicious tongue; also known as *ah huay*
aiyo!	'Oh, dear!'
alamak!	exclamation of disbelief or frustration, like 'Oh my God!'
angmoh	common term for Westerner (Caucasian), with derogatory undertone; literally 'red-haired monkey' in Hokkien
ayam	Malay word for chicken; adjective for something inferior or weak

blur	slow or uninformed; popular phrase is *'blur like sotong'*
buaya	womaniser, from the Malay for crocodile
can?	'Is that OK?'
can!	'Yes! That's fine'
charbor	babe, woman
cheena	derogatory term for old-fashioned Chinese in dress or thinking
confirm	used to convey emphasis when describing something or someone, as in *'He confirm blur one'* (He's not very smart)
go stun	to reverse, as in *'Go stun the car'* (from the naval expression 'go astern')
heng	luck, good fortune (Hokkien)
hiao	vain
inggrish	English
kambing	foolish person, literally 'goat' (Malay)
kaypoh	busybody
kena	Malay word close to the meaning of the English word 'got', describing something that happened, as in *'He kena arrested for drunk driving'*
kena ketok	ripped off
kiasee	scared, literally 'afraid to die'; a coward
kiasu	literally 'afraid to lose'; selfish, pushy, always on the lookout for a bargain
kopitiam	coffeeshop
lah	generally an ending for any phrase or sentence; can translate as 'OK', but has no real meaning, added for emphasis to just about everything
lai dat	'like that'; used for emphasis, as in *'I so boring lai dat'* (I'm very bored)
looksee	take a look
minah	girlfriend
or not?	general suffix for questions, as in *'Can or not?'* (Can you or can't you?)
see first	wait and see what happens
shack	tired; often expressed as *'I damn shack sial'*
shiok	good, great, delicious
sotong	Malay for 'squid', used as an adjective meaning clumsy, or generally not switched on
steady lah	well done, excellent; an expression of praise
wah!	general exclamation of surprise or distress
ya ya	boastful, as in *'He always ya ya'*; also expressed *'He damn ya ya papaya'*

Survival Guide

Transport

ARRIVING IN SINGAPORE

Singapore is one of Asia's major air hubs, serviced by both full-service and budget airlines. The city state has excellent and extensive regional and international connections. You can also catch trains and buses to Malaysia and Thailand.

Changi Airport

Changi Airport (Map p213; ☑6595 6868; www.changi airport.com; Airport Blvd; ☎; Ⓜ Changi Airport), 20km northeast of Singapore's central business district (CBD), has four main terminals (the latest opened in 2017) and a fifth already in the works. Regularly voted the world's best airport, it is a major international gateway, with frequent flights to all corners of the globe. You'll find free internet, courtesy phones for local calls, foreign-exchange booths, medical centres, left luggage, hotels, day spas, showers, a gym and swimming pool.

The 10-storey Jewel complex features a canopy park, forest and rain vortex as well as retail, accommodation and dining offerings.

Taxi

Taxi lines at Changi are fast moving and efficient. The fare structure is complicated, but count on spending anywhere between S\$20 to S\$40 into the city centre, depending on the time of travel. The most expensive time is between 5pm and 6am, when a whole raft of surcharges kick in.

A four-seater limousine taxi costs S\$55 to anywhere on the island, plus S\$15 surcharge per additional stop. A seven-seater limousine taxi costs \$60, plus S\$15 surcharge per additional stop. You can book via the self-service kiosk in the arrivals hall of all terminals.

Train

The MRT is the best low-cost way to get into town. The station is located below Terminal 2 and 3, the fare to the city centre is S\$1.69 and takes around 40 minutes. The first train leaves at 5.31am Monday to Saturday and at 5.59am Sunday, the last train goes at 11.18pm daily.

Bus

Public bus 36 runs from Terminals 1, 2 and 3 to Orchard Rd and the Colonial District (S\$1.78, one hour). Buses leave roughly every five to 15 minutes, the first departing after 6am and the last just before midnight.

Faster and more convenient are the airport shuttle buses (adult/child S\$9/6, 20 to 40 minutes) that leave from the arrivals halls at Terminals 1, 2 and 3 and drop passengers at most downtown hotels. Waiting times are up to 15 minutes during peak hours (6 to 9am and 5pm to 1am) and up to 30 minutes at all other times. You can book via the self-service kiosk in the arrivals hall of all terminals.

Bus

If you are travelling beyond Johor Bahru, the simplest option is to catch a bus straight

from Singapore, though there are more options and lower fares travelling from JB.

Numerous private companies run comfortable bus services to Singapore from many destinations in Malaysia, including Melaka and Kuala Lumpur, as well as from destinations such as Hat Yai in Thailand. Many of these services terminate at **Golden Mile Complex Bus Terminal** (5001 Beach Rd; Ⓜ Lavender, Nicoll Hwy), close to Kampong Glam. Golden Mile Complex houses numerous bus agencies specialising in journeys from Singapore to Malaysia or Thailand. You can book online at www. busonlineticket.com.

First Coach (☑6822 2111; www.firstcoach.com.my; 03-33 Novena Sq, 238 Thompson Rd; ☺7am-7pm) has daily buses to Kuala Lumpur departing from Novena Sq, while **Phya Travel** (☑6294 5415; www. phyatravel.com; 02-25, Golden Mile Complex, 5001 Beach Rd) runs buses departing from Golden Mile Complex for Hat Yai, Thailand, from where travellers can catch onward buses.

From Johor Bahru, Malaysia, commuter buses with **Causeway Link Express** (www.causewaylink.com.my) run regularly to various locations in Singapore (one way S\$3.30/RM3.40, every 15 to 30 minutes, roughly 6am to 11.30pm), including Newton Circus, Jurong East Bus Terminal and Kranji MRT station.

Sea

Regular ferry services from Johor in Malaysia and the Riau Archipelago in Indonesia

CLIMATE CHANGE & TRAVEL

Every form of transport that relies on carbon-based fuel generates CO_2, the main cause of human-induced climate change. Modern travel is dependent on aeroplanes, which might use less fuel per kilometre per person than most cars but travel much greater distances. The altitude at which aircraft emit gases (including CO_2) and particles also contributes to their climate change impact. Many websites offer 'carbon calculators' that allow people to estimate the carbon emissions generated by their journey and, for those who wish to do so, to offset the impact of the greenhouse gases emitted with contributions to portfolios of climate-friendly initiatives throughout the world. Lonely Planet offsets the carbon footprint of all staff and author travel.

arrive at various ferry terminals in Singapore.

Changi Point Ferry Terminal (Map p141; ☑6545 2305; 51 Lorong Bekukong; ☺24hr; ☑2)

HarbourFront Cruise & Ferry Terminal (Map p222; ☑6513 2200; www.singaporecruise.com; 1 Maritime Sq; ☑HarbourFront)

Tanah Merah Ferry Terminal (Map p213; ☑6513 2200; www.singaporecruise.com; 50 Tanah Merah Ferry Rd; ☑35)

Indonesia

Direct ferries run between the Riau Archipelago islands of Pulau Batam and Pulau Bintan and Singapore. The ferries are modern, fast and air-conditioned. A small ferry also runs to Tanjung Belungkor in Malaysia.

BatamFast (☑HarbourFront terminal 6270 2228, Tanah Merah terminal 6542 6310; www.batamfast.com) Ferries from Batam Centre, Sekupang and Harbour Bay in Pulau Batam terminate at HarbourFront Ferry Terminal. Ferries from Nongsapura, also in Pulau Batam, terminate at the Tanah Merah Ferry Terminal.

Bintan Resort Ferries (Map p213; ☑6542 4369; www.brf.com.sg; 01-21 Tanah Merah Ferry Terminal, 50 Tanah Merah Ferry Rd; ☺7am-8pm Mon-Fri, 6.30am-8pm Sat & Sun; ☑Tanah Merah, then bus 35) Ferries to Bandar Bentan Telani

in Pulau Bintan depart from Tanah Merah Ferry Terminal.

Limbongan Maju Ferry Services (☑Tangjung Belungkor 07-827 8001; www.tanjungbelungkor.com) Ferries from Tanjung Belungkor, Malaysia, arrive at Changi Point Ferry Terminal.

Sindo Ferries (Map p213; ☑HarbourFront terminal 6331 4123, Tanah Merah terminal 6331 4122; www.sindoferry.com.sg; 01-15 Tanah Merah Ferry Terminal, 50 Tanah Merah Ferry Rd; ☑35) Ferries to Batam Centre, Sekupang, Waterfront and Tanjung Balai depart from HarbourFront Ferry Terminal. Ferries to Tanjung Pinang depart from Tanah Merah Ferry Terminal.

Train
Malaysia & Thailand

As of July 2015, it's no longer possible to catch a direct train from Singapore to Kuala Lumpur. Instead, Malaysian company **Keretapi Tanah Melayu Berhad** (www.ktmb.com.my) operates a shuttle train from **Woodlands Train Checkpoint** (Map p205; 11 Woodlands Crossing; ☑170, Causeway Link Express from Queen St terminal) to JB Sentral with a connection to Kuala Lumpur. Tickets for the shuttle (S$5) can be bought at the counter. Trains leave from here to Kuala Lumpur, with connections on to Thailand.

You can book tickets at the Woodlands or JB Sentral stations or via the dreadful KTM website.

The luxurious **Eastern & Oriental Express** (☑6395 0678; www.belmond.com/eastern-and-oriental-express) departs Bangkok on the two-night, 1943km journey to Singapore – one of the world's great train journeys. Don your linen suit, sip a gin and tonic and dig deep for the fare: itineraries (including side tours) start from US$2664 per person for three days/two nights.

GETTING AROUND

Get the credit-card-sized electronic EZ-Link card to use on MRT trains and local buses. Just tap on and off at the sensors. You can buy one, and top up your card's credit, at all MRT stations.

Singapore is the easiest city in Asia to get around. Maps showing the surrounding area are printed on the walls in MRT stations – great for figuring out which exit to use.

The smartphone app gothere.sg will guide you from your location to your destination via different public transport options; it also provides an approximate taxi fare guide.

➡ **MRT** The local subway – the most convenient way to get around between 5.30am and midnight.

⇒ **Bus** Go everywhere the trains do and more. Great for views. Run from 6am till midnight, plus some later night buses from the city.

⇒ **Taxis** These are fairly cheap if you're used to Sydney or London prices, though there are hefty surcharges during peak hours and from midnight to 6am. Flag one on the street or at taxi stands. Good luck getting one on rainy days.

⇒ **Uber** Singapore has a fast-growing Uber tribe.

Mass Rapid Transit

The efficient Mass Rapid Transit (MRT) subway system is the easiest, quickest and most comfortable way to get around Singapore. The system operates from 5.30am to midnight, with trains at peak times running every two to three minutes, and off-peak every five to seven minutes.

In the inner city, the MRT runs underground, emerging overground out towards the suburban housing estates. It consists of five colour-coded lines: North–South (red), North–East (purple), East–West (green), Circle Line (orange) and Down-town (blue). You'll find a map of the network at www.smrt.com.sg.

Fares & Fare Cards

Single-trip tickets cost from S$1.40 to S$2.50 (plus a 10¢ refundable deposit), but if you're using the MRT a lot it can become a has-sle buying and refunding tickets for every journey. A lot more convenient is the EZ-Link card. Alternatively, a **Singapore Tourist Pass** (www.thesingaporetouristpass.com.sg) offers unlimited train and bus travel (S$10 plus a S$10 refundable deposit) for one day.

Bus

Singapore's extensive bus service is clean, efficient and regular, reaching every corner of the island. The two main operators are **SBS Transit** (☏1800 287 2727; www.sbstransit.com.sg) and **SMRT** (☏1800 336 8900; www.smrt.com.sg). Both offer similar services. For informa-tion and routes, check the websites. Alternatively down-load the 'SG Buses' smart-phone app, which will give you real-time bus arrivals.

Bus fares range from S$1 to S$2.10 (less with an EZ-Link card). When you board the bus, drop the exact money into the fare box (no change is given), or tap your EZ-Link card or Singapore Tourist Pass on the reader as you board, then again when you get off.

Train operator SMRT also runs late-night bus services between the city and various suburbs from 11.30pm to 2.30am on Fridays, Satur-days and the eve of public holidays. The flat rate per journey is S$4.50. See the website for route details.

Taxi

You can flag down a taxi any time, but in the city centre taxis are technically not allowed to stop anywhere except at designated taxi stands.

Finding a taxi in the city at certain times is harder than it should be. These include during peak hours, at night, or when it's raining. Many cab drivers change shifts between 4pm and 5pm, mak-ing it notoriously difficult to score a taxi then.

The fare system is also complicated, but thankfully it's all metered, so there's no haggling over fares. The basic flagfall is S$3 to S$3.40 then S$0.22 for every 400m.

There's a whole raft of surcharges to note, among them:

⇒ 50% of the metered fare from midnight to 6am

⇒ 25% of the metered fare between 6am and 9.30am Monday to Friday, and 6pm to midnight daily

⇒ S$5 for airport trips from 5pm to midnight Friday to Sunday, and S$3 at all other times

⇒ S$3 city-area surcharge from 5pm to midnight

⇒ S$2.30 to S$8 for telephone bookings

Payment by credit card incurs a 10% surcharge. You can also pay using your EZ-Link transport card. For a comprehensive list of fares and surcharges, visit www.taxisingapore.com.

THE EZ-LINK AROUND TOWN

⇒ If you're staying in Singapore for more than a day or two, the easiest way to pay for travel on public transport is with the EZ-Link card (www.ezlink.com.sg). The card allows you to travel by train and bus by simply swiping it over sensors as you enter and leave a station or bus.

⇒ EZ-Link cards can be purchased from the customer service counters at MRT stations for S$12 (this includes a S$5 nonrefundable deposit).

⇒ The card can also be bought at 7-Elevens for S$10 (including the S$5 nonrefundable deposit).

⇒ Cards can be topped up with cash or by ATM cards at station ticket machines. The minimum top-up value is S$10 while the maximum stored value allowed on your card is S$500.

Comfort Taxi & CityCab
(☑6552 1111; www.cdgtaxi.com.sg)
Premier Taxis (☑6363 6888; www.premiertaxi.com.sg)
SMRT Taxis (☑6555 8888; www.smrt.com.sg)

Bicycle

Avoid cycling on roads. Drivers are sometimes aggressive and the roads themselves are uncomfortably hot. A much safer and more pleasant option for cyclists is Singapore's large network of parks and park connectors, not to mention the dedicated mountain-biking areas at Bukit Timah Nature Reserve, Chestnut Park, Tampines and Pulau Ubin.

Other excellent places for cycling include East Coast Park, Sentosa, Pasir Ris Park and the route linking Mt Faber Park, Telok Blangah Hill Park and Kent Ridge Park.

Only fold-up bikes are allowed on trains and buses, with only one fold-up bike allowed on buses at any time, so you might as well ride if you have to.

Hire

Bikes can be rented at several places along East Coast Park and on Sentosa Island and Pulau Ubin, with adult prices starting from S$5 a day on Pulau Ubin and around S$8 an hour elsewhere.

Bike-sharing platforms made an appearance in Singapore in 2017 and they're extremely popular. So far there are three players in the market, **Mobike** (www.mobike.com), **oBike** (www.o.bike) and **ofo** (www.ofo.so) – each are still working out the kinks in their systems but basically you download the app, pay a deposit (between S$40 and S$50), find a bike and off you go. You're charged for the time you ride.

Boat

Visit the islands around Singapore from the Marina South Pier. There are regular ferry services from Changi Point Ferry Terminal to Pulau Ubin (S$3). To get there, take bus 2 from Tanah Merah MRT.

Car & Motorcycle

Singaporeans drive on the left-hand side of the road and it is compulsory to wear seat belts in the front and back of the car. The *Mighty Minds Singapore Street Directory* (S$14.90) is invaluable and available from petrol stations, bookshops, FairPrice supermarkets and stationery stores. However, the island has good internet coverage so Google Maps is also a reasonable option.

Driving

If you plan on driving in Singapore, bring your current home driver's licence. Some car-hire companies may also require you to have an international driving permit.

The roads are immaculate and well signed. However, drivers tend to change lanes quickly and sometimes do so without signalling. Motorcycles have a bad habit of riding between cars, especially when traffic is slow.

Hire

If you want a car for local driving only, it's worth checking smaller operators, where the rates are often cheaper than the big global rental firms. If you're going into Malaysia, you're better off renting in Johor Bahru, where the rates are significantly lower (besides which, Malaysian police are renowned for targeting Singapore licence plates).

Rates start from around S$60 a day. Special deals may be available, especially for longer-term rental. Most rental companies require

that drivers are at least 23 years old.

All major car-hire companies have booths at Changi Airport as well as in the city.

Avis (☑6737 1668; www.avis.com.sg; 01-07 Waterfront Plaza, 390A Havelock Rd; ⊙8am-8pm; ☒5, 16, 75, 175, 195, 970)
Hawk (Map p221;☑6466 2366; www.hawkrentacar.com.sg; 01-11 Ispace, 7 Soon Lee St; ⊙9am-6pm Mon-Fri, to 1pm Sat; Ⓜ Pioneer)
Hertz (Map p213;☑6542 5300; www.hertz.com; Terminals 2 & 3, Changi Airport; ⊙7am-11pm; Ⓜ Changi Airport)

Restricted Zone & Car Parking

At various times through the day, from Monday to Saturday, much of central Singapore is considered a restricted zone. Cars are free to enter but they must pay a toll. Vehicles are automatically tracked by sensors on overhead Electronic Road Pricing (ERP) gantries, so cars must be fitted with an in-vehicle unit, into which drivers must insert a cash card (available at petrol stations and 7-Elevens). The toll is extracted from the card. The same system is also in operation on certain expressways. Rental cars are subject to the same rules. Check www.onemotoring.com.sg for ERP rates and hours of operation.

Parking in the city centre is expensive, but relatively easy to find – almost every major mall has a car park. Outdoor car parks and street parking spaces are usually operated by the government – you can buy booklets of parking coupons, which must be displayed in the window, from petrol stations and 7-Elevens. Many car parks are now run using the same in-vehicle unit and cash card and ERP gantries instead of the coupon system.

Directory A–Z

Accessible Travel

A large government campaign has seen ramps, lifts and other facilities progressively installed around the island. The footpaths in the city are nearly all immaculate, all MRT stations have lifts and there are some buses and taxis equipped with wheelchair-friendly equipment.

The **Disabled People's Association Singapore** (www.dpa.org.sg) can provide information on accessibility in Singapore.

Download Lonely Planet's free Accessible Travel guide from https://shop.lonelyplanet.com/categories/accessible-travel.com.

Customs Regulations

You are not allowed to bring tobacco into Singapore unless you pay duty. You will be slapped with a hefty fine if you fail to declare and pay.

You are permitted 1L each of wine, beer and spirits duty free. Alternatively, you are allowed 2L of wine and 1L of beer, or 2L of beer and 1L of wine. You need to have been out of Singapore for more than 48 hours and to anywhere but Malaysia.

It's illegal to bring chewing gum, firecrackers, obscene or seditious material, gun-shaped cigarette lighters, endangered species or their by-products and pirated recordings or publications with you.

Discount Cards

If you arrived on a Singapore Airlines or SilkAir flight, you can get discounts at shops, restaurants and attractions by presenting your boarding pass. See www.singaporeair.com/boardingpass for information.

Electricity

230V/50Hz

Emergency

Country Code	☑65
Ambulance & Fire	☑995
Police	☑999

Health

Hygiene in Singapore is strictly observed and the tap water is safe to drink. However, hepatitis A does occasionally occur. You only need vaccinations if you come from a yellow-fever area. Singapore is not a malarial zone, though dengue fever is an increasing concern and there have been cases of zika reported.

Dengue Fever

Singapore has suffered a sharp rise in cases of this nasty mosquito-borne disease in recent years. Peak biting periods are dawn and dusk, though it's best to use insect-avoidance measures at all times. Symptoms include high fever, severe headache and body ache. Some people develop a rash and diarrhoea. There is no specific treatment – just rest and paracetamol. Do not take aspirin. See a doctor to be diagnosed and monitored. For more information, visit www.dengue.gov.sg.

Zika Virus

The first case of Zika virus was recorded in Singapore in 2016 and for a few weeks afterwards, shops sold out of mosquito repellent throughout Singapore. After the initial outbreak, the number of confirmed cases diminished steadily. Check www.nea.gov.sg/public-health/zika for up-to-date information. Symptoms can be similar to those caused by the flu, and may include fever, skin rash, joint and muscle pain, headache, red eyes and lack of energy. See a doctor for diagnosis.

Prickly Heat

This is an itchy rash caused by excessive perspiration trapped under the skin. It usually strikes people who have just arrived in a hot climate. Keep cool, bathe often, dry the skin and use a mild talcum or prickly heat powder, or resort to air conditioning.

Internet Access

Most hotels offer internet access. All backpacker hostels offer free internet access and wi-fi. Unlike many other modern, major cities around the world, very few cafes offer free wi-fi.

SingTel (www.singtel. com), **StarHub** (www. starhub.com) and **M1** (www. m1.com.sg) are local providers of broadband internet via USB modem dongles. Bring your own or buy one from them. You can get prepaid data SIM cards if you have your own dongle.

LGBTIQ+ Travellers

Sex between males is illegal in Singapore, carrying a minimum sentence of 10 years. In reality, nobody is ever

---

likely to be prosecuted, but the ban remains as a symbol of the government's belief that the country is not ready for the open acceptance of what it deems as 'alternative lifestyles'.

Despite that, Singapore has a string of popular LGBTIQ+ bars. A good place to start looking for information is on the websites of **Travel Gay Asia** (www. travelgayasia.com), **PLUguide** (www.pluguide.com) or **Utopia** (www.utopia-asia.com), which provide coverage of venues and events.

Singaporeans are fairly conservative about public affection, though it's more common to see displays of familiarity among lesbian couples these days. A gay male couple doing the same would definitely draw negative attention.

Medical Services

Singapore's medical institutions are first-rate and generally cheaper than private healthcare in the West. But needless to say, travel insurance is advisable. Check with insurance providers as to which treatments and procedures are covered before you leave home.

Clinics

Your hotel or hostel should be able to direct you to a local GP: there are plenty around.

International Medical Clinic (Orchard Clinic; Map p216; ✆6733 4440; www.imc-health care.com; 14-06 Camden Medical Centre, 1 Orchard Blvd; ☺8am-5.30pm Mon-Fri, 9am-1pm Sat; ⓂOrchard) Specialising in family and travel medicine.

Raffles Medical Clinic (✆6311 2233; www.rafflesmedical group.com; Level 2, Raffles Hospital, 585 North Bridge Rd; ☺8am-10pm; ⓂBugis) A walk-in clinic at Raffles Hospital.

Singapore General Hospital (Map p209; ✆6222 3322; www. sgh.com.sg; Block 1, Outram Rd; ⓂOutram Park) Also has an emergency room.

Emergency Rooms

There are several 24-hour emergency rooms.

Gleneagles Hospital (✆6575 7575; www.gleneagles.com.sg; 6A Napier Rd; 🚌7, 75, 77, 106, 123, 174)

Mount Elizabeth Hospital Novena (✆6933 0000; www. mountelizabeth.com.sg; 38 Irrawaddy Rd; ⓂNovena)

Mount Elizabeth Hospital Orchard (Map p216; ✆6731 2218; www.mountelizabeth. com.sg; 3 Mt Elizabeth Rd; ⓂOrchard)

Raffles Hospital (Map p210; ✆6311 1111; www.raffles medicalgroup.com; 585 North Bridge Rd; ⓂBugis)

PRACTICALITIES

→ **Newspapers** English daily newspapers in Singapore include broadsheets the *Straits Times* and *Business Times*, and afternoon tabloid the *New Paper.*

→ **Magazines** Pornographic publications are strictly prohibited, but toned-down local editions of *Cosmopolitan* and lads' magazines such as *FHM* and *Maxim* are allowed.

→ **Weights & Measures** Singapore uses the metric system for weights and measures. Weights are in grams and kilograms and volume in millilitres and litres.

Singapore General Hospital (Map p209; ☑6222 3322; www.sgh.com.sg; Block 1, Outram Rd; Ⓜ Outram Park)

Money

The country's unit of currency is the Singapore dollar (S$), locally referred to as the 'singdollar', which is made up of 100 cents. Singapore uses 5¢, 10¢, 20¢, 50¢ and S$1 coins, while notes come in denominations of S$2, S$5, S$10, S$50, S$100, S$500 and S$1000. The Singapore dollar is a highly stable and freely convertible currency.

ATMs

Cirrus-enabled ATMs are widely available at malls, banks, MRT stations and commercial areas.

Changing Money

Banks change money, but virtually nobody uses them for currency conversion because the rates are better at the moneychangers dotted all over the city. These tiny stalls can be found in just about every shopping centre (though not necessarily in the more modern malls). Rates can be haggled a little if you're changing amounts of S$500 or more.

Credit Cards

Credit cards are widely accepted, apart from at local hawkers and food courts. Cases of smaller stores charging an extra 2% to 3% for credit-card payments have decreased in recent years.

Opening Hours

Opening hours can vary between individual businesses. General opening hours are as follows.

Banks 9.30am to 4.30pm Monday to Friday (some branches open at 10am and some close at 6pm or later); 9.30am to noon or later Saturday

Government and Post Offices Between 8am and 9.30am to between 4pm and 6pm Monday to Friday; between 8am and 9am to between 11.30am and 1.30pm Saturday.

Restaurants Top restaurants generally noon–2.30pm for lunch and 6–11pm for dinner. Casual restaurants and food courts open all day.

Shops 10am or 11am to 6pm; larger shops and department stores open until 9.30pm or 10pm. Some smaller shops in Chinatown and Arab St close Sunday.

Post

Postal delivery in Singapore is very efficient. Call ☑1605 to find the nearest post office or check www.singpost.com.sg.

The following post offices are in convenient locations:

Killiney Rd (Map p216; ☑24/7 Customer Care Hotline 1605; www.singpost.com; 1 Killiney Rd; ⊙9.30am-9pm Mon-Fri, to 4pm Sat, 10.30am-4pm Sun & public holidays; Ⓜ Somerset) Open on Sundays.

Orchard Rd (Map p216; ☑24/7 Customer Care Hotline 1605; www.singpost.com; B2-62 ION Orchard, 2 Orchard Turn; ⊙11am-7pm; Ⓜ Orchard) Open on Sundays.

Changi Airport Post office (Map p213; ☑1605; www.singpost.com; Terminal 2; ⊙9am-6pm Mon-Fri; Ⓜ Changi Airport) in the departure check-in hall of Terminal 2.

Public Holidays

Listed here are the public holidays in Singapore. For those days not based on the Western calendar, the months in which they are likely to fall is provided. The only holiday that has a major effect on the city is Chinese New Year, when virtually all shops shut down for two days.

New Year's Day 1 January

Chinese New Year Three days in January/February

Good Friday March/April

Labour Day 1 May

Vesak Day June

Hari Raya Puasa July

National Day 9 August

Hari Raya Haji September

Deepavali October

Christmas Day 25 December

Taxes & Refunds

Tourists are entitled to claim a refund of the GST paid on purchases made at participating retail stores before leaving the country. This refund is applicable for purchases above S$100. See the Treasure Hunt chapter (p41) for more information.

Telephone

➜ Singapore's country code is 🗲65.

➜ There are no area codes within Singapore; telephone numbers are eight digits unless you are calling toll-free (🗲1800).

➜ You can make local and international calls from public phone booths. Most phone booths take phonecards.

➜ Singapore also has credit-card phones that can be used by running your card through the slot.

➜ Calls to Malaysia (from Singapore) are considered to be STD (trunk or long-distance) calls. Dial the access code 🗲020, followed by the area code of the town in Malaysia that you wish to call (minus the leading zero) and then the phone number. Thus, for a call to 🗲346 7890 in Kuala Lumpur (area code 🗲03) you would dial 🗲02-3-346 7890.

➜ Mobile-phone numbers start with 🗲9 or 🗲8.

Mobile Phones

In Singapore, mobile-phone numbers start with 9 or 8.

You can buy a tourist SIM card for around S$15 from post offices, convenience

stores and telco stores – by law you must show your passport. Local carriers include:

M1 (www.m1.com.sg)

SingTel (www.singtel.com)

StarHub (www.starhub.com)

Phonecards

Phonecards are particularly popular among Singapore's migrant workers – the domestic maids and construction workers who keep the city ticking over – so there are plenty on sale. There's a small, thriving phonecard stall outside the Centrepoint shopping centre on Orchard Rd, and there are plenty of retailers around Little India, but check which countries they service before you buy.

Time

Singapore is eight hours ahead of GMT/UTC (London), two hours behind Australian Eastern Standard Time (Sydney and Melbourne), 13 hours ahead of American Eastern Standard Time (New York) and 16 hours ahead of American Pacific Standard Time (San Francisco and Los Angeles).

So, when it's noon in Singapore, it is 8pm in Los Angeles and 11pm in New York the previous day, and 4am in London and 2pm in Sydney and Melbourne.

Tourist Information

Before your trip, a good place to check for information is the website of the **Singapore Tourism Board** (Map p216; 🗲1800 736 2000; www.yoursingapore.com; 216

Orchard Rd; ⊙8.30am-9.30pm; 🛜; Ⓜ Somerset).

In Singapore, there are several tourism centres offering a wide range of services, including tour bookings and event ticketing. Its main branch, **Singapore Visitors Centre @ Orchard** (Map p216; 🗲1800 736 2000; www.yoursingapore.com; 216 Orchard Rd; ⊙8.30am-9.30pm; 🛜; Ⓜ Somerset), is conveniently located on Orchard Rd, near the Somerset MRT station, and is filled with knowledgeable staff who can help you organise tours, buy tickets and book hotels.

A smaller branch, **Singapore Visitors Centre @ ION** (Map p216; 🗲1800 736 2000; www.yoursingapore.com; Level 1 Concierge, ION Orchard, 2 Orchard Turn; ⊙10am-10pm; 🛜; Ⓜ Orchard), is found at the Concierge Desk in ION Orchard Mall.

Chinatown's very own visitors centre, **Singapore Visitor Centre@Chinatown** (Map p206; 🗲1800 736 2000; www.yoursingapore.com; 2 Banda St; ⊙9am-9pm; 🛜; Ⓜ Chinatown), offers free maps and can book walking tours of the area for you. A small range of quality souvenirs is also available for sale.

Visas

Citizens of most countries are granted 90-day entry on arrival. Citizens of India, Myanmar and certain other countries must obtain a visa before arriving.

Visa extensions can be applied for at the **Immigration & Checkpoints Authority** (Map p210; 🗲6391 6100; www.ica.gov.sg; Level 4, ICA Bldg, 10 Kallang Rd; ⊙8am-4.30pm Mon-Fri, 8am-12.30pm Sat; Ⓜ Lavender).

Behind the Scenes

SEND US YOUR FEEDBACK

We love to hear from travellers – your comments keep us on our toes and help make our books better. Our well-travelled team reads every word on what you loved or loathed about this book. Although we cannot reply individually to your submissions, we always guarantee that your feedback goes straight to the appropriate authors, in time for the next edition. Each person who sends us information is thanked in the next edition – the most useful submissions are rewarded with a selection of digital PDF chapters.

Visit **lonelyplanet.com/contact** to submit your updates and suggestions or to ask for help. Our award-winning website also features inspirational travel stories, news and discussions.

Note: We may edit, reproduce and incorporate your comments in Lonely Planet products such as guidebooks, websites and digital products, so let us know if you don't want your comments reproduced or your name acknowledged. For a copy of our privacy policy visit lonelyplanet.com/legal.

OUR READERS

Many thanks to the travellers who used the last edition and wrote to us with helpful hints, useful advice and interesting anecdotes:
Elgin Tay, Indraneel Bhanap, Kandhasamy Muthu, Michael Holloway, Patricio de la Fuente

WRITER THANKS

Ria de Jong

Thank you to my destination editors Dora Ball and Clifton Wilkinson for all their help and advice guiding me through my Lonely Planet adventure, and to all those who I met along my travels and who kindly shared their knowledge, time and Singapore secrets with me. To my parents and sister who nurtured my love of the road less travelled, to my travelling circus tribe Craig, Cisca and William, and to Jen, who keeps us all in line.

ACKNOWLEDGEMENTS

Cover photograph: Singapore skyline, Roel van Wanrooy/ Shutterstock ©

THIS BOOK

This 12th edition of Lonely Planet's *Singapore* guidebook was researched and written by Ria de Jong. The 11th edition was also written by Ria and the 10th edition was written by Cristian Bonetto. This guidebook was produced by the following:

Destination Editor Dora Ball, Clifton Wilkinson
Senior Product Editor Daniel Bolger
Product Editors Ronan Abayawickrema, Kate Chapman, Sandie Kestell, Amanda Williamson
Senior Cartographer Julie Sheridan
Book Designer Gwen Cotter, Wibowo Rusli

Assisting Editors Judith Bamber, Nigel Chin, Victoria Harrison, Kate James, Kristin Odijk
Cover Researcher Ania Bartoszek
Thanks to Hannah Cartmel, Fergal Condon, Karen Henderson, Liz Heynes, Jenna Myers, Lauren O'Connell, Ambika Shree, Tony Wheeler

See also separate subindexes for:

✖ **EATING P195**

🍷 **DRINKING & NIGHTLIFE P196**

☆ **ENTERTAINMENT P197**

🛍 **SHOPPING P197**

🛏 **SLEEPING P198**

Index

✕ EATING

INDEX SLEEPING

Skyline Luge Sentosa 140
Snow City 134
Spa Esprit 101
Tomi Foot Reflexology 101
TreeTop Walk 118
Ubin Adventure (Pulau Ubin) 144
Ultimate Drive 68
Wild Wild Wet 113
Willow Stream 68

SLEEPING

5Footway.Inn Project Boat Quay 156

A
Adler Hostel 157-8
Ambassador Transit Hotel 164
Amoy 158

B
Banyan Tree Bintan (Pulau Bintan) 147
Betel Box 162
Bunc@Radius 159

C
Capella Singapore 163
Carlton City 153
Citrus Hotel (Johor Bahru) 149
COO 157
Crowne Plaza 164

D
Days Hotel Singapore at Zhongshan Park 163
D'Kranji Farm Resort 133

F
Fernloft 158
Fisher BnB 160
Five Stones Hostel 159
Fullerton Bay Hotel 156
Fullerton Hotel 157

G
Goodwood Park Hotel 161

H
hangout@mt.emily 160-1
Hilton DoubleTree (Johor Bahru) 149
Holiday Inn Express Clarke Quay 156
Hotel 1929 159
Hotel Fort Canning 157
Hotel Indigo 162
Hotel Jen (Iskandar Malaysia) 152
Hotel Jen Tanglin 162
Hotel Mono 158-9

I
Ibis Singapore on Bencoolen 160
InnCrowd 160

J
Jelutong (Pulau Ubin) 144

K
Kam Leng Hotel 159

L
Legoland Hotel (Johor Bahru) 149
Lloyd's Inn 161

M
Marina Bay Sands 157

N
Naumi 157

P
Park Regis 156
Parkroyal on Pickering 159
Pod 159
Port by Quarters Hostel 156

Q
Quincy 162

R
Raffles Hotel 156
Ramada Singapore at Zhongshan Park 163
Rendezvous Hotel 161
Ritz-Carlton Millenia Singapore 156

S
Scarlet 159
Shangri-La Hotel 162
Shangri-La's Rasa Sentosa Resort & Spa 164
Shophouse the Social Hostel 160
Singapore Marriott 162
St John's Holiday Bungalow (Southern Islands) 146
St Regis 161

T
Trikora Beach Club (Pulau Bintan) 147

V
Venue Hotel 162-3
Village Hotel Albert Court 161
Village Hotel Changi 163
Villa Samadhi 163

W
Wangz 158
Warehouse 157
Wink Hostel 158
W Singapore - Sentosa Cove 163-4
York Hotel 161-2

Singapore Maps

Sights

- Beach
- Bird Sanctuary
- Buddhist
- Castle/Palace
- Christian
- Confucian
- Hindu
- Islamic
- Jain
- Jewish
- Monument
- Museum/Gallery/Historic Building
- Ruin
- Shinto
- Sikh
- Taoist
- Winery/Vineyard
- Zoo/Wildlife Sanctuary
- Other Sight

Activities, Courses & Tours

- Bodysurfing
- Diving
- Canoeing/Kayaking
- Course/Tour
- Sento Hot Baths/Onsen
- Skiing
- Snorkelling
- Surfing
- Swimming/Pool
- Walking
- Windsurfing
- Other Activity

Sleeping

- Sleeping
- Camping

Eating

- Eating

Drinking & Nightlife

- Drinking & Nightlife
- Cafe

Entertainment

- Entertainment

Shopping

- Shopping

Information

- Bank
- Embassy/Consulate
- Hospital/Medical
- Internet
- Police
- Post Office
- Telephone
- Toilet
- Tourist Information
- Other Information

Geographic

- Beach
- Gate
- Hut/Shelter
- Lighthouse
- Lookout
- Mountain/Volcano
- Oasis
- Park
- Pass
- Picnic Area
- Waterfall

Population

- Capital (National)
- Capital (State/Province)
- City/Large Town
- Town/Village

Transport

- Airport
- Border crossing
- Bus
- Cable car/Funicular
- Cycling
- Ferry
- Metro/MTR/MRT station
- Monorail
- Parking
- Petrol station
- Skytrain/Subway station
- Taxi
- Train station/Railway
- Tram
- Underground station
- Other Transport

Note: Not all symbols displayed above appear on the maps in this book

Routes

- Tollway
- Freeway
- Primary
- Secondary
- Tertiary
- Lane
- Unsealed road
- Road under construction
- Plaza/Mall
- Steps
- Tunnel
- Pedestrian overpass
- Walking Tour
- Walking Tour detour
- Path/Walking Trail

Boundaries

- International
- State/Province
- Disputed
- Regional/Suburb
- Marine Park
- Cliff
- Wall

Hydrography

- River, Creek
- Intermittent River
- Canal
- Water
- Dry/Salt/Intermittent Lake
- Reef

Areas

- Airport/Runway
- Beach/Desert
- Cemetery (Christian)
- Cemetery (Other)
- Glacier
- Mudflat
- Park/Forest
- Sight (Building)
- Sportsground
- Swamp/Mangrove

MAP INDEX

COLONIAL DISTRICT & THE QUAYS

COLONIAL DISTRICT & THE QUAYS

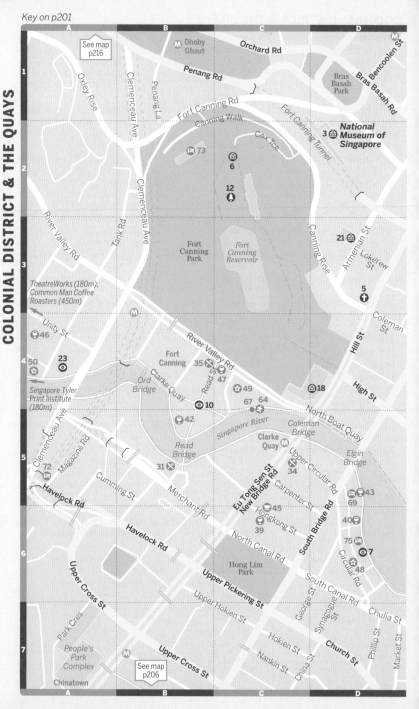

Key on p201

See map p216

Dhoby Ghaut

Orchard Rd

Penang Rd

Oxley Rise

Clemenceau Ave

Penang La

Penang Rd

Fort Canning Rd

Canning Walk

Fort Canning Tunnel

Cox Tce

Bras Basah Park

Bras Basah Rd

Bencoolen St

National Museum of Singapore
3

73

6

12

Fort Canning Park

Fort Canning Reservoir

Clemenceau Ave

Tank Rd

River Valley Rd

Canning Rise

Armenian St

Lokeyew St
21

5

Coleman St

Hill St

TheatreWorks (180m);
Common Man Coffee
Roasters (450m)

Unity St

46

River Valley Rd

50

23

Fort Canning

35

47

Ord Bridge

Clarke Quay

49

18

High St

Singapore Tyler
Print Institute
(180m)

10

67 64

North Boat Quay

42

Read Bridge

Singapore River

Coleman Bridge

Clarke Quay

Elgin Bridge

Clemenceau Ave

72

Magazine Rd

Cumming St

31

Merchant Rd

Read St

Upper Circular Rd

34

Eu Tong Sen St

New Bridge Rd

Carpenter St

Hongkong St

45

39

South Bridge Rd

43

69

40

75

7

48

Havelock Rd

Havelock Rd

North Canal Rd

Hong Lim Park

Upper Pickering St

Upper Hokien St

South Canal Rd

George St

Synagogue St

Circular Rd

Chulia St

Upper Cross St

Park Cres

People's Park Complex

Upper Cross St

See map p206

Hokien St

Nankin St

Chulia St

Church St

Phillip St

Market St

Chinatown

A   B   C   D

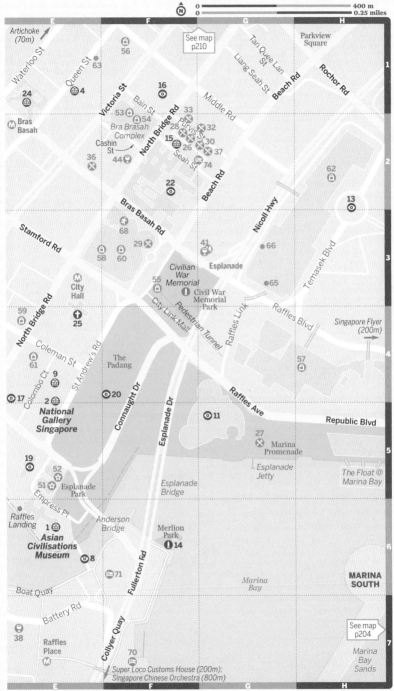

MARINA BAY

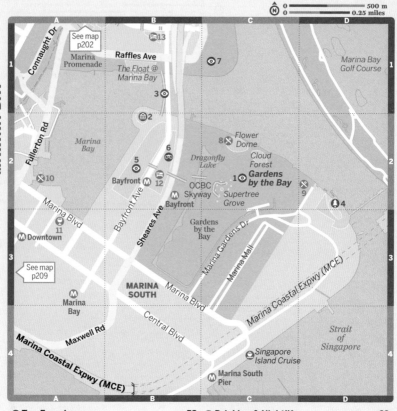

0 ——— 500 m
0 ——— 0.25 miles

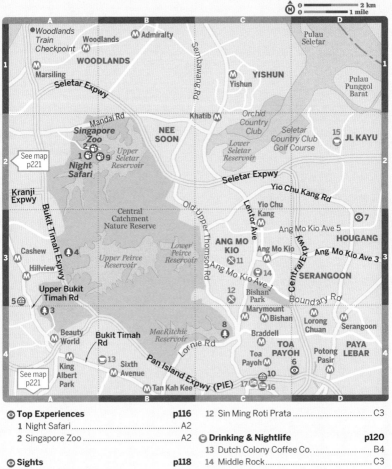

Key on p208

CHINATOWN

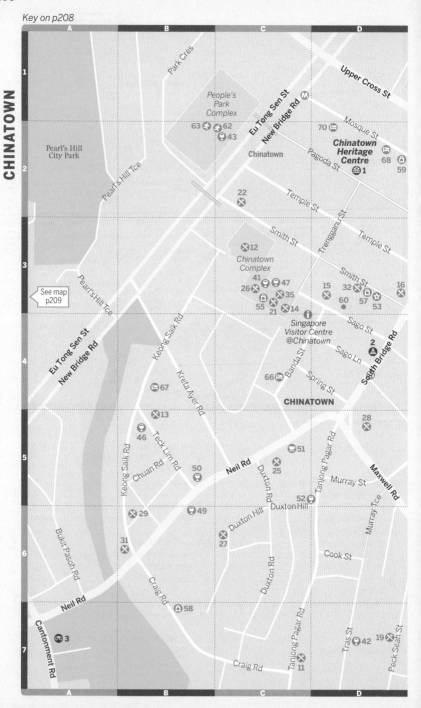

Park Cres

Upper Cross St

People's
Park
Complex

Eu Tong Sen St

New Bridge Rd

Mosque St

70

Chinatown
Heritage
Centre

68

59

63 62
43

Chinatown

Pagoda St

1

Pearl's Hill
City Park

Pearl's Hill Tce

Temple St

Trengganu St

Temple St

22

Smith St

See map
p209

Pearl's Hill Tce

12

Chinatown
Complex

Smith St

41 47

26 35

55 14

21

Singapore
Visitor Centre
@Chinatown

Sago St

2

Sago Ln

15 32

60 57 53

16

Keong Saik Rd

Kreta Ayer Rd

67

13

Banda St

66

Spring St

South Bridge Rd

CHINATOWN

28

46

Teck Lim Rd

Chuan Rd

50

51

25

Neil Rd

Duxton Rd

Tanjong Pagar Rd

Murray St

Maxwell Rd

Keong Saik Rd

Duxton Hill

52

Duxton Hill

Murray Tce

29

49

Bukit Pasoh Rd

27

Duxton Rd

Cook St

31

Craig Rd

58

Neil Rd

Cantonment Rd

3

Tanjong Pagar Rd

Tras St

42 19

Peck Seah St

11

Craig Rd

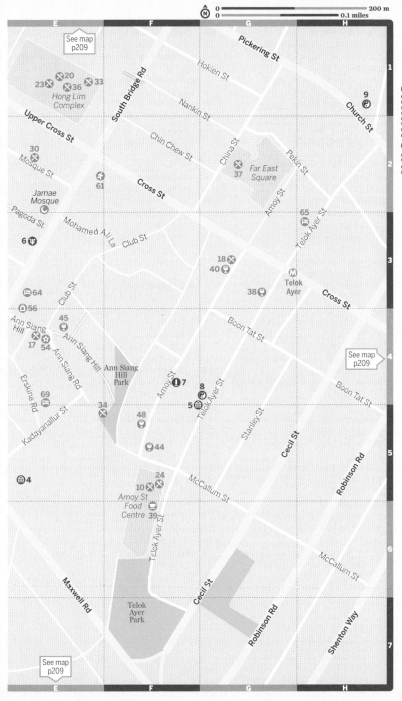

0 —————————— 200 m
0 —————————— 0.1 miles

See map p209

Pickering St

Hokien St

Church St

9

South Bridge Rd

Nankin St

Upper Cross St

Chin Chew St

China St

Far East Square

Pekin St

30
Mosque St

37

Amoy St

Cross St

61

Jamae Mosque

Mohamed Ali La

Club St

65

Telok Ayer St

Pagoda St

6

18
40

Telok Ayer

64

Club St

38

Cross St

56

Boon Tat St

Ann Siang Hill

45

17
54

Ann Siang Hill

Ann Siang Hill Park

See map p209

Boon Tat St

Ann Siang Rd

Erskine Rd

69

Amoy St

7

8

5

Telok Ayer St

Kadayanallur St

34

48

Stanley St

Cecil St

Robinson Rd

4

44

24

McCallum St

10

Amoy St Food Centre

39

Telok Ayer St

McCallum St

Maxwell Rd

Cecil St

Telok Ayer Park

Robinson Rd

Shenton Way

See map p209

CHINATOWN

CHINATOWN, TANJONG PAGAR & THE CBD

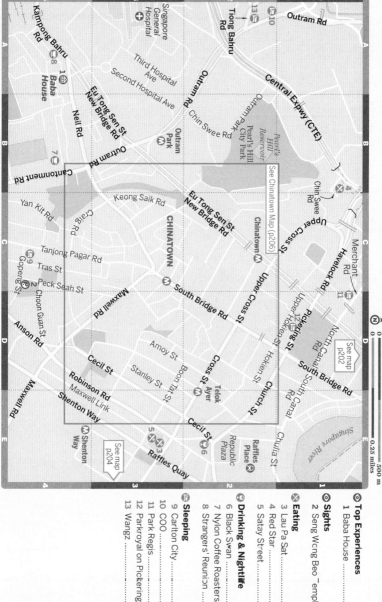

LITTLE INDIA & KAMPONG GLAM

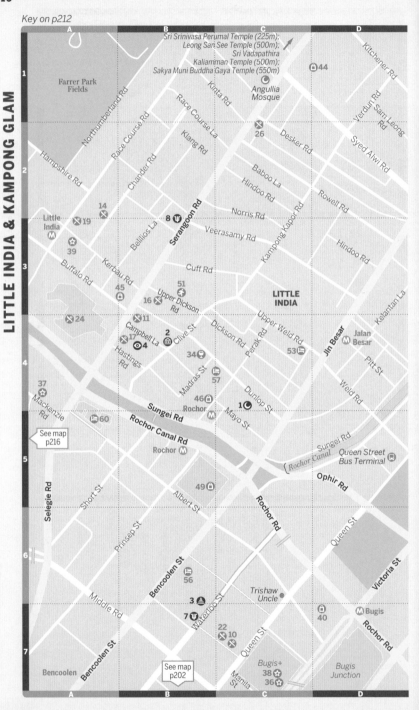

Sri Srinivasa Perumal Temple (225m);
Leong San See Temple (500m);
Sri Vadapathira
Kaliamman Temple (500m);
Sakya Muni Buddha Gaya Temple (550m)

Farrer Park
Fields

Angullia
Mosque

44

Northumberland Rd

Race Course Rd

Race Course La

Klang Rd

Kinta Rd

Kitchener Rd

Verdun Rd

Sam Leong Rd

Syed Alwi Rd

Hampshire Rd

Chander Rd

Baboo La

Hindoo Rd

Desker Rd

Rowell Rd

26

Little
India

14

19

39

Bellios La

Serangoon Rd

8

Norris Rd

Veerasamy Rd

Kampong Kapor Rd

Hindoo Rd

Buffalo Rd

Kerbau Rd

Cuff Rd

LITTLE
INDIA

45

51

16

Upper Dickson Rd

Upper Weld Rd

Kelantan La

24

11

Campbell La

17

4

2

Clive St

Dickson Rd

Perak Rd

53

Jln Besar

Jalan
Besar

Pitt St

Hastings Rd

34

Madras St

57

46

Dunlop St

1

Weld Rd

37

Mackenzie Rd

Rochor

Mayo St

Sungei Rd

60

Rochor Canal Rd

Rochor

Sungei Rd

Rochor Canal

Queen Street
Bus Terminal

Ophir Rd

Selegie Rd

Short St

49

Albert St

Rochor Rd

Queen St

Victoria St

Prinsep St

Bencoolen St

56

Trishaw
Uncle

40

Bugis

Rochor Rd

Middle Rd

3

7

22

10

Waterloo St

Queen St

Bugis+

38

36

Bugis
Junction

Bencoolen

Bencoolen St

See map
p216

See map
p202

Manila St

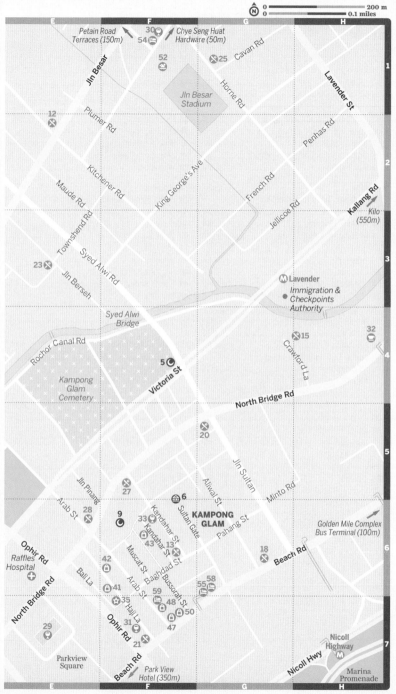

LITTLE INDIA & KAMPONG GLAM

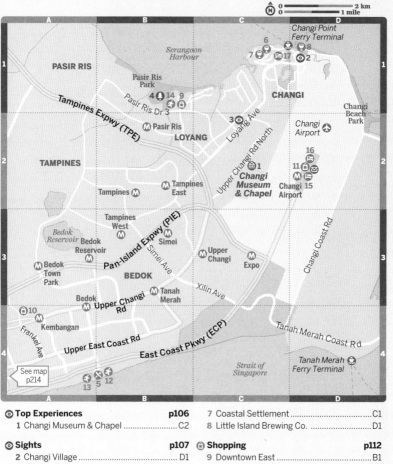

◎ **Top Experiences**   **p106**
  1 Changi Museum & Chapel C2

◎ **Sights**   **p107**
  2 Changi Village D1
  3 Loyang Tua Pek Kong Temple C2
  4 Pasir Ris Park... B1

✗ **Eating**   **p109**
    Changi Village Hawker Centre ....(see 2)
  5 East Coast Lagoon Food Village B4
    International Nasi Lemak ....(see 2)
    Makan Melaka.....................................(see 2)
    Mei Xiang Goreng Pisang...................(see 2)

◉ **Drinking & Nightlife**   **p112**
  6 Coachman Inn C1

  7 Coastal Settlement C1
  8 Little Island Brewing Co. D1

🛍 **Shopping**   **p112**
  9 Downtown East B1
 10 Isan Gallery A4
 11 Jewel D2

✚ **Sports & Activities**   **p113**
 12 Bike Stop B4
 13 Singapore Wake Park A4
 14 Wild Wild Wet B1

🛏 **Sleeping**   **p163 & p164**
 15 Ambassador Transit Hotel D2
 16 Crowne Plaza Changi Airport D2
 17 Village Hotel Changi..................................C1

EASTERN SINGAPORE

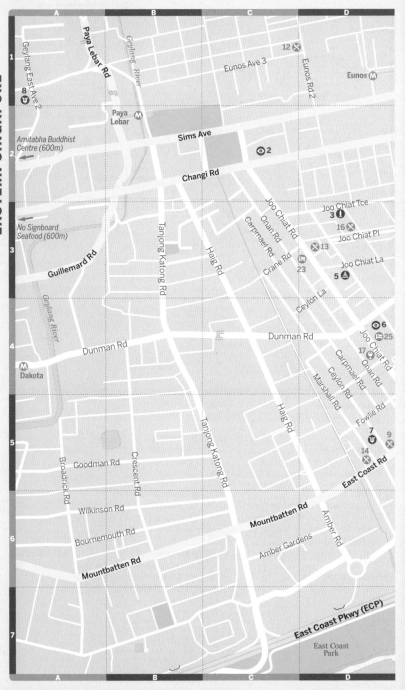

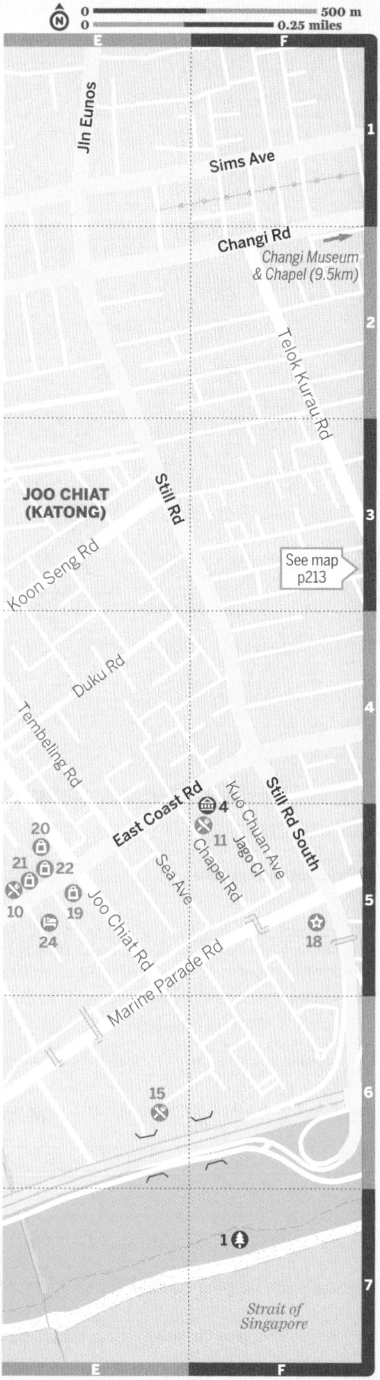

0 500 m
0 0.25 miles
E
F
Jln Eunos
Sims Ave
Changi Rd
Changi Museum & Chapel (9.5km)
Telok Kurau Rd
JOO CHIAT (KATONG)
Still Rd
Koon Seng Rd
See map p213
Duku Rd
Tembeling Rd
East Coast Rd
Kuo Chuan Ave
Jago Cl
Still Rd South
Chapel Rd
Sea Ave
Joo Chiat Rd
Marine Parade Rd
Strait of Singapore
1
2
3
4
5
6
7

Sights p107

1 East Coast Park ... F7
2 Geylang Serai New Market ... C2
3 Jousting Painters Mural by Ernest Zacharevic ... D3
4 Katong Antique House ... F5
5 Kuan Im Tng Temple ... D3
6 Peranakan Terrace Houses ... D4
7 Sri Senpaga Vinayagar Temple ... D5
8 Sri Sivan Temple ... A1

Eating p109

9 328 Katong Laksa ... D5
10 Birds of Paradise ... E5
11 Chin Mee Chin Confectionery ... F5
12 Le Chasseur ... C1
13 Long Phung ... D3
14 Lower East Side ... D5
15 Roland Restaurant ... E6
16 Smokey's BBQ ... D3

Drinking & Nightlife p112

17 Cider Pit ... D4

Entertainment p112

18 Necessary Stage ... F5

Shopping p112

19 112 Katong ... E5
20 Cat Socrates ... E5
21 Kim Choo Kueh Chang ... E5
22 Rumah Bebe ... E5

Sports & Activities p113

Betel Box: The Real Singapore Tours ... (see 23)

Sleeping p162

23 Betel Box ... D3
24 Hotel Indigo ... E5
25 Venue Hotel ... D4

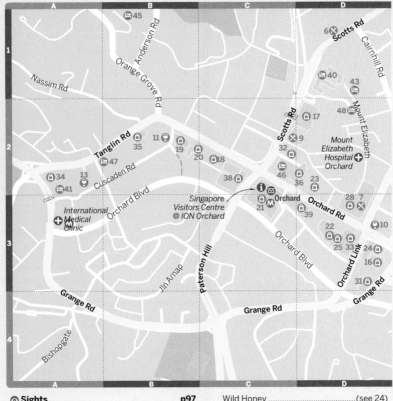

ORCHARD ROAD

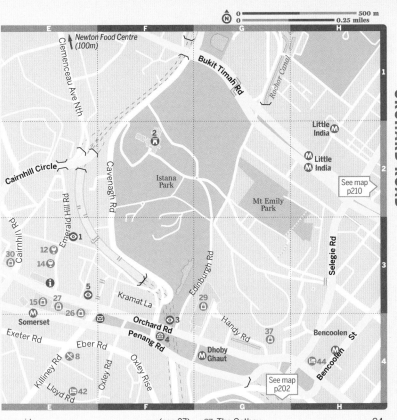

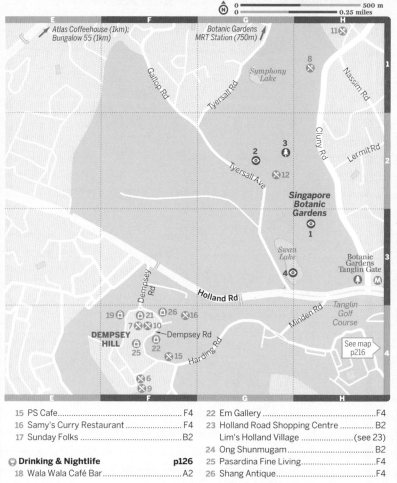

HOLLAND VILLAGE, DEMPSEY HILL & THE BOTANIC GARDENS

SOUTHWEST SINGAPORE

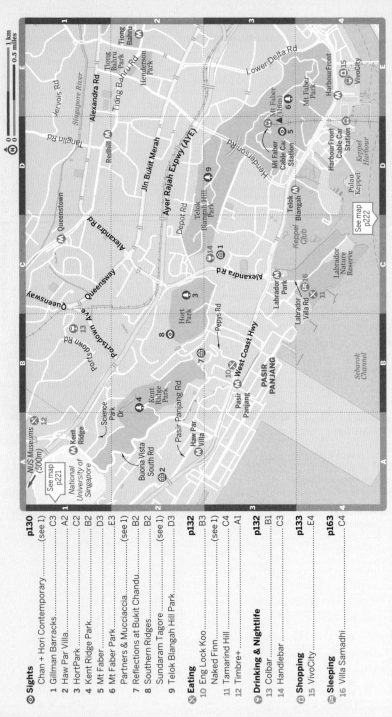

WEST SINGAPORE

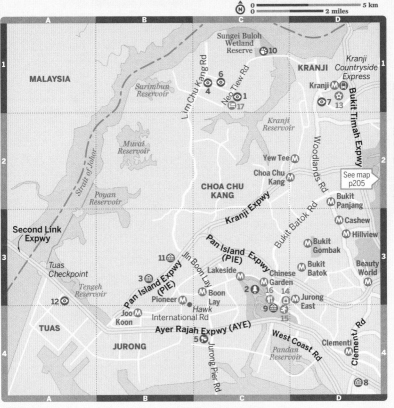

SENTOSA ISLAND

See map p220

Reflections at Keppel Bay

Pulau Keppel

Keppel Harbour

HarbourFront M

HarbourFront

VivoCity

West Coast Hwy

Sentosa Boardwalk

Pulau Brani

Selat Sengkir

Waterfront Resorts World

Universal Studios

☉ 1

☒ 6

⊕ 4

Cable Car

Sentosa Cable Car Station

Sentosa Cable Car Line

12

Siloso Point

Siloso Beach

19

☆ 2

☆ 16

Imbiah Lookout

Imbiah

Merlion

Beach

3

14

17

9

8

15

13

11

Palawan Beach

Artillery Ave

☒ 5

18

Sentosa Island

Serapong Golf Course

Mt Serapong

Serapong Hill Rd

Allanbrooke Rd

Bukit Manis Rd

Tanjong Golf Course

Buran Darat

☒ 7

20

0   0.5 miles
0   1 km

Strait of Singapore

10
Tanjong Beach

SENTOSA ISLAND

Our Story

A beat-up old car, a few dollars in the pocket and a sense of adventure. In 1972 that's all Tony and Maureen Wheeler needed for the trip of a lifetime – across Europe and Asia overland to Australia. It took several months, and at the end – broke but inspired – they sat at their kitchen table writing and stapling together their first travel guide, *Across Asia on the Cheap*. Within a week they'd sold 1500 copies. Lonely Planet was born.

Today, Lonely Planet has offices in the US, Ireland and China, with a network of over 2000 contributors in every corner of the globe. We share Tony's belief that 'a great guidebook should do three things: inform, educate and amuse'.

Our Writer

Ria de Jong

Ria started life in Asia, born in Sri Lanka to Dutch-Australian parents; she has always relished the hustle and excitement of this continent of contrasts. After growing up in Townsville, Australia, Ria moved to Sydney as a features writer before packing her bags for a five-year stint in the Philippines. Moving to Singapore in 2015 with her husband and two small children, Ria is loving discovering every nook and cranny of this tiny city, country, nation. This is Ria's third Singapore update for Lonely Planet.

Published by Lonely Planet Global Limited
CRN 554153
12th edition – December 2021
ISBN 978 1 78701 648 4
© Lonely Planet 2021 Photographs © as indicated 2021
10 9 8 7 6 5 4 3 2
Printed in China

Although the authors and Lonely Planet have taken all reasonable care in preparing this book, we make no warranty about the accuracy or completeness of its content and, to the maximum extent permitted, disclaim all liability arising from its use.